SECRETS of the CODE

BY THE "SECRETS" TEAM

Secrets of the Code: The Unauthorized Guide to the Mysteries Behind The Da Vinci Code, edited by Dan Burstein
www.SecretsOfTheCode.com

Secrets of Angels & Demons: *The Unauthorized Guide to the Bestselling Novel,* edited by Dan Burstein and Arne de Keijzer
www.SecretsOfAngelsAndDemons.com

Secrets of The Widow's Son, by David A. Shugarts
www.SecretsOfTheWidowsSon.com

Secrets of Mary Magdalene
(Fall 2006)

SECRETS of the CODE

The Unauthorized Guide to the Mysteries Behind *The Da Vinci Code*

Edited by Dan Burstein

MANAGING EDITOR: *Arne de Keijzer*

CONTRIBUTING EDITOR: *David A. Shugarts*

CONSULTING EDITORS:
Peter Bernstein and Annalyn Swan / ASAP Media LLC
Paul Berger, Jennifer Doll, John Castro, Kate Stohr, Brian Weiss, Nicole Zaray

Published by
CDS Books
In association with Squibnocket Partners LLC

For Julie,
who represents the spirit of the sacred feminine
in my life every day
—D.B.

Published by CDS Books

 Printed in the United States of America. For information and inquiries, address CDS Books, 425 Madison Ave., New York, NY 10017, or call (212) 223-2969, or fax (212) 223-1504.

Cataloging-in-Publication Data for this book is available from the Library of Congress.

ISBN-10: 1-59315-367-8
ISBN-13: 978-1-59315-367-0

CDS books are available at special discounts for bulk purchases in the U.S. by corporations, institutions, and other organizations. For more information, please contact the Special Markets Department at the Perseus Books Group, 11 Cambridge Center, Cambridge, MA 02142, or call (800) 255-1514 or (617) 252-5298, or email special.markets@perseusbooks.com.

06 07 08 / 10 9 8 7 6 5 4 3 2 1

Contents

Part II
Echoes of the Hidden Past

BOOK II
The Da Vinci Code Revealed

Part I
Reviews and Commentary

Editor's Note

Secrets of the Code: The Unauthorized Guide to the Mysteries Behind The Da Vinci Code is a compendium of original thought and writing, excerpts from numerous books, websites, and magazines, and interviews with key writers and scholars active in their fields.

This paperback edition is much more than a reprint of the original hardcover. Three years have gone by since *The Da Vinci Code* was first published; two years since our own *Secrets of the Code* burst onto the scene—and the *New York Times* bestseller list. Yet the phenomenon around *The Da Vinci Code* shows no signs of slowing down. With the film version starring Tom Hanks arriving in theaters in May 2006, more people than ever will have questions and become engaged with the search for answers.

Indeed, the impact of the novel just seems to get bigger and go deeper into the collective cultural psyche—and we have tried to bring our readers along with us in this revised, updated edition of *Secrets of the Code*. What's new in this edition? Among other highlights:

- A revelatory advance look at the ideas, issues, themes, and symbols likely to be in *The Solomon Key,* the announced title for Dan Brown's as-yet unpublished sequel to *The Da Vinci Code*. We crack the codes we found buried in the prior Dan Brown novels and "reverse engineer" his arguments, to show you the way he will mine the mysteries of early American history for the next novel, just as he mined the mysteries of early Christianity for *The Da Vinci Code.*

- Modern-day Holy Grail hunters: We look at real-life scholarship and research on new archeological finds and new interpretations of ancient documents. From the recently found *Genealogy of Jesus* in Wales to new finds involving ancient relics, we show you many of the new theories, ideas, and speculations about the life of Jesus and the world of the Holy Land two thousand years ago.
- *The Da Vinci Code* and Jewish culture: A prominent Rabbi with a flair for the mystical looks at the Jewish symbols and rituals discussed in *The Da Vinci Code.* These range from Kabbalah to the sacred feminine force of Shekinah, from the speculation about Jesus as a Jewish rabbi and whether he would or would not have been married, to the interpretation of the Star of David as an intertwined chalice and blade.
- We take you on the "Da Vinci Code tour" of the Louvre art museum, pairing you up for this excursion through Paris with an American art historian who shows you the treasures of the Louvre in a whole new light, from Mithras to Mary Magdalene to the *Mona Lisa.*
- The latest in Leonardo scholarship: several new Leonardo paintings have recently been found or attributed to the great Renaissance master, including a bare-breasted painting of Mary Magdalene that was recently displayed in Italy for the first time in many years. We catch our readers up on everything that has been happening in the world of Leonardo scholarship in the wake of *The Da Vinci Code.*
- From the *Village Voice* to the *Times of London,* from *New York Times* columnist Maureen Dowd to an investiga-

tion into Opus Dei by a reporter for *GQ*: the best things ever said about *The Da Vinci Code*.

- We analyze the charges of plagiarism that have swirled against Dan Brown. We know he borrowed heavily from works that preceded his, but did he borrow *too* heavily from prior books on similar topics?
- Why a powerful cardinal in the Vatican called for banning *The Da Vinci Code*—and how the world has reacted.
- More revalatory material about what Opus Dei really is and isn't. . . . Expanded interviews with key *Da Vinci Code* sources like Margaret Starbird. . . . More in-depth commentary from Bart Ehrman, the leading academic expert on lost and alternative scriptures. . . . More insight from Notre Dame's Rev. McBrien, a consultant to the filmmakers of *The Da Vinci Code*. . . . More on the hoax of the Priory of Sion, created in the 1950s by Pierre Plantard. . . . And the many ways *The Da Vinci Code* has had an impact upon our culture and our lives . . .

A few housekeeping notes to bear in mind as you wander through this rich library of history and mystery:

As with the original edition, this sequel contains a wide range of source materials, including transcriptions of ancient texts. We have tended to regularize spellings and naming conventions in our own work, while leaving undisturbed the original spellings and conventions that appear in the many works that are excerpted here from other books or materials. In some cases, we have renumbered footnotes for ease of reading. The careful reader will enjoy some variations within the book. For example, references to the name Leonardo da Vinci within the text generally follow the convention art history has assigned to Leonardo, but when the name is reproduced as part of the title of *The Da Vinci Code,* the D is capitalized, as it was throughout Dan Brown's book. Elsewhere, some sources spell Magdalene with the final e, some without. Wherever possible, we have tried to leave original material from other sources untouched, even at the risk of inconsistencies.

We have taken great care to set off each type of material so that it will be clear when we are excerpting from previously published works and when we are providing our own original writing and speaking in our own editorial voice. Except for the essays that begin each chapter, which conform to the typestyle of the book as a whole, the editor's introductions and notes that precede the excerpted materials, essays, or interviews are set off in a notably different typestyle. So are the interstitial materials within excerpts from books. On the other hand, guest contributions, interviews, and excerpts from previously published materials are clearly identified with bylines and/or copyright and reprint permission notices. If we have inadvertently missed any explanations of the provenance of the material or otherwise misidentified any of the pieces in this text, the editors apologize in advance.

Throughout the book, we have tried to find short selections and excerpts from much larger bodies of works to give our readers a quick taste of the content in a certain book, or the ideas of a certain expert. It was incredibly difficult to make these editorial decisions and to leave so much great material on the cutting room floor. We want to thank all the authors, publishers, periodicals, websites, and experts who have so generously made their content available to us for this book. And we want to encourage readers to buy the books that are excerpted here, visit the websites that are mentioned, and pursue all the multitude of ideas referred to within these pages from the original sources.

We would also like to call the reader's attention to several other books the "Secrets" team has published since the original *Secrets of the Code.* The first is *Secrets of Angels & Demons,* which illuminates the historical labyrinth of conspiracies, cover-ups, and the ongoing conflict between science and religion touched on in Dan Brown's novel *Angels & Demons,* published before *The Da Vinci Code.* We have also published *Secrets of the Widow's Son,* by David A. Shugarts, which is a fascinating "prequel" to the *next* Dan Brown book, *The Solomon Key.* And we will soon publish *Secrets of Mary Magdalene.*

Each of our books has its own website as well. Visit us at any of the following websites and share your own thoughts, questions, journeys, and explorations with us:

www.SecretsOfTheCode.com
www.SecretsOfAngelsAndDemons.com
www.SecretsOfTheWidowsSon.com

Introduction
Searching for Sophia

By Dan Burstein

Like many of you, I came across *The Da Vinci Code* by Dan Brown in the summer of 2003. It was already the number one book on the *New York Times* bestseller list. It sat by my bedside for a while, along with dozens of other unread books, piles of magazines, business presentations I needed to review, and all the other things typical of the competition for mind share in the complex, chaotic, information-intense world in which we all live.

Then one day I picked up *The Da Vinci Code* and started reading. I read all night, fascinated. I literally couldn't put it down. It is an experience I used to have frequently, but not so often in this season of my life, as I was turning fifty. At one point, around 4 a.m., as I read Leigh Teabing's explanation to Sophie Neveu of why and how he saw Mary Magdalene in *The Last Supper,* I got out of bed and pulled the art books down from our library shelves. I looked at the Leonardo painting that I had encountered, of course, hundreds of times previously. *Yes, it really does look like a woman seated next to Jesus!* I thought.

By morning, when I had finished the book, I was as intellectually challenged as I had been by any book I had read in a long time. I wanted to know what was true and what was not, what was fact, what was fiction, what was informed speculation, and what was pure flight of literary fancy. As soon as my local bookstore opened, I was there, sipping latte and rummaging through scores of books that had been mentioned or alluded to in *The Da Vinci Code: Holy Blood, Holy Grail, The Templar Revelation, Gnostic Gospels, The Woman with the Alabaster Jar, The Nag Hammadi Library,* and many more. I discovered, to my surprise, that there were dozens of recent books about Mary Magdalene, goddess culture, the sacred feminine, the roots of Christianity, and about how the Bible was written and codified, as well as all the Gnostic and other alternative gospels. I found shelves full of occult books on Templar traditions, secret societies, and several places mentioned by *The Da Vinci Code* that I had never heard of before, including Rennes-le-Château in France and Rosslyn Chapel in Scotland. I left the store with hundreds of dollars' worth of books and went home to absorb all this material, only later discovering that Dan Brown had a website with a bibliography on it.

For weeks, I continued to buy books that I discovered were relevant to *The Da Vinci Code.* I raced through Elaine Pagels's new book, *Beyond Belief,* having already had my eyes opened to the world of alternative scriptures through her path-breaking 1979 book, *The Gnostic Gospels.* I discovered a world of scholars who were experts in Coptic, Greek, Hebrew, and Latin, and who had painstakingly translated and parsed ancient documents to discern new information and discover new possible interpretations of events described in the Bible. I read all of the books by Baigent, Leigh, and Lincoln, Lynn Picknett, and others who have been mining much of the same raw material as Dan Brown for years. I soaked up the richly detailed book on Mary Magdalene by Susan Haskins that documented two thousand years of myth and metaphor about the woman who Dan Brown suggests was the bride of Christ.

I rediscovered books I had read previously: Jonathan Kirsch's powerful biography *Moses,* in which he tried to tease the true story of Moses's life out of oblique passages from the Old Testament, including fascinating references to the idea that Miriam was not the sister of Moses, as the Bible tells us, but a priestess with her own cult following and her own role in liberating the Jewish slaves from Egypt. I reread the following passage: "Some scholars argue that Miriam is real but Moses is made up. Others suggest that both of them existed but were not really brother and sister—Miriam, they argue, was a priestess and prophetess in her own right," who was ultimately merged into the Bible story as the "sister" of Moses as a kind of ancient form of politically correct storytelling. Perhaps this longstanding habit of biblical redactors—changing relationships, merging deeds performed by women with deeds performed by men, changing the earlier forms of the story to fit later political needs—had manifested itself in the way New Testament redactors edited the story of Jesus, Mary Magdalene, and the others in their circle.

I reread Umberto Eco's *Foucault's Pendulum* (a literary pastiche and send-up of much of the same occult material treated in *The Da Vinci Code*). Eco would later tell interviewers from *Jesus, Mary, and da Vinci* (the ABC news special that was devoted to exploring Dan Brown's thesis) that *The Da Vinci Code*'s premises were based on nineteenth-century fairy tales equivalent to Pinocchio and Little Red Riding Hood—"wrong theories," as false as believing that the world was flat.

I recommuned with Norman O. Brown's 1960s classic, *Love's Body,* a favorite of mine at an earlier time in my life, with all its brilliant synthesis of myth and archetype concerning the sacred feminine and the role of mythic ideas in the creation of Western consciousness. Many of the quotations from interdisciplinary fields and diverse cultures that Brown assembled seemed to be right up Robert Langdon's symbological alley. Langdon sees chalices and blades as universal female and male symbols. And he sees them everywhere: from the adoption of the six-pointed Star of David in ancient Jewish history, to the interplay of the space between Jesus and the person seated next to him in *The Last Supper,* to I. M. Pei's downward- and upward-pointed pyramids at the Louvre. As Norman O. Brown argued, "All metaphors are sexual; a penis in every convex object and a vagina in every concave one." Langdon would have also appreciated Brown's frequent invocation of Yeats, seeking to understand how the sacred unity that was divided into male and female may someday be restored to a unified state: "Nothing can be sole or whole / That has not been rent."

I revisited a 1965 bestseller, *The Passover Plot,* that I remember my parents reading and discussing. The vintage copy I bought had these interesting words emblazoned on the flap copy: "*The Passover Plot* asserts—and presents detailed evidence from the Bible and from the newly discovered Dead Sea Scrolls to prove—that Jesus planned his own arrest, crucifixion, and resurrection, that he arranged to be drugged on the cross, simulating death so that he could later be safely removed and thus bear out the Messianic prophecies . . . Never before has so eminent an authority presented so challenging a thesis—or backed it up with such irrefutable evidence." Déjà vu all over again for readers of Dan Brown's bestselling book forty years later.

I read Nikos Kazantzakis's *The Last Temptation of Christ* from half a century ago, and watched the Martin Scorsese movie adaptation of it, which I had never seen. These works certainly painted a vivid picture of a possible romantic relationship between Jesus and Mary Magdalene (or Willem Dafoe and Barbara Hershey, as the case may be).

As I absorbed all these books and materials and as I continued to talk to friends about their experience of reading *The Da Vinci Code* (*DVC*), the idea occurred to me that I should try to bring some of these diverse strands together into a single volume, so that other *DVC* readers and enthusiasts could benefit from the same body of knowledge and criticism that I was exploring. Thus, the idea for this book was born.

Shortly after I decided to dig into this material with the vision of creating an unauthorized reader's guide to the novel, I read a report that indicated there were approximately ninety books that were selling better at bookstores around the country because of the proximity of their subject matter to *DVC*. I realized that other readers were indeed embarked on exactly the same quest that I was, reaffirming my instinct and desire to create this book. Fortunately, Gilbert Perlman and his colleagues at CDS shared my vision and moved heaven and earth to support the publication of this book on a time cycle sufficiently accelerated to provide relevant context to the thousands of new readers who were buying *The Da Vinci Code* with each passing day. Now, the millions of filmgoers who will see *The Da Vinci Code* movie will have *Secrets of the Code* as a resource as well.

In my "day job" as a venture capitalist, our firm often hears interesting but outlandish claims about new technologies and innovations. We then undertake what is known as the "due diligence" process to evaluate these claims. We look to see if, beneath all the hype, there is a real business that can be built successfully. Our approach usually begins with a list of questions.

My research on *The Da Vinci Code* was somewhat analogous. Here was my initial list:

- What do we really know about Mary Magdalene? Was she a prostitute, as Christian tradition has portrayed her? If she was not, why was she portrayed as such for so long in church history, and why did the Vatican change its mind in the 1960s?
- Is there real evidence that Jesus and Mary Magdalene were married? When gospel accounts in the New Testament speak of a woman anointing Jesus with luxurious aromatic oils from an alabaster jar and drying his feet with her hair—was this Mary Magdalene or a different Mary, who may have actually been a reformed prostitute? And if it was Mary Magdalene who performed these acts, are they ritual acts of respect or metaphors for sexual relations?
- Does the *Gospel of Philip* found at Nag Hammadi really say that Jesus frequently kissed Mary Magdalene on the mouth—and if we have the right translation and the right words, is this too a metaphor? Or is it an actual reference to a romantic relationship?
- Is it possible Jesus and Mary Magdalene had a child and fostered a bloodline that continued into modern times? How valid are the many legends about Mary Magdalene's escape to France? Could her progeny have been the basis for the Merovingian kings? And what of the cults of the "black Madonna" in France and elsewhere? Could Mary Magdalene have possibly been a black woman from Egypt or Ethiopia?
- Was the historical Jesus essentially a Jewish rabbi, teacher, or spiritual leader and, as such, would it be likely and even probable that he would be married?

Or was there already a tradition at that time of celibacy and asceticism among Jewish male leaders?

- Is it possible that Mary Magdalene was an important spiritual figure in her own right, the romantic companion and/or wife of Jesus, and the person whom he wished to lead his movement after his death? Is there a historical record of arguments and jealousies on the part of the male apostles over Mary Magdalene's role? Is the *DVC*'s assertion that Jesus was the "original feminist" plausible in any way?
- Are the Gnostic Gospels and other alternative scriptures credible—or at least as credible as the mainstream, traditional gospels? Do they really tell a significantly different story? What do they add to our understanding of the intellectual and philosophical ferment of the first few hundred years of the Common Era?
- Did leaders of the Roman church, from Constantine to Pope Gregory, carry out a concerted attack on alternative beliefs and scriptures? Did they edit what became the accepted canon for political purposes? Did they deliberately conflate Mary Magdalene with another Mary in the gospels who was, indeed, a prostitute?
- Did these early church fathers not only slander Mary Magdalene as a prostitute, but do so as part of a larger effort to cover up Christianity's archaic inheritances from goddess cults and in order to suppress the role of women in the church?
- Did the Gnostics practice sacred sexual rituals? Is there a tradition of *hieros gamos* that runs from Egypt through Greece, through early Christianity and on to the Templars and Priory of Sion members?

- Who were the Knights Templar and what might they have found in excavating the Temple Mount during the Crusades?
- How did the Templars gain power and influence and how did they lose it? Is there any evidence that the Templars ever found the Holy Grail?
- Is there any evidence that the Templars or other secret societies of that time believed the Holy Grail to be related not to a chalice or wine cup, but to Mary Magdalene, her relics, documents about her role in the early church, her progeny, and the future of the Jesus-Mary bloodline?
- Is the Priory of Sion a real organization in history? If so, did it continue uninterrupted into modern-day France, with the involvement of the great figures of European culture alleged by *DVC* to have been its grand masters: Leonardo, Newton, Victor Hugo, Claude Debussy, Jean Cocteau, etc.?
- If, as seems more likely, the idea of the Priory of Sion as a secret society continuously operating into the modern era is a mid-twentieth-century hoax invented by Pierre Plantard, did Dan Brown fall for this story, not understanding that it was a hoax? Did he try to remarket it as "fact" knowing that it was fiction simply to spin a good yarn and sell more books? Or did he find in this strange brew of rural legend and manipulative fraud a literary device with sufficient mythopoetic power to entrance readers and induce them to contemplate much more important and meaningful issues?
- What is going on within the church today to reevaluate doctrine, reconsider fundamental principles, and rethink the role of women? Why do movies like *The Passion* stir such passion? How is the church responding to sex abuse and other scandals, and what does his-

tory tell us is likely to happen? What is Opus Dei, and what role does it play in the Catholic Church?

- Did Leonardo da Vinci embed secret symbolic messages in *The Last Supper* and other works? Does *The Last Supper* depict a female Mary Magdalene to the right of Christ, rather than the male apostle John? And whether this interpretation of *The Last Supper* has any validity or not, did Leonardo and his contemporaries have access to lost, secret, heretical knowledge of any type that they may have tried to communicate in one way or another through their artworks?

In this volume, readers will find materials that address all of these questions and more. The materials include excerpts from books, periodicals, websites, original articles, commentaries, and interviews with scholars, experts, and thinkers who have been working on aspects of these issues for years. It is my sincere hope that readers will find these resources as useful to the process of drawing their own conclusions and formulating their own ideas as I have found them to mine.

Before setting readers off into the stacks contained in this volume of what we like to call "Sophie's Library," I would like to share a variety of observations about why I think *The Da Vinci Code* has struck such a nerve among the reading public and resonates so deeply with the contemporary zeitgeist.

1) *DVC* is a novel of ideas. Say what you will about some of the ham-fisted dialogue and improbable plot elements, Dan Brown has wrapped large complex ideas, as well as minute details and fragments of intriguing thoughts, into his action-adventure-murder mystery. Our culture is hungry for the opportunity to feed the collective mind with something other than intellectual junk food. Even

among much higher-brow, more literary writers, all too few are writing novels that deal with big philosophical, cosmological, or historical concepts. And among those who are, most of the books they are producing are simply too inaccessible for even the average sophisticated, educated reader. Dan Brown has given us an incredible array of fascinating ideas and concepts. We get to partake in all this with no academic prerequisites. We open the first page with Saunière staggering through the Louvre's Grand Gallery at 10:46 p.m. and we then get swept away into Brown's fast-paced scavenger hunt through the history of Western civilization. We never have to do any heavy mental lifting if we don't want to, but for those who want to pursue the ideas, the novel leaves the key words at every turn.

2) Like James Joyce's *Ulysses, DVC* takes place essentially in one twenty-four-hour period. Like Joyce's *Finnegan's Wake,* it ends where it begins. Clearly, Dan Brown takes literary form quite seriously. He may play faster and looser with facts than some would like, but his ability to compress extensive intellectual and religious arguments into quickly accessible sound bites is an art form. This is not to say that *DVC* is "great literature." I am not certain it will stand the test of time, popular as it is right now. But our society should appreciate, more highly than it does, the artistry of the great mystery, spy thriller, and action-adventure novelists. Dan Brown, it will turn out, is this type of literary artist.

3) Our materialistic, technological, scientific, information-flooded culture is hungry, not only for the intellectual allure of big ideas, but for a sense of mission and meaning. People are looking for a recovery of their spiritual sensibility, or at least a context for their lives. *DVC,* like the Harry Potter novels that parallel it in this same

zeitgeist, is a classic hero's journey (only in this case the heroine is not only a full and equal partner, she is actually more important). *DVC* can be read as a modern odyssey through myth, archetypes, symbolic language, and religious practice. The characters will not only save the most precious secrets from falling into the wrong hands, in the process they will gain knowledge of self, identity, and their place in the world.

4) Like other times in history—the legendary days of Arthur, the Crusades, the nineteenth century—we are living in an era when the romance of the hunt for the Holy Grail is being renewed. This is true in the narrow sense of a huge flourishing of new literature about the Holy Grail of Christian history. Dan Brown draws extensively on this body of occult, New Age, and mysterious work. But there is also a flourishing of the Holy Grail hunt in the widest, most metaphoric sense. The search to unlock the secrets of the human genome, to go to Mars, understand the Big Bang, and shrink communication into wireless digital bits—all of these are Holy Grail quests of a kind. Perhaps this is all a bit of delayed millennialism: when the actual change of the millennium occurred a few years ago, many trend-watchers were surprised at how little millennial fever was exhibited. But then came the shock of September 11, apocalyptic acts of terrorism, wars in Afghanistan and Iraq, explosions of violence throughout the Middle East, all accented by religious extremism and Crusades-era rhetoric about faith and infidels. The birth of our new era has started to look more millennial after all. *DVC* strikes right into this vein, drawing its key plot elements from two thousand and one thousand years ago—the birth of the Christian era and the Crusades. In a remarkable book that came out shortly after *DVC, The Holy Grail: Imagination and Belief,* Britain's

leading medieval historian, Richard Barber, traces the role of the Holy Grail in firing artistic imaginations from Wagner to T. S. Eliot to Monty Python. He also charts the use of the phrase "Holy Grail" by mainstream newspapers not usually given to spending much time on religious matters. According to Barber, the *New York Times* mentioned the Holy Grail only 32 times in 1995–96, but 140 in 2001–02. The *Times* of London upped its Grail score from 14 in 1985–86 to 171 in 2001–02; *Le Figaro* from 56 in 1997–98 to 113 in 2001–02.

5) Women are a large constituency of *DVC* readers, and the book responds in many ways to new thinking about women in our culture. Dan Brown has rescued Mary Magdalene from her reputation of sin, penitence, and prostitution. In the book, even the smart, sophisticated Sophie Neveu still thinks of Mary Magdalene as a prostitute until Langdon and Teabing set her straight. I am willing to go out on a limb and guess that far more people may have learned from *The Da Vinci Code* that Mary Magdalene is no longer considered a prostitute than from the official church clarifications of the 1960s. Fourteen hundred years of being seen as a fallen woman is a tough reputation to overcome. But *DVC* has moved the church's correction off the proverbial page 28 of the third section and on to the front page of the public's consciousness. Not only that. *DVC* makes the case that Mary Magdalene was much more than "not a prostitute." In the novel's estimation, she was a strong, independent figure, patron of Jesus, cofounder of his movement, his only believer in his greatest hour of need, author of her own gospel, his romantic partner, and the mother of his child. To the millions of women who feel slighted, discriminated against, or unwelcome in churches of all faiths today, the novel is a chance to see early religious history in an entirely different light. Just as women

have found new pioneering female heroines in every pursuit from science to the arts to sports over the last thirty years, *The Da Vinci Code* opens everyone's eyes to a startlingly different view of the powerful role of women in the birth of Christianity. These themes have become mainstream at Harvard's divinity school and other intellectual centers, but it is *DVC* that brought this perspective into focus for literate women (and men) who dwell outside academe. For Catholic women in particular—many of whom have long been embittered by the church's stance against abortion, birth control, divorce, and women being ordained as priests—the book illuminates how the feminine half of the human equation may have been deliberately suppressed for political reasons by the rise of the institutional, centralized power of the Roman church. Facts presented in *DVC*—real, verifiable facts—tell a story many people do not know. For example, there was no prohibition against women being priests in the early years of the church, and male celibacy in the priesthood did not become the rule until six centuries after Christ. Moreover, it was not only Mary Magdalene who was an important figure in the traditional gospels. There are a variety of other leading women mentioned by name, most of whom have remained ciphers even to the faithful all these years. Of course the Virgin Mary, mother of Jesus, has long had a deeply devoted following. In recent years, she has emerged as an even more important figure in the church—a trend Pope John Paul II actively encouraged. But the new vision of Mary Magdalene that Dan Brown paints—powerful, strong, independent, smart, the standard-bearer of Christianity long after the death of Jesus and, yes, sexy—makes Mary Magdalene a much more accessible, more human character to contemplate than the aloof, saintly, perfect Virgin Mary.

6) In a time of growing fundamentalism and religious extremism in the world, *DVC* offers an important study of Western history. First, it highlights the diversity and ferment that existed in the Judeo-Christian world two thousand years ago—diversity and ferment that was later suppressed by the antiheresy campaigns of the church. It suggests that some of the pagan and Eastern ideas that found their way into eastern Mediterranean thought may have had value and validity. In reminding us of the Crusades and Inquisitions as well as the intense ideological battles over interpretation, and in contrast to Mel Gibson's 2004 movie, *The Passion of the Christ,* which seeks to present a version of the true way these well-known events unfolded, *DVC* challenges readers to imagine that what they have always heard or believed may not be the truth after all. The novel suggests a multitude of conspiracies and covert worlds: the mainstream church's great cover-up and conspiracy to eradicate the Priory of Sion, the Priory's own conspiracy of secrecy, Opus Dei's conspiracy to gain power in the church, and the Teacher's conspiracy to murder and bring forward his own version of the truth. In doing so, *DVC* is an implicit critique of intolerance, of madness in the name of God, and of all those who believe there is only one true God, one true faith, and one true way to practice religious devotion.

7) Tapping into world-shaking twentieth-century archaeological finds—such as the Nag Hammadi texts and the Dead Sea Scrolls—as well as doing art history analysis of Leonardo and other painters, symbol interpretation, and cryptography, *DVC* weaves together various strands from the scientific and archaeological reports of our times. In doing so, the novel sketches out elements of the greatest detective story ever told: we are living in an era where we are uncovering authentic evidence about hu-

man origins as well as the origins of many ideas and beliefs. Sophie's journey of self-discovery is really an analog of our own. Sophie may be descended directly from Jesus, but we are all descended from people who walked the earth at that time, thought those thoughts, practiced those customs. When we are able to share the insights that Gnostic philosophers may have had sitting in the Egyptian desert sixteen or eighteen centuries ago, it is a startling experience. We are simultaneously cracking the codes of our biological DNA as well as our cultural DNA. With new research and with new scientific tools, we may well learn what Leonardo was trying to tell us—or if he was trying to tell us anything at all.

8) The idea that Robert Langdon is a symbologist—an academic pursuit that appears to be Dan Brown's own coinage—and that Langdon has such a terrific knack for explaining signs and symbols, is another aspect of the book's appeal. We are moving at full throttle out of the Gutenberg age and into the webified world of interactive media and the blogosphere. It is a transition from the world of hierarchical, literal, structured, rational thought into a futuristic soup of image, idea, motion, emotion, randomness, and interconnection. In a sense, we are moving backward in time to a period when visual signs and symbols were much more important. The icons on our computer screens are the reincarnation of cave paintings in France. That Dan Brown is attuned to the rich meanings and inputs coming into our lives from nonliteral, nonrational sources is a critical part of the experience of reading the book. Indeed, reading *DVC* is similar to the experience Langdon describes when he says that, for him, watching a Disney movie is like being "barraged by an avalanche of allusion and metaphor." The Langdon character, as pointed out elsewhere in this book, is an

attractive mix of Indiana Jones and Joseph Campbell. The fact that Brown has strewn codes, symbols, and anagrams throughout the book makes it all the more interesting and interactive for us as participants in the experience.

9) Conspiracy, secrecy, privacy, identity theft, technology and its problems—these are themes in all of Dan Brown's books, and they are very appropriate themes for our time. Reading *DVC* stimulates thought and discussions on all these subjects. The modern American church concealed heinous cases of sexual abuse for years; the president of the United States may have launched an invasion of a foreign country based on concocted evidence of weapons of mass destruction; executives of companies like Enron and WorldCom deceived shareholders and regulators about billions and billions in nonexistent value. One can't read *The Da Vinci Code* without hearing the echoes of these contemporary incidents of lying and cover-up—and the truth coming out in the end.

Is *The Da Vinci Code* fact or fiction? My primary goal is to give you the materials so you can draw your own conclusion. Let me make it perfectly clear that I do not claim to have great prior expertise on the subjects covered by *The Da Vinci Code.* I have an intense interest and abiding curiosity about these subjects, but no academic, religious, or artistic credentials. I see myself as very much like most of the novel's readers. I became engaged with these ideas and I went out to research them in more depth, find the most well-regarded experts I could to interview, identify the most compelling source material, and bring it all together in a handy single volume designed for other interested, curious readers.

As a businessperson, however, I feel I owe my readers at least an executive summary of the case I think the materials in this book present in aggregate. My personal conclusion is that the novel is a fascinating, well-crafted work of fiction that is informed throughout by interesting bits of little-known facts and stimulating, but highly speculative thought provocations. It is most valuable when read as a book of ideas and metaphors—a notebook, Leonardo style, that helps the reader think through his or her own philosophy, cosmology, religious beliefs, or critiques.

With those caveats, let me offer a quick overview of my personal conclusions on the "fact versus fiction" question. There are at least two very different parts to answering this question.

First, I would say that the further Dan Brown goes back in time, the more he stands on credible intellectual ground. For example, you can find many anthropologists, archaeologists, and other experts who would endorse the broad strokes of the argument made in *DVC* about the sacred feminine. Serious academic literature abounds making the case that prior to the emergence of Judeo-Christian monotheism, many polytheistic pagan belief systems tended to pay much more attention to goddesses as well as gods, and to the spiritual and divine nature of sex, procreation, fertility, and birth. Similarly, on the question of Mary Magdalene not being confused with the prostitute of the New Testament, or on the matter of Mary having a much more important role in the founding moments of Christianity than has been previously emphasized, you can find a large body of independent academic work, as well as research by religious scholars and theologians, making the same points. Of course serious academics are not going to leap to a conclusion for which there is no hard evidence, so you don't find a lot of mainstream academics who are positively convinced that Jesus and Mary were married. But you can find very serious, credible academics—and even theologians—who are open to the possibility, and even the probability, of a romantic relationship between them. As the distinguished Notre Dame theologian Rev. Richard McBrien likes to point out, it is only a "short putt" from the evidence we have to the conclusion that Jesus and Mary may have actually been married. The world of academic research and scholarship can't actually make that putt with the evidence we have, and may never be able to do so. But the point is that Dan Brown is not inventing something out of whole cloth here. He is *not* making a cosmic leap; he's making a short putt of the imagination.

The Da Vinci Code tackles big topics, from the role of the sacred feminine in prehistory, Mary Magdalene, early Christianity, the diversity of thought two thousand years ago, and the ensuing consolidation of the institution of the Roman church. In addressing these issues, the novel starts from the work of serious scholars and bits of real evidence, such as the Nag Hammadi finds. Dan Brown interprets this material in the most dramatic, exaggerated, plot-driven way possible. Of course he does: this is a novel. But the roots of the ideas for these themes seem to me—and to many of the experts whose voices and research we present in these pages—to have rough approximate validity.

However, as we fast forward through history, *The Da Vinci Code* remains a fascinating story, but it becomes further and further uncoupled from serious scholarship. The early history of the Crusades and the Templars, as it is presented, is not out of synch with mainstream views. But by the time we get to matters such as the Holy Grail being synonymous with Mary Magdalene and the royal bloodline of Jesus, or the Priory of Sion's enduring commitment to the spirit of the sacred feminine, or the argument that *The Last Supper* is a coded message from Leonardo about the real history of Jesus and Mary, or that the Priory of Sion continued into modern times with an unbroken chain of grand masters from Leonardo to Pierre Plantard, Dan Brown has left mainstream scholarship behind. He has plunged into the world of the medieval legend and occult and New Age myths. Almost all of this is recycled from legend and lore documented by other writers over the last few decades. A great deal of it falls so far below the standards of evidence for historical credibility that it's not worth discussing as history or as fact. To some, it is a lot of occult hogwash. To me, and perhaps many others, it is hogwash as history, but great material for storytelling and folklore, endlessly fascinating to discuss from the point of view of myth, metaphor, and our cultural DNA.

Many commentators are arguing over Dan Brown's portrayal of religious doctrine and Christian history. In fact, most of the more than twenty books now available in English as guides to *The Da Vinci Code* offer readers a critique of the book from a religious point of view. If you are really interested in the issues raised by *The Da Vinci Code,* I encourage you to read those too. Each has a unique point of view and adds to the overall mosaic of understanding. But whether or not Dan Brown got his theology right is not the focus of this book, although we have presented some arguments along those lines here. Instead, I have chosen to emphasize the ideas, metaphors, and their interconnections that can be discerned by engaging in the dialogue over this book. It is not my desire to enter into polemics or to be critical or disrespectful of anyone's religious beliefs. Nor is it my desire to uphold or disparage the works that *DVC* relies on for source material that are excerpted here. The fact that material is presented here doesn't mean I think the arguments presented are true. It only means I think you should hear the arguments and make up your own mind.

What follows in *Secrets of the Code* is a compilation of ideas and opinions from a wide spectrum of thinkers. This book is designed to help the reader on his or her hunt for personal knowledge and insight—*sophia,* if you will.

Let me be crystal clear: *The Da Vinci Code* is a novel. It is an entertainment. It is something to enjoy. Part of the enjoyment, for me anyway, is to follow up on its threads and ideas, to pursue its interconnections. That's what *Secrets of the Code* is all about.

SECRETS of the CODE

1 Mary Magdalene

How a Woman of Substance Was Harlotized by History

Christ loved her more than all the disciples and used to kiss her often on the [mouth]. The rest of the disciples were offended by it and expressed disapproval. They said to him, "Why do you love her more than all of us?" The Savior answered and said to them, "Why do I not love you like I love her?"

—GOSPEL OF PHILIP

Mary Magdalene is, in many ways, the star of *The Da Vinci Code,* and it is fitting that she should be the starting point for this book's odyssey into exploring the histories and mysteries in Dan Brown's novel. But who was this woman who plays such a key role at critical moments in the traditional gospels? She is clearly one of the closest companions of the itinerant Jesus. She is mentioned twelve times by name in the New Testament. She is among the only followers of Jesus to be present at his crucifixion and she attends to him after his death. She is the person who returns to his tomb three days later and the person to whom the resurrected Jesus first appears. When he appears, he instructs—indeed, he empowers—her to spread the news of his resurrection and to become, in effect, the most important apostle, the bearer of the Christian message to the other apostles and to the world.

All of that is according to statements made in the officially accepted New Testament accounts. If you study the alternative accounts—various lost scriptures and the Gnostic Gospels—you quickly find the hints that Mary Magdalene and Jesus may have had kan extremely close relationship, an intimate relationship of man and wife. You find that she may have been a leader and thinker in her own right to whom Jesus may have entrusted secrets that he did not even share with the male apostles. She may have been caught up in a jealous rivalry among the other apostles, some of whom, notably Peter, may have disdained her role in the movement on the basis of her gender and found her relationship with Jesus problematic. She may have represented a more humanistic, individualized philosophy, perhaps closer to that which Jesus actually preached than to what became accepted by the Roman Empire in the time of Constantine as official, standardized, mainstream Christian thinking.

She is perhaps best known in history as a prostitute. But was she ever a prostitute? Did Jesus simply forgive her—and did she simply repent and change her ways—to illustrate traditional Christian principles about sin, forgiveness, penance, and redemption? Or was she not a prostitute at all, but a wealthy financial patron and supporter of the Jesus movement who was later declared by Pope Gregory in the sixth century to be identical to a different Mary in the gospels who was, indeed, a prostitute? And when Pope Gregory conflated three different Marys in the gospels into one, did he do this deliberately to brand Mary Magdalene with the stigma of prostitution? Was it an honest mistake of interpretation in a dark age when few original documents were in hand and biblical language was a mélange of Hebrew, Aramaic, Greek, and Latin? Did the church need to simplify and codify the Gospels and to play up the themes of sin, penance, and redemption? Or was it a far more Machiavellian stratagem (a millennium before Machiavelli) to ruin Mary Magdalene's reputation in history and, by doing so, destroy the last vestiges of the influences of pagan goddess cults and the "sacred feminine" on early Christianity, to undermine the role of women in the church and bury the more humanistic side of Christian faith?

Did it go even further? When Pope Gregory placed the scarlet letter of prostitution on Mary Magdalene—who would remain officially a reformed prostitute for the next fourteen centuries—was it the beginning of the great cover-up to deny the marriage of Jesus and Mary Magdalene and, ultimately, the royal, sacred bloodline of their offspring?

Their offspring? Well, yes. If Jesus and Mary Magdalene were married or at least had an intimate relationship, there might well have been a child or children. And what did happen to Mary Magdalene after the crucifixion? The Bible is silent, but around the Mediterranean, from Ephesus to Egypt, there is legend and lore suggesting Mary Magdalene, with her child (or children), escaped from Jerusalem and eventually settled down to the life of an evangelist. The most interesting stories have her living out her years in France . . . a theme Dan Brown picks up and makes integral to the plot of *The Da Vinci Code.*

Representing issues about sin and redemption, the Madonna and the whore, penitence and virtue, the faithful and the fallen, it is no surprise that Mary Magdalene has always been a towering figure in literature and culture. Male churchgoers took to the stage to portray her in the passion plays, the very first theater works produced in western Europe over a thousand years ago. And she has been a constant figure in church art ever since.

In much more recent times, Dan Brown is not the first author to be fascinated with Mary Magdalene, nor the first to play up the issue of her possible marriage to Jesus. Nikos Kazantzakis posited a romantic relationship between them in his novel *The Last Temptation of Christ* more than fifty years ago (well before Martin Scorsese turned it into a movie in the 1980s and raised the issue again). William E. Phipps addressed many of these same issues in his book *Was Jesus Married?,* more than thirty years ago. The rock opera *Jesus Christ Superstar,* another work that hails from more than thirty years ago, also assumes a romantic relationship between Jesus and Mary Magdalene. Given our society's interest in issues about gender roles, women as leaders, and all the permutations of love, marriage, and sex one can imagine, the "new" Mary Magdalene fits right in, and *The Da Vinci Code* is right on time.

In the pages of this chapter, some of the world's leading experts on Mary Magdalene discuss and debate different versions of who she may have been in history, the meaning of her role in the traditional gospels, and how the Gnostic and other alternative Gospels may further augment our ability to understand her today. Some of the experts are interested in teasing out the meaning of only what is in the Bible. Others want to deepen and enrich the debate with new evidence and new interpretations. Still others are focused less on what texts say and much more on the meaning of Mary Magdalene in the context of archetype, myth, and metaphor.

Every issue that could be debated has come into the twenty-first-century debate about Mary Magdalene. Was she from Magdala on the Sea of Galilee and was she therefore likely to be a Jewish woman? Or was she from a similarly named town in Egypt or Ethiopia? Was she fair and auburn-haired as she was often depicted in medieval times or was she a black African woman? Was she an "insider" to the Holy Land's customs and way of life or was she an outsider, much like Jesus is sometimes portrayed? Was she very wealthy and able to finance Jesus' movement from her personal means? How do we know that she was wealthy—because she came from a prosperous fishing town? Because *spikenard,* the perfume she used to anoint Jesus, was considered an expensive luxury product? Because she appears to have arranged for the food and lodging of Jesus and his followers who had renounced worldly things? Since she is just one of several women who appear to be patrons of Jesus, what of the other women, several of whom are mentioned by name? Was she descended from the House of Benjamin, as some accounts suggest Jesus was descended from the House of David, and would their marriage have been politically important, bringing these two clans together? Would Jesus have been married in the normal course of events anyway? After all, most of the rabbis of Jewish culture in those days were married, and Jesus is called "rabboni" by Mary Magdalene and many of his followers in the New Testament. If he was a Jewish rabbi, wouldn't the expectation be that he would be married? Weren't Peter and several of the other apostles explicitly referred to as married? Why would Jesus have practiced celibacy when biblical language is so full of the injunctions to be "fruitful" and "to go forth and multiply"?

In the scene in the Gospels where Mary Magdalene anoints Jesus with perfumed unguents from an alabaster jar and washes his feet with her tears, drying them with her hair—is this really she or a different Mary? If it is Mary Magdalene, are these actions indicators of ceremonial respect or metaphors for sexual relations? And if sexual relations, is this an allusion to her former life as a prostitute? Is it a clue that Jesus and Mary Magdalene are actually married? Is it a poetic metaphor not just for sexual relations, but specially charged, sacred sexual relations, such as the *hieros gamos* (sacred marriage) practices that come from even more ancient Greek, Minoan, and Egyptian cultures? Could she be a "prostitute" in the sense that in some ancient cultures, men engaged in sexual acts with "temple prostitutes" in order to have ecstatic, divine, mystical, religious experiences? Is the wedding at Cana, described in the New Testament, really a metaphoric description of the wedding of Mary Magdalene and Jesus Christ and does it, in turn, hearken back to the Song of Solomon in the Old Testament? And don't these stories, in turn, harken even further back to what Carl Jung or Joseph Campbell would see as universal archetypes and myths of sacred unity between male and female, of the need for wholeness and the need for love—not just love in the New Testament sense, but love in the full-bodied, erotic, humanistic sense as well?

Are there sacred texts and other kinds of documents that shed light on the true history of what happened in Israel in the time of Christ and what happened between Jesus, Mary Magdalene, and their followers? Could documents and relics referring to these events have been buried under the Temple Mount in Jerusalem and become the Holy Grail sought by crusading knights? Could the Knights Templar have found this material, spirited it out of the Holy Land, and taken it to France in medieval days? And if this material is ever found—whether in the cavity under Rosslyn Chapel in Scotland or under the Louvre's pyramid, or anywhere else—will it fundamentally change Christian history and belief the way the fragmentary

Gnostic Gospels and Dead Sea Scrolls have already proven influential?

Dan Brown has done quite a job in *The Da Vinci Code* of alluding to many of those questions. In a handful of pages, in the midst of a murder mystery–thriller–detective story, he manages to refer to all of the key issues above and much more . . . most notably the possibility that Leonardo da Vinci knew and understood the real history of Jesus Christ and Mary Magdalene and that's why he painted Mary Magdalene into *The Last Supper.* Moreover, the image of a leering Peter, slicing his bladelike hand in Mary Magdalene's direction in the painting, is meant, according to *The Da Vinci Code,* to suggest the animosity between Peter and Mary Magdalene over the future of the church. In the novel, Sophie Neveu asks her late-night teachers, Teabing and Langdon, "You're saying the Christian Church was to be carried on by a woman?"

"That was the plan," says Teabing. "Jesus was the original feminist. He intended for the future of His Church to be in the hands of Mary Magdalene."

One can see why the issues of *The Da Vinci Code* have people talking, arguing, searching—however improbable some aspects of the plot may be and however rewoven or spun out of whole cloth the religious history may be. In this chapter, we hear from a wide range of experts on many aspects of the Mary Magdalene debate. Some, like Lynn Picknett and Margaret Starbird, are part of the original source material for the ideas in *The Da Vinci Code.* Their ideas may be at the extreme end of the continuum, but they are always thought-provoking and challenging. Authorities like Susan Haskins, Deirdre Good, Karen King, and Richard McBrien are well-credentialed academics who have spent years studying the most arcane details from the available information about Mary Magdalene and related issues. They all believe that she has been mistreated in history. They eschew the most extreme ideas about her, but are consciously working to create a new multifaceted, nuanced view of Mary Magdalene restored to her rightful place in history. Katherine Ludwig Jansen and Kenneth Woodward are more conservative. Yet even the conservatives today are willing to assign a dramatically stronger role to Mary Magdalene in history than the traditional church view.

We start the discussion off with a mainstream, up-the-middle piece from *Time* magazine, occasioned by the extraordinary fascination with Mary Magdalene and the ideas of *The Da Vinci Code* in 2003.

Mary Magdalene

Saint or Sinner?

BY DAVID VAN BIEMA

The gorgeous female cryptographer and the hunky college professor are fleeing the scene of a ghastly murder they did not commit. In the midst of their escape, which will eventually utilize an armored car, a private jet, electronic-surveillance devices and just enough unavoidable violence to keep things interesting, our heroes seek out the one man who holds the key not only to their exoneration but also to a mystery that could change the world. To help explain it to them, crippled, jovial, fabulously wealthy histo-

Excerpted from *Time* magazine, August 11, 2003.

rian Sir Leigh Teabing points out a figure in a famous painting.

"Who is she?" Sophie asked.

"That, my dear," Teabing replied, "is Mary Magdalene."

Sophie turned. "The prostitute?"

Teabing drew a short breath, as if the word had injured him personally. "Magdalene was no such thing. That unfortunate misconception is the legacy of a smear campaign launched by the early Church."

Summer page turners tend to sidestep the finer points of sixth century church history. Perhaps that is their loss. *The Da Vinci Code,* by Dan Brown . . . is one of those hypercaffeinated conspiracy specials with two-page chapters and people's hair described as "burgundy." But Brown, who by book's end has woven Magdalene intricately and rather outrageously into his plot, has picked his MacGuffin cannily. Not only has he enlisted one of the few New Testament personages whom a reader might arguably imagine in a bathing suit (generations of Old Masters, after all, painted her topless). He has chosen a character whose actual identity is in play, both in theology and pop culture.

Three decades ago, the Roman Catholic Church quietly admitted what critics had been saying for centuries: Magdalene's standard image as a reformed prostitute is not supported by the text of the Bible. Freed of this lurid, limiting premise and employing varying ratios of scholarship and whimsy, academics and enthusiasts have posited various other Magdalenes: a rich and honored patron of Jesus, an apostle in her own right, the mother of the Messiah's child and even his prophetic successor. The wealth of possibilities has inspired a wave of literature, both academic and popular, including Margaret George's 2002 best-selling historical novel *Mary, Called Magdalene*. And it has gained Magdalene a new following among Catholics who see in her a potent female role model and a possible argument against the all-male priesthood. The woman who three Gospels agree was the first witness to Christ's resurrection is having her own kind of rebirth. Says Ellen Turner, who played host to an alternative celebration for the saint on her traditional feast day on July 22: "Mary [Magdalene] got worked over by the church, but she is still there for us. If we can bring her story forward, we can get back to what Jesus was really about."

In 1988, the book *Mary Magdalene: A Woman Who Showed Her Gratitude,* part of a children's biblical-women series and a fairly typical product of its time, explained that its subject "was not famous for the great things she did or said, but she goes down in history as a woman who truly loved Jesus with all her heart and was not embarrassed to show it despite criticism from others." That is certainly part of her traditional resume. Many Christian churches would add her importance as an example of the power of Christ's love to save even the most fallen humanity, and of repentance. (The word *maudlin* derives from her reputation as a tearful penitent.) Centuries of Catholic teaching also established her colloquial identity as the bad girl who became the hope of all bad girls, the saved siren active not only in the overheated imaginations of parochial-school students but also as the patron of institutions for wayward women such as the grim nun-run laundries featured in the new movie *The Magdalene Sisters* . . .

The only problem is that it turns out that she wasn't bad, just interpreted that way. Mary Magdalene (her name refers to Magdala, a city in Galilee) first appears in the Gospel of Luke as one of several apparently wealthy women Jesus cures of possession (seven demons are cast from her), who join him and the apostles and "provided for them out of their means." Her name does not come up again until the crucifixion, which she and other women witness from the foot of the cross, the male disciples having fled. On Easter Sunday morning, she visits Jesus' sepulcher, either alone or with other women, and discovers it empty. She learns—in three Gospels from angels and in one from Jesus himself—that he is risen. John's recounting is the most dramatic. She is solo at the empty tomb. She alerts Peter and an unnamed disciple; only the latter seems to grasp the Resurrection, and they leave. Lingering, Magdalene encounters Jesus, who asks her not to cling to him, "but go to my brethren and say unto them, I ascend unto my Father . . . and my God." In Luke's and Mark's versions, this plays out as a bit of a farce: Magdalene and other women try to alert the men, but "these words seemed to them an idle tale, and they did not believe them." Eventually they came around.

Discrepancies notwithstanding, the net impression is of a woman of substance, brave and smart and devoted, who plays a crucial—perhaps irreplaceable—role in Christianity's defining moment. So where did all the juicy stuff come from? Mary Magdalene's image became distorted when early church leaders bundled into her story those of several less distinguished women whom the Bible did not name or referred to without a last name. One is the "sinner" in Luke who bathes Jesus' feet with her tears, dries them with her hair, kisses them and anoints them with ointment. "Her many sins have been forgiven, for she loved much," he says. Others include Luke's Mary of Bethany and a third unnamed woman, both of whom anointed Jesus in one form or another. The mix-up was made official by Pope Gregory the Great in 591: "She whom Luke calls the sinful woman, whom John calls Mary [of Bethany], we believe to be the Mary from whom seven devils were ejected according to Mark," Gregory declared in a sermon. That position became church teaching, although it was not adopted by Orthodoxy or Protestantism when each later split from Catholicism.

What prompted Gregory? One theory suggests an attempt to reduce the number of Marys—there was a similar merging of characters named John. Another submits that the sinning woman was appended simply to provide missing backstory for a figure of obvious importance. Others blame misogyny. Whatever the motivation, the effect of the process was drastic and, from a feminist perspective, tragic. Magdalene's witness to the Resurrection, rather than being acclaimed as an act of discipleship in some ways greater than the men's, was reduced to the final stage in a moving but far less central tale about the redemption of a repentant sinner. "The pattern is a common one," writes Jane Schaberg, a professor of religious and women's studies at the University of Detroit Mercy and author of last year's *The Resurrection of Mary Magdalene,* "the powerful woman disempowered, remembered as a whore or whorish." As shorthand, Schaberg coined the term "harlotization."

In 1969, in the liturgical equivalent of fine print, the Catholic Church officially separated Luke's sinful woman, Mary of Bethany and Mary Magdalene as part of a general revision of its missal. Word has been slow in filtering down into the pews, however. (It hasn't helped that Magdalene's heroics at the tomb are still omitted from the Easter Sunday liturgy, relegated instead to midweek.) And in the meantime, more scholarship has stoked the fires of those who see her eclipse as a chauvinist conspiracy. Historians of Christianity are increasingly fascinated with a group of early followers of Christ known broadly as the Gnostics, some of whose writings were unearthed only fifty-five years ago. And the Gnostics were fascinated by Magdalene. The so-called Gospel of Mary [Magdalene], which may date from as early as AD 125 (or about forty years after John's Gospel), describes her as having received a private vision from Jesus, which she passes on to the male disciples. This role is a usurpation of the go-between status the standard Gospels normally accord to Peter, and Mary depicts him as mightily peeved, asking, "Did [Jesus] really speak with a woman without our knowledge?" The disciple Levi comes to her defense, saying, "Peter, you have always been hot-tempered. . . . If the Savior made her worthy, who are you to reject her? Surely, the Savior loves her very well. That is why he loved her more than us."

Them's fightin' words, especially when one remembers that the papacy traces its authority back to Peter. Of course, the Gnostic Gospels are not the Bible. In fact, there is evidence that the Bible was standardized and canonized precisely to exclude such books, which the early church leaders regarded as heretical for many non-Magdalene reasons. Nonetheless, feminists have been quick to cite Mary as evidence both of Magdalene's early importance, at least in some communities, and as the virtual play-by-play of a forgotten gender battle, in which church fathers eventually prevailed over the people who never got the chance to be known as church mothers. "I think it was a power struggle," says Schaberg, "and the canonical texts that we have [today] come from the winners."

Schaberg goes further. In her book, she returns to John in light of the Gnostic writings and purports to find "fragments of a claim" that Jesus may have seen Magdalene as his prophetic successor. The position is thus far quite lonely. But it serves nicely to illustrate the way in which any retrieval of Magdalene as a "winner" inevitably shakes up current assumptions about male church leadership. After Pope John Paul II prohibited even the discussion of female priests in 1995, he cited "the example recorded in the Sacred Scriptures of Christ choosing his Apostles only from among men . . ." That argument would seem weakened in light of the "new" Magdalene, whom the Pope himself has acknowledged by the once unfashionable title "Apostle to the Apostles." Chester Gillis, chair of the department of theology at Georgetown University, says conventional Catholics still feel that Mary Magdalene's absence from many biblical scenes involving the male disciples, and specifically from the ordination-like ritual of the Last Supper, rule her out as a priest precedent. Gillis agrees, however, that her recalibration "certainly makes a case for a stronger role for women in the church."

Meanwhile, the combination of Catholic rethinking and Gnostic revelations have reanimated wilder Magdalene speculations, like that of a Jesus-Magdalene marriage. ("No other biblical figure," Schaberg notes, "has had such a vivid and bizarre postbiblical life.") The Gnostic Gospel of Philip describes Magdalene as "the one who was called [Jesus'] companion," claiming that he "used to kiss her on her [mouth]." Most scholars discount a Jesus-Magdalene match because it finds little echo in the canonical Gospels once the false Magdalenes are removed. But it fulfills a deep narrative expectation: for the alpha male to take a mate, for a yin to Jesus' yang, or, as some neopagans have suggested, for a goddess to his god. Martin Luther believed that Jesus and Magdalene were married, as did Mormon patriarch Brigham Young.

The notion that Magdalene was pregnant by Jesus at his crucifixion became especially entrenched in France, which already had a tradition of her immigration in a rudderless boat, bearing the Holy Grail, his chalice at the

Last Supper into which his blood later fell. Several French kings promoted the legend that descendants of Magdalene's child founded the Merovingian line of European royalty, a story revived by Richard Wagner in his opera *Parsifal* and again in connection with Diana, Princess of Wales, who reportedly had some Merovingian blood. . . . The idea that Magdalene herself was the Holy Grail—the human receptacle for Jesus' blood line—popped up in a 1986 bestseller *Holy Blood, Holy Grail,* which inspired Brown's *Da Vinci Code.* When Brown said recently, "Mary Magdalene is a historical figure whose time has come," he meant a figure with a lot of mythic filagree. . . .

Sacred Sex and Divine Love

A Radical Reconceptualization of Mary Magdalene

By Lynn Picknett

Lynn Picknett is a writer, researcher, and lecturer on the paranormal, the occult, and historical and religious mysteries. The essay that follows below has been excerpted from *Mary Magdalene,* one of the earliest popular books re-assessing the historical Mary Magdalene. Together with Clive Prince, she has written *The Templar Revelation,* a bestseller and an important source for Dan Brown's book. She and Mr. Prince also wrote *Turin Shroud: In Whose Image? The Truth Behind the Centuries-Long Conspiracy of Silence,* which propounded the thesis that it was Leonardo who staged the revered shroud as a hoax. Ms. Picknett's reaction to being so heavily relied upon for a key theme in *The Da Vinci Code* can be found as the lead essay in chapter 10.

Who was the mysterious Mary Magdalene, so carefully squeezed to the very outside edge of the New Testament by the Gospel writers? Where did she come from, and what made her so threatening to the men of the emergent Roman Church?

In *The Templar Revelation* . . . I write about the enduring controversy surrounding this pivotal biblical character:

> The identification of Mary Magdalene, Mary of Bethany (Lazarus' sister) and the 'unnamed sinner' who anoints Jesus in Luke's Gospel has always been hotly debated. The Catholic Church decided at an early date that these three characters were one and the same, although it reversed this position as recently as 1969. Mary's identification as a prostitute stems from Pope Gregory I's *Homily 33,* delivered in 591 c.e. in which he declared:
>
> "She whom Luke calls the sinful woman, whom John calls Mary, we believe to be Mary from whom seven devils were ejected according to Mark. And what did these seven devils signify, if not all the vices? . . . It is clear, brothers, that the woman previously used the unguent to perfume her flesh in forbidden acts."
>
> The Eastern Orthodox Church has always treated Mary Magdalene and Mary of Bethany as separate characters.

The Catholic Church has always been canny in its presentation of the Magdalene, recognizing her value as role model for the hopeless women under their control, such as the Magdalene laundresses. As David Tresemer and Laura-Lea Cannon write in their preface to Jean-Yves

Leloup's 1997 translation of the Gnostic *Gospel of Mary Magdalene:*

> Only in 1969 did the Catholic Church officially repeal Gregory's labeling of Mary as a whore, thereby admitting their error—though the image of Mary Magdalene as the penitent whore has remained in the public teachings of all Christian denominations. Like a small erratum buried in the back pages of a newspaper, the Church's correction goes unnoticed, while the initial and incorrect article continues to influence readers.

Yet perhaps it would be unduly hasty to dissociate her from all suspicion of "prostitution" in an excess of modern zeal to rehabilitate her. Several researchers have pointed out that the "seven devils" that were allegedly cast out of her may be a garbled reference to the seven underworld gatekeepers of the pagan mysteries, and may provide a valuable clue about her real background. Indeed, in the pagan world there were the so-called "temple prostitutes," women who literally embodied and passed on the sacred "whore wisdom" through transcendental sex: clearly, outside their own culture they would be viewed as little more than streetwalkers, especially among the male disciples, imbued with the moral and sexual strictures of the Judaic Law, in the Holy Land . . .

Luke's choice of words in describing her moral status is very interesting: it is *harmartolos,* meaning one who has committed a crime against the Jewish law, although this does not necessarily imply prostitution. It is a term taken from the sport of archery, meaning missing the target, and may refer to someone who for whatever reason does not keep the religious observances—or does not pay the taxes, possibly because she was not actually Jewish.

Mary of Bethany is also described as having unbound or uncovered hair, which no self-respecting Judaean Jewish woman would do, for it represented sexual licence, as it does to Orthodox Jews and Muslims in today's Middle East. Indeed, Mary wipes Jesus' feet with her hair—a curiously intimate, not to say iconoclastic, action for an apparently unknown woman to perform in public. This would have been regarded as utterly scandalous by the disciples. . . .

A woman could even be divorced on the grounds of appearing in public with unbound hair—so heinous was the sin—and here Mary of Bethany, a "harmartolos" woman, one who somehow misses the Jewish mark or is outside the religious law, seems utterly oblivious to the outcry her actions would cause. More significantly, not only does Jesus not rebuke her for flouting the Judaic law, but he tacitly encourages her by turning on those who criticize her behaviour.

Both of them are behaving like foreigners in a strange land: no wonder they are not understood, particularly by the Twelve who, time after time, we are told, fail to understand Jesus' teaching or the whole point of his mission. Mary of Bethany may be an outsider, but she appears to share some kind of private secret with Jesus—and they are both outsiders.

If the anointing were not a Jewish custom, then to what tradition did it belong? In their time there was a sublimely sacred *pagan* rite that involved a woman anointing a chosen man both on the head and feet—and also on the genitals—for a very special destiny. This was the anointing of the sacred king, in which the priestess singled out the chosen man and anointed him, before bestowing his destiny upon him in a sexual rite known as the *hieros gamos* (sacred marriage). The anointing was part of the ritual preparation for penetration during the rite—which did not have the same emotional or legal ramifications as the more usual form of marriage—in which the priest-king was flooded with the power of the god, while the priestess-queen became possessed by the great goddess. Without the power of the woman, the chosen king could never reign and would be powerless. . . . This was the original meaning of "holy matrimony" *(hieros gamos)*. . . .

The concept of the sacred marriage is essential to the understanding of Jesus and his mission, and his relationship with the most important woman in his life—not to mention two highly significant men. . . . The persistent image of Mary of Bethany/Mary Magdalene as a whore begins to make sense when it is realized that this ritual is the ultimate expression of what the Victorian historians called "temple prostitution"—of course with their arrogant and hypocritical puritanism and sexual repression, this should not surprise us—although the original term for the priestess involved was *hierodule,* or "sacred servant." It was only through her that a man could achieve knowledge of himself and of the gods. In the epitome of the sacred servant's work, the *hieros gamos,* the king is sanctified and set apart—and of course immediately after the biblical anointing, Judas betrays Jesus and the machinery for his ultimate destiny through the crucifixion is set in motion. . . .

The sacred marriage was a familiar concept to pagans of Jesus' day: versions of it were commonly performed by the devotees of various other dying-and-rising god cults, such as that of Tammuz (to whom there was a temple in Jerusalem at that time) and the Egyptian god Osiris, whose consort Isis breathed life into his dead body long enough for her to conceive the magical child, the hawk-headed god of courage, Horus. Indeed, Tresemer and Cannon state unequivocally that: "Her appearances with special oils to use in anointing Jesus Christ place her in the tradition of priests and priestesses of Isis, whose unguents were used to achieve the transition over the threshold of death while retaining consciousness."[1] Indeed, this places her in the specific context of the shamanic tradition of Egypt, which is only now being acknowledged. . . .

In all versions of the sacred marriage, the representative of the goddess, in the form of her priestess, united sexually with the chosen king before his sacrificial death. Three days afterwards the god rose again, and the land was fertile once more. . . .

Clearly, this woman who anointed Jesus was very special, a great priestess of some ancient pagan tradition—but was she also Mary Magdalene, as the Church claimed until 1969? . . . Let us consider the clues concerning the true nature of the mysterious woman known as the Magdalene.

Where was Magdala?

This enigmatic woman, who was so obviously a central part of the mission of Jesus, is referred to in the Bible as "Mary Magdalene" or simply "the Magdalene," which conveys a pervasive sense that the Gospel writers expected their readers to know who she was, recognizing her name immediately. . . . This early twentieth century analysis gives a largely conventional interpretation which is still generally accepted today:

> Mary Magdalene is probably named from the town of Magdala or Magadan . . . now Medjdel, which is said to

1. Leloup, pp. xx–xxi.

> mean "a tower." It was situated at a short distance from Tiberias, and is mentioned . . . in connection with the miracle of the seven loaves. An ancient watchtower still marks the site. According to Jewish authorities it was famous for its wealth, and for the moral corruption of its inhabitants. . . .[2,3]

In fact, nowhere in the New Testament does it spell out where Mary comes from, which has led scholars and churchgoers merely to assume that she hailed from the shores of Lake Galilee—even though it must be said that there are more compelling reasons to believe she may have come from elsewhere: perhaps as a truly exotic foreigner. Indeed, . . . there is persuasive evidence that Jesus himself was not from those parts, although the assumption that he was a Jew from Galilee is so entrenched as to be deemed an unassailable fact. . . .

In fact, there is no necessity to endeavour to crowbar her into a Galilean setting, for there are at least two other intriguing alternatives for her place of origin: although there was no "Magdala" in Judaea in her day, there was a Magdolum in Egypt—just across the border—which was probably the Migdol mentioned in Ezekiel. There was a large and flourishing Jewish community in Egypt at that time, which was particularly centred on the great seaport of Alexandria, a seething cosmopolitan melting pot of many races, nationalities and religions, where John the Baptist had his headquarters, and perhaps where the Holy Family had fled to escape the depredations of Herod's

2. Edersheim, vol. i. p. 571.

3. *A Dictionary of the Bible: Dealing with its language, literature, and contents including the Biblical theology,* edited by James Hastings, M.A., D.D., Edinburgh, 1900, p. 284.

men. . . . If the Magdalene really was from the Egyptian town of Magdolum, this could provide a clue as to why she was so sidelined—after all, despite the exciting mix of nations and religions in Galilee at that time, human nature has always been suspicious of foreigners, and the gospels make it clear that few were more insular in their attitudes than the likes of Simon Peter, at least at the beginning of the mission. . . .

However, if the Magdalene was a *priestess* from Egypt, that would increase the Jewish men's hostility to her a thousandfold. Not only was she an outspoken and independent woman of means, but also invested with pagan authority! . . . They would have had great reservations about the foreign priestess who constantly tagged along. . . .

Perhaps there was another reason why the Magdalene was treated so badly by the men of Jesus' following. While she may have lived in Egypt—after all, we know that both the Baptist and Jesus himself lived there for several years—perhaps that is not where she came from originally. Indeed, it may be significant that for many years there was a Magdala in Ethiopia. . . . This rocky outcrop is now called Amra *Mariam* (Mary): although the Ethiopians today generally revere the Virgin Mary over Mary Magdalene, these place names indicate that there is a long association with the latter in that area, perhaps—unthinkably to many—it may even have been her birthplace or home.

An Ethiopian background would certainly have made her extremely exotic and perhaps disturbing to the insular men of Jesus' mission such as Simon Peter. Despite what politically correct revisionists may claim now, the British Empire did not invent racism: if the Magdalene were *black,* outspoken, rich, a pagan priestess—and Jesus' closest ally (to say the least)—the Twelve might well have floundered in a sea of uneducated emotions at the sight of her, born of fear of the alien, the unknown. . . .

Bride of Christ?

Was the obviously close relationship between the Magdalene and Jesus due to their being legally man and wife, as some—most seminally Baigent, Leigh and Lincoln in their 1982 book *Holy Blood, Holy Grail*—have claimed? If they were, there is a very strange silence about it in the New Testament, for despite what Christians (especially Catholics) may think today, priests and rabbis in the Holy Land were *supposed* to be married, for to abstain from procreation was (and still is, among Orthodox Jews) seen as an insult to God. Indeed, celibacy won censure from the elders of the synagogue, and perhaps also mutterings about unnatural lusts among the congregation. For a Jewish rabbi, it would have been very odd if Jesus were *not* married, but if he had a wife, surely she would have been mentioned—as "Miriam the wife of the Saviour," or "Mary the wife of Jesus." There is never any phrase that might remotely be interpreted as alluding to his legal spouse, but was this because there was no such person, or because his wife was known but disliked so intensely and on such a scale that the canonical Gospel writers decided to ignore her? Or because they had married in a ceremony that the Jews did not recognize? But if, as the Gnostic Gospels overwhelmingly suggest, Jesus and the Magdalene were committed and passionate lovers, why did they stop short of putting their relationship on an official footing? . . .

Apart from there being some kind of legal proscription on their love—such as being close blood relatives or being legally married to someone else at the time—there seems little reason for them not to have made a public commitment to each other. Could this reluctance to tie the knot have been because they were not, in fact, Jewish at all in the generally accepted sense and therefore could not be married in a synagogue? And it is significant that pagan priestesses, even those involved in sacred sex, were often required to be otherwise celibate and remain unmarried. . . .

The French Connection

There are several legends about Mary Magdalene travelling to France (or Gaul as it was then) after the crucifixion, together with a varied assortment of people, including a black servant girl called Sarah, and Mary Salome and Mary Jacobi—allegedly Jesus' aunts—besides Joseph of Arimathea, the rich man who owned the tomb in which Christ was laid prior to the resurrection, and St Maximin (Maximus), one of the seventy-two closest disciples of Jesus and the first bishop of Provence. Although the details of the story differ from version to version, it appears that the Magdalene and her party were forced to flee from Palestine under less than perfect conditions—their boat was leaky, rudderless, oarless and without a sail, which is believed to have been the result of deliberate sabotage on the part of certain factions in their homeland. Even allowing for the inevitable exaggeration of myth-making—the ruinous state of their boat seems rather unlikely—given the Gnostic Gospels' depiction of the volatile situation between Mary and Simon Peter, it is not difficult to hazard a guess at the possible, even probable, identity of at least one of the plotters who would have wished her and her companions at the bottom of the sea. In the light of the legend of the leaky boat, it is chilling to recall Mary's words from the *Pistis Sophia:* "I am afraid of Peter, because he threatened me and hateth our sex." But whoever sought to kill them, miraculously they survived, allegedly ending up on the wild coast of what is now Provence. . . .

The story goes that they landed (no doubt very gratefully, after wallowing about in floods of seawater for weeks) at what is now the town of Saintes-Maries-de-la-Mer in the Camargue, in the wetlands where the Rhone meets the Mediterranean. Three Marys—Magdalene, Mary Jacobi and Mary Salome—are the focus for great reverence in the grand church that rises like a stately sailing ship from the surrounding marshes, while in the crypt there is an altar dedicated to Sarah the Egyptian, allegedly the Magdalene's black servant girl, now the much-loved patron saint of the gypsies, who converge on the town for her annual feast day of 25 May. Surrounded by thousands of adoring devotees, Sarah's statue is paraded to the sea, where it is ceremoniously dipped. As medieval folk thought of gypsies as being from Egypt—"egypsies"—it made sense for them to venerate this young woman who originated from that country. Indeed, the colour of her skin, and the fact that Egypt was known as the land of "*Khem,*" or blackness, may be very significant. Judging by the New Testament's division of one woman into three—the Magdalene, Mary of Bethany and the unnamed "sinner"—perhaps the assorted women in the leaky boat were also merely different aspects of one woman . . .

The Woman with the Alabaster Jar

Mary Magdalen and the Holy Grail

BY MARGARET STARBIRD

Margaret Starbird holds a master's degree from the University of Maryland and has studied at Christian Albrechts University in Kiel, Germany, and at Vanderbilt Divinity School. In great demand as a leader of workshops and media commentator, she has written extensively on the concept of the sacred feminine. Her books—which Dan Brown acknowledges as having had a strong influence on his exploration of the same themes—include *Magdalen's Lost Legacy: Symbolic Numbers and the Sacred Union in Christianity, The Goddess in the Gospels: Reclaiming the Sacred Feminine,* and *The Feminine Face of Christianity.* In this excerpt from her most famous book, *The Woman with the Alabaster Jar: Mary Magdalen and the Holy Grail,* she makes the case that Mary Magdalene and Jesus were not simply man and wife, but had a holy, dynastic marriage.

I have come to suspect that Jesus had a secret dynastic marriage with Mary of Bethany and that she was a daughter of the tribe of Benjamin, whose ancestral heritage was the land surrounding the Holy City of David, the city Jerusalem. A dynastic marriage between Jesus and a royal daughter of the Benjamites would have been perceived as a source of healing to the people of Israel during their time of misery as an occupied nation.

Israel's first anointed King Saul was of the tribe of Benjamin, and his daughter Michol was the wife of King

David. Throughout the history of the tribes of Israel, the tribes of Judah and Benjamin were the closest and most loyal of allies. Their destinies were intertwined. A dynastic marriage between a Benjamite heiress to the lands surrounding the Holy City and the messianic Son of David would have appealed to the fundamentalist Zealot faction of the Jewish nation. It would have been seen as a sign of hope and blessing during Israel's darkest hour.

In the novel *King Jesus* (1946), Robert Graves, the twentieth-century mythographer, suggests that Jesus' lineage and marriage were concealed from all but a select circle of royalist leaders. To protect the royal bloodline, this marriage would have been kept secret from the Romans and the Herodian tetrarchs, and after the crucifixion of Jesus, the protection of his wife and family would have been a sacred trust for those few who knew their identity. All reference to the marriage of Jesus would have been deliberately obscured, edited, or eradicated. Yet the pregnant wife of the anointed Son of David would have been the bearer of the hope of Israel—the bearer of the Sangraal, the royal bloodline.

Magdal-eder, the Tower of the Flock

In chapter 4 of the Hebrew prophet Micah, we read a beautiful prophecy of the restoration of Jerusalem, when all nations shall beat their swords into plowshares and be reconciled under God. Beginning with verse 8 we find:

> As for you, O [Magdal-eder], watchtower of the flock,
> O stronghold of the Daughter of Zion!
> the former dominion will be restored to you;
> kingship will come to the Daughter of Jerusalem.
> Why do you now cry aloud—

have you no king?
Has your counselor perished,
that pain seizes you like that of a woman in labor?
Writhe in agony, O Daughter of Zion,
like a woman in labor,
for now you must leave the city
and camp in the open field.

It is probable that the original references to Mary Magdalen in the oral tradition, the "pericopes" of the New Testament, were misunderstood before they were ever committed to writing. I suspect that the epithet "Magdalen" was meant to be an allusion to the "Magdal-eder" found in Micah, the promise of the restoration of Sion following her exile. Perhaps the earliest verbal references attaching the epithet "Magdala" to Mary of Bethany's name had nothing to do with an obscure town in Galilee, as is suggested, but were deliberate references to these lines in Micah, to the "watchtower" or "stronghold" of the daughter of Sion who was forced into political exile.

The place name *Magdal-eder* literally means "tower of the flock," in the sense of a high place used by a shepherd as a vantage point from which to watch over his sheep. In Hebrew, the epithet *Magdala* literally means "tower" or "elevated, great, magnificent." This meaning has particular relevance if the Mary so named was in fact the wife of the Messiah. It would have been the Hebrew equivalent of calling her "Mary the Great," while at the same time referring to the prophesied return of dominion to "the daughter of Jerusalem" (Mic. 4:8).

In Old French legend, the exiled "Magdal-eder," the refugee Mary who seeks asylum on the southern coast of France, is Mary of Bethany, the Magdalen. The early French legend records that Mary "Magdalen," traveling with Martha and Lazarus of Bethany, landed in a boat on the coast of Provence in France. Other legends credit Joseph of Arimathea as being the custodian of the Sangraal, which I have suggested may be the *royal bloodline of Israel* rather than a literal chalice. The vessel that contained this bloodline, the archetypal chalice of medieval myth, must have been the wife of the anointed King Jesus.

The image of Jesus that emerges in our story is that of a charismatic leader who embodies the roles of prophet, healer, and Messiah-King, a leader who was executed by the Roman Army of Occupation and whose wife and bloodline were secretly taken from Israel by his loyal friends and transplanted in Western Europe to await the fullness of time and the culmination of prophecy. The friends of Jesus who believed so fervently that he was the Messiah, the Anointed of God, would have perceived the preservation of his family as a sacred duty. The vessel, the chalice that embodied the promises of the Millennium, the "Sangraal" of medieval legend, was, I have come to believe, Mary Magdalen . . .

But tradition derived from [another] Old French legend from the Mediterranean coast tells us that . . . Joseph of Arimathea was the custodian of the "Sangraal" and that the child on the boat was Egyptian, which means quite literally "born in Egypt." It seems likely that after the crucifixion of Jesus, Mary the Magdalen found it necessary to flee for the sake of her unborn child to the nearest refuge. The influential friend of Jesus, Joseph of Arimathea, could very well have been her protector.

If our theory is correct, the child actually *was* born in Egypt. Egypt was the traditional place of asylum for Jews whose safety was threatened in Israel; Alexandria was easily reached from Judea and contained well-established Jewish communities at the time of Jesus. In all probability, the emergency refuge of Mary Magdalen and Joseph of Arimathea was Egypt. And later—years later—they left Alexandria and sought an even safer haven on the coast of France.

Scholars of archaeology and linguistics have found that place names and legends of an area contain "fossils" from that area's remote past. The truth may be embellished by changes and stories may suffer abridgment through the years of telling, but traces of the truth remain in fossil form, buried in the names of people and places. In the town of Les Saintes-Maries-de-la-Mer in France, there is a festival every May 23 to 25 at a shrine in honor of Saint Sarah the Egyptian, also called Sara Kali, the "Black Queen." Close scrutiny reveals that this festival, which originated in the Middle Ages, is in honor of an "Egyptian" child who accompanied Mary Magdalen, Martha, and Lazarus, arriving with them in a small boat that came ashore at this location in approximately AD 42. The people seem to have assumed that the child, being "Egyptian," was dark-skinned and, by further interpolation, that she must have been the servant of the family from Bethany, since no other reasonable explanation could be found for her presence.

The name Sarah means "queen" or "princess" in Hebrew. This Sarah is further characterized in local legends as "young," no more than a child. So we have, in a tiny coastal town in France, a yearly festival in honor of a young, dark-skinned girl-child called Sarah. The fossil in this legend is that the child is called "princess" in Hebrew. A child of Jesus, born after Mary's flight to Alexandria, would have been about twelve years of age at the time of the voyage to Gaul recorded in the legend. She, like the princes of David's line, is *symbolically* black, "unrecognized in the streets" (Lam. 4:8). The Magdalen was herself the "Sangraal," in the sense that she was the "chalice" or vessel that once carried the royal bloodline *in utero.* The symbolic blackness of the Bride in Canticles and the Davidic princes of Lamentations is extended to this hidden Mary and her child. . . .

In summary, the two royal refugees from Israel, mother and daughter, might logically be represented in early European art as a dark-skinned mother and child, the hidden ones. The Black Madonnas of the early shrines in Europe (fifth to twelfth centuries) might then have been venerated as symbolic of this other Mary and her child, the Sangraal, which Joseph of Arimathea brought in safety to the coast of France. The symbol for a male of the royal house of David would be a flowering or budding staff, but the symbol for a woman would be the chalice—a cup or vessel containing the royal blood of Jesus. And that is exactly what the Holy Grail is said to have been!

Mary Magdalen
The Model for Women in the Church

An Interview with Susan Haskins

Susan Haskins is an editor, researcher, translator, and the author of *Mary Magdalen: Myth and Metaphor.* She has given lectures around the world, appeared on various television programs to discuss Mary Magdalene, and is currently translating from the Italian and editing *Three Marian Writings* (texts on the life of the Virgin by three sixteenth-century Italian female writers). In this interview, she departs sharply from many of her colleagues who claim knowledge of Mary Magdalene beyond what is written in the New Testament. Yes, she says, Mary Magdalene was "the leading apostle," and even a "Christian goddess," but we have absolutely no direct evidence about her personal life.

In your opinion, who was the true Mary Magdalene?

The true Mary Magdalene is the figure in the gospels: the leading woman follower of Christ, who, together with the other women named in Luke, supported and contributed to the living expenses of the itinerant group. She was present at his crucifixion, witnessed it, and according to John's gospel, was one of the privileged few, along with the Virgin Mary, wife of Cleophas, and St. John, to be beneath the cross. She was witness to the putting of his body in Joseph of Arimathea's sepulcher; she came at dawn with either one or two other Marys to bring unguents. In John's gospel, it was to her alone and first that Christ appeared after his resurrection, and it was to her alone and first that he gave the message of the new Christian life. Mark's gospel, in a later addition, says that she had had seven devils driven from her. We have no idea of what she looked like. She is shown with long red or golden hair in medieval and later art, because blond hair was the attribute of ideal feminine beauty. We do not know what her life was like. It is assumed that because she, along with the other women followers, supported the group "of their own substance," that she was mature—among the other women were ones who were married or separated—and comparatively well off and independent. So I agree with those who see her as a patron and supporter of Jesus.

What are the representations of Mary Magdalene that have occurred throughout history? Do any of them fit with Dan

Brown's theory in The Da Vinci Code *that she may have been married to Jesus and had his child?*

Dan Brown's theory that Mary Magdalene may have been married to Jesus and had his child has a long history. It was made particularly public by *Holy Blood, Holy Grail,* and followed up by Bishop Spong and others. Luther seems to have thought that she had a sexual relationship with Christ as far back as the sixteenth century! As there is no concrete evidence of either a marriage or child, I would give no credence to this hypothesis.

Why did the church depict Mary Magdalene as a prostitute for so many years? Was she simply a victim of bad luck to be confused with all of the other Marys in the New Testament, or was there a kind of foul play involved?

The church depicted Mary Magdalene as a prostitute because of the various commentaries on the Gospels made by early church fathers from the third century, trying to work out who all the gospel characters were. There are several females called Mary in the New Testament, which led to confusion. Because Luke's first mention of Mary Magdalene, following Christ from Galilee with the other women, and the male disciples follows his account of the unnamed woman named as a sinner, forgiven by Christ in the house of the Pharisee, Pope Gregory the Great (AD 595) conflated these two figures, as well as that of Mary of Bethany. Although the woman is only called a "sinner," the assumption was that her sin was that of the flesh, even though the word *porin,* used to describe her, does not mean "prostitute." Making Mary Magdalene a repentant prostitute diminished her role as first apostle, an otherwise extremely powerful and important role. We cannot know for sure whether foul play was involved, but certainly ecclesiastical politics were. The early church had women priests and bishops, but by the fifth century the sacerdotal role was not allowed to women, although tomb monuments in southern Italy show that women were still carrying out the priestly role. Diminishing Mary Magdalene's role to both penitent and prostitute puts her on a par with Eve, whose sexuality and gender were deemed by the male ecclesiastical hierarchy as being responsible for the Fall.

Do you think that Jesus and Mary Magdalene could have been married?

I personally do not think Jesus and Mary Magdalene were married. That an important relationship existed between them is undeniable, but was it any more than the fact that she was his leading woman disciple? People find the idea compelling for many reasons: there is this enigmatic relationship in the Gospels—even more so in the Gnostic Gospels—so a kind of logical progression would be marriage. Rabbis were often, if not usually, married, so it has often been suggested that Christ must also have been, although there is nothing in the Gospels to suggest this. We have no evidence of a child, and the Merovingian link is very unlikely.

How does The Da Vinci Code *character of Mary Magdalene fit in with other characters in prior religious belief systems? Is there a woman comparable to Mary Magdalene in Greek, Egyptian, Jewish, or pagan/tribal cultures?*

The Da Vinci Code is interesting for its narrative re: the goddess figure, suppressed by the early church. The theme of resurrection is found in Egyptian, Sumerian, and Christian belief systems: Isis and Osiris, Ishtar and Tammuz, Mary Magdalene and Christ. Mary Magdalene can be seen as the Christian goddess.

What do you think the Gospel of Philip *tells us about the relationship between Jesus and Mary Magdalene, and about the rivalries with Peter for control of the church?*

The *Gospel of Philip* is regarded by scholars as an allegory of the relationship between Christ and his church, his love for his church. Elaine Pagels sees the antagonism between Peter and Mary Magdalene as—if I remember rightly—a metaphor of the antagonism between the evolving early church in the second and third centuries, based on a hierarchy of bishops, deacons, and priests, and Gnosticism, which valued individual inspiration or knowledge, without the intermediary of the church. Peter was also jealous of Mary Magdalene because of gender issues.

Why was Mary Magdalene one of the few at the crucifixion? Why might she have attended when other disciples did not? And what is the importance of Mary Magdalene being the first to see Jesus after the resurrection?

It is interesting that Mary Magdalene was one of the few at the crucifixion. But this is only in John's account; in the others, she witnesses it from a distance, with other women. We do not know who edited the Gospel texts or why they are only approximately identical, but presumably they come from different oral traditions. The women disciples were there, but not the males because the males had taken fright, particularly Peter, who denied Jesus thrice.

It is, or should be, of the utmost importance to

Christians that it was to Mary Magdalene that Jesus appeared first after the resurrection, because the keystone to Christianity is the promise of everlasting life—the very message Christ gave to her to tell the world. It was male prejudice in both the Judaic and Hellenistic systems that disallowed women as witnesses and therefore allowed the male disciples to claim the right to give the news of the resurrection. But, of course, it can be seen as equally important—as a matter of editing the canon, Christian apologetics, and ecclesiastical politics—for the church to deny this role and to assert the premise that "You are Peter and upon this rock I will found my church."

Why is the topic of Mary Magdalene so compelling in itself? She is a beautiful image of an independent woman, who follows a charismatic preacher and offers an ethical and theological framework for his followers. She is also dynamic, a leader and a model of fidelity. She witnesses the crucifixion, unlike the male disciples. She is courageous. She goes alone, or with others, to the sepulcher at dawn. She meets Christ. Christ is egalitarian. He heals women of their afflictions without criticism and social stigma—the "sinner" in Luke, the Samaritan woman, the woman with the issue of blood, the woman taken in adultery, Mary Magdalene with her seven devils. He appears to a woman, Mary Magdalene, first after his resurrection, and he gives one woman, Mary Magdalene, the role of delivering the Christian message of everlasting life.

She has represented the sinner redeemed since the sixth century, and for this reason has been a model for all Christians, male and female. She offers them hope. Her closeness to Christ has been a topic of fascination since early Christianity; her cult burgeoned from the eleventh century. She represents the fallible female redeemed, as well as her role as intercessor with God. Renewed interest in her in our times is due in part to feminism, particularly in recent scholarship about women's roles in religion and the reassertion of their right to be priests, which has been denied for seventeen centuries. Mary Magdalene, as first apostle and disciple, is the model for women in the church, both Catholic and Protestant, and in the synagogue.

Mary Magdalen
Myth and Metaphor

By Susan Haskins

In four excerpts from Susan Haskins's seminal book, *Mary Magdalen: Myth and Metaphor,* we sample the author's view on the role of the female apostles, how Mary's relationship to Christ is portrayed in the *Gospel of Philip,* what the exact relationship between Jesus and Mary Magdalene might have been, and where Mary went after the crucifixion—and how French towns built mini-industries around worshipping Mary Magdalene. Haskins does not mince words. She states her case boldly:

> And so the transformation of Mary Magdalen was complete. From the gospel figure with her active role as herald of the New Life—the Apostle before the Apostles—she became the redeemed whore and Christianity's model of repentance: a manageable, controllable figure, an effective weapon and instrument of propaganda against her own sex.

De Unica Magdalena

We know very little about Mary Magdalen. The predominant image we have of her is of a beautiful woman with long golden hair, weeping for her sins, the very incarnation of the age-old equation between feminine beauty, sexuality and sin. For nearly two thousand years, the traditional conception of Mary Magdalen has been that of the prostitute who, hearing the words of Jesus Christ, repented of her sinful past and henceforth devoted her life and love to him. She appears in countless devotional images, scarlet-cloaked and with loose hair, kneeling below the cross, or seated at Christ's feet in the house of Mary and Martha of Bethany, or as the beauteous prostitute herself, sprawled at his feet, unguent jar by her side, in the house of the Pharisee. Her very name evokes images of beauty and sensuality, yet when we look for this creature in the New Testament, we look for her in vain. All we truly know of her comes from the four gospels, a few brief references which yield an inconsistent, even contradictory vision. These shifting reflections converge, however, on four salient aspects: that Mary Magdalen was one of Christ's female followers, was present at his crucifixion, was a witness—indeed, according to the gospel of St. John, *the* witness—of his resurrection, and was the first to be charged with the supreme ministry, that of proclaiming the Christian message. She brought the knowledge that through Christ's victory over death, life everlasting was offered to all who believe . . .

One of the most striking aspects about the gospel accounts is the role given to Christ's female followers as supporters and witnesses during the events of that first Easter. Their faith and tenacity were acknowledged by early Christian commentators, but later cast into the background as new emphases and interpretations increasingly reduced their importance. The true significance of their witness was for the most part ignored, while Mary Magdalen herself was in the late sixth century recreated as an entirely different character to serve the purposes of the ecclesiastical hierarchy. This refashioning by the early Church Fathers has distorted our view of Mary Magdalen and the other women; we need therefore to turn again to the gospels in order to see them more clearly.

Mark tells us that Mary Magdalen was among the women who when Christ was in Galilee "followed him and *ministered* unto him" (my italics; 15:41; see also Matt. 27:55). "To minister" is translated from the Greek verb *diakonein,* to serve or to minister. It is also the root of the word "deacon," which establishes the important function given to the women within the group of both female and male disciples. Luke, from whom we also hear that the group has been part of Christ's entourage for some considerable time before the crucifixion (8:1–4), corroborates their ministering role, and amplifies it with the words "of their own substance" (v.3). This role has often been assumed to have been domestic, as women's lives in Jewish society of the first century AD were circumscribed within their traditional household environment. They carried out such tasks as grinding flour, baking and laundering, feeding children, bed-making and woolworking. Until modern times the role of the women amongst Christ's followers has also been taken to have been merely domestic, and therefore less important, an assumption which has only recently been questioned by scholars. But "of their own substance" indicates that the women contributed the means to enable the travelling preachers to carry out their work. Whilst women are known to have supported rabbis with money, possessions and food, their participation in the practice of Judaism was negligible. Although they were allowed to read the Torah at congregational services, they were forbidden to recite lessons in public in order to "safeguard the honor of the congregation."

In the first century AD, one Rabbi Eliezer was quoted as saying, "Rather should the words of the Torah be burned than entrusted to a woman!"[1] It was for much the same reason that in the synagogue itself, women were seated apart from the men. They were restricted to a gallery above, unable to wear the phylactery—the small leather box containing verses from the Old Testament attached to the head and arm by leather thongs—or to carry out any liturgical functions. Their exclusion from the priesthood was based on their supposed uncleanness during menstruation, as defined in a Temple ordinance (Leviticus 15), a taboo which was also invoked by the Christian Church and still used until recently as a powerful weapon against the entry of women into ecclesiastical office. A priest, according to Leviticus 21 and 22, was to be clean and holy at all times to offer sacrifice. Women were, nonetheless, allowed to be prophetesses, as the Old Testament bears witness, and even, as in the case of Anna, daughter of Phanuel, celebrated as such in Christ's day (Luke 2:36–8).

It is in this context that Luke's phrase has a special significance, as it suggests that Christ's women followers were central to the group as a whole, in that they donated their own property and income to provide Christ and the male disciples with the means to live as they travelled around the countryside preaching and healing. This, in turn, sheds further light on the women, since their ability

1. Mishnah Sotah 3, 4, quoted in Leonard Swidler, *Biblical Affirmations of Woman*, Philadelphia, 1979, p. 163.

to dispose of their money presupposes their financial independence, and possibly their maturity, which is corroborated by the statement that one of the Marys is the "mother of James," presumably referring to the apostle (Mark 15:40 and 16:1). Even more important is the recent suggestion that, contrary to a general assumption that the women disciples did not preach, and in this way differed from their male counterparts, they may well have done so, since the term "to follow" as used by Mark to describe those at the crucifixion—"who also when he was in Galilee followed him, and ministered unto him" (15:41)—was used technically to imply their full participation, both in belief and in the activities of the travelling preachers, as is borne out by the accounts in Acts and in Paul's letters of the women's involvement. Nowhere in the texts is there any indication that Christ regarded the women's contribution as inferior or subsidiary to that of his male disciples. Indeed, it could be argued that the women's contribution both during and after the crucifixion showed greater tenacity of purpose and courage, though not necessarily greater faith, than that of the men who fled. Unlike the eleven male disciples who feared for their own lives, the women disciples followed, were present at the crucifixion, witnessed the burial, discovered the empty tomb and, as true disciples, were rewarded with the first news of the resurrection and, in the case of Mary Magdalen, the first meeting with the risen Christ.

Christ's disinterest in the conventions of his day and his desire to radically alter certain social *mores* are made manifest in his treatment of women, not least because they actually formed part of his retinue. Although women might assist rabbis financially, it was certainly uncommon for them to accompany preachers as travelling disciples. Christ also welcomed into the group the kind of women whom Luke describes as having been healed of "evil spirits and infirmities" (8:2–3), those who might otherwise have been regarded as social outcasts. Of the few women in the community who are named, one, Joanna, is or has been married to Chuza, Herod's steward, and must therefore have left her family and the royal court to follow Christ. It perhaps should be noted that the reference to Joanna's social status, as a married woman, has the effect of further determining that of Mary Magdalen: of the women described, she alone stands out undefined by a designation attaching her to some male as wife, mother or daughter; and she is the only one to be identified by her place of birth. It is therefore as an *independent* woman that she is presented: this implies that she must also have been of some means, to have been able to choose to follow and support Christ. . . .

Mary Magdalen's "seven devils" to which both Luke and Mark refer were a focus for speculation amongst early Christian commentators; their link with the "evil spirits and infirmities" ascribed to some of the women may well have led to their identification with the seven deadly sins. It has been suggested that Mary Magdalen was the best known of the women because her "healing was the most dramatic," as the seven demons may have indicated a "possession of extraordinary malignity."[2] However, nowhere in the New Testament is demoniacal possession regarded as synonymous with sin.[3] That Mary Magdalen's condition might have been psychological, that is, seen as madness, rather than moral or sexual, seems never to have entered

2. Ben Witherington III, *Women in the Ministry of Jesus,* Cambridge, 1984, p. 117.

3. Although in John 8:46–9 direct comparison is made between being a sinner and having a devil.

into the considerations of the early biblical commentators, although it preoccupied her interpreters from the nineteenth century onwards. There is, after all, no implication in the story of the man possessed of devils that his "unclean spirit" is sexual (Luke 8:26–39). . . . Mrs. Balfour, the noted nineteenth-century Evangelical, was one of the first to deny that Mary Magdalen's malaise was anything other than psychological, and more recently J. E. Fallon has written that rather than being in a state of sinfulness, she probably suffered from a "violent and chronic nervous disorder."

To the ascription to her of the ambiguous "seven devils" was added the putative disadvantage of her birthplace: Mary Magdalen's second name, *Magdalini* in Greek, signified her belonging to el Mejdel, a prosperous fishing village on the northwest bank of the lake of Galilee, four miles north of Tiberias. Its apparent notoriety in the early centuries of Christianity—it was destroyed in AD 75 because of its infamy and the licentious behaviour of its inhabitants—may have helped later to colour the name and reputation of Mary Magdalen herself.[4] (Today, a rusting sign by the lake tells the passing tourist that Magdala, or Migdal, had been a flourishing city at the end of the period of the Second Temple, and was also the birthplace of Mary of Magdala who "followed and ministered to Jesus.")

It might be argued that none of the elements detailed above offers sufficient grounds in itself for proving that Mary Magdalen was a sinner or prostitute. Indeed, these assertions might never have achieved currency—at least not to the extent they did—had she not also been confused with other female characters from the gospels, some of whom are explicitly described as sinners; and one who,

4. J. E. Fallon, "Mary Magdalen," NCE, vol. IX, p. 387.

from her story, appears to have been a prostitute. To later commentators, and in an ecclesiastical environment which was becoming more entrenched in its attachment to the ideal of celibacy, her femaleness would only have served to lend credence to this misidentification. By such means could the seven devils with which she was possessed assume the social and moral stigma, the monstrous proportions, of lust and temptation—those vices which early Christian interpreters of Genesis traditionally associated with the Female—that they did. Mary Magdalen, chief female disciple, first apostle and beloved friend of Christ, would become transformed into a penitent whore . . .

Companion of the Saviour

Her close relationship to Christ is emphasised in the *Gospel of Philip*, where she is depicted as one of the "three who always walked with the Lord: Mary his mother, her sister and Magdalene [*sic*], the one who was called his companion. His sister and his mother and his companion were each a Mary. And the companion of the Saviour is Mary Magdalene." The Greek word *koinonōs* used to describe Mary Magdalen, whilst often rendered as "companion," is more correctly translated as "partner" or "consort," a woman with whom a man has had sexual intercourse. Two pages on is another passage, which amplifies in sexual imagery the relationship already described:

> But Christ loved her more than all the disciples and used to kiss her often on the mouth. The rest of the disciples were offended by it and expressed disapproval. They said to him, "Why do you love her more than all of us?" The Saviour answered and said to them, "Why do I not love you like [I love] her?"

Erotic love has often been the vehicle used to express mystical experiences, perhaps most notably in that great spiritual epithalamium, the *Canticle of Canticles,* or *Song of Songs,* which describes in the most sensual and voluptuous imagery what the rabbis were to read as an allegory of Yahweh's love for Israel, and early Christian commentators to interpret as Christ's love for the Church, for the Christian soul—sometimes in the person of Mary Magdalen—and for the Virgin Mary. In the *Gospel of Philip,* the spiritual union between Christ and Mary Magdalen is couched in terms of human sexuality; it is also a metaphor for the reunion of Christ and the Church which takes place in the bridal chamber, the place of fullness or *pleroma*. While the tractate itself deals with sacramental and ethical arguments, its main theme is the idea, common to many Gnostic and later Christian writings, that mankind's woes had been brought about by the differentiation of the sexes caused by the separation of Eve from Adam, which destroyed the primal androgynous unity found in Genesis 1:27, after which the Gnostic spirit would forever yearn. As the author of the *Gospel of Philip* explains: "When Eve was still in Adam death did not exist. When she was separated from him, death came into being. If he again becomes complete and attains his former self, death will be no more." The *Gospel of Philip* uses the bridal chamber as a metaphor for the reunion between "Adam" and "Eve," in which the polarities of male and female would be abolished, and androgyny, or the spiritual state, would be effected through the coming of Christ, the Bridegroom.[5] The relationship between Christ and Mary Magdalen symbolises that perfect spiritual union. Some Gnostics, however, were believed by their adversaries to put erotic

5. Wesley W. Isenberg, introduction, *Gospel of Philip,* NHL, p. 131.

concepts into practice, and to take part in sexual orgies which were profane re-enactions of Christian ritual: according to Epiphanius, the Gnostics had a book called the "Great Questions of Mary" which represented Christ as a revealer to Mary Magdalen of obscene ceremonies which a sect had to perform for its salvation. He wrote indignantly:

> For in the Questions of Mary which are called "Great" . . . they assert that he [Jesus] gave her [Mary] a revelation, taking her aside to the mountain and praying; and he brought forth from his side a woman and began to unite with her, and so, forsooth, taking his effluent, he showed that "we must so do, that we may live"; and how when Mary fell to the ground abashed, he raised her up again and said to her: "Why didst thou doubt, O thou of little faith?"[6]

The sequence in the *Gospel of Philip* can be seen at two different levels, one symbolic of the love of Christ for the Church—in the person of Mary Magdalen—and the other as representing an historical situation in which she symbolises the feminine element in the Church. As we have seen, the preferential treatment that Mary Magdalen receives from Christ in both the *Gospel of Mary* and the *Gospel of Philip* gives rise to jealousy among the other disciples, notably Peter. In the *Pistis Sophia,* one of the few tractates found before the writings at Nag Hammadi, a similar argument breaks out between Mary and Peter, who complains on behalf of the male disciples that Mary dominates the conversation about Pistis Sophia's fall from

6. Epiphanius (Panarion, 26.8, 2–3), quoted in H.-Ch. Puech, "Gnostic Gospels and Related Documents," in NTA, vol. I, pp. 338–9.

the realm of Light, and so prevents them from speaking. Jesus rebukes him. Mary later tells Jesus that she fears Peter, "because he is wont to threaten me, and he hateth our sex." (Jesus tells her that anyone who is inspired by the divine spirit may come forward to speak, implying that inspiration nullifies sexual differentiation, and reiterating the theme of androgyny found in the *Gospel of Philip.*) It has been suggested that Peter's antagonism towards Mary Magdalen may reflect the historical ambivalence of the leaders of the orthodox community towards the participation of women in the Church. But by the end of the second century, the egalitarian principles defined in the New Testament, and adhered to in this context by St. Paul, had been discarded in favour of a return to the patriarchal system of Judaism which had preceded them. Thus at the level of historical interpretation, the Gnostic texts may have referred to a political tension in the early Church. It is a situation inferred in the synoptics through the disciples' disbelief of the women's account of the resurrection, and in Paul's omission of the women's witness of the resurrection, but never alluded to directly by the orthodox Christians, namely the suppression of the feminine element within the Church which had gradually been taking place from the second century.

Much Malign'd Magdalen

Christ's genuine humanity, and therefore his sexuality, has been the subject of several serious studies over the past three decades. Unlike the Renaissance images which drew attention to his genitalia in order to stress his humanity, recently the problem has been how to deal with his sexuality in the context of his human existence. The suggestion that he may have been married, as a rabbi of his age would probably have been, has led one writer, as we have seen, to conjecture that he might even have been married to Mary Magdalen. This was argued by the Protestant theologian William E. Phipps in his book *Was Jesus Married? The Distortion of Sexuality in the Christian Tradition,* first published in 1970 and reissued in 1989. Marriage to Mary Magdalen, he suggests, might have taken place during the second decade of Christ's life; she may even, in a further extension of the hypothesis, have been unfaithful, and Christ, out of unwavering love, may well have duly forgiven her. This experience, according to Phipps, rendered Christ far more understanding about the nature of adultery and love, *agape,* and convinced him to reject all notion of divorce. Phipps' "intriguing conjecture" could therefore be taken to accord to Mary Magdalen the power to influence to some extent Christ's views of human relationships, a theme which has been resumed recently, and with rather less authority, by other more populist writers. A book published in 1992, Dr. Barbara Thiering's *Jesus the Man,* goes so far as to claim that Mary Magdalen was not only married to Jesus, but left him after the crucifixion (which he survived for thirty years), having borne him a girl and two boys. Christ, it seems, then married again. The author, a lecturer in the school of divinity at Sydney University, bases her claims on a new reading of the Dead Sea Scrolls.

The idea that Mary Magdalen might have been married to Christ, and the bearer of his children, receives an airing in [Baigent, Leigh, and Lincoln's] *Holy Blood, Holy Grail,* one of the more bizarre manifestations of the late twentieth-century popular interest both in the story of Christ and in conspiracy theory. Following a staged crucifixion, in which Jesus is either taken down from the cross in a drugged state or replaced by Simon of Cyrene, his family is obliged to flee from those, headed by St. Peter, who were not part of the plot and are bent on preserving the reputation of Christ the Messiah. Mary Magdalen, together with brother Lazarus and others, arrive in the south of France, she bearing the *Sang Raal,* or Holy Grail, which the authors interpret as the holy blood of Christ in the form of his child or children. Once established within the Jewish community in the south of France, the family intermarries with the Merovingian kings and so on down through Godfroi de Bouillon (who almost becomes king of Jerusalem), the house of Lorraine, the Hapsburgs, and the ever shadowy, but ever present, Prieuré de Sion, who hold the secret of it all, whatever it may be (and are also poised to create a unified state of Europe with a descendant of Christ, and of course Mary Magdalen, on its throne), which is rumoured to be hidden near the town of Rennes-le-Château, whose *curé* Saunière discovered coded documents in the church and constructed the mysterious Tour de Magdala to house his library. The authors breathlessly bend to their purpose whatever information comes their way, and the book offers no new insights into the historical figure of Mary Magdalen, but concentrates on trying to assemble proof for some of the more far-fetched of the legends which have accumulated around her over the centuries, using as their guiding principle the idea that there is no smoke without a fire. . . .

In a dense, complex, and brilliant analysis, Susan Haskins recounts the many-faceted history of how a cult of Mary Magdalene came to be so prominent in France. She traces the arc of far-flung myth and legend that has Mary fleeing Jerusalem and heading in all directions—Ephesus, where there was a long-standing Greek goddess cult around Diana and where the Virgin Mary is thought to have gone (visitors today are still shown the house where the Virgin Mary allegedly lived); thirty years in the Egyptian desert as a hermit; and even to Northumbria in England, where she, Joseph of Arimathea, and the Holy Grail become bound up in the legends of Avalon and King Arthur. But in medieval France, an industry arose, creating provenance about how Mary Magdalene arrived and lived in France. The fascinating tale of human mythmaking, fraud, and credulity that Haskins tells is worth every *Da Vinci Code* reader's attention. If you think Pierre Plantard and the Dossier Secrets are a fraud, or if you think Baigent, Leigh, and Lincoln—or Dan Brown, for that matter—have played too fast and loose with history, you should have seen what the abbots, bishops, and enterprising noblemen did during the Crusades: they dreamed up relics having to do with Mary Magdalene—some bits of her hair, some of her teardrops. They brought back alleged holy objects from the Holy Land, made big profits in the trade in relics, and mined them for the snake oil of purported medicinal value. They also created processionals, pilgrimages, festivals, and some of the first outdoor theater productions, all of which brought tourist dollars, trade and commerce to small French towns. And wherever Mary Magdalene's name and image as a penitent were invoked, it was usually to provide a cover for festivals of debauchery. As Haskins puts it:

The *Grandes Heures* of Vézelay

In the twelfth and thirteenth centuries, huge pilgrimages grew around the more famous shrines, with vast crowds in the hope of cures, deliverance from demons, and other such manifestations of divine intervention. These were not the only purposes, however, of such festivities, for dissoluteness and debauchery were often companions to the relics being processed. . . . Seduction, it seems, was rife, and procuresses plying their trade were often much in evidence. But . . . the local town council would have been extremely loath to abolish its pilgrimage, since such processions brought the town large profits as all the pilgrims had to be fed and lodged, and anyway, it seemed such decadence was all part of the occasion.

Pilgrims flocked from all over France to touch the tomb of Mary Magdalen at Vézelay; some even came from as far as England to be healed, forgiven, and dispossessed of their devils at the holy site. And with these faithful came the merchants too, ever ready to profit from the pious . . .

The cult of Mary Magdalene was so potent, and her spirit was credited with such intercessory powers with God, that Mary received credit for everything from bringing peace to Burgundy to putting dead knights back in the saddle. Papal bulls issued by Lucius III, Urban III, and Clement III all confirmed that Mary Magdalene's body was, indeed, resting in the French town of Vézelay. But how did she get from Jerusalem to France, and what did she do during her years there? Haskins picks up the story as follows:

There was always, however, the awkward question of how Mary Magdalen's body had come to its resting place in Burgundy, so far way from her birthplace in Judaea. Reverence was paid to a tomb, but although the body of the "blessed Magdalen" was said to rest in the monastery's church, it had never been seen, nor had adequate account been given of its arrival from Palestine after the ascension. In the eleventh century, the simple answer given to tiresome questions could be "summed up in a few words," as a document issued by Vézelay rather testily pointed out. "All is possible to God who does what he pleases.

Nothing is difficult for him when he has decided to do it for the well-being of men." When this reply proved unsatisfactory, the narrator told of how Mary Magdalen had appeared to him standing outside her tomb, saying, "It is me, whom many people believe to be here." Warnings of the divine chastisement which had befallen previous doubters were given to those who queried the existence of the Magdalen's body. An excuse for not exposing the remains appears in a late twelfth-century manuscript which told of the occasion when Geoffrey [abbot of Vézelay] himself had decided to remove the Magdalen's relics from the little crypt where they had been found to put them in a precious reliquary. The church had suddenly been plunged into thick darkness, and the people assisting had fled terrified, and all those present had suffered; it had henceforth been decided to relinquish all ideas of opening the holy tomb as such acts clearly provoked wrath from above. Faith was all that was required, the monks at Vézelay told their faint-hearted pilgrims.

Documents issued by the abbey in the thirteenth century to justify its claims to possess Mary Magdalen's relics relate how the pilgrims' faith had so dwindled that it was clear to the monks that they had to engineer some way of making their claim credible. A flood of hagiographical material henceforth issued from the abbey in which a new element in the Magdalen story emerged. Tales, often entirely contradictory, were told of how the body had arrived, not directly from Palestine, but from somewhere in Provence where she had been buried between the years 882 and 884, and how a "holy theft" by one Aléaume had been perpetrated to bring the precious remains to their final resting place. . . .

However, the most widely believed story was that she had arrived by boat, like other saints and apostles who

Remembrance of Things Past

The famous French sweet, the madeleine, is associated with Mary Magdalene. This cross between a cookie and a pastry is traditionally made of eggs, butter, flour, and sugar. It is the act of biting into the madeleine, with all the nostalgic memories it conjures, that sets Marcel Proust off on the telling of his long, long novel, *Remembrance of Things Past.* Legend holds that the nuns of a convent dedicated to Mary Magdalene in the town of Commercy either invented or perfected the madeleine, later selling their recipe to commercial bakers for a fabulous sum in order to support themselves after their convent was abolished in the wake of the French Revolution. Madeleines became ubiquitous in France, but were made in particularly great quantity on Mary Magdalene's feast day, July 22.

made their way to France, and had been accompanied by Maximinus—in the first account—one of the seventy-two disciples (for, as Duchesne wryly remarked, "a woman could not have come alone as she always has need of support"). They had disembarked at Marseille and there preached the gospel. In this account, our saint had once more become the *apostola apostolorum* who, having been the first apostle of the gospels, now, through her arrival in France, and her preaching, continued her apostolic career, and in the process had converted the pagan prince of Marseille. (A later monkish narrator, however, clearly felt it his duty to explain discreetly how a woman could have taken part in these apostolic and by definition masculine activities, remembering that ecclesiastical discipline was disinclined to favour female apostolacy, and told instead of how, having arrived on French soil, Mary

Magdalen had not preached but retired in solitude.[7]) According to this same legend, Maximinus had subsequently become the first bishop of Aix. Mary Magdalen had predeceased her companion, who buried her and was then himself buried near her. A special altar at the church of St. Sauveur at Aix was dedicated to Maximinus and Mary Magdalen as first founders of the city, which also claimed the honour of having been evangelised in the first century. A false charter purporting to be dated 7 August 1103 refers to this consecration, written by the archbishop and canons of the church in support of their claims at the end of the twelfth century that the bones of its illustrious founders were still in the tomb from which Vézelay had fabricated its *furtum sacrum*.

A later version, recalling the Magdalen's relationship to Lazarus and Martha, recounted the family from Bethany's flight from Palestine during the Jewish persecution—where, as close friends of Christ, they would have been prime targets—their journey across the sea, and arrival at Aix. In this, Lazarus had become first bishop of Marseille, Martha had lived at Tarascon, and overcome the wicked dragon, and they had all died; the bones of Lazarus and Mary Magdalen had been taken to Burgundy, but those of Martha had remained in Provence, where they were "discovered" in 1187.

By the thirteenth century, an alarmingly confusing array of versions existed of Mary Magdalen's voyage, sometimes featuring Maximinus, sometimes Lazarus and Martha, sometimes including Sidonius and Marcellina, Martha's servant, and sometimes apostolising Marseille and lower Gaul. But the results were uniform: the relics

7. Baudouin de Gaiffier, "Hagiographie bourguignonne," *Anlaecta Bollandiana,* vol. LXIX, 1951, p. 140.

were now at Vézelay, brought by Badilon in an heroic "holy" theft. . . .

Without the monastic rivalries of the Middle Ages, and the pilgrimage to Vézelay, Mary Magdalen might never have become as popular as she did. Without the claim of the monks of St. Maximin, and her consequent adoption by the Dominicans, the concept of the penitent Magdalen, who had spent thirty years in the desert, might never have been taken to Italy, where it appeared in liturgica and in frescoes painted in churches and monasteries all over the peninsula from the thirteenth century. Through Charles of Anjou, king of Naples and Sicily, the idea of Mary Magdalen was taken to Naples, and through marriage alliances between his own royal house and that of Spain, she also reached the Iberian peninsula. And the movement founded in her name in Germany in 1225 for the moral relief of prostitutes and fallen women, which grew to enormous proportions throughout the Middle Ages, and lasted in various forms until early in the twentieth century, might never have existed had it not been for Vézelay's claims to have in its possession the relics of Christianity's most loved and illustrious penitent.

"*The Da Vinci Code* uses fiction as a means to interpret historical obscurity . . ."

An Interview with Deirdre Good

Deirdre Good, a professor of the New Testament at the General Theological Seminary of the Episcopal Church in New York City, discusses what we know—and don't know—about Mary Magdalene, why there has been such resurgence of interest in her, and the question of celibacy versus marriage. Good earned her doctorate at Harvard Divinity School, speaks frequently on Mary Magdalene and *The Da Vinci Code,* and is a contributing editor to the forthcoming *Secrets of Mary Magdalene.*

Who was the true Mary Magdalene and what was her life like?

According to Luke's gospel, she was a wealthy follower and disciple of Jesus from whom he cast out seven demons. Her name suggests whence she came: from Magdala, a city on the shore of Galilee known in Roman times for fish salting. Migdal is just north of Tiberias. She was one of a group of women disciples who came to the tomb in the early morning of the third day after Jesus' death, perhaps to bring spices. In several gospel accounts, the women were met by an angel who announced, "He is risen!" She had a vision of the resurrected Jesus according to John's gospel. This makes her both prophet and apostle. We do not know what she looked like, but we certainly have representations of her in art of the Christian East and West and in the medieval mystery plays.

As a scholar of Christian Origins, I can identify Mary Magdalene in the Gospels of Luke, John, the longer text of Mark, and the extracanonical *Gospels of Thomas, Mary, Philip, Peter,* and in the later *Pistis Sophia* and the *Manichaean Psalms.* In early texts, her fidelity to Jesus causes her, along with two other women, to visit his tomb. Subsequently, in several texts, she is apostle and prophet to whom the resurrected Jesus appears. Her insight is conveyed in reports of her vision of Jesus (John 20; *Gospel of Mary*). In John 20, Jesus addresses her by her Semitic name: Mariam! She recognizes him by replying: Rabboni! In a few texts (longer ending of Mark; *Gospel of Mary; Gospel of Thomas; Pistis Sophia*) she encounters hostility from other apostles (Peter especially) and her testimony is disbelieved. But other apostles (Levi) speak on her behalf. Thus in Christian tradition, she is the apostle to the apostles. In the *Manichaean Psalms,* Jesus reminds her of their resurrection encounter and confirms that she is to go to the other disciples, especially Peter.

What do you think of the picture that is painted of Mary Magdalene in The Da Vinci Code?

What *The Da Vinci Code* does is use fiction as a means to interpret historical obscurity and fill the gaps. This is an approach used successfully by other—and better—novelists: Charles Dickens, for example. It's an approach worth pursuing, once we dismiss Brown's claim that what he writes is true. Thus the claim that Jesus and Mary Magdalene were married is a fiction designed to express the particularity of their relationship. However, Jesus also had distinctive relationships with others—for example, the "Beloved Disciple" of John's gospel, with Peter, and so on. Thus one must ask whether Brown's assertion that Jesus and Mary Magdalene were married is a restrictive way to describe the particular relationship of a man Jesus with a woman Mary Magdalene. If one assumes this limited particularity, one then looks for it anywhere and everywhere. Actually it isn't in da Vinci's *Last Supper* because art historians, looking at sketches of figures drawn by the artist to prepare for the painting, identify the figure to Jesus' right with John. Representations of John always depict him as young and thus beardless.

Why do you think there is so much contemporary interest in Mary Magdalene?

New interest in Mary Magdalene coincides with the appearance of feminist research—now established as a credible discipline in its own right—on the role of women and the subject of gender as culturally constructed in the field of Christian origins. In this regard, the discovery and publication of original Coptic texts from Nag Hammadi in English have stimulated interest in early material outside the canon among those interested in gender categories and women. The success of Elaine Pagels' book *The Gnostic Gospels,* and publication of these Nag Hammadi texts on the Internet, created access to a new body of material. Investigating all the historical material about Mary Magdalene raised the question about the role of women in the early Christian movements. Mary Magdalene was clearly identified as a prominent apostle and prophet.

You have worked on the comparative names and meaning of Mary Magdalene of the New Testament and Miriam of the Old Testament. What is your thesis on this subject?

I believe there is a connection in name and function between Miriam of the Hebrew Bible and both Mary Magdalen and Mary, the mother of Jesus. This is the argument of my new book, *Mariam, the Magdalen, and the Mother,* published in 2005 by Indiana University Press. The name Miriam in the Greek translation of Hebrew Scripture is Mariam. This form of the name is used to describe the woman to whom Gabriel speaks in Luke 2 and the woman to whom Jesus appears in the garden in John 20. Moreover, like Miriam the prophet, Jesus' mother praises God (in the song called the Magnificat) for the reversal of fortunes God has accomplished in the past. She also anticipates what God will accomplish in the ministry of her son, Jesus, described in Luke's gospel. The prophetic role of Jesus' mother continues in the *Protevangelium* of James, one of the noncanonical birth stories.

Like Miriam, Mary Magdalen is disbelieved when she proclaims her vision of the resurrected Lord, undoubtedly because of her gender. Ultimately, she is vindicated. This feature resonates with the experience of most women who have felt a call to ministry.

Can you comment on the background of celibacy versus marriage that would have prevailed in biblical times?

In Matthew 19:12, in a discussion of marriage and divorce, Jesus tells his disciples:

> For there are some eunuchs which were so born from their mother's womb: and there are some eunuchs, which were made eunuchs of men: and there be eunuchs, which have made themselves eunuchs for the kingdom of heaven's sake. He that is able to receive it, let him receive it.

Some commentators interpret this passage as a commendation of celibacy. And when celibacy was viewed as a higher state than marriage in subsequent Christian tradition, Jerome could understand Matthew 19:10–12 to indicate that "Christ loves virgins more than others."

Modern commentators have tended to follow this view by interpreting this passage as an invitation to celibacy for some or by linking the passage explicitly to Paul's teaching in I Cor. 7 commending celibacy over marriage. But in Matthew's Gospel, eunuchs, like someone voluntarily humbling him- or herself, forego being "great" or exercising authority over others. Since Matthew 20:26–7 equates status within the Matthean community to being a servant or a slave, we can entertain the thesis that the eunuch within the Matthean community is the perfect servant. Eunuchs in the Matthean community, having voluntarily given up all honor deriving from their own family, possessions, and wealth, are exclusively loyal to the kingdom. To Peter's question: "Look, we have left everything and followed you. What then will we have?" Jesus offers status and power not in this world, but in the next: "At the renewal of all things, when the Son of Man is seated on the throne of his glory, you who have followed me will also sit on twelve thrones, judging the twelve tribes of Israel. And every one who has left houses or brothers or sisters or father or mother or children or lands, for my name's sake, will receive a hundredfold, and inherit eternal life" (19:27–30).

Many people believe the fragmentary Gospel of Philip *to say that Jesus kissed Mary Magdalene often on her mouth. Do you believe that to be true? And, if so, what is its meaning?*

The *Gospel of Philip* is actually in far better shape than the *Gospel of Mary!* Although both texts were published in the same collection, *The Nag Hammadi Library in English,* they presuppose different symbolic worlds. For example, we should not assume, because the *Gospel of Philip* speaks of men and women, that it is describing real men and women. The *Second Apocalypse of James* reports that Jesus called James his beloved and grants him deeper understanding of things that others have not known. In both the *First* and the *Second Apocalypse of*

James, Jesus and James kiss and embrace each other as an indication of their special relationship. In the so-called *Secret Gospel of Mark,* Jesus reveals the mystery of the kingdom of God to a young man he loves. In the fourth-century Coptic text *Pistis Sophia,* Philip, John, James, and Matthew, along with Mariamne (Mary), are all spoken of as beloved by Jesus. This probably indicates their special capacity for spiritual insight. It is easy to imagine that others would be jealous of such people.

Critiquing the Conspiracy Theory

An Interview with Katherine Ludwig Jansen

Katherine Ludwig Jansen, associate professor of History at Catholic University, is the author of *The Making of the Magdalen: Preaching and Popular Devotion in the Later Middle Ages.* She believes in hewing to the historical evidence—emphasizing facts that come from the texts of accepted biblical documents and official church history. Jansen argues against the cover-up thesis and presents the defense for Pope Gregory and church officialdom on the issue of Mary Magdalene, sin, and penitence. On the other hand, she also concludes that the Dark Ages may have been more enlightened than our own times in one respect: Mary Magdalene, a woman, was understood to be an apostle in her own right, whereas today there remains a battle in many religious groups over whether women should assume leadership roles in preaching their faiths.

In your opinion, who was the true Mary Magdalene?

As a historian, I am trained to base my opinions and analysis on historical evidence. In the case of Mary

Magdalene, the only evidence we have to document her existence is that which is contained in the New Testament. All told, the four gospels contain just twelve references to this woman, eleven of which are directly related to the passion and resurrection narratives. Only Luke 8:2–3 adds the detail that "Mary who is called Magdalene" was the woman from whom Jesus cast out seven demons. After he did so, Mary from Magdala became one of Jesus' most steadfast disciples, ministering to him from her own financial resources (Luke 8:3). Based on this textual evidence, it seems clear that Mary Magdalene was a financially independent woman who used her resources to support Jesus and his band of disciples.

Why did the church depict Mary Magdalene as a prostitute for so many years? Do you feel that they benefited from this "cover-up" in any way?

In my view, "cover-up" and "conspiracy" are not useful ways to understand the historical confusion about Mary Magdalene's identity. We must begin by noting that, in addition to the Virgin Mary and Mary Magdalene, there are five women mentioned in the gospels who are also called Mary—that very fact has created ample room for confusion. Nonetheless, early church writers tended to keep all these women distinct in their discussions of Mary Magdalene, as does the Eastern Orthodox Church, which never conflated the figure of Mary of Magdala with Mary of Bethany, let alone the unnamed sinner of Luke (7:37–50). Indeed, the Orthodox Church has always kept separate feasts for separate women.

It was only at the end of the sixth century that the figure of Mary Magdalene was fused together with the figures of Mary of Bethany and the unnamed sinner in Luke. Pope Gregory the Great collapsed into one individual the identities of three distinct gospel figures. The moment Pope Gregory the Great grafted Luke's sinner onto Mary Magdalene's identity, was the moment at which Mary Magdalene was transformed into a prostitute, largely because women's sins were inevitably construed as sexual sins. Had Mary Magdalene been married, that sin might have been construed as adultery. As a single woman, her sin was construed as wantonness, which was tantamount to prostitution.

What were Gregory's motives for compounding the characters of sinners with Mary Magdalene?

It would be a gross misrepresentation of history to view it as a conspiracy or an act of maliciousness on his part. One has to see Gregory in his own context, a period beset by intense dislocation: Germanic invasions, plague, and famine were just a few of the major catastrophes he had to face during his pontificate, which demanded that he be not only a spiritual leader, but a political leader, as well. In this period of flux and uncertainty, Gregory was attempting to create some sort of stability and certainty for his community. The text in which Gregory creates a new identity for Mary Magdalene was a sermon in which he was clearly responding to questions about Magdalenian identity that had been posed by the people of his community, who were, it seems, looking for clarity in their faith to serve as a bulwark against the late Roman world crumbling beneath their feet. Gregory's composite Magdalene figure had the virtue of seeming to answer definitively all the questions that his Christian community had been asking about the relation of one Mary to another.

The identification stuck because it filled a deep-seated need, theologically speaking. Mary Magdalene, now reconfigured as the great sinner, was poised to become the great saint. Gregory suggested that she achieved this through penance, which in her case was the penitential act of washing Christ's feet with her tears and drying them with her hair. As the sacrament of penance continued to be reformulated and given primacy during the Middle Ages and the early modern period, so Mary Magdalene's image as sinner-saint grew correspondingly. The image of the sinner-saint became increasingly important at historical moments when the sacrament of penance came to the fore. In my view, the image of the sinner-saint was certainly one of the reasons that so many people were attracted to Mary Magdalene throughout the centuries: She provided hope to ordinary sinners—both men and women—that they too could be redeemed.

Why was Mary Magdalene one of the few at the crucifixion? Why might she have attended when other disciples did not? What is the importance of Mary Magdalene being the first to see Jesus after the resurrection?

After Jesus' arrest, most of the other disciples went into hiding for fear that they too would be arrested. Mary Magdalene and the other women did not. Whether this is because the Romans did not consider the female disciples a danger or because the women were more steadfast in their loyalty to Jesus is an open question. Nonetheless, their faith did not waiver. They appeared at and witnessed the crucifixion. In my view, Mary Magdalene's most important role is as first witness to Jesus' resurrection. Jesus charges her with the duty of bearing the news of his resurrection to the other disciples. At that moment, she earned the title given her by medieval scriptural commentators: *apostolorum apostola*—the apostle of the apostles, a title that endured throughout the Middle Ages. Thus, one of the most important tenets of Christianity—the resurrection—was both witnessed and announced by a woman. The title "apostle of the apostles" is as appropriate now to celebrate her role in the history of Christianity as it was in the medieval period.

The Beliefnet Debate

Beliefnet.com describes itself as a "multi-faith e-community" designed to help individuals meet their religious and spiritual needs. Since the publication of *The Da Vinci Code,* a number of Beliefnet articles and postings have focused on discussions about Mary Magdalene and other issues raised by the book. Here, we excerpt key arguments from a point-counterpoint between Kenneth L. Woodward and Karen King. Woodward is a contributing editor at *Newsweek.* King is Winn Professor of Ecclesiastical History at Harvard University Divinity School.

A Quite Contrary Mary

By Kenneth Woodward

Like Jesus, Mary Magdalene is now the subject of a cultural makeover. What agenda do feminist scholars have in mind?

Why the sudden interest in Mary Magdalene? Yes, I know about the two or three new books on the subject, as well as the bestselling book *The Da Vinci Code* and the new movie *The Magdalene Sisters.* But is anything new being said about this familiar Biblical figure?

Not really. Scholars have known for decades, if not longer, that Mary Magdalene was not a prostitute, and that she had been erroneously conflated in early Christian tradition with the penitent woman in Luke who anoints the feet of the soon-to-be-crucified Jesus and dries them with her hair. It's certainly not news that her greatest claim to fame was the commission she received from Christ to go tell the apostles the news of his resurrection. Those kinds of "redefinitions" were readily available in the entry under her name in the *New Catholic Encyclopedia,* published in 1967—hardly an arcane resource for any journalist willing to check out claims that something new is being said.

That Jesus was married—possibly to Mary Magdalene—is also a hoary notion going well beyond William E. Phipps' theological potboiler of 1970, *Was Jesus Married?* Phipps' answer—that he probably was, since most Jewish men of the time married—was hardly persuasive. Nor is the contrary view, that Jesus was gay and had a thing for John, the "beloved disciple," a new idea; I came upon it in the 1960s, when the notion of Jesus as the ultimate "outsider" was popular in Existentialist circles. The conceit was that by virtue of his "illegitimate birth" and his rural origins, Jesus was an outsider to the power groups of his day. Anglican bishop Hugh Montefiore added homosexuality to the mix so as to complete the outsider image. Like Jesus, Mary Magdalene is now the subject of a cultural makeover.

When it comes to Biblical figures, it is not enough to say that every generation entertains notions already imagined and discarded by previous generations. In the case of Mary Magdalene, the news is not what is being said about her, but the new context in which she is being placed—and who is doing the placing and why. In other words, Mary Magdalene has become a project for a certain kind of ideologically committed feminist scholarship. That's the real news. . . .

In the 13th century, no less a figure than Peter Abelard preached a sermon in which he saw symmetry between Miriam and Mary Magdalene as proclaimers of good news. (Even then, Mary Magdalene was known as "apostle to the apostles.") Finding symmetries between Old and New Testament figures was an important aspect of medieval Biblical exegesis. In the current context, some exegetes focus on Exodus 15:20–21, where Miriam is called a "prophet" and leads the Israelite women in dance and song. For those feminists who are looking for any signs of female leadership in the Hebrew Bible (not to mention grounds for doing their own song and dance), this passage has led to the creation of a story of their own. According to that narrative, Miriam was regarded as a prophet, just as her brother Moses was, producing a rivalry among the ancient Israelites between the party of Moses and the party of Miriam.

But—so the story goes—the male editors of the Bible expunged the stories of Miriam's leadership that they believe existed in ancient oral traditions. Moreover, a few feminist scholars insist that the ancient Israelites actually created an egalitarian society before the rise of male kingship. Thus, we have a classic case of patriarchy—feminism's equivalent of original sin—excising the evidence of female leadership, indeed, of female prophethood. Similarly, the Biblical myth of an original Eden is replaced by the feminist idea of an original egalitarian society which was eventually covered up by the male redactors of the Exodus story, Judaism's foundation event.

Whether any of this is true—or even likely—is not something a mere journalist is equipped to judge. Nonetheless, a journalist might note that not many Biblical scholars, male or female, give these speculations credence. The evidence simply isn't there, which is why those who advance them rely on what is called "rhetorical analysis" of Biblical texts rather than historical or archeological evidence. A journalist might also note that within religious feminism, the truth or falsity of these speculations doesn't matter. Thus, at least since the late 1970s, some Jewish women have staged feminist seders in which a cup is set aside for Miriam as well as the traditional one for Elijah. They do this not because they believe that Miriam, like Elijah, was taken bodily into heaven and so will return in the fullness of time, but just to make things, well, egalitarian.

We find the same pattern in the feminist redefinition of Mary Magdalene. Here the narrative framework functions like this: the early movement led by Jesus was egalitarian and gender-inclusive (though some second-generation Jewish feminists now reject this on the grounds that it makes Jesus an exception among Jewish men of his day and so is anti-Semitic). Among the women who follow Jesus, Mary of Magdala is the most prominent: she is mentioned more often (12 times) than any other woman but the mother of Jesus. The most important mention is in John 20:11–18, where the resurrected Jesus appears to Mary alone and commissions her to relay the news to his (male) apostles. Hence her traditional title: "apostle to the apostles."

Now, it should be clear to any reader of the New Testament that the women who followed Jesus often acted more like disciples than did some of Jesus' chosen Twelve. For example, the synoptic gospels (Mark, Matthew and Luke) have *only* women at the foot of the cross. (The Gospel of John adds John, the beloved disciple.) But a small cadre of feminist scholars—especially those tutored and credentialed at Harvard Divinity School—go much further. Their headline-making claim is that in the early church there was a party of Magdalene and a party of Peter—again, men versus women, as in the case of Miriam—and that the party of Peter not only won, but also proceeded to expunge the evidence and memory of the Magdalene faction from the New Testament and to tarnish the reputation of Magdalene to boot. A sermon preached by Pope Gregory in 591 is frequently cited on the latter point, as if he had invented an anti-woman tradition and sealed it with (retroactive) infallibility. Blaming a pope fits the feminist agenda here, injecting an anti-hierarchical, indeed, anti-papal note. In short, patriarchy is again the culprit.

But there is a difference between the two Marys—Miriam and the Magdalene. To make their case, Mary Magdalene's feminist defenders have switched to a different deck of cards. Just as a feminist hermeneutics of suspicion—biblical scholarship based on suspicion of male authorship—dictates that the text of the New Testament, being the work of males, must be distrusted for that very reason, so a feminist hermeneutics of retrieval—in this case, retrieving the suppressed evidence of the party of Mary Magdalene—must go to other sources. These sources are the various texts that did not make it into the New Testament as it was fixed in the 4th century. And the very fact of this exclusion by male church hierarchs makes the extra texts all the more authoritative for scholars whose aim is showing that patriarchy suppressed female leadership in the church. Among these texts, the *Gospel of Mary* is paramount; it reads as if the author had obtained a D.D. degree from Harvard Divinity School.

As second-century documents, the *Gospel of Mary,* the *Gospel of Philip* (in which Jesus and Mary kiss), and other apocryphal texts come much too late to provide any reliable historical information about Jesus, Peter, or Mary Magdalene. But they do suggest what some groups—traditionally considered Gnostics—understood about the story of Jesus and his followers . . .

Karen King, a professor at the Harvard Divinity School, argues that there is a relationship between the *Gospel of Mary,* which exalts the role of Mary Magdalene, and Paul's Letter to Timothy, which counsels women to be silent in church. Her argument is that both were produced about the same time, 125 C.E., and taken together reflect a raging gender war in the early church. But she does this by taking certain liberties with the dating of these two texts. No one knows when either was written, but some scholars put Timothy in the 90s C.E., and some scholars put the *Gospel of Mary* in the late—not early—second century. King maximizes the dates of both, like bookends with nothing in between, for her purposes. In short, the new Mary Magdalene is an old Gnostic.

Even so, how credible is the assumption that the church's rejection of Gnosticism in all its forms was essentially a gender war? In his rigorously balanced "Introduction to the New Testament," the late scholar Raymond E. Brown summarizes how the scriptures written by Christians were preserved and accepted—and what criteria were used. Among them were apostolic origin, real or putative, and conformity to the rule of faith. None of them involved gender. Furthermore, there is no reason to believe that whole communities of Christians used the *Gospel of Mary,* or *of Phillip,* as authoritative texts. Yes, they were in circulation, but so are a number of books in my own library, several of them including the Gnostic gospels, but that does not make me a Gnostic . . .

For several years I have kept an anthology of selections from the various world religions that on the cover invites the reader to choose from them those that they find appealing and thereby "create your own scriptures." That anyone would package this material, I thought, was indicative of one wind blowing in the mixed weather pattern of contemporary American religion. The operative assumption is that all sacred texts are of equal value and the reader is free to make sacred those that provide personal appeal. . . . It is the ultimate in consumer-oriented religion, of course, and has the added advantage of bypassing the authority of any community as to which texts count as sacred and which do not.

Something similar is, I think, happening with the Gnostic texts that support poor Mary Magdalene in the role thrust upon her as a leader of the church—and, if author Lynn Picknett is to be believed, as "Christianity's Hidden Goddess." At least the minority of feminist scholars pushing the Gnostic texts as equal in standing to those of the New Testament can argue that at an early period in Christian history they were available to Christians and occasionally read. From that it apparently follows that if you don't like the established canon, create one of your own. If the *Gospel of Mary* is just as authoritative as, say, the *Gospel of Mark,* then of course Mary Magdalene can be whatever today's feminists want her to be.

Were I to write a story involving Mary Magdalene, I think it would focus on this: that a small group of well-educated women decided to devote their careers to the pieces of Gnostic literature discovered in the last century, a find that promised a new academic specialty within the somewhat overtrodden field of Biblical studies, on which they could build a career. They became experts in this literature, as others become experts in the biology of the hermit crab. But unlike those who study marine decapod crustaceans, some of them came to identify with the objects of their study—in some cases, perhaps, because they had no other religious community to identify with other than that formed by common academic pursuit; others perhaps because they were in rebellion against whatever authoritative religious community nurtured their interest in religion in the first place. . . .

And the next step? That is already upon us in the form of a new book from Harvard's Karen King, *What Is Gnosticism?* which aims at showing the great diversity among Gnostics—true and pluralizing Gnosticism—fair enough—but also at divesting Gnostics of their opposition to orthodox Christianity, thereby dissolving the very category of heresy. In short, if there is no error, then anything can be true. How very American. How inclusive and nonjudgmental. And in this age of postmodernism, so Now. In this kind of environment, even the figure of Mary Magdalene can be prostituted for polemical purposes.

Letting Mary Magdalene Speak

By Karen L. King

Tradition is not fixed. Newly discovered texts like the Gospel of Mary *let us hear other voices in an ancient Christian debate.*

In an article about recent interest in Mary Magdalene, Kenneth Woodward writes: "The news is not what is being said about her, but the new context in which she is being placed—and who is doing the placing and why." As he points out, scholars have agreed at least since the 1960s that she was not a prostitute. Likewise, the speculation that Mary and Jesus were married is hardly new. "The real news," he says, is found in the work of "ideologically committed feminist scholarship"—a statement I heartily agree with.

The rest of his article, however, is more an expression of Woodward's distaste for feminism than a review or even a critique of that scholarship. Readers may want to evaluate for themselves examples of the best work in rhetorical criticism and feminist scholarship on Mary of Magdala, such as Elisabeth Schussler Fiorenza's classic work, *In Memory of Her,* and Jane Schaberg's recent book, *The Resurrection of Mary Magdalene.*

Part of the recent excitement about Mary Magdalene has to do with discoveries of previously unknown early Christian writings from Egypt, like the *Gospel of Mary,* the *Dialogue of the Savior,* and the *Gospel of Thomas.* The *Gospel of Mary* is found in a fifth-century c.e. papyrus book that came onto the Cairo antiquities market in 1896. It was purchased by a German scholar and taken to Berlin, where it was first published in 1955. In 1945, two Egyptian peasants made an astonishing discovery while digging for fertilizer at the foot of the Jabel al-Tarif, a cliff near the town of Nag Hammadi in Middle Egypt. They uncovered a sealed clay jar containing a hoard of papyrus manuscripts. Known as the Nag Hammadi Codices, these fourth-century c.e. papyrus books included a wealth of ancient Christian literature, a total of forty-six different works in all, almost all of which were previously unknown. These and other original writings are offering new perspectives on Christian beginnings. They show that early Christianity was much more diverse than we had ever imagined.

Early Christians intensely debated such basic issues as the content and meaning of Jesus' teachings, the nature of salvation, the value of prophetic authority, the roles of women and slaves, and competing visions of ideal community. After all, these first Christians had no New Testament, no Nicene Creed or Apostles Creed, no commonly established church order or chain of authority, no church buildings, and indeed no single understanding of Jesus. All of the elements we might consider essential to define Christianity did not yet exist. Far from being starting points, the Nicene Creed and the New Testament were the end products of these debates and disputes. They represent the distillation of experience and experimentation—and not a small amount of strife and struggle.

One consequence of these struggles is that the winners were able to write the history of this period from their perspective. The viewpoints of the losers were largely lost since their ideas survived only in documents denouncing them. Until now. The recent discoveries provide a wealth of primary works that illustrate the plural character of early Christianity and offer alternative voices. They also help us to understand the winners better because their ideas and practices were shaped in the crucible of these early Christian debates . . .

Placing the figure of Mary Magdalene in this new context helps us understand how the erroneous portrait of her as a prostitute could have been invented and how it could have flourished in the West for well over a millennium without any evidence to support it. Several of the newly discovered works portray her as a favored disciple of Jesus and apostle after the resurrection. In the *Gospel of Mary,* for example, she calms the other disciples when they are afraid and gives them special teaching that Jesus had conveyed to her alone. The text states that Jesus knew her completely and loved her more than the others. It also draws upon a tradition of Peter in conflict with Mary, a topic handled with great sophistication by Anne Brock in her new book, *Mary Magdalene, the First Apostle: The Struggle for Authority.*

But in these newly discovered books, Mary is the apostolic guarantor of a theological position that lost out in the battle for orthodoxy. The *Gospel of Mary,* for example, presents a radical interpretation of Jesus' teachings as a path to inner spiritual knowledge, not apocalyptic revelation; it acknowledges the reality of Jesus' death and his resurrection, but it rejects his suffering and death as the path to eternal life; it also rejects the immortality of the physical body, asserting that only the soul will be saved; it presents the most straightforward and convincing argument in any early Christian writing for the legitimacy of women's leadership; it offers a sharp critique of illegitimate power and a utopian vision of spiritual perfection; it challenges our romantic views about the harmony of the first Christians; and it asks us to rethink the basis for church authority. All written in the name of a woman.

The *Gospel of Mary* lets us see that by making Mary Magdalene into a repentant prostitute, the leaders of the Church could achieve two aims at once. They succeeded both in undermining appeals to Mary Magdalene to support women's leadership, and at the same time they were able to undermine the kind of theology being promoted in her name—theology which the Church Fathers condemned as heresy.

Mr. Woodward is quite right that the discovery of such sources challenges the traditional portrait of Christian history, a history which states that Jesus gave the true teaching to male apostles who passed it down untainted to the bishops who succeeded them. The purity of this gospel is secured especially through the Nicene Creed and orthodox interpretation of the Biblical canon.

While the new texts do not show a "raging gender war" in the early churches, they do provide evidence that one issue being debated concerned women's leadership. In the *Gospel of Mary,* Peter is portrayed as a hothead—just as he is in many episodes in the New Testament gospels. Here he is jealous of Mary and refuses to believe that Jesus would give her special teaching. This portrait seems to suggest that Christians who, like Peter, reject women's right to teach do so out of jealousy and lack of understanding . . .

The *Gospel of Mary* lets us hear another voice in the ancient debate, one that was lost for almost two thousand years. It expands our understanding of the dynamics of early Christianity, but it does not offer a voice that is beyond criticism. For example, the *Gospel of Mary*'s rejection of the body as one's true self is highly problematic for contemporary feminism, which affirms the dignity of the human body.

Of course the issue of women's leadership has not gone away. It is not just an ancient controversy. In our own

Mary Magdalene, Patron Saint of Elite Education

Both Oxford and Cambridge, the tradition-steeped leading universities of England, have colleges named for Mary Magdalene.

Oxford's Magdalen College was founded in 1448 and was among the first colleges in the world to teach science. Magdalen Choir—with a history that goes back to the beginnings of the college—is famous for welcoming spring ceremonies held in May at its famed tower. The movie *Shadowlands,* about the life of C. S. Lewis, depicted these tower ceremonies. Some of the experts whose work we present in this volume would, no doubt, see intriguing connections of myth and metaphor between the pagan-influenced spring rites of pre-Christian history, the Magdalen College tower (recall the etymology of Magdala is derived from an ancient word for tower), and the interests of C. S. Lewis in faith, theology, symbolism, and myth. Magdalen College counts nine Nobel laureates among its students or professors.

At Cambridge, Magdalene College, founded in 1542, is spelled with a final *e* to differentiate it from Oxford. Historically, however, this college's name was pronounced Maudleyn, a compressed double meaning in the word (Dan Brown fans, take note) having to do with its founder, Lord Audley. Meanwhile, the word *maudlin* (excessively sentimental, often teary-eyed) comes into English from this Renaissance-era pronunciation of Mary Magdalene, whose tears are among the most famous in history.

time, feminists are working to ensure that the true story of Mary Magdalene, as well as other ancient alternative voices, are heard—not only by readers of the 1967 *New Catholic Encyclopedia,* but also by a broader range of the public as well. On the other hand, scholars and others who find these new works challenging tend to dismiss them as heresy and try to marginalize their impact on current debates. It would seem, then, that all this commotion about Mary Magdalene is just another episode in the long history of Christians arguing amongst themselves. Why should anyone pay attention?

This is why: since so much in Christian belief and practice rests upon historical claims, an accurate view of history is crucial. One criterion for good history is accounting for all the evidence and not marginalizing the parts one doesn't like or promoting unfairly the parts one does like. Whether or not communities of faith embrace or reject the teaching found in these newly discovered texts, Christians will better understand and responsibly engage their own tradition by attending to an accurate historical account of Christian beginnings.

Moreover, given the importance of religion in today's world—especially notable in the intersection of religion and violence—I believe it is important for non-Christians as well as Christians to recognize that all religious traditions contain many voices and offer a variety of possibilities for addressing the complex issues of our day. In that sense, tradition is not fixed, but is continually being constructed as believers draw upon the past to address the present . . . Therefore religion is not simply given—something one can only accept or reject. Religions are constantly being interpreted . . . An accurate historical account will not ensure that the figure of Mary Magdalene won't continue to be prostituted for polemical purposes as she has been for centuries—but it does restore some dignity to this important woman disciple of Jesus.

Is It Sinful to Engage in Sex within Marriage?

An Interview with Rev. Richard P. McBrien

By far the most controversial aspect of *The Da Vinci Code,* of course, is Dan Brown's hypothesis that Jesus and Mary Magdalene were married, and that the Holy Grail wasn't simply a chalice but a symbolic vessel of Mary's child and the continuing holy bloodline. Scores of books, articles, and TV specials have since explored, debated, and attacked Brown's rendering of sacred religious history. The Rev. Richard P. McBrien has been a very visible figure in this debate. McBrien's interest in ecclesiology—the relationship between religion and politics—as well as the doctrinal dimensions of the Catholic tradition makes him a knowledgeable source both on the larger cultural themes involved in the debate and on the finer points of theology. His assertion that Jesus's divinity would not have been compromised had he married generated considerable controversy and comment. At the same time, McBrien does not blindly accept the theory that Jesus was married, pointing out that there is no evidence in any known gospels, both canonical and noncanonical, that he was.

In the interview that follows—updated and considerably expanded for this edition of *Secrets of the Code*—McBrien renders his pithy and expert opinions on, among other things, why the church transmogrified Mary Magdalene into a prostitute, how likely it is that Jesus was married, and how celibacy became entrenched in the early church. He also addresses the differing reactions to Dan Brown's novel both within and outside the Catholic Church. Rev. McBrien is Crowley-O'Brien Professor of Theology at the University of Notre Dame. A frequent presence in the media, he was also an advisor on the making of *The Da Vinci Code* movie.

You say that the church might possibly have depicted Mary Magdalene as a prostitute for so many years "because some church leaders couldn't face up to the fact that Mary

Magdalene was one of Jesus's main disciples, a close friend, and a primary witness of the resurrection." If not, why not?

I wouldn't say that none have been able to "face the fact," but those who have not haven't paid close attention to the New Testament. Jesus had several women among his disciples and supporters and clearly had a special relationship (not necessarily sexual) with Mary Magdalene. According to three of the five Resurrection narratives, Jesus appeared first to her upon his resurrection from the dead. Nonetheless, women were not considered the equal of men in that society and, therefore, it was not at all surprising that she was not considered as a successor to Judas as a member of the Twelve, even though she was not only a witness of the Resurrection, but a primary one at that.

When, and why, did the church begin to reassess its portrayal of Mary Magdalene as prostitute and penitent?

I don't know when, exactly, the church came to appreciate Mary Magdalene as an important disciple of Jesus rather than a "fallen woman." I suspect, however, that the change came about with the maturing of Catholic biblical scholarship, which occurred after Pope Pius XII's encyclical, *Divino Afflante Spiritu,* in 1943. That encouraged Catholic biblical scholars to use the same tools of critical scholarship that Protestant biblical scholars had been employing since the end of the nineteenth century.

Why do so many people find Mary Magdalene such a compelling character today?

Perhaps because they have been so alienated from the church for its negative, rigid, and censorious views on human sexuality. Thinking about Mary Magdalene raises the question of Jesus's sexuality and also makes people reconsider the place of women in the church. If Jesus had been married, that would undermine centuries of bias against sexual intimacy.

You have said on an ABC special entitled Jesus, Mary and Da Vinci, *as well as in our previous interview, that it would not have compromised the divinity of Jesus for him to have been married. Can you explain why?*

I don't mean to be flippant, but why not? The Epistle to the Hebrews (4:15) says that Jesus was like us in all things except sin. Is it sinful to engage in sexual relations within marriage?

You've also said that, had Jesus ever married, it's just "a short putt" to his bride having been Mary Magdalene. Why Mary Magdalene?

Because she was the female disciple closest to him during his life. Unlike the cowardly males, she and other women stuck by him to the end. She is the one who, according to at least three traditions in the New Testament, was the first to see him after his resurrection. He also had to warn her not to "touch" him because he had not yet ascended to his Father in heaven.

As a teacher and theologian, you undoubtedly have been sharply criticized by conservative Catholics for your widely expressed views on Jesus's sexuality and your willingness to consider whether or not he might have been married.

Yes, but there is very little I haven't been criticized for saying or writing by the ultraconservative wing of the Catholic Church. Most of the criticisms I have received come via email and they are from ultraconservative Christians—all lay people—most of whom I assume are Catholics, but I cannot always tell. On the other hand, I've received a preponderance of positive comments in response to my initial appearance on the ABC documentary *Jesus, Mary and Da Vinci,* which has been reaired several times. I have received no criticisms from non-Christians, and none that I can recall from fellow priests.

To put this discussion in context, would all the leading religious figures of the time have been married?

Perhaps not all, but certainly most. It is clear that some of the apostles were married, including Peter.

Having said that, what are the chances, in your opinion, that Jesus himself was married?

There is no evidence that Jesus was married, and there are at least three reasons against such a hypothesis. First, the gospels make no mention of a marriage. Second, the antierotic bias of the New Testament churches came very early into Christianity, and it can be supposed that if Jesus had been married, that tendency would have been checked decisively. Third, when St. Paul invoked his own right to marry (1 Corinthians 9:5), why did he not appeal to Jesus's own marriage to support his argument?

From its earliest days, the church seemed to equate saintliness with celibacy. Was priestly celibacy suggested in the Bible? Was it practiced from the very beginning of Christianity?

There is a tradition of virginity in the early church, practiced by women and men alike. But they constituted a small minority. The New Testament says nothing about the celibacy of priests. In fact, no individual except Jesus himself is called a priest in the New Testament. Indeed, several of the apostles were married, including Peter himself.

While recommendations for priestly celibacy came early on in the church, especially when monks became bishops, the discipline was never formalized for the Western Church, and certainly not in the East, until at least the eleventh century. Even then it was not universally observed in the West. The Council of Trent in the sixteenth century had to reaffirm the discipline. It has been a general rule of the Roman Catholic Church (as distinct from the various Eastern Catholic churches) since Trent.

Dan Brown argues that, prior to the Council of Nicea, Jesus was seen as mortal, not divine. In the novelist's interpretation, in other words, the church anointed Jesus a deity when the Council voted him the Son of God in AD 325. Does Dan Brown have this right? If so, what was the alternative belief that was not accepted?

No, Dan Brown does not have it right. The Council voted against a sect of early Christianity called Arianism, which held that Jesus was "merely" the greatest of creatures. The Council of Nicea held that Jesus was not a creature like other human beings, but was "generated" from all eternity as the Son of God. In other words, that he was "of the same substance" as God the Creator. The church did not define the divinity of Christ until this common belief of the church was explicitly challenged, as it was by Arianism. And that practical principle also applies to other major tenets of the faith.

In The Da Vinci Code, *Brown returns again and again to the theme of the sacred feminine—the fact that, before the rise of monotheism, ancient peoples worshipped goddesses as well as gods. He alleges the Catholic Church suppressed the idea that a feminine spirit like Sophia, the spirit of Wisdom, ever had any presence in the gospels. Did Jesus's preaching ever seem to indicate that he acknowledged or endorsed a goddess theme in religion?*

No.

Turning to the reaction to Brown's novel, there has been a wide divergence of opinion even within the Catholic Church. Earlier this year, Cardinal Tarcisio Bertone of Genoa told people not to buy or read The Da Vinci Code*—"a castle of lies," as he put it. Meanwhile Alec Knight, the dean of Lincoln Cathedral in England—the Anglican cathedral where the movie version of the book has been filmed—recently took the opposite view to Bertone's. He said that though parts of the book are "heretical," he welcomed the encouragement it has given to people to think about Christianity. Do you think Cardinal Bertone spoke for the church in general, or just for himself? Do you personally lean toward one side or the other in what has become a rather stark debate? And, from your own observation, how have Catholics in general reacted to the novel?*

Cardinal Bertone's remarks, made in March 2005, were rather late in coming. The book had already been a bestseller for some two years. His reaction was akin to the proverbial locking of the barn door after all the horses have galloped off. Second, the book is a work of fiction. One should not treat it otherwise. In any case, no one is forced to buy it or read it. As to whether that was his own opinion, I would guess that he spoke on his own. He had been second-in-command of the Congregation for the Doctrine of the Faith, under then Cardinal Joseph Ratzinger. Perhaps he felt a special obligation to speak up, although, significantly, Cardinal Ratzinger did not.

One must also recall that Cardinal Bertone's statement came less than a month before John Paul II's death. The pope was already very ill and there was increasing speculation about likely successors. Cardinal Bertone's name was on some of the longer lists. Was it a way of trying to draw attention to himself as someone who could speak up on behalf of Catholic orthodoxy, as the next pope?

There has been no official statement from the church itself. The reaction of ordinary Catholics seems to be the same as society at large. Many thousands of Catholics have read the novel and have enjoyed it. Others have denounced the book, but probably without reading it. As for the comments by the Dean of Lincoln Cathedral, I should raise a question about the dean's use of the term "heretical." Heresy is a technical theological term. It refers to the formal denial of a dogma of the church. I am aware of no formal denials of any dogma of the church in this book. It wouldn't be technically heretical anyway, since the book is a work of fiction.

Finally, do you think the movie will stir up as much reaction—and, in some quarters criticism—as has the novel? Or, given The Passion of Christ, *be even more of a tinderbox?*

Most of the novel's critics, from what I have heard and on the basis of my own experience as a writer, have not read the book. I expect that critics of the film, particularly those who might be disposed to picket theaters that show it, will not have seen the movie, nor will they ever do so. But I would expect the film to be a great commercial success.

2 The Sacred Feminine

The sacred feminine is that other face of God that has not been honored over the two millennia of Christianity—at least not as a fully equal partner.

—Margaret Starbird

In this chapter, we explore the background to the "sacred feminine" thesis that lies at the heart of *The Da Vinci Code*'s plot. As readers of the novel will recall, almost on arrival in the middle of the night at Leigh Teabing's Château Villette, Sophie Neveu finds herself immersed in explanations and theoretical pyrotechnics from Teabing and Langdon about the Holy Grail, Mary Magdalene, and the sacred feminine. Langdon tells Sophie: "The Holy Grail represents the sacred feminine and the goddess . . . The power of the female and her ability to produce life was once very sacred, but it posed a threat to the rise of the predominantly male Church, and so the sacred feminine was demonized and called unclean. . . . When Christianity came along, the old pagan religions did not die easily. Legends of chivalric quests for the lost Grail were in fact stories of forbidden quests to find the lost sacred feminine. Knights who claimed to be 'searching for the chalice' were speaking in code as a way to protect themselves from a Church that had subjugated women, banished the Goddess, burned nonbelievers, and forbidden the pagan reverence for the sacred feminine."

The case for the sacred feminine—suppressed goddess—Mary Magdalene analysis that Langdon and Teabing lay out for Sophie raises some of the most intellectually fascinating questions in the novel. To be sure, it is implausible in many respects, especially the way this set of mysteries has been wrapped into the enigmas of the plot. But it is profoundly interesting. In making his late-night case, the fictional Langdon draws heavily on several of the experts whose work is represented in this chapter—Margaret Starbird, Elaine Pagels, Timothy Freke and Peter Gandy, Riane Eisler, and others.

In the following pages, these experts put forward their own arguments about the role of the sacred feminine in the development of Western culture, thought, politics, philosophy, and religion. They recall the goddess-worshipping cults in Egypt, Greece, Crete, and Rome, and gender roles in the context of the Judeo-Christian biblical era. They sift through the Christian experience of the early and medieval church. And they examine spirituality, myths, legends, and traditions that associate special sacred significance with women in general—and with Mary Magdalene in particular.

Readers should note: much of this material is, by definition, mystical, mythical, and poetic; much of the original source material comes in fragments and has been handed down through a variety of languages and translations. In many cases, a short passage from a biblical or Gnostic source has been the subject of extensive analysis and commentary elsewhere. We can only give it shorthand treatment here.

God Does Not Look Like a Man

An Interview with Margaret Starbird

Two of Margaret Starbird's real-life books are specifically mentioned in *The Da Vinci Code* when they attract Sophie Neveu's interest on Leigh Teabing's library shelves in Château Villette: *The Woman with the Alabaster Jar: Mary Magdalen and the Holy Grail* and *The Goddess in the Gospels: Reclaiming the Sacred Feminine.* In the interview below for this book, Starbird briefly explains her view of the sacred feminine. She also declares that "characterizing Mary Magdalen as an apostle, equal to Peter, or perhaps even more important than Peter, does not go nearly far enough." Our interview presents an introduction to Starbird's thinking. Following the interview, we present brief excerpts from the aforementioned books.

How does the concept of the sacred feminine differ from the way most religions seem to assume the primacy of male deities?

More and more, we are becoming aware that the Divine we call "God" does not really look like the patriarch on the ceiling of the Sistine Chapel in the Vatican. For two millennia Christians have been attributing exclusively masculine images to God, using masculine pronouns when speaking of the Creator. But intellectually, we realize that God is not male. God is beyond gender, the "weaver" beyond "the veil" and beyond our ability to conceive God. So we limit God by ascribing attributes to "Him." God is neither male nor female, which is why the Jews were always told never to make images of God. But Christians dropped this idea, and ascribed to God and Jesus the epithets "Father" and

"Son." When the Greek words for "Holy Spirit" were translated into Latin, they became masculine: *Spiritus Sanctus*. The entire trinity was characterized as masculine from the fifth century onward in Western Europe.

The sacred feminine is that *other* face of God that has not been honored over the two millennia of Christianity—at least, not as a fully equal partner. The Virgin Mary certainly embodies one aspect of "God" as feminine: the Blessed Mother, our advocate at the throne of her Son. But in Christianity, the paradigm of partnership, the life-giving principle on planet earth, has not been celebrated or even acknowledged.

I believe we need to reclaim the lost feminine at all levels: physical, psychological, emotional, and spiritual. We have been gravely impoverished by the loss of the bride and the mandala of sacred partnership that was to have been the birthright of Christians. We have suffered the loss of Eros/relationship and deep connection with the feminine—the body, the emotions, the intuitive, the kinship of all the living, the blessings of the beautiful and bountiful planet.

Who is "the lost bride" of the Christian tradition? How does she tie in with the concept of the sacred feminine?

There is only one model for life on planet earth—and that model is "sacred union." In ancient cultures, this fundamental reality was honored in cults that celebrated the mutuality and "symbiosis" of the masculine and feminine as intimate partners. Examples are Tammuz/Ishtar, Ba'al/Astarte, Adonis/Venus, Osiris/Isis. In these cultures, the joy from their bridal chambers spread out into the crops and herds, and into the people of their realm. Similar rites were acknowledged in various liturgies throughout the Near East. The Song of Songs is a redaction of ancient liturgical poetry from the *hieros gamos* rites of Isis and Osiris. Invariably the king is executed and his bride seeks him, mourning his death, and is eventually reunited with him. In the Song of Songs, the fragrance of the bride is nard [spikenard, an eastern perfume or ointment] which wafts around the bridegroom at the banquet table. And in the Gospel, again it is nard with which Mary anoints Jesus, and the fragrance "filled the house" (John 12:3).

On seven of eight lists of women who accompanied Jesus, Mary Magdalene is mentioned first, and yet, her status as "first lady" was later denied. It suited the church fathers of the fourth century to officially elevate the mother of Jesus as "Theotokos" (God-bearer, Mother of God) but to ignore his bride/beloved. The result has been a distortion of the most basic model for life on our planet—the "sacred union" of devoted partners.

You just referred to hieros gamos, *which is mentioned in* The Da Vinci Code *and is understood to be a translation from the Greek of "sacred marriage." But what does it really mean? And how is it connected to Jesus?*

I believe that Jesus embodied the archetype of the sacred bridegroom and that he and his bride together manifested the mythology of *hieros gamos.* Their union was, in my opinion, the cornerstone of the early Christian community, a radical new way of living a partnership. In 1 Corinthians 9:5, Paul mentions that the brothers of Jesus and the other apostles travel around with their "sister-wives," a phrase that is often translated as "Christian sisters." But it actually says "sister-wives." What is a "sister-wife"? There is another place in Scripture where sister and wife occur together and that is in the Song of Songs. There, the bridegroom calls his beloved "my sister, my bride." This phrase speaks of an intimate relationship that is beyond that of an arranged marriage. It is a relationship of mutual interest, affection, and special kinship. According to Paul, these apostles were traveling as missionary couples, not as pairs of men as we have been inclined to believe. I firmly believe the model for this relationship was Jesus traveling with his own beloved. It is this intimacy to which the *Gospel of Philip* alludes when it states: "There were three Marys who walked with Jesus. His mother, his sister, and his consort were each a Mary," and goes on to say that Jesus used to kiss Mary Magdalene and the other disciples were jealous.

What is the significance of the chalice—or grail—symbolism?

The chalice or vessel is ubiquitous as a symbol for the feminine "container." I have a picture of a pitcher with breasts from about 6000 b.c.e. It represents the feminine as nurturer. Marija Gimbutas [pioneering archaeologist and commentator on goddess symbols and goddess-worshipping cultures of pre-historic Europe and the Near East] noted examples of the letter *V* on cave walls dating from prehistoric times. The downward-pointing triangle is universally understood as the female pubic triangle, and the hexagram is a very ancient symbol for the cosmic dance of the chalice and the blade, the male and female triangles representing the deities Shiva and Shakti in India.

What role did women play in the earliest days of the Christian church?

Before the Gospels were ever written, women were

apparently very much involved in the leadership of the early Christian communities. In his epistles, written in the 50s C.E., Paul mentions various women, including Phoebe, a deaconess, Prisca, and Junia, who exercised leadership in early Christian communities. In the epistle to the Romans (16:6,12), Paul commends several women—Mary, Persis, Tryphosa, and Tryphena—for their hard work. Wealthy women supported Jesus' ministry from the beginning, and were faithful to him until the end, standing at the foot of the cross while the male apostles cowered in hiding. Women opened their homes as meeting places and communal living space in the early community, and some served as deaconesses and even priests in the early days of the church. Dr. Dorothy Irvin has discovered and published numerous murals and mosaics from early Christian communities depicting women in priestly robes and regalia. Following the guidelines found in the epistle 1 Timothy, the hierarchy later denied women the right to teach and prophecy in the assembly.

How do you feel about efforts by modern feminist scholars to recast Mary Magdalene as the preeminent apostle?

Although I'm very much in sympathy with research establishing Mary Magdalene as the most faithful of all those who accompanied Jesus during his ministry, I don't think that styling her as an apostle, equal to Peter, or perhaps even more important than Peter, goes nearly far enough. There is no doubt that Mary Magdalene shows total devotion and faithfulness to Christ. But the Gospel also tells a different story. In the earliest Christian texts, Mary Magdalene is not merely equal in status to Peter. She is identified as the archetypal bride of the eternal bridegroom and provides the model for the quest and desire of the human soul (and the entire human community) for union with the Divine. She models the way of "eros" relatedness, the way of the heart, and together with her bridegroom, provides the paradigm for imaging the Divine as partners. Her role of apostle or "emissary" fades in comparison.

Some people, taking this argument too literally, seem to feel that styling Mary Magdalene as the wife of Jesus somehow demeans her. The argument seems to be that it defines her in terms of her relationship with a man which somehow diminishes her own stature. I believe this is far too narrow a view. One needs to realize that the "sacred marriage" we are discussing here is not merely about a first-century Jewish rabbi and his wife. It is really about the archetypal pattern for wholeness, the harmony of the polarities and the "syzygy" of *logos/sophia* (reason/wisdom) representing the Divine as a union of opposites.

Throughout the Gospels Jesus is presented as bridegroom, but it is now widely claimed that he had no bride. In the ancient rites of *hieros gamos,* the royal bride proclaimed and even conferred kingship by her anointing of the bridegroom. Clearly the woman with the alabaster jar who anointed Jesus embodies that ancient archetype, immediately recognized in every corner of the Roman Empire. There was nothing subservient in the mythic act of recognition and endorsement Mary performed in anointing Jesus in the rite of *hieros gamos.*

Mary and Jesus
Re-Enacting Ancient Fertility Cults?

By Margaret Starbird

Early Christian renderings of the Virgin and her child were modeled on the far more ancient images of the Egyptian goddess Isis, the Sister-Bride of Osiris, holding the sacred child Horus, god of light, on her lap. Ritual poetry from the cult of Isis and Osiris parallels the Song of Songs, in some places word for word. Both lunar and Earth goddesses of the ancient world were often rendered dark to represent feminine principle in juxtaposition to the solar/masculine, a dualism common in the early civilizations of the Mediterranean. Numerous goddesses were rendered black: Inanna, Isis, Cybele, and Artemis, to name only a few.

For the earliest Christians, the goddess in the Gospels was Mary Magdalene, whose epithet meant "elevated" or "watchtower/stronghold" . . .

After peaking in the twelfth century, the unique importance of the Magdalene in Western Europe was gradually downgraded from around the mid-thirteenth century—a date that corresponds rather dramatically with the Albigensian crusade against the Cathars and the adherents of the "Church of Love." The rise of the Inquisition in the thirteenth century was especially virulent in southern France in response to several Gospel-oriented versions of Christianity, popular heretical sects that severely threatened the hegemony of the Church of Rome. With collab-

---

Excerpted from *The Goddess in the Gospels: Reclaiming the Sacred Feminine.*

oration from the French king, the pope mounted a crusade against the Albigensian heretics, a bloody war of devastation that lasted for a generation, wiping out whole towns and destroying the cultural flowering of the region known as the Languedoc.

During this same era, beautiful and important epithets that once belonged to the Magdalene were shifted to the Blessed Virgin Mary and churches built to "Our Lady" ostensibly honored the mother of Jesus as the preeminent bearer of the archetypal feminine—"alone of all her sex." Statues and effigies of the Virgin proliferated, most often with her child on her lap, reminiscent of the Egyptian statues of Isis and Horus. After the mid–thirteenth century, the "voice of the Bride" was effectively silenced, although it is whispered that the masons of Europe kept the true faith and built its symbols into the very stones of their Gothic cathedrals. . . .

The anointing of Jesus in the Gospels is an enactment of rites from the prevailing fertility cult of the ancient Middle East. In pouring her precious unguent of nard over the head of Jesus, the woman whom tradition has identified with "the Magdalene" ("the Great"!) performed an act identical to the marriage rite of the *hieros gamos*—the rite of the anointing of the chosen Bridegroom/King by the royal representative of the Great Goddess!

Jesus recognized and acknowledged this rite himself, in the context of his role as the sacrificed king: "She has anointed me in preparation for burial" (Mark 14:8b). Those who heard the Gospel story of the anointing at the feast in Bethany would certainly have recognized the rite as the ceremonial anointing of the Sacred King, just as they would have recognized the woman, "the woman with the alabaster jar," who came to the garden sepulcher on the third day to finish the anointing for burial and to lament her tortured Bridegroom. She found an empty tomb. . . .

In the pagan rituals surrounding the ancient myths, the Goddess (the Sister-Bride) goes to the tomb in the garden to lament the death of her Bridegroom and rejoices to find him resurrected. "Love is stronger than death" is the poignant promise in the Song of Songs and similar love poetry of the Middle East celebrating these ancient rites of the Sacred Marriage. . . .

Royal Blood and Mary's Vine

By Margaret Starbird

The Sangraal

Medieval poets writing in the twelfth century, when the Grail legends first surfaced in European literature, mention a "Grail Family," presumably the custodians of the chalice who were later found unworthy of this privilege. A connection is sometimes drawn by Grail scholars between the word *sangraal* and *gradales,* a word that seems to have meant "cup," "platter," or "basin" in the Provençal language. But it has also been suggested that if one breaks the word *sangraal* after the *g,* the result is *sang raal,* which in Old French means "blood royal."

This second derivation of the French *sangraal* is extremely provocative, and perhaps enlightening. Suddenly

---

Excerpted from *The Woman with the Alabaster Jar: Mary Magdalen and the Holy Grail.*

one is faced with a new reading of the familiar legend: instead of a cup or chalice, the story now states that Mary Magdalen brought the "blood royal" to the Mediterranean coast of France. Other legends credit Joseph of Arimathea with bringing the blood of Jesus to France in some kind of vessel. Perhaps it was really Mary Magdalen, under the protection of Joseph of Arimathea, who carried the royal bloodline of David the King to the Mediterranean coast of France.

The Merovingian Connection

There is evidence to suggest that the royal bloodline of Jesus and Mary Magdalen eventually flowed in the veins of the Merovingian monarchs of France. The name *Merovingian* may itself be a linguistic fossil. The lore surrounding the royal family of the Franks mentions an ancestor Merovee. But the word *Merovingian* breaks down phonetically into syllables that we can easily recognize: *mer* and *vin,* Mary and the vine. Broken down this way, it may be seen to allude to the "vine of Mary" or perhaps the "vine of the Mother."

The royal emblem of the Merovingian King Clovis was the fleur-de-lis (the iris). The Latin name for the iris flower, which grows wild in countries of the Middle East, is *gladiolus,* or "small sword."The trefoil fleur-de-lis of the royal house of France is a masculine symbol. In fact, it is a graphic image of the covenant of circumcision in which are inherent all the promises of God to Israel and to the House of David. Thomas Inman discusses the masculine nature of the "flower of light" at length in his nineteenth-century work, *Ancient Pagan and Modern Christian Symbolism.* It is almost amusing that this same male symbol, the "little sword," is today the international emblem for the Boy Scouts!

Two Years Later

Margaret Starbird Assesses The Da Vinci Code *Phenomenon*

A Follow-Up Interview with Margaret Starbird

The past two years have been eventful, not only for Dan Brown but for Margaret Starbird, whose deep belief in the sacred feminine has propelled her books into significant sales and has kept her on the road giving interviews, lectures, and retreats. We wanted to know what impact the "Code" effect has had on her life. And also her beliefs—has she learned things or heard things that have caused her to modify her views? Along the way, she offers thoughts ranging from Gnosticism to Carl Jung, and from the state of the Catholic Church and the symbolism in Leonardo's paintings to the Grail bloodline.

The Da Vinci Code *has not only been at the top of worldwide bestseller lists since it appeared in the spring of 2003—it has truly become a cultural phenomenon. To what do you attribute the success of Dan Brown's novel and, in particular, the continuing fascination with the religious themes Dan Brown has raised?*

The idea of the "Sacred Union" of Christ and Mary Magdalene at the heart of Christianity apparently resonates at a very deep level. At this point of crisis in the Roman Catholic Church, it is clear to many that the institution has a fundamental flaw—the dissociation of its doctrines and hierarchy from the Feminine. The egalitarian community embodying the enlightened teachings of its "Rabbi Yeshua" has become gravely distorted over the two millennia of its history.

Suddenly we begin to wonder if there is something else they forgot to tell us.

Dan Brown has acknowledged the impact of your works—particularly The Woman with the Alabaster Jar—*on the thinking that went behind the novel. How faithful has he been to them, particularly that of the sacred marriage and Mary's sojourn in France to start the holy bloodline?*

Those who read my books realize that my work is not about restoring an elite bloodline, but rather centers on the balancing of masculine and feminine/Logos and Sophia. I believe the stories and legends of the child of Jesus and Mary Magdalene—the princess locked in the tower or inadvertently lost—reflect a folk memory of the "Union" of the archetypal Bride and Bridegroom. The "child" proves that the union existed at all levels: physical, psychological, metaphorical. It was the ultimate partnership of "Divine Complements" enabling us to image God as a loving Oneness.

How has the "Code" affected you personally? Did you feel any backlash from the vociferous critiques of the theology behind The Da Vinci Code? *What about the call by a bishop closely tied to the Vatican that all but told people not to read it?*

When I wrote *The Woman with the Alabaster Jar,* I gave it to my Roman Catholic pastor to read before I sent it to the publisher. His response was, "This could heal the Church." He must have sensed that reclaiming the Bride would restore the "wasteland," just as the Grail legends suggest. Other priests and prelates have endorsed and embraced my vision of the "Sacred Union," and I am invited to speak at a surprising and increasing number of mainstream Christian churches. I also receive hundreds of emails every week from people, including many Catholics and other Christians, thanking me for my work. I would venture to guess that the Cardinal assigned to denigrate *The Da Vinci Code* has not yet read my books.

How about in terms of scholarship? The Da Vinci Code *has brought out a cornucopia of scholarship and commentary. Has any of it led to the modification of your own views? If so, what and how?*

Someone asked me recently if I changed my message in my new book, *Mary Magdalene, Bride in Exile*. The answer is no. I am saying the same thing only louder, with more evidence, more medieval art, more footnotes and documentation. In answer to critics who state that there is no evidence for the intimate partnership of Jesus and Mary Magdalene, I have provided an additional mountain of circumstantial evidence in support of the "Sacred Marriage." My work is not about one fact or another but rather, an entire body of facts that provide a mosaic attesting to the Union at the heart of Christian mythology.

Is there any more evidence—or a debunking thereof—relating to Mary Magdalene's journey to Egypt and then to France, or the continuity of the bloodline?

Since there are no historical facts available, all proponents of the various theories are relying on a body of legend, tradition, and hearsay. When I wrote the fictional piece at the beginning of *Alabaster Jar,* I suggested that Joseph of Arimathea had taken Mary Magdalene to safety in Egypt. My theory was based on three elements: the "flight of the Holy Family to Egypt" in Matthew's Gospel; the prophecy of Hosea 11:1, "Out of Egypt I called my child"; and the fact that in the French tradition, Sarah, whose name means "Princess" in Hebrew, is called "Sarah the Egyptian." In *Mary Magdalene, Bride in Exile,* I published a photograph of a probably second-century prayer rug depicting the exiled Christians, including a mother and child with halos, traveling in boats, along with the story of the amazing survival of this artifact.

Wouldn't lands to the east of Palestine have been seen as more hospitable than France, for example? There were only "barbarians" in Europe, while it's believed other disciples wandered north and east; there is even a monument to Peter in western India.

The oral tradition of the refugee family from Palestine—Mary Magdalene, Lazarus, Martha, the other Marys—and their friends in Gaul is of great antiquity, supported by local place names and prayers in very old breviaries in the region. Again, we don't have any travelogue or ticket receipts for these émigrés from Palestine seeking asylum in Gaul, but there is evidence of a large Jewish presence in Provence, so France is a plausible speculation. There are legends in Ephesus and to the east as well.

In your book, Magdalene's Lost Legacy, *you explore archaic symbols, hidden meanings in biblical texts, sacred numbers in the ancient world, symbolic architecture, and even numerical "evidence" that Jesus and Mary symbolized the harmonious union of opposing principles. Could it not be argued that all this is modern-day, unfounded conjecture based on selective coincidences?*

Gematria is an ancient literary device confirmed in writings of Plato and other Greek philosophers, reaffirmed in the Hebrew Bible, and employed also in the Greek New Testament. There is nothing "modern" or "New Age" about *gematria.* And its prevalence in these texts seems to confirm that it is certainly NOT accidental. I get numerous emails supporting my work and conclusions from people who actually study sacred geometry and the corresponding *gematria* in the sacred texts reflecting cosmic principles.

When the subject of archetypes and symbolism comes up in your work as well as the novel, do we detect the influence of Carl Gustav Jung?

I mention Carl Jung in my books when discussing the integration of the masculine "Logos" and Feminine "Eros" principles implied by the "Sacred Union." I think Carl Jung would have been absolutely ecstatic to learn that the Great Secret hidden in Western civilization was the "Sacred Union" of Jesus and Magdalene. In fact, in *Aion,* Jung says that the "Self" is often conceived as a royal, distinguished or Divine Couple. Each of us is a living composite of both "left"- and "right"-brained gifts. The "Sacred Union" is a reconciliation of these imagined "opposites," integrated into wholeness.

Dan Brown places a lot of emphasis on the Gnostic Gospels. Beyond citing them as further evidence of the role of the sacred union, you have written little about

Gnosticism. What are your views on the Gnostic tradition?

I think the Gnostic texts (CE 125–300), with the possible exception of the Gospel of Thomas, are late. Most are at least three or four generations late. They are too late to be the original testimony about the relationship of Jesus and Mary Magdalene. In laying out my evidence for the "Sacred Marriage," I rely solely on the Christian canon. The Gnostic Gospels eloquently affirm the testimony of the canonical texts that Mary Magdalene was the preeminent and most beloved of the followers of Jesus, but one need look no further than the Christian Gospels for that information.

The argument about whether or not it was Mary Magdalene who was painted into The Last Supper *has also continued over the past couple of years. As a believer in "lost symbols," do you agree that Leonardo may have indeed invoked symbols in this painting?*

Clearly, Leonardo used symbols, although my work does not focus on his paintings. Dan Brown's assertion that there is no chalice on the table of Leonardo's *Last Supper* is apparently correct, but if you look above the head of the apostle on the far left (the feminine side!) of the painting, you will find the chalice floating as a decoration in the wall. Leonardo seems to be saying, "The Grail is not a cup, but rather, look for the Grail on a different plane."

Do you have an opinion on whether or not the figure in The Last Supper *is that of Mary Magdalene?*

The figure at the right hand of Jesus certainly appears to be a woman. Alignment in a painting was an artist's device for linking elements in the work. Given that a line drawn from the middle of the floating chalice goes through the face of the figure asserted to be a woman and then touches the left hand of Jesus, I think it's a safe guess that Leonardo was deliberately linking the "Grail" to Jesus and his Beloved in this painting. The distance between the floating chalice and the woman is the same as the distance between her and the left hand of Jesus, further establishing their apparent connection.

What long-term impact, if any, do you think the novel—and the currency of your views—will have?

When I published *The Woman with the Alabaster Jar,* pouring the hidden tradition into the mainstream, I had no idea where the ripples would go. With the encouragement of my pastor, I felt the work would be seen to be a blessing for Christianity, allowing the hierarchy to welcome the Bride and embrace her after her centuries of exile. That is still the prayer of my heart. The focus of my subsequent books is to ensure that the mountain of circumstantial evidence in support of the Sacred Partnership of the archetypal Bride and Bridegroom survives in spite of "dungeon, fire, and sword."

The Gnostic Tradition and the Divine Mother

BY ELAINE PAGELS

Elaine Pagels is a preeminent figure in the theological community and bestselling author. The Harrington Spear Paine Professor of Re-

---

ligion at Princeton University, Pagels was awarded the Rockefeller, Guggenheim, and MacArthur Fellowships in three consecutive years. As a young researcher at Barnard College, she changed forever the historical landscape of the Christian religion by exploding the myth of the early Christian Church as a unified movement. Her findings were published in the bestselling book, *The Gnostic Gospels,* an analysis of 52 early Christian manuscripts known collectively as the Nag Hammadi Library, which show the pluralistic nature of the early church and the role of women in the developing Christian movement (see Chapter 3). *The Gnostic Gospels,* from which the following is an excerpt, won both the National Book Critic's Circle Award and the National Book Award and was chosen by the Modern Library as one of the 100 best books of the 20th Century. Pagels is also the author or the bestseller *Beyond Belief: The Secret Gospel of Thomas.*

One group of gnostic sources claims to have received a secret tradition from Jesus through James and through Mary Magdalene. Members of this group prayed to both the divine Father and Mother: "From Thee, Father, and through Thee, Mother, the two immortal names, Parents of the divine being, and thou, dweller in heaven, humanity, of the mighty name. . . ."

Since the Genesis account goes on to say that humanity was created "male and female" (1:27), some concluded that the God in whose image we are made must also be both masculine and feminine—both Father and Mother.

How do these texts characterize the divine Mother? I find no simple answer, since the texts themselves are extremely diverse. Yet we may sketch out three primary characterizations. In the first place, several gnostic groups describe the divine Mother as part of an original couple. Valentinus, the teacher and poet, begins with the premise that God is essentially indescribable. But he suggests that the divine can be imagined as a dyad; consisting, in one part, of the Ineffable, the Depth, the Primal Father; and, in the other, of Grace, Silence, the Womb and "Mother of the All." Valentinus reasons that Silence is the appropriate complement of the Father, designating the former as feminine and the latter as masculine because of the grammatical gender of the Greek words. He goes on to describe how Silence receives, as in a womb, the seed of the Ineffable Source; from this she brings forth all the emanations of divine being, ranged in harmonious pairs of masculine and feminine energies.

Followers of Valentinus prayed to her for protection as the Mother, and as "the mystical, eternal Silence." For example, Marcus the magician invokes her as Grace (in Greek, the feminine term *charis*): "May She who is before all things, the incomprehensible and indescribable Grace, fill you within, and increase in you her own knowledge." In his secret celebration of the mass, Marcus teaches that the wine symbolizes her blood. As the cup of wine is offered, he prays that "Grace may flow" into all who drink of it. A prophet and visionary, Marcus calls himself the "*womb* and *recipient* of Silence" (as she is of the Father). The visions he received of the divine being appeared, he reports, in female form.

Another gnostic writing, called the *Great Announcement,* quoted by Hippolytus in his *Refutation of All Heresies,* explains the origin of the universe as follows: From the power of Silence appeared "a great power, the Mind of the Universe, which manages all things, and is a male . . . the other . . . a great Intelligence . . . is a female which produces all things." Following the gender of the Greek words for "mind" (*nous*-masculine) and "intelligence" (*epinoia*-feminine), this author explains that these powers, joined in union, "are discovered to be duality. . . . This is Mind in Intelligence, and these are separable from one another, and yet are one, found in a state of duality." This means, the gnostic teacher explains, that

> there is in everyone [divine power] existing in a latent condition . . . This is one power divided above and below; generating itself, making itself grow, seeking itself, finding itself, being mother of itself, father of itself, sister of itself, spouse of itself, daughter of itself, son of itself—mother, father, unity, being a source of the entire circle of existence.

How did these gnostics intend their meaning to be understood? Different teachers disagreed. Some insisted that the divine be considered masculofeminine—the "great male-female power." Others claimed that the terms were meant only as metaphors, since, in reality, the divine is "neither male nor female." A third group suggested that one can describe the primal Source in either masculine or feminine terms, depending on which aspect one intends to stress. Proponents of these diverse views agreed that the divine is to be understood in terms of a harmonious, dynamic relationship of opposites—a concept that may be akin to the Eastern view of *yin* and *yang*, but remains alien to orthodox Judaism and Christianity. . . .

If some gnostic sources suggest that the Spirit constitutes the maternal element of the Trinity, the *Gospel of Philip* makes an equally radical suggestion about the doctrine that later developed as the virgin birth. Here again, the Spirit is both Mother and Virgin, the counterpart—and consort—of the Heavenly Father: "Is it permitted to utter a mystery? The Father of everything united with the virgin who came down"—that is, with the Holy Spirit descending into the world. But because this process is to be understood symbolically, not literally, the Spirit remains a virgin. The author goes on to explain that "Adam came into being from two virgins, from the Spirit and from the virgin earth," so "Christ, therefore, was born from a virgin" (that is, from the Spirit). But the author ridicules those literal-minded Christians who mistakenly refer the virgin birth to Mary, Jesus' mother, as though she conceived apart from Joseph: "They do not know what they are saying. When did a woman ever conceive by a woman?" Instead, he argues, virgin birth refers to that mysterious union of the two divine powers, the Father of All and the Holy Spirit.

In addition to the eternal, mystical Silence and the Holy Spirit, certain gnostics suggest a third characterization of the divine Mother: as Wisdom. Here the Greek feminine term for "wisdom," *sophia,* translates a Hebrew feminine term, *hokhmah*. Early interpreters had pondered the meaning of certain Biblical passages—for example, the saying in Proverbs that "God made the world in Wisdom." Could Wisdom be the feminine power in which God's creation was "conceived"? According to one teacher, the double meaning of the term conception—physical and intellectual—suggests this possibility: "The image of thought [*ennoia*] is feminine, since . . . [it] is a power of conception."

The Godman and the Goddess

An Interview with Timothy Freke

In this interview, Timothy Freke introduces some of the argument in *Jesus and the Lost Goddess,* excerpts from which follow. Freke, along with his collaborator and regular co-author Peter Gandy, are key architects of the argument that holds that the belief system of the original Christians was thoroughly subverted as the Roman Empire institutionalized Christianity. The early Christian movement's beliefs in the Gnostic experience of mystical enlightenment and the mystical union of the Godman (Jesus) and the Goddess (Mary Magdalene) were so threatening to the Roman church's vision that they had to be brutally suppressed. The Goddess, as well as the mystical and Gnostic traditions, was then written out of the documents, beliefs, and practices of Christianity. For the original Christians, as Teabing tells Sophie in *The Da Vinci Code* about the Priory of Sion's efforts to keep alive the Goddess tradition, Mary Magdalene represents "the Goddess, the Holy Grail, the Rose, and the Divine Mother."

Timothy Freke has a degree in philosophy. Peter Gandy has an M.A. in classical civilizations, specializing in ancient pagan mystery religions. They are the coauthors of *Jesus and the Lost Goddess: The Secret Teachings of the Original Christians,* as well as *The Jesus Mysteries: Was the "Original Jesus" a Pagan God?* and more than twenty other books.

What was the importance of Goddess worship in pagan cultures?

Along with the myth of the Godman, the pagan mysteries told an allegorical myth of the lost and redeemed Goddess, that was an allegory about the fall and redemption of the soul. The most famous pagan version of this myth is Demeter and Persephone. The original Christians adapted this into their myth of Sophia—the Christian Goddess whose name means "wisdom."

What is distinctly "feminine" about Sophia?

The Goddess represents the All, the universe, all that we sense, all that we imagine—the flow of appearances, forms, experience. God—the male archetype—represents the One, the mysterious source of all consciousness which conceives and witnesses the flow of appearances we call life. (Life, or Zoë, was another name of the Christian Goddess). Sophia was already being venerated by Jewish and pagan mystics before the rise of Christianity.

But the Goddess is not always portrayed in only one light.

Christian mythology is deep and multilayered. This relationship plays out in many ways on many levels. From the arising of something from nothing, it eventually becomes the relationship between Jesus and the two Marys who represent the two aspects of the Goddess—virgin mother and fallen and redeemed whore. Again, these are images taken from ancient pagan mythology.

How does Eve fit into the "lost Goddess" tradition?

She represents half (not a rib as is often mistranslated) of Adam (whose name means "human"). Her myth mirrors pagan myths of the fall of the soul into incarnation, which the Jesus myth seeks to redress.

What is the philosophical concept behind the sacred feminine?

The male principle for the ancients was indivisible consciousness. The female principle was the multitude of appearances, experiences, what is being witnessed. This duality is fundamental to life. Without it there is nothing. Wisdom is the state of the soul (feminine principle) when it is pure enough to recognize its true nature, to be the One Consciousness in all, which was symbolized for Paul and company by the Christ or "King."

Sophia's Journey

The Pagan Goddess of the Centuries Lost in the Modern Christian World

BY TIMOTHY FREKE AND PETER GANDY

In this excerpt from Freke and Gandy's *Jesus and the Lost Goddess,* the authors trace the tradition of the Goddess back to the Greek myths and Jewish sources. They build their image of the Goddess from Old Testament quotations, Greek myths, and pagan traditions that range from Helen of Troy to Plato's view of Psyche as female, to mysteries of Eleusis that regularly reenacted the myth of Demeter and Persephone. In the end, they find the theme of the lost Goddess even in the Sleeping Beauty legend.

The Christian Goddess

The myth of the Godman Jesus can only be properly understood alongside the myth of the Goddess Sophia. After so many centuries of patriarchal Christianity it is both shocking and reassuring to discover a Goddess at the very heart of Christianity. She is, like her son/brother/lover Jesus, a syncretic figure created from both Pagan and Jewish sources.

Sophia, whose name means "wisdom," had been the Goddess of pagan philosophers for centuries. Indeed, the word for "philosopher," first used by Pythagoras, means "lover of Sophia." Although often pictured today as dry academics, these brilliant intellectuals were actually mystics

---

Excerpted from *Jesus and the Lost Goddess: The Secret Teachings of the Original Christians,* by Timothy Freke and Peter Gandy.

and devotees of the Goddess. Parmenides, for example, is usually remembered as the founder of Western logic, yet his masterwork is a visionary poem in which he descends to the underworld to be instructed by the Goddess.

Sophia was also an important mythical figure for Jewish Gnostics, such as Philo [Jewish-Hellenistic philosopher based in Alexandria, 25 b.c.e.–50 c.e.]. Although later rejected by Jewish literalists, there had always been a Jewish Goddess tradition. At one time Israelites had worshipped the Goddess Asherah as the consort of the Jewish God Jehovah. In the fifth century b.c.e. she was known as Anat Jahu. In texts written between the fourth and fifth centuries b.c.e., such as *Proverbs, The Sophia of Solomon,* and the *Sophia of Jesus the Son of Sirach,* she becomes God's companion and cocreator Sophia.

Origins of the Christian Goddess

As with all Christian mythology, the myth of the lost Goddess is a synthesis of preexisting Jewish and Pagan myths. Let's examine some of these sources.

Jewish Sources

The Exegesis on the Soul [one of the most intriguing lost gospels found among the books in the Nag Hammadi Library] draws attention to some of the Jewish mythological motifs which it develops in the myth of Sophia. It quotes *Jeremiah,* in which God proclaims to Israel, as if to the lost Goddess:

> You prostituted yourself to many shepherds and then you returned to me. Take an honest look and see where you prostituted yourself. You became shameless with every-

> one. You did not call on me as kinsman or as Father or author of your virginity.

Likewise, in *Ezekiel* God announces:

> You built yourself a brothel on every lane, and you wasted your beauty, and you spread your legs in every alley, and you multiplied your acts of prostitution. You prostituted yourself to the sons of Egypt, those who are your neighbors, men great of flesh.

The *Exegesis on the Soul* decodes the allegorical meaning of this text:

> What does "the sons of Egypt, men great of flesh" mean, if not the world of the body and the realm of the senses and the affairs of this Earth, by which the psyche has become contaminated?

The Exegesis on the Soul also points out the resonance between the myth of Sophia and the *Genesis* myth. In *Genesis* Adam represents Consciousness and Eve represents psyche. In the beginning there was originally a primordial human being, Adam, from whom God took "one side" and created Eve (not a "rib" as it says in traditional translations!). This represents the projection of psyche from Consciousness. The two are essentially one, but appear as opposites. The psyche (Eve) leads Consciousness (Adam) into identification with the body. This is symbolized by the Fall from Eden. The mystical marriage repairs the primal separation of Adam and Eve, Consciousness and psyche. *The Exegesis on the Soul* quotes Paul's teaching, "They will become a single body," and comments:

They were originally joined one to another when they were with the Father, before the woman led astray the man, who is her brother. This marriage has brought them back together again and the psyche has been joined to her true lover.

In another Jewish text, *Proverbs,* the two fundamental states of the psyche are represented by Lady Wisdom and Lady Folly, According to Philo, Lady Folly is like a whore who leads those who listen to her to Hell. Lady Wisdom, however, is compared to an invitation to a wedding and a faithful wife—images which refer to the motif of the mystical marriage.

The Myth of Helen

As with the Jesus story, the most important source for the Christian Goddess myth is Pagan mythology. *The Exegesis on the Soul* compares the Christian myth of Sophia to Homer's initiatory tales *The Iliad* and *The Odyssey,* in which Helen has been abducted and must be rescued. According to the Pythagoreans, Helen is a symbol of the psyche and her abduction represents the fall of the psyche into incarnation . . .

The Helen myth was important to the first Christians . . . Deliberately imitating the myth of Jesus and the Goddess, these Gnostic masters identified themselves with the role of the savior come to reveal Gnosis to their lost followers, symbolized by Helen/Sophia.

Plato's Phaedo

In *Phaedo* Plato gives us an account of the fall and redemption of the psyche which was undoubtedly drawn on by the original Christians when they created their own version of the myth of the lost Goddess:

> The Psyche is dragged by the body into the region of the changeable, where she wanders in confusion. The world spins around her and she is like a drunkard under its influence. But returning to herself, she reflects. Then she passes into the realm of purity, eternity, immortality and unchangeableness, which are her kindred. When she is herself and not obstructed or hindered she is ever with them. When she ceases from her erring ways and is in communion with the unchanging, she is herself unchanging. This state of the psyche is called Sophia.

The Myth of Aphrodite

The Pagan myth of the Goddess Aphrodite tells fundamentally the same tale as the later Christian myth of the lost Goddess. Like Sophia, Aphrodite has a pristine and fallen nature. Plotinus [Egyptian-Roman philosopher of the third century c.e.] explains that in essence she is "Aphrodite of the Heavens," but "here she has turned whore." He writes, "Zeus represents consciousness and Aphrodite his daughter who issues from him is psyche," commenting:

> The nature of the psyche is to love God and long to be at one with Him in the noble love of a daughter for a noble Father. But coming to human birth and lured by the courtships of this sphere, she takes up with another lover, a mortal, leaves her Father and falls. But one day, coming to hate her shame, she puts away the evil of Earth, once more seeks her Father and finds peace. The psyche's true good lies in devotion to Consciousness its kin. Evil to the psyche lies in frequenting strangers. But suppose the psyche has attained the highest, or rather it has revealed its presence to her. Then as long as the presence holds all distinctions fade. It is like the merging of lover and beloved.

Once she has this she would not trade it for anything in the whole universe.

The Myth of Demeter and Persephone

The most influential of all the myths of the Goddess in her two aspects is the myth of Demeter and Persephone, taught in the Mysteries of Eleusis. The Pagan Gnostic Sallustius [who lived around 360 C.E., was an advisor to the Roman Emperor Julian and sought a Pagan revival] tells us that this myth is an allegory for descent of the Psyche into incarnation. Olympiodorus likewise explains, "The Psyche descends after the manner of Persephone." Lucius Apuleius talks of the "dark descending rites" and "luminous ascending rites" of Persephone, writing of his own initiation:

> I approached the confines of death, and trod on the threshold of Persephone, and being carried through all the elements, I came back again to my pristine condition.

The Literalist Christian Hippolytus describes the teachings of the descent and ascent of the Psyche as the mystery revealed to those "admitted to the highest grade of the Eleusinian rites" and states that initiates of the Naassene school [Gnostic sect during the time of Hadrian—110–140 C.E.—which believed in the divinity of the serpent and held mystery rites dedicated to the Great Mother] of Christian Gnosticism had developed their teachings specifically from this source.

Plato tells us the name "Persephone" comes from *sophe* and means "wise," so it derives from the same root as "Sophia." Persephone, who was known as Kore, meaning "Daughter" or "Girl," represents the fallen psyche. In the Christian *Acts of Thomas,* the psyche is called Kore. Demeter means "Mother." She is the Celestial Queen who represents the pure psyche.

In the myth, Demeter's daughter Persephone is abducted by Hades, god of the underworld. This represents the fall into incarnation. Before they were initiated, initiates into the Mysteries of Eleusis had to imitate the grief felt by Demeter and Persephone at their separation. This represents the experience of *metanoia* which results from the initiates' grief at becoming separated from their deeper nature and lost in the world. Hermes goes to the underworld to rescue Persephone and reunite her with her mother Demeter. This represents rescuing the psyche from identification with the circumference of the circle of self and reuniting it with its true nature at the center.

Hades secretly gives Persephone pomegranate seeds to eat, however, and because she eats these seeds she must return to the underworld for a third of every year. The pomegranate seeds represent the seeds of future lives which we create in this life, which bring us back into human incarnation to continue the journey of awakening. They represent what the ancients called our "fate," which in modern spiritual jargon is generally known as our "karma." The motif of returning to the underworld for "a third of the year" is an allusion to the threefold nature of the Self: Consciousness, psyche, body. A third of our identity—the body—is in the underworld.

The figures of Demeter and Persephone were developed by the Greeks from ancient Egyptian mythology. Porphyry [pagan philosopher, 232–303 C.E.] tells us that the Egyptian Isis is equivalent to both Demeter and Persephone . . . In Egyptian mythology the higher and lower aspects of the Goddess are represented by Isis and her sister Nephthys, the wife of the evil god Set, who, like Hades, represents the material world.

These Egyptian myths are the earliest sources of what was to become the Christian myth of the lost and redeemed Goddess. Although this perennial story has been expunged from Christianity, it survived in the form of fairy tales such as *Sleeping Beauty.* As her name suggests, Sleeping Beauty is an image of the psyche fallen asleep in the world. The story portrays her as a princess cursed to sleep forever, imprisoned in a dark castle surrounded by deep impenetrable forest, but finally rescued by her lover, the hero prince.

The Goddess in the Gospels

In the Christian myth of Sophia, the Goddess, representing the psyche, is the central figure, while her brother-lover, representing Consciousness, is an incidental character. In the Jesus myth, it is the opposite. The God-man is the central character. Yet the myth of the lost Goddess forms an important subtext to the Jesus story, which would have been obvious to Christian initiates familiar with both allegories. The Sophia myth makes clear the nature of Jesus' mythical mission—he comes to rescue his sister-lover Sophia, the psyche lost in identification with the body. "Christ came for her sake," states *The Tripartate Tractate* [another of Nag Hammadi's Gnostic Gospels].

Virgin and Prostitute

In the gospels the Virgin Mary and Mary Magdalene represent the higher Sophia and the fallen Sophia. They are called by the same name to emphasize the fact that mythologically they are aspects of the same figure. As in the Sophia myth, the first Mary is a virgin, like Sophia when she was living with her Father, and the second is a

Did Early Gnostic Christians Engage in Sacred Sexual Acts?

Most of our experts find little evidence on this subject. However, Freke and Gandy comment briefly, noting that "Gnostics deliberately violated social norms as a way of deconditioning themselves from their social personae and so becoming aware of their true spiritual identity. For some, such as the Cainite school, this was done through ascetic abstinence. For others, such as the Carpocratian school, this was done through libertine indulgence . . ."

Apparently Carpocrates, an Alexandrian Platonist Gnostic, who founded a sect of Gnostic Christians in the early second century CE—a group described by Freke and Gandy as radical communists who abhorred private property—taught students to "enjoy life, including the pleasures of sex that are so often condemned by religious Literalists . . . Such Gnostics saw sexuality as a celebration of the union of God and Goddess, from which all life springs. They are said to have sometimes practiced sacramental nudity in church and even ritual intercourse."

prostitute who is redeemed by her lover Jesus, like Sophia when lost in the world.

The Goddess as mother and prostitute is alluded to in the genealogy created for Jesus by *The Gospel of Matthew*. As we would expect, this genealogy follows the patriarchal line, but breaks this pattern to specifically mention four famous Jewish "fallen women." Tamar was a temple prostitute. Ruth indulged in shameless sexual exploitation. Baathsheba was committed for adultery with King David. Rahab was the madam of a brothel. In the *Exodus* allegory, when Jesus/Joshua arrives in the Promised Land he rescues the prostitute Rahab, symbolizing the psyche, from the walled city of Jericho, symbolizing the body. By specifically naming Rahab as one of Jesus Christ's ancestors *The Gospel of Matthew* points to the mythological resonance between this story and the gospel story of Jesus redeeming the prostitute Mary Magdalene.

Mary Magdalene, representing Jesus' sister-lover Sophia, is the "Beloved Disciple" who is consistently portrayed in Christian texts as having a particularly close relationship with Jesus. *The Gospel of the Beloved Disciple* (aka *The Gospel of John)* [another Gnostic work] portrays Jesus and Mary as so close that, during the Last Supper, she is lying in his lap. *The Gospel of Philip* relates that Jesus "loved her more than the other disciples, and often used to kiss her on the lips." In *The Gospel of Luke* Mary wipes her hair on Jesus' feet. According to Jewish law, only a husband was allowed to see a woman's hair unbound, and if a woman let down her hair in front of another man, this was a sign of impropriety and grounds for mandatory divorce. This incident, then, can be seen as portraying Jesus and Mary either as man and wife or as libertine lovers with scant regard for moral niceties.

Images of the Awakening Psyche

Women play a prominent role throughout the Jesus story, particularly in *The Gospel of the Beloved Disciple,* and all of them represent Sophia in her various states of awakening. *The Exegesis on the Soul* portrays Sophia at her most desperate as a barren old woman. It is in this state that she experiences *metanoia* and calls out to the Father to rescue her. In the Jesus story this aspect of Sophia is represented by Elizabeth, the mother of John the Baptist. She is a partner figure to the Virgin Mary. Mary is young and unimpregnated. Elizabeth is old and barren. In this condition, like Sophia, she calls out to the Father for help, representing the barren psyche in which the call for help arises. The answer is John the Baptist, who represents the *psychic* initiation of purification through baptism with water, which is the start of the Gnostic path of self-knowledge.

Throughout his mission Jesus has various encounters with women who are Sophia figures and symbolize the progressive states of awakening of the psyche. In one incident Jesus prevents an adulterous woman from being stoned to death by pointing out that none of her accusers are themselves blameless. This is an allusion to the fallen Sophia being abused by her adulterous lovers. The woman in this story is a helpless victim surprised to be rescued. This represents the early stage of awakening in which the embodied psyche is a recipient of unasked-for assistance from essential Self, which it experiences as "grace."

In a further incident, Jesus meets an adulterous Samaritan woman representing the fallen Sophia. Jesus reveals to the woman that he is Christ and offers her the "waters of life." This story takes the relationship between Sophia, representing the psyche, and Jesus, representing Consciousness, a step further. Here, Jesus directly offers the teaching which leads to Gnosis, represented by the waters of eternal life, and reveals that he is the Christ. This represents a state in which initiates glimpse their true nature for the first time, and understand the possibility of knowledge. The scene is set at Jacob's Well, which is designed to reinforce the allusion to the Sophia myth. In Jewish mythology, Rebecca, the mother of Jacob, draws water from this well, which Philo tells us represents receiving the wisdom of Sophia.

In the next episode, we meet two important Sophia figures, Martha and her sister Mary. Their brother Lazarus has died, but they believe that if Jesus had been present he could have saved him. Moved by their faith, Jesus goes to the cave in which Lazarus is buried and miraculously raises him from the dead. In this remarkable little story Lazarus represents the *hylic* [i.e., material, corporeal] state of being spiritually dead in the underworld. He is brought to life by the power of the Christ, representing Consciousness, through the faith of Martha and Mary, representing the *psychic* and *pneumatic* stages of awakening. . . .

Another significant episode also happens whilst Jesus is visiting the house of Lazarus, Martha and Mary. Martha is again serving whilst Lazarus, now returned from the dead, sits at the table. Meanwhile, Mary takes "very costly ointment" and anoints Jesus, thus formally making him the "Anointed" or Christ/King. These events represent the stage of awakening in which initiates are no longer spiritually dead in the *hylic* state, which is represented by the resurrected Lazarus eating at the table. They are engaged in the *psychic* process of awakening, represented by Martha, who is serving, and have progressed sufficiently in the *pneumatic* level of awakening to clearly recognize their true identity as Consciousness, represented by Mary anointing Jesus as the Christ/King.

Jesus is portrayed as having expelled "seven demons" from "Mary called Magdalene." The number seven is significant. In the Gnostic mythical schema, the cosmos has seven levels, represented by the sun, moon, and five visible planets. These were sometimes imagined as demonic forces which entrap us in materiality. Above these is the *ogdoad* or "eighth," represented by the starry skies, which is the mythological home of the Goddess. The Gnostic journey of awakening from incarnation is sometimes conceived of as mounting a sevenfold ladder to the *ogdoad*. That Mary has been freed from seven demons represents

Jesus having helped her to ascend the seven rungs of the ladder to the heavens.

At the culmination of the Jesus story, it is Mary Magdalene who finds Jesus' empty tomb and to whom the resurrected Christ first appears. This represents the fulfillment of the process of initiation. For the Gnostics the body is a "tomb" in which we exist as the spiritually dead. Mary finding that the tomb is empty represents the understanding that we are not the physical body. Her encounter with the resurrected Christ represents the realization that our essential nature is the one Consciousness of God.

After this Mary represents the wise psyche, truly worthy of the name "Sophia." As *The Dialogue of the Saviour* puts it, Mary is now "a woman who completely understands." In *The Gospel According to Mary* the resurrected Jesus imparts the Inner Mysteries of Christianity to Mary, who reveals these secret teachings to the other disciples. They then go forth to preach "the gospel according to Mary." Despite the misogyny of the Christian Literalists, the tradition of Mary Magdalene as the *apostola apostolorum,* the "apostle to the apostles," remains Catholic doctrine to this day.

Motifs of the Mystical Marriage

According to the Christian Gnostics, there are many allusions to the mystical marriage in the Jesus story. The most important is the Eucharist ritual, which is based on the ancient rites of the mystical marriage in the Pagan Mysteries. In the Mysteries of Eleusius, the Goddess Demeter was represented by bread and the Godman Dionysus by wine. The original Christians, likewise, associated bread with Mary and wine with Jesus, who is called "the true vine" in *The Gospel of John*. The Literalist Epiphanius records with horror that initiates of the Colyridian school of Christianity celebrated the Eucharist in the name of "Mary Queen of Heaven," writing:

> They adorn a chair or a square throne, spread a linen cloth over it, and, at a certain solemn time, place bread on it and offer it in the name of Mary; and all partake of this bread.

In the act of ceremonially eating the bread and drinking the wine, the Godman and the Goddess, representing Consciousness and psyche, commune in the mystical marriage. It is obviously significant that as Jesus officiates at the Last Supper Eucharist celebration, the "Beloved Disciple" Mary Magdalene rests intimately in his lap.

Earlier, Jesus miraculously turns water into wine at a marriage ceremony at Cana, which according to Christian Gnostics represents the mystical marriage. Water becoming wine is an archaic symbol representing the ecstatic intoxication of spiritual transformation. The creators of the Jesus story borrowed this motif from Pagan mythology, in which the Godman Dionysus turns water into wine at his marriage to Ariadne. In the Christian version of this tale Jesus is not portrayed as the bridegroom. However, in the New Testament Jesus refers to himself, and is repeatedly referred to by others, as "the bridegroom." . . .

In one intriguing non-canonical Christian tale, Jesus takes Mary Magdalene up a mountain, whereupon one side of him becomes a woman with whom he makes love. Going up a mountain is a perennial image of walking the spiritual path to Heaven. The image of Jesus producing a woman from his side is an allusion to the *Genesis* myth in which Eve is created from one side of Adam, representing

Consciousness objectifying itself as psyche. In the Christian parable, Jesus (Consciousness) shows Mary (fallen psyche) the magical woman (higher psyche), who is Mary's original nature. Jesus then makes love with the woman, representing the consummation of the mystical marriage in which Consciousness and psyche commune in the realization of their essential Oneness.

Summary

- The Christian myth of the lost Goddess is the partner myth to the Jesus myth. Jesus and the Goddess represent Consciousness and psyche, or spirit and soul. The Goddess is portrayed as having two aspects, representing the pure psyche and the embodied psyche. These two aspects can be thought of as the two ends of the radius circle of self, one connecting to Consciousness at the center and the other to the body at the circumference.
- The myth of Sophia tells the story of the fall of the psyche into incarnation and her redemption by her lover-brother, representing Consciousness. Sophia's fall, repentance, redemption and marriage represent the *hylic, psychic* and *pneumatic* states of awareness an initiate passes through on their journey towards the realization of Gnosis.
- The myth of Sophia forms the subtext to the Jesus story. The most important Sophia figures in the gospels are the two Marys, Jesus' virgin mother and prostitute lover, representing the higher Sophia and the fallen Sophia. . . .

The Chalice and the Blade

Archaeology, Anthropology, and the Sacred Feminine

By Dan Burstein

In her well-known work, *The Chalice and the Blade: Our History, Our Future,* Riane Eisler lays the archeological and historical foundation for the central role of the Goddess and the feminine in early culture—a role she argues was later pushed aside by hierarchies that implicitly fostered domination, patriarchy, and rigidity. Eisler is a cofounder of the Center for Partnership Studies, which promotes a way of life based on "harmony with nature, nonviolence, and gender, racial, and economic equity." Her book is mentioned in Dan Brown's bibliography for *The Da Vinci Code* and informs some of *The Da Vinci Code*'s discussion of symbols and representations of goddess culture in history.

"There is abundant evidence that spirituality, and particularly the spiritual vision characteristic of wise seers, was once associated with woman," writes Eisler. "From Mesopotamian archaeological records we learn that Ishtar of Babylon . . . was still known as the Lady of Vision, She Who Directs Oracles, and the Prophetess." In Egypt, where there is ample evidence of strong queens and female pharaohs, records show that "the picture of a cobra was the hieroglyphic sign for the word *goddess* and the cobra was known as the Eye, *uzait,* a symbol of mystic insight and wisdom . . ."

Turning to Greece, Eisler points out that "the well-

---

known oracular shrine at Delphi also stood on a site originally identified with the worship of the Goddess. And even in classical Greek times, after it was taken over for the worship of Apollo, the oracle still spoke through the lips of a woman."

Archaeological records from many Near East and eastern Mediterranean countries note a propensity to associate justice (law) and medicine (healing powers) with women. Apparently, the Egyptian goddess Isis was associated with these traits. "Even writing, long assumed to date back to around 3200 b.c.e. in Sumer, appears to have much earlier, and possibly feminine, roots. In Sumerian tablets the Goddess Nidaba is described as the scribe of the Sumerian heaven as well as the inventor of both clay tablets and the art of writing. In Indian mythology the Goddess Sarasvati is credited with inventing the original alphabet."

The Minoan society left an artistic and archaeological record that indicates its daily life centered on the worship of the Goddess. "The evidence indicates that in Crete power was primarily equated with the responsibility of motherhood," says Eisler, arguing that Minoan Crete offered a male-female "partnership model of society in which women and traits associated with women were not systematically devalued." Democracy was practiced before its rise in Athens, the arts flourished, peace prevailed, and the culture exhibited a love for life that included what Eisler refers to as a "pleasure bond" between males and females. Clothing and art emphasized a relaxed and uninhibited sexuality, according to Eisler and many other researchers. Some scholars suggest that Minoan civilization was particularly successful, artistic, rich, and peaceful because the aggressive tendencies of its males were well channeled into sports, ecstatic dancing, music, and sex, rather than warfare.

While other goddess-worshipping cultures were abandoning their female deities for male gods of war, the Crete of four thousand years ago clung to its goddess traditions. Perhaps that is why, as Eisler puts it, "In the island of Crete where the Goddess was still supreme, there are no signs of war. Here the economy prospered and the arts flourished." The Goddess remained at the center of religious and ritual practice in Minoan society for hundreds more years, before the Goddess was lost here too and male God figures gained sway. The process of the fall of the Goddess is one that may well have echoes in the story of the Christian experience and how Mary Magdalene was treated by the early church and even today. Langdon, Teabing, and Sauniere are no doubt on to one of male-written history's greatest cover-ups.

If you go to Knossos, the Minoan palace in Crete, even today, the limestone frescoes still tell the story of the Goddess, her priestesses, and sacred, mystical practices—including sacred sexual practices. These and other archaeological finds give us many clues to understanding that looking for the "sacred feminine" in the collective unconscious of Western thought or the Judeo-Christian experience is an intriguing, productive, and historically important endeavor.

3 The Lost Gospels

"Liberated" Christianity

What I find interesting about Dan Brown's book is that it raises a very important question: If they—meaning the leaders of the church—suppressed so much of early Christian history, what else don't we know about? What else is there to be known? And as a historian, I think it's a really important question because the answer means a great deal.

—Elaine Pagels

The religious girders that frame the edifice of Dan Brown's plot are built upon the foundations of early Christian history and, in particular, the set of Gnostic Gospels found in 1945 near the Egyptian town of Nag Hammadi. These documents, which have led to remarkable discoveries about an alternate tradition later suppressed, form the backdrop of another artful blending of fact and fiction in *The Da Vinci Code.* In Chapter 58, which takes place in Lee Teabing's sumptuous study, Sophie Neveu and Robert Langdon are handed a copy of these lost Gospels in a "leather-bound . . . poster-sized" edition to demonstrate with irrevocable proof that "the marriage of Jesus and Mary Magdalene is part of the historical record."

As the following excerpts and interviews with some of the world's leading experts elaborate, there is no doubt the Nag Hammadi texts have yielded a treasure trove of documents permitting a richer, more nuanced and, perhaps, even more radical interpretation of the words of Jesus, the role of his followers, and the interpretation of early Christianity. They help shed light on a time when the many contending schools of Christian worship were interwoven and the definitive canon had not yet been created. Specifically, they give our era a glimpse into a different tradition—the Gnostic tradition—that conflicted with the interpretation of Jesus's preaching found today in the orthodoxy of the New Testament. More explosively, in terms of the history of the church, they suggest a much more important role for Mary Magdalene as a disciple and close companion to Jesus. They also suggest more interest in seeking inner knowledge and self-development than what we traditionally understand as the philosophy of the New Testament. And the Gnostics of Nag Hammadi seemed to feel less need for churches and priests. They seemed perfectly comfortable interpreting their own gospels and sacred books without intermediation—an idea institutionalized Christianity would find threatening.

In this chapter, we invite readers to join in the search for the meaning and implications of these "Lost Gospels." Certainly they seem to emphasize a balance between the masculine and the feminine, the good and the evil in mankind, and the importance of Mary Magdalene as an apostle. Beyond that, did the word *companion* mean "marriage" or was it simply a fellow traveler? What of the seemingly explicit reference in the *Gospel of Philip* to Jesus kissing Mary Magdalene frequently on the mouth? Factual description or metaphor? And if metaphor, metaphor for what? Are these Gnostic Gospels really telling us that a more humane, more "the spirit is within you" emphasis and a strongly anti-authoritarian, pro-feminine tradition existed that was purposely marginalized and shoved aside as heresy by history's Christian "winners"?

In the hands of the experts who have lived and breathed this material their whole professional lives, the reader will be guided through the existing scholarship as well as translations of the original documents that play such a prominent role in *The Da Vinci Code.*

An Astonishing Find

The Keys to the Alternate Tradition and Their Meaning for Today

By Elaine Pagels

In December 1945 an Arab peasant made an astonishing archeological discovery in Upper Egypt. Rumors obscured the circumstances of this find—perhaps because the discovery was accidental, and its sale on the black market illegal. For years even the identity of the discoverer remained unknown. One rumor held that he was a blood avenger; another, that he had made the find near the town of Naj 'Hammadi at the Jabal al-Tārif, a mountain honeycombed with more than 150 caves. Originally natural, some of these caves were cut and painted and used as grave sites as early as the sixth dynasty, some 4,300 years ago.

Elaine Pagels is Harrington Spear Paine Professor of Religion at Princeton University and author of the bestselling *Beyond Belief* as well as *The Gnostic Gospels,* from which this selection has been excerpted.

Thirty years later the discoverer himself, Muhammad 'Alī al-Samman, told what happened. Shortly before he and his brothers avenged their father's murder in a blood feud, they had saddled their camels and gone out to the Jabal to dig for *sabakh,* a soft soil they used to fertilize their crops. Digging around a massive boulder, they hit a red earthenware jar, almost a meter high. Muhammad 'Alī hesitated to break the jar, considering that a *jinn,* or spirit, might live inside. But realizing that it might also contain gold, he raised his mattock, smashed the jar, and discovered inside thirteen papyrus books, bound in leather. Returning to his home in al-Qasr, Muhammad 'Alī dumped the books and loose papyrus leaves on the straw piled on the ground next to the oven. Muhammad's mother, 'Umm-Ahmad, admits that she burned much of the papyrus in the oven along with the straw she used to kindle the fire.

A few weeks later, as Muhammad 'Alī tells it, he and his brothers avenged their father's death by murdering Ahmed Ismā'īl. Their mother had warned her sons to keep their mattocks sharp: when they learned that their father's enemy was nearby, the brothers seized the opportunity, "hacked off his limbs . . . ripped out his heart, and devoured it among them, as the ultimate act of blood revenge."

Fearing that the police investigating the murder would search his house and discover the books, Muhammad 'Alī asked the priest, al-Qummus Basiliyus Abd al-Masīh, to keep one or more for him. During the time that Muhammad 'Alī and his brothers were being interrogated for murder, Raghib, a local history teacher, had seen one of the books, and suspected that it had value. Having received one from al-Qummus Basiliylus, Raghib sent it to a friend in Cairo to find out its worth.

Sold on the black market through antiquities dealers in Cairo, the manuscripts soon attracted the attention of officials of the Egyptian government. Through circumstances of high drama, as we shall see, they bought one and confiscated ten and a half of the thirteen leather-bound books, called codices, and deposited them in the Coptic Museum in Cairo. But a large part of the thirteenth codex, containing five extraordinary texts, was smuggled out of Egypt and offered for sale in America.

Word of this codex soon reached Professor Gilles Quispel, distinguished historian of religion at Utrecht, in the Netherlands. Excited by the discovery, Quispel urged the Jung Foundation in Zürich to buy the codex. But discovering, when he succeeded, that some pages were missing, he flew to Egypt in the spring of 1955 to try to find them in the Coptic Museum. Arriving in Cairo, he went at once to the Coptic Museum, borrowed photographs of some of the texts, and hurried back to his hotel to decipher them. Tracing out the first line, Quispel was startled, then incredulous, to read: "These are the secret words which the living Jesus spoke, and which the twin, Judas Thomas, wrote down." Quispel knew that his colleague H. C. Puech, using notes from another French scholar, Jean Doresse, had identified the opening lines with fragments of a Greek *Gospel of Thomas* discovered in the 1890s. But the discovery of the whole text raised new questions: Did Jesus have a twin brother, as this text implies? Could the text be an authentic record of Jesus's sayings? According to its title, it contained the *Gospel According to Thomas;* yet, unlike the gospels of the New Testament, this text identified itself as a *secret* gospel. Quispel also discovered that it contained many sayings known from the New Testament; but these sayings, placed in unfamiliar contexts, suggested other dimensions of meaning. Other passages, Quispel found, differed entirely from any known Christian tradition: the "living Jesus," for example, speaks in sayings as cryptic and compelling as Zen *koans:*

> Jesus said, "If you bring forth what is within you, what you bring forth will save you. If you do not bring forth what is within you, what you do not bring forth will destroy you."

What Quispel held in his hand, the *Gospel of Thomas,* was only one of the fifty-two texts discovered at Nag Hammadi (the usual English transliteration of the town's name). Bound into the same volume with it is the *Gospel of Philip,* which attributes to Jesus acts and sayings quite different from those in the New Testament:

> . . . the companion of the [Savior is] Mary Magdalene. [But Christ loved] her more than [all] the disciples, and used to kiss her [often] on her [mouth]. The rest of [the disciples were offended] . . . They said to him, "Why do you love her more than all of us?" The Savior answered and said to them, "Why do I not love you as [I love] her?"

Other sayings in this collection criticize common Christian beliefs, such as the virgin birth or the bodily resurrection, as naïve misunderstandings. Bound together with these gospels is the *Apocryphon* (literally, "secret book") of *John,* which opens with an offer to reveal "the mysteries [and the] things hidden in silence" which Jesus taught to his disciple John.

Muhammad 'Alī later admitted that some of the texts were lost—burned up or thrown away. But what remains is astonishing: some fifty-two texts from the early centuries of the Christian era—including a collection of early Christian gospels, previously unknown. Besides the *Gospel of Thomas* and the *Gospel of Philip,* the find included the *Gospel of Truth* and the *Gospel to the Egyptians,* which identifies itself as "the [sacred book] of the Great Invisible [Spirit]." Another group of texts consists of writings attributed to Jesus's followers, such as the *Secret Book of James,* the *Apocalypse of Paul,* the *Letter of Peter to Philip,* and the *Apocalypse of Peter.*

What Muhammad 'Alī discovered at Nag Hammadi, it soon became clear, were Coptic translations, made about 1,500 years ago, of still more ancient manuscripts. The originals themselves had been written in Greek, the language of the New Testament: as Doresse, Puech, and Quispel had recognized, part of one of them had been discovered by archeologists about fifty years earlier, when they found a few fragments of the original Greek version of the *Gospel of Thomas.*

About the dating of the manuscripts themselves there is little debate. Examination of the datable papyrus used to thicken the leather bindings, and of the Coptic script, places them c. AD 350–400. But scholars sharply disagree about the dating of the original texts. Some of them can hardly be later than c. AD 120–150, since Irenaeus, the orthodox Bishop of Lyons, writing c. 180, declares that heretics "boast that they possess more gospels than there really are," and complains that in his time such writings already have won wide circulation—from Gaul through Rome, Greece, and Asia Minor.

Quispel and his collaborators, who first published the *Gospel* of *Thomas,* suggested the date of c. AD 140 for the original. Some reasoned that since these gospels were heretical, they must have been written later than the gospels of the New Testament, which are dated c.

60–110. But recently Professor Helmut Koester of Harvard University has suggested that the collection of sayings in the *Gospel of Thomas,* although compiled c. 140, may include some traditions even *older* than the gospels of the New Testament, "possibly as early as the second half of the first century" (50–100)—as early as, or earlier, than Mark, Matthew, Luke, and John.

Scholars investigating the Nag Hammadi find discovered that some of the texts tell the origin of the human race in terms very different from the usual reading of Genesis: the *Testimony of Truth,* for example, tells the story of the Garden of Eden from the viewpoint of the serpent! Here the serpent, long known to appear in gnostic literature as the principle of divine wisdom, convinces Adam and Eve to partake of knowledge while "the Lord" threatens them with death, trying jealously to prevent them from attaining knowledge, and expelling them from Paradise when they achieve it. Another text, mysteriously entitled the *Thunder, Perfect Mind,* offers an extraordinary poem spoken in the voice of a feminine divine power:

> For I am the first and the last.
> I am the honored one and the scorned one.
> I am the whore and the holy one.
> I am the wife and the virgin . . .
> I am the barren one,
> and many are her sons . . .
> I am the silence that is incomprehensible . . .
> I am the utterance of my name.

These diverse texts range, then, from secret gospels, poems, and quasi-philosophic descriptions of the origin of the universe, to myths, magic, and instructions for mystical practice.

Why were these texts buried—and why have they remained virtually unknown for nearly 2,000 years? Their suppression as banned documents, and their burial on the cliff at Nag Hammadi, it turns out, were both part of a struggle critical for the formation of early Christianity. The Nag Hammadi texts, and others like them, which circulated at the beginning of the Christian era, were denounced as heresy by orthodox Christians in the middle of the second century. We have long known that many early followers of Christ were condemned by other Christians as heretics, but nearly all we knew about them came from what their opponents wrote attacking them. Bishop Irenaeus, who supervised the church in Lyons, c. 180, wrote five volumes, entitled *The Destruction and Overthrow of Falsely So-called Knowledge,* which begin with his promise to

> set forth the views of those who are now teaching heresy . . . to show how absurd and inconsistent with the truth are their statements . . . I do this so that . . . you may urge all those with whom you are connected to avoid such an abyss of madness and of blasphemy against Christ.

He denounces as especially "full of blasphemy" a famous gospel called the *Gospel of Truth.* Is Irenaeus referring to the same *Gospel of Truth* discovered at Nag Hammadi? Quispel and his collaborators, who first published the *Gospel of Truth,* argued that he is; one of their critics maintains that the opening line (which begins "The gospel of truth") is not a title. But Irenaeus does use the same source as at least one of the texts discovered at Nag Hammadi—the *Apocrypbon* (Secret Book) *of John*—as ammunition for his own attack on such "heresy." Fifty years later Hippolytus, a teacher in Rome, wrote another massive *Refutation of All Heresies* to "expose and refute the wicked blasphemy of the heretics."

This campaign against heresy involved an involuntary admission of its persuasive power; yet the bishops prevailed. By the time of the Emperor Constantine's conversion, when Christianity became an officially approved religion in the fourth century, Christian bishops, previously victimized by the police, now commanded them. Possession of books denounced as heretical was made a criminal offense. Copies of such books were burned and destroyed. But in Upper Egypt, someone, possibly a monk from a nearby monastery of St. Pachomius, took the banned books and hid them from destruction—in the jar where they remained buried for almost 1,600 years.

But those who wrote and circulated these texts did not regard *themselves* as "heretics." Most of the writings use Christian terminology, unmistakably related to a Jewish heritage. Many claim to offer traditions about Jesus that are secret, hidden from "the many" who constitute what, in the second century, came to be called the "catholic church." These Christians are now called gnostics, from the Greek word *gnosis,* usually translated as "knowledge." For as those who claim to know nothing about ultimate reality are called agnostic (literally, "not knowing"), the person who does claim to know such things is called gnostic ("knowing"). But *gnosis* is not primarily rational knowledge. The Greek language distinguishes between scientific or reflective knowledge ("He knows mathematics") and knowing through observation or experience ("He knows me"), which is *gnosis.* As the gnostics use the term, we could translate it as "insight," for *gnosis* involves an intuitive process of knowing oneself. And to know oneself, they claimed, is to know human nature and human destiny. According to the gnostic teacher Theodotus, writing in Asia Minor (c. 140–160), the gnostic is one who has come to understand

> who we were, and what we have become; where we were . . . whither we are hastening; from what we are being released; what birth is, and what is rebirth.

Yet to know oneself, at the deepest level, is simultaneously to know God; this is the secret of *gnosis.* Another gnostic teacher, Monoimus, says:

> Abandon the search for God and the creation and other matters of a similar sort. Look for him by taking yourself as the starting point. Learn who it is within you who makes everything his own and says, "My God, my mind, my thought, my soul, my body." Learn the sources of sorrow, joy, love, hate . . . If you carefully investigate these matters you will find him *in yourself.*

What Muhammad 'Alī discovered at Nag Hammadi is, apparently, a library of writings, almost all of them gnostic. Although they claim to offer secret teaching, many of these texts refer to the Scriptures of the Old Testament, and others to the letters of Paul and the New Testament gospels. Many of them include the same *dramatis personae* as the New Testament—Jesus and his disciples. Yet the differences are striking.

Orthodox Jews and Christians insist that a chasm separates humanity from its creator: God is wholly other. But some of the gnostics who wrote these gospels contradict this: self-knowledge is knowledge of God; the self and the divine are identical.

Second, the "living Jesus" of these texts speaks of illusion and enlightenment, not of sin and repentance, like the Jesus of the New Testament. Instead of coming to save us from sin, he comes as a guide who opens access to spiritual understanding. But when the disciple attains enlightenment, Jesus no longer serves as his spiritual master: the two have become equal—even identical.

Third, orthodox Christians believe that Jesus is Lord and Son of God in a unique way: he remains forever distinct from the rest of humanity whom he came to save. Yet the gnostic *Gospel of Thomas* relates that as soon as Thomas recognizes him, Jesus says to Thomas that they have both received their being from the same source:

> Jesus said, "I am not your master. Because you have drunk, you have become drunk from the bubbling stream which I have measured out. . . . He who will drink from my mouth will become as I am: I myself shall become he, and the things that are hidden will be revealed to him."

Does not such teaching—the identity of the divine and human, the concern with illusion and enlightenment, the founder who is presented not as Lord, but as spiritual guide—sound more Eastern than Western? Some scholars have suggested that if the names were changed, the "living Buddha" appropriately could say what the *Gospel of Thomas* attributes to the living Jesus. Could Hindu or Buddhist tradition have influenced gnosticism?

The British scholar of Buddhism, Edward Conze, suggests that it had. He points out that "Buddhists were in contact with the Thomas Christians (that is, Christians who knew and used such writings as the *Gospel of Thomas*) in South India." Trade routes between the Greco-Roman world and the Far East were opening up at the time when gnosticism flourished (AD 80–200); for generations, Buddhist missionaries had been proselytizing in Alexandria. We note, too, that Hippolytus, who was a Greek-speaking Christian in Rome (c. 225), knows of the Indian Brahmins—and includes their tradition among the sources of heresy. . . .

Could the title of the *Gospel of Thomas*—named for the disciple who, tradition tells us, went to India—suggest the influence of Indian tradition? These hints indicate the possibility, yet our evidence is not conclusive. Since parallel traditions may emerge in different places at different times, such ideas could have developed independently. What we call Eastern and Western religions, and tend to regard as separate streams, were not clearly differentiated 2,000 years ago. Research on the Nag Hammadi texts is only beginning: we look forward to the work of scholars who can study these traditions comparatively to discover whether they can, in fact, be traced to Indian sources.

Even so, ideas that we associate with Eastern religions emerged in the first century through the gnostic movement in the West, but they were suppressed and condemned by polemicists like Irenaeus. Yet those who called gnosticism heresy were adopting—consciously or not—the viewpoint of that group of Christians who called themselves orthodox Christians. A heretic may be anyone whose outlook someone else dislikes or denounces. According to tradition, a heretic is one who deviates from the true faith. But what defines that "true faith"? Who calls it that, and for what reasons?

We find this problem familiar in our own experience. The term "Christianity," especially since the Reformation, has covered an astonishing range of groups. Those claiming to represent "true Christianity" in the twentieth century can range from a Catholic cardinal in the Vatican to an African Methodist Episcopal preacher initiating revival in Detroit, a Mormon missionary in Thailand, or the member of a village church on the coast of Greece. Yet Catholics, Protestants, and Orthodox agree that such diversity is a recent—and deplorable—development. According to Christian legend, the early church was different. Christians of every persuasion look back to the primitive church to find a simpler, purer form of Christian faith. In the apostles' time, all members of the Christian community shared their money and property; all believed the same teaching, and worshiped together; all revered the authority of the apostles. It was only after that golden age that conflict, then heresy emerged: so says the author of the Acts of the Apostles, who identifies himself as the first historian of Christianity.

But the discoveries at Nag Hammadi have upset this picture. If we admit that some of these fifty-two texts represent early forms of Christian teaching, we may have to recognize that early Christianity is far more diverse than nearly anyone expected before the Nag Hammadi discoveries.

Contemporary Christianity, diverse and complex as we find it, actually may show more unanimity than the Christian churches of the first and second centuries. For nearly all Christians since that time, Catholics, Protestants, or Orthodox, shared three basic premises. First, they accept the canon of the New Testament; second, they confess the apostolic creed; and third, they affirm specific forms of church institution. But every one of these—the canon of Scripture, the creed, and the institutional structure—emerged in its present form only toward the end of the second century. Before that time, as Irenaeus and others attest, numerous gospels circulated among various Christian groups, ranging from those of the New Testament, Matthew, Mark, Luke, and John, to such writings as the *Gospel of Thomas*, the *Gospel of Philip*, and the *Gospel of Truth*, as well as many other secret teachings, myths, and poems attributed to Jesus or his disciples. Some of these, apparently, were discovered at Nag Hammadi; many others are lost to us. Those who identified themselves as Christians entertained many—and radically differing—religious beliefs and practices. And the communities scattered throughout the known world organized themselves in ways that differed widely from one group to another.

Yet by AD 200, the situation had changed. Christianity had become an institution headed by a three-rank hierarchy of bishops, priests, and deacons, who understood themselves to be the guardians of the only "true faith." The majority of churches, among which the church of Rome took a leading role, rejected all other viewpoints as heresy. Deploring the diversity of the earlier movement, Bishop Irenaeus and his followers insisted that there could be only one church, and outside of that church, he declared, "there is no salvation." Members of this church alone are orthodox (literally, "straight-thinking") Christians. And, he claimed, this church must be *catholic*—that is, universal. Whoever challenged that consensus, arguing instead for other forms of Christian teaching, was declared to be a heretic, and expelled. When the orthodox gained military support, sometime after the Emperor Constantine became Christian in the fourth century, the penalty for heresy escalated.

The efforts of the majority to destroy every trace of heretical "blasphemy" proved so successful that, until the discoveries at Nag Hammadi, nearly all our information concerning alternative forms of early Christianity came from the massive Orthodox attacks upon them. Although gnosticism is perhaps the earliest—and most threatening—of the heresies, scholars had known only a handful of original gnostic texts, none published before the nineteenth century. The first emerged in 1769, when a Scottish tourist named James Bruce bought a Coptic manuscript near Thebes (modern Luxor) in Upper Egypt. Published only in 1892, it claims to record conversations of Jesus with his disciples—a group that here includes both men and women. In 1773 a collector found in a London bookshop an ancient text, also in Coptic, that contained a dialogue on "mysteries" between Jesus and his disciples. In 1896 a German Egyptologist, alerted by the previous publications, bought in Cairo a manuscript that, to his amazement, contained the *Gospel of Mary* (Magdalene) and three other texts. Three copies of one of them, the *Apocryphon* (Secret Book) *of John,* were also included among the gnostic library discovered at Nag Hammadi fifty years later. . . .

Yet even the fifty-two writings discovered at Nag Hammadi offer only a glimpse of the complexity of the early Christian movement. We now begin to see that what we call Christianity—and what we identify as Christian tradition—actually represents only a small selection of specific sources, chosen from among dozens of others. Who made that selection, and for what reasons? Why were these other writings excluded and banned as "heresy"? What made them so dangerous? Now, for the first time, we have the opportunity to find out about the earliest Christian heresy; for the first time, the heretics can speak for themselves.

Gnostic Christians undoubtedly expressed ideas that the orthodox abhored. For example, some of these gnostic texts question whether all suffering, labor, and death derive from human sin, which, in the orthodox version, marred an originally perfect creation. Others speak of the feminine element in the divine, celebrating God as Father *and* Mother. Still others suggest that Christ's resurrection is to be understood symbolically, not literally. A few radical texts even denounce catholic Christians themselves as heretics, who, although they "do not understand mystery . . . boast that the mystery of truth belongs to them alone." Such gnostic ideas fascinated the psychoanalyst C. G. Jung: he thought they expressed "the other side of the mind"—the spontaneous, unconscious thoughts that any orthodoxy requires its adherents to repress.

Yet orthodox Christianity, as the apostolic creed defines it, contains some ideas that many of us today might find even stranger. The creed requires, for example, that Christians confess that God is perfectly good, and still, he created a world that includes pain, injustice, and death; that Jesus of Nazareth was born of a virgin mother; and that, after being executed by order of the Roman procurator, Pontius Pilate, he arose from his grave "on the third day."

Why did the consensus of Christian churches not only accept these astonishing views but establish them as the only true form of Christian doctrine? Traditionally, historians have told us that the orthodox objected to gnostic views for religious and philosophic reasons. Certainly they did; yet investigation of the newly discovered gnostic sources suggests another dimension of the controversy. It suggests that these religious debates—questions of the nature of God, or of Christ—simultaneously bear social and political implications that are crucial to the development of Christianity as an institutional religion. In simplest terms, ideas which bear implications contrary to that development come to be labeled as "heresy"; ideas which implicitly support it become "orthodox."

By investigating the texts from Nag Hammadi, together with sources known for well over a thousand years from orthodox tradition, we can see how politics and religion coincide in the development of Christianity. We can see, for example, the *political* implications of such orthodox doctrines as the bodily resurrection—and how gnostic views of resurrection bear opposite implications. In the process, we can gain a startlingly new perspective on the origins of Christianity.

What the Nag Hammadi Texts Tell Us about "Liberated" Christianity

An Interview with James M. Robinson

James Robinson is Professor of Religion Emeritus, Claremont Graduate University, and general editor, *The Nag Hammadi Library*. He is one of the world's leading authorities on early Christianity and supervised the team of scholars and translators who brought these "Lost Gospels" to life.

As one of the leading scholars of what we know as the lost gospels, what is your reaction to seeing these historic ideas suddenly being propelled onto the bestseller list with the popularity of The Da Vinci Code?

The book has had a sensationalist kind of success, which worries scholars such as myself who are trying to stick to the facts. I think there is a certain built-in problem of this book being a novel, and therefore saying it's fiction but, at the same time, using enough facts, well-known names and things like the Nag Hammadi discovery to give it a semblance of factual accuracy. It is hard for the lay public to distinguish where one begins and the other leaves off. So, strictly from that point of view, it's very misleading.

Moreover, it is clear to me that Dan Brown doesn't know much about the scholarly side of things in my field and he sort of fudges the evidence to make it more sensational than it is. As an example, he refers to the Nag Hammadi find as "scrolls," but they are not. They are codexes—books with individual pages. Indeed, it is actually the oldest example we have of leather-bound books. Elsewhere, Dan Brown refers to the *Gospel Q*, writing, "Allegedly it is a book of Jesus's teachings, possibly written with His own hand." What is interesting is that while it is mentioned, it is not discussed—perhaps because it would not help his argument since we know Jesus didn't write it. These are just some of the ideas thrown into the novel that are more sensational than factual.

So how would you characterize the Nag Hammadi texts?

The canonical gospels, Matthew, Mark, Luke, and John, are a sort of theological biography of Jesus. By contrast, the Nag Hammadi Gospels are not gospels in the traditional use of that word to mean narrative history, but what we now call a sayings gospel. The *Gospel of Philip*, for example, is a scattering of materials that is not an original document, but some sort of collection of excerpts from various sources. The *Gospel of Truth* is a quasi-philosophical theological treatise, but it doesn't tell the story of Jesus in any sense of the word. The only one that can claim in some sense to be what we might call a gospel is the fourth Nag Hammadi text (the *Gospel of Thomas*), which uses the word *gospel* as a secondary title appended at the end. The opening of the text, however, calls it "secret sayings." It's a collection of sayings, like the sayings behind Matthew and

Luke, which is called theoretically *Q*, and which is mentioned once in *The Da Vinci Code.*

Do we know anything about the people who might have written these texts?

They were most likely written by different people at different times. If they were written in the second and third centuries, the authors would likely have been Gnostics, part of a Gnostic movement that was almost competing with emerging orthodox Christianity for who had the right form of Christianity. The orthodox movement had books called gospels that are known as Mathew, Mark, Luke, and John. The Gnostic side attached the word *gospel* to some of their tracts, which really weren't gospels, like those in the New Testament, since the canonical gospels are narratives that speak to the theological biography of Jesus. The Nag Hammadi Gospels are more like a collection of scattered excerpts.

Would you flesh out this idea of competing Christianities?

The writers of these codices were attempting to influence what we might call left-wing Christianity—somewhat similar to the New Age phenomenon in our time. They thought that the dominant church of the day (in *The Da Vinci Code* called the Roman Catholic Church) was too earth bound, too worldly, too materialistic, too physical and had missed the spiritual, allegorical, higher, heavenly secret meaning of all of this. And that's what they were supporting.

Talking about New Age, does the word companion in the Gospel of Philip imply for you, as it does for some students of these documents, that Jesus and Mary were married? And even that they kissed?

No, it doesn't automatically mean married or unmarried. *Companion* is not necessarily a sex-related term as it might be construed in our day and age. It seems to me it might have been simply a way to pump up the story, to make it more intriguing. If one reads the entire *Gospel of Philip* it becomes clear that the writer disdains physical sex as beastly, literally comparing it to animals. In the early church, a kiss was known as a metaphor for giving birth. And too much has been made out of this kiss. It was also called the Kiss of Peace, somewhat analogous to a modern church service where they ask you to shake hands with everybody and say, "May the peace of Christ be with you."

Regarding designating Mary Magdalene as Jesus's companion, Brown says Aramaic scholars know this means wife. But the *Gospel of Philip* is in Coptic, translated from Greek, so there is no word in the text for Aramaic scholars to consider.

I think the only relevant text for historical information about Mary Magdalene is the New Testament, and it does not go beyond saying that she was one of the circle of women who accompanied the wandering Jesus and his male followers. I think the seven demons that Jesus cast out of her may have referred to some sort of nervous problem or mental illness, like epilepsy. She was challenged, he helped her, and she became a disciple, loyal to the bitter end. I also think she was alone after the execution because the other disciples were cowards. They were likely to have been arrested. The Romans felt women were not important enough to arrest, so they let Mary grieve, figuring she would soon enough melt into the crowds. No doubt the New Testament gives an accurate portrayal of all of these Marys having been there at the time of the crucifixion and on Easter Sunday, to the extent that one gives historical credence to any of the empty-tomb stories.

While you seem to believe her role to be more circumscribed than some of the radicals would have it, would you nevertheless agree that whoever wrote the Gnostic Gospels was more sympathetic to women and their role in spiritual life than was the case with the orthodox tradition?

Yes, certainly. I think the Gnostics were more liberated—if I can use a more modern term—on many issues. Their view of women in the church, for example, was based more on the perceived quality of their religious experience than on the relationship between bishop and supplicant or other forms of authority. They believed women to have religious experiences, spiritual insights, and even visions. The idea that the men were keeping the women in their place, I think, is a historically accurate description of those early centuries, and the fact that there were some women who were trying to get everybody (including the men) to accept them as equal partners is a historical fact of the second and third centuries. The *Gospel of Mary* is a good documentation for that.

That said, people should not override that which is known with that which can only be speculated about. Even with these texts in hand, one must not interpret the specific role of Mary beyond what is known about her as related in the New Testament—and the New Testament does not say anything about Jesus having more time with Mary than the other disciples. This starts to get into the realm of what could be called wishful thinking, about which we historians have to be cautious. It is not the scholarly method to use wishful thinking to weigh the evidence one way or the other—as saint or sinner, married or not. That's not the method that we historians can use.

The Gospel of Thomas

Introduced by Helmut Koester

The *Gospel of Thomas* is a collection of traditional sayings of Jesus. These sayings or small groups of sayings are introduced in most instances by "Jesus said [to them]," sometimes by a question or a statement of the disciples. Only in one instance is a saying expanded into a longer discourse between Jesus and the disciples. . . .

The authorship of this Gospel is attributed to Didymos Judas Thomas, that is, Judas "the twin." In the Syrian church, (Judas) Thomas was known as the brother of Jesus who founded the churches of the East, particularly of Edessa (in a somewhat later tradition, he even travels to India). Other Christian writings of the Eastern churches have been attributed to the same apostle.

A large number of the sayings of the *Gospel of Thomas* have parallels in the Gospels of the New Testament, in the Synoptic Gospels (Matthew, Mark, and Luke), as well as the *Gospel of John* (parallels with the latter are especially striking).

The theme of recognizing oneself is further elaborated in sayings which speak of the knowledge of one's divine origin which even Adam did not share, although "he came into being from a great power. . . ." The disciples must "pass by" the present corruptible existence. The existence of the ideal Gnostic disciple is characterized by the term *solitary one,* which describes the one who has left behind everything that binds human beings to the world. Even women can obtain this goal, if they achieve the "maleness" of the solitary existence.

The Gospel of Thomas

TRANSLATED BY THOMAS O. LAMBDIN

These are the secret sayings which the living Jesus spoke and which Didymos Judas Thomas wrote down.

(1) And he said, "Whoever finds the interpretation of these sayings will not experience death."

(2) Jesus said, "Let him who seeks continue seeking until he finds. When he finds, he will become troubled. When he becomes troubled, he will be astonished, and he will rule over the all."

(3) Jesus said, "If those who lead you say to you, 'See, the kingdom is in the sky,' then the birds of the sky will precede you. If they say to you, 'It is in the sea,' then the fish will precede you. Rather, the kingdom is inside of

you, and it is outside of you. When you come to know yourselves, then you will become known, and you will realize that it is you who are the sons of the living father. But if you will not know yourselves, you dwell in poverty and it is you who are that poverty. . . ."

(5) Jesus said, "Recognize what is in your sight, and that which is hidden from you will become plain to you. For there is nothing hidden which will not become manifest. . . ."

(16) Jesus said, "Men think, perhaps, that it is peace which I have come to cast upon the world. They do not know that it is dissension which I have come to cast upon the earth: fire, sword, and war. For there will be five in a house: three will be against two, and two against three, the father against the son, and the son against the father. And they will stand solitary. . . ."

(37) His disciples said, "When will you become revealed to us and when shall we see you?"

Jesus said, "When you disrobe without being ashamed and take up your garments and place them under your feet like little children and tread on them, then [will you see] the son of the living one, and you will not be afraid. . . ."

(70) Jesus said, "That which you have will save you if you bring it forth from yourselves. That which you do not have within you [will] kill you if you do not have it within you. . . ."

(114) Simon Peter said to them, "Let Mary leave us, for women are not worthy of life." Jesus said, "I myself shall lead her in order to make her male, so that she too may become a living spirit resembling you males. For every woman who will make herself male will enter the kingdom of heaven."

The Gospel of Philip

INTRODUCED AND TRANSLATED BY
WESLEY W. ISENBERG

The *Gospel of Philip* is a compilation of statements pertaining primarily to the meaning and value of sacraments within the context of a Valentinian conception of the human predicament and life after death [Valentinians rejected the way most of their fellow Christians interpreted the Bible as being overly literal —Ed.].

Like the Gospels of the New Testament canon these statements employ a variety of literary types: aphorism, analogy, parable, paraenesis, polemic, narrative dialogue, dominical sayings, biblical exegesis, and dogmatic propositions. However, the *Gospel of Philip* is not a Gospel like one of the New Testament Gospels.

To be sure, it does provide the occasional word or deed of Jesus. . . . [But] these few sayings and stories about Jesus . . . are not set in any kind of narrative framework like one of the New Testament Gospels. In fact, the *Gospel of Philip* is not organized in a way that can be conveniently outlined. Although some continuity is achieved through an association of ideas, a series of contrasts, or by catchwords, the line of thought is rambling and disjointed. Complete changes of subject are common.

This is the Gospel famed for its passage "He kissed her frequently on her. . . ." which is highlighted in bold type.

The Gospel of Philip

. . . Christ came to ransom some, to save others, to redeem others. He ransomed those who were strangers and made them his own. And he set his own apart, those whom he gave as a pledge according to his plan. It was not only when he appeared that he voluntarily laid down his life, but he voluntarily laid down his life from the very day the world came into being. Then he came first in order to take it, since it had been given as a pledge. It fell into the hands of robbers and was taken captive, but he saved it. He redeemed the good people in the world as well as the evil.

Light and Darkness, life and death, right and left, are brothers of one another. They are inseparable. Because of this neither are the good good, nor evil evil, nor is life life, nor death death. For this reason each one will dissolve into its earliest origin. But those who are exalted above the world are indissoluble, eternal. . . .

Some said, "Mary conceived by the Holy Spirit." They are in error. They do not know what they are saying. When did a woman ever conceive by a woman? Mary is the virgin whom no power defiled. She is a great anathema to the Hebrews, who are the apostles and [the] apostolic men. This virgin whom no power defiled [. . .] the powers defile themselves. And the lord [would] not have said "My [father who is in] heaven" (Mt 16:17), unless [he] had had another father, but he would have said simply "[My father]." . . .

Faith receives, love gives. [No one will be able to receive] without faith. No one will be able to give without love. Because of this, in order that we may indeed receive, we believe, and in order that we may love, we give,

The *Gospel of Philip*. Fragments like this one are what remain of the alternative Gospels found in the Egyptian desert at Nag Hammadi in 1945. The fragmentary nature of the *Gospel of Philip* is particularly tantalizing. The passage refers to the apparently well-known fact (in Gnostic circles at the time) that Jesus kissed Mary Magdalene frequently on the m. . . . The first letter of the Coptic word for mouth follows, then the hole in the fragment renders the rest of the word indiscernible.
INSTITUTE FOR ANTIQUITY AND CHRISTIANITY, CLAREMENT, CA.

since if one gives without love, he has no profit from what he has given. He who has received something other than the lord is still a Hebrew. . . .

As for the Wisdom who is called "the barren," she is the mother [of the] angels. And the companion of the [. . .] Mary Magdalene. **[. . . loved] her more than [all] the disciples, [and used to] kiss her [often] on her [. . .].** The rest of [the disciples . . .]. They said to him, "Why do you love her more than all of us?" The Savior answered and said to them, "Why do I not love you like her? When a blind man and one who sees are both together in darkness, they are no different from one another. When the light comes, then he who sees will see the light, and he who is blind will remain in darkness."

Great is the mystery of marriage! For [without] it the world would [not exist]. Now the existence of [the world . . .], and the existence of [. . . marriage]. Think of the [. . . relationship], for it possesses [. . .] power. Its image consists of a [defilement].

The forms of evil spirit include male ones and female ones. The males are they that unite with the souls which inhabit a female form, but the females are they which are mingled with those in a male form, though one who was disobedient. And none shall be able to escape them, since they detain him if he does not receive a male power or a female power, the bridegroom and the bride. . . .

A bridal chamber is not for the animals, nor is it for the slaves, nor for defiled women; but it is for free men and virgins.

The world came about through a mistake. For he who created it wanted to create it imperishable and immortal. He fell short of attaining his desire. For the world never was imperishable, nor, for that matter, was he who made the world. For things are not imperishable, but sons are. Nothing will be able to receive imperishability if it does not first become a son. But he who has not the ability to receive, how much more will he be unable to give? . . .

The Gospel of Mary

Introduced by Karen L. King

The extant text of the *Gospel of Mary* can easily be divided into two parts. The first section (7:1–9:24) describes the dialogue between the (risen) Savior and the disciples. He answers their questions concerning matter and sin. . . . The Savior argues, in effect, that sin is not a moral category, but a cosmological one; it is due to the improper mixing of the material and the spiritual. In the end all things will be resolved into their proper root. After finishing his discourse, the Savior gives them a final greeting, admonishes them to beware of any who may try to lead them astray, and commissions them to go and preach the Gospel of the kingdom. After he departs, however, the disciples are grieved and in considerable doubt and consternation. Mary Magdalene comforts them and turns their hearts toward the Good and a consideration of the Savior's words.

The second section of the text . . . contains a description by Mary of special revelation given to her by the Savior. At Peter's request, she tells the disciples about things that were hidden from them. The basis for her knowledge is a vision of the Lord and a private dialogue with him. Unfortunately four pages of the text are missing here so that only the beginning and end of Mary's revelation are extant.

The revelation is in the form of a dialogue. The first question Mary asks the Savior is how one sees a vision. The Savior replies that the soul sees through the mind which is between the soul and the spirit. At this point the text breaks off. When the text resumes . . . Mary is in the midst of describing the Savior's revelation concerning the rise of the soul past the four powers. The four powers are most probably to be identified as essential expressions of the four material elements. The enlightened soul, now free of their bonds, rises past the four powers, overpowering them with her *gnosis,* and attains eternal, silent rest.

After Mary finishes recounting her vision to the disciples, Andrew and then Peter challenge her on two grounds. First of all, Andrew says, these teachings are strange. Secondly, Peter questions, would the Savior really have told such things to a woman and kept them from the male disciples? Levi admonishes Peter for contending with the woman as against the adversaries and acknowledges that the Savior loved her more than the other disciples. He entreats them to be ashamed, to put on the perfect man, and to go forth and preach as the Savior had instructed them to do. They immediately go forth to preach and the text ends.

The confrontation of Mary with Peter, a scenario also found in the *Gospel of Thomas, Pistis Sophia,* and the *Gospel of the Egyptians,* reflects some of the tensions in second-century Christianity. Peter and Andrew represent orthodox positions that deny the validity of esoteric revelation and reject the authority of women to teach. The *Gospel of Mary* attacks both of these positions head-on through its portrayal of Mary Magdalene. She is the Savior's beloved, possessed of knowledge and teaching superior to that of the public apostolic tradition. Her superiority is based on vision and private revelation and is demonstrated in her capacity to strengthen the wavering disciples and turn them toward the Good. . . .

The *Gospel of Mary* was originally written in Greek sometime in the second century. Unfortunately the two extant copies of the *Gospel of Mary* are extremely fragmentary.

The Gospel of Mary

TRANSLATED BY GEORGE W. MACRAE AND R. MCL. WILSON

. . . Peter said to him, "Since you have explained everything to us, tell us this also: What is the sin of the world?" The Savior said, "There is no sin, but it is you who make sin when you do the things that are like the nature of adultery, which is called 'sin.' That is why the Good came into your midst, to the (essence) of every nature, in order to restore it to its root." Then he continued and said, "That is why you [become sick] and die, for [. . .] of the one who [. . . He who] understands, let him understand. [Matter gave birth to] a passion that has no equal, which proceeded from (something) contrary to nature. Then there arise a disturbance in the whole body. That is why I said to you, 'Be of good courage,' and if you are discouraged [be] encouraged in the presence of the different forms of nature. He who has ears to hear, let him hear." . . .

When he had said this, he departed.

But they were grieved. They wept greatly, saying, "How shall we go to the gentiles and preach the gospel of the kingdom of the Son of Man? If they did not spare him, how will they spare us?" Then Mary stood up, greeted them all, and said to her brethren, "Do not weep and do not grieve nor be irresolute, for his grace will be entirely with you and will protect you. But rather let us praise his greatness, for he has prepared us and made us into men." When Mary said this, she turned their hearts to the Good, and they began to discuss the words of the [Savior].

Peter said to Mary, "Sister, we know that the Savior loved you more than the rest of women. Tell us the words of the Savior which you remember—which you know [but] we do not, nor have we heard them." Mary answered and said, "What is hidden from you I will proclaim to you." And she began to speak to them these words: "I," she said, "I saw the Lord in a vision and I said to Him, 'Lord I saw you today in a vision.' He answered and said to me, 'Blessed are you, that you did not waver at the sight of me. For where the mind is, there is the treasure.' I said to Him, 'Lord, how does he who sees the vision see it, [through] the soul [or] through the spirit?' The Savior answered and said, 'He does not see through the soul nor through the spirit, but the mind which [is] between the two—that is [what] sees the vision and it is [. . .].' "

When Mary had said this, she fell silent, since it was to this point that the Savior had spoken with her. But Andrew answered and said to the brethren, "Say what you [wish to] say about what she has said. I at least do not believe that the Savior said this. For certainly these teachings are strange ideas." Peter answered and spoke concerning these same things. He questioned them about the Savior: "Did he really speak with a woman without our knowledge [and] not openly? Are we to turn about and all listen to her? Did he prefer her to us?"

Then Mary wept and said to Peter, "My brother Peter, what do you think? Do you think that I have thought this up myself in my heart, or that I am lying about the Savior?" Levi answered and said to Peter, "Peter, you have always been hot-tempered. Now I see you contending against the woman like the adversaries. But if the Savior made her worthy, who are you indeed to reject her? Surely the Savior knows her very well. That is why he loved her more than us. Rather let us be ashamed and put on the perfect man, and acquire him for ourselves as he commanded us, and preach the gospel, not laying down any other rule or other law beyond what the Savior said." When [. . .] and they began to go forth [to] proclaim and to preach.

The Sophia of Jesus Christ

INTRODUCED AND TRANSLATED BY
DOUGLAS M. PARROTT

In form, the *Sophia of Jesus Christ* is a revelation discourse given by the risen Christ in response to the questions of his disciples. This text allows one to see the process by which a non-Christian tractate was modified and transformed into a Christian gnostic one . . . It would not be surprising if it had been composed soon after the advent of Christianity in Egypt—the latter half of the first century C.E. That possibility is supported by the tractate's relatively nonpolemical tone.

The *Sophia of Jesus Christ* was directed to an audience for whom Christianity was an added element in their religious environment (i.e., not its primary one). . . . In it, the Savior (Christ) came from the supercelestial region. Sophia is the one responsible for the fall of drops of light from the divine realm into the visible world; and, a god exists who, with his subordinate powers, directly rules this world to the detriment of those who come from the divine realm.

Sex, it is suggested, is the means by which enslavement to the powers is perpetuated. But the Savior (Christ) broke the bonds imposed by the powers, and taught others to do the same . . . In addition, it should be noted that the disciples named in the *Sophia of Jesus Christ,* Philip, Matthew, Thomas, Bartholomew, and Mary, reflect a tradition within Gnosticism of disciples who are distinctively gnostic, and who are contrasted with some regularity, and in various ways, with "orthodox" or "orthodox turned gnostic" disciples (principally, Peter and John).

The Sophia of Jesus Christ

After he rose from the dead, his twelve disciples and seven women continued to be his followers and went to Galilee onto the mountain called "Divination and Joy." When they gathered together and were perplexed about the underlying reality of the universe and the plan and the holy providence and the power of the authorities and about everything the Savior is doing with them in the secret of the holy plan, the Savior appeared—not in his previous form, but in the invisible spirit. And his likeness resembles a great angel of light. But his resemblance I must not describe. No mortal flesh could endure it, but only pure, (and) perfect flesh, like that which he taught us about on the mountain called "Of the Olives" in Galilee. And he said: "Peace be to you! My peace I give you!" And they all marveled and were afraid.

The Savior laughed and said to them: "What are you thinking about? [Why] are you perplexed? What are you searching for?" Philip said: "For the underlying reality of the universe and the plan."

The Savior said to them: "I want you to know that all men born on earth from the foundation of the world until now, being dust, while they have inquired about God, who he is and what he is like, have not found him. Now the wisest among them have speculated from the ordering of the world and [its] movement. But their speculation has not reached the truth. For it is said that the ordering is directed in three ways by all the philosophers, [and] hence they do not agree. For some of them say about the world that it is directed by itself. Others, that it is providence [that directs it]. Others, that it is fate. But it is none of these. Again, of the three voices I have just mentioned, none is close to the truth, and [they are] from man. But I, who came from Infinite Light, I am here—for I know him [Light]—that I might speak to you about the precise nature of the truth. For whatever is from itself is a polluted life; it is self-made. Providence has no wisdom in it. And fate does not discern. . . .

Matthew said to him: "Lord, no one can find the truth except through you. Therefore teach us the truth."

The Savior said: "He Who Is is ineffable. No principle knew him, no authority, no subjection, nor any creature from the foundation of the world until now, except he alone, and anyone to whom he wants to make revelation through him who is from First Light. From now on, I am the Great Savior. For he is immortal and eternal. Now he is eternal, having no birth; for everyone who has birth will perish. He is unbegotten, having no beginning; for everyone who has a beginning has an end. Since no one rules over him, he has no name; for whoever has a name is the creation of another. . . . And he has a semblance of his own—not like what you have seen and received, but a strange semblance that surpasses all things and is better than the universe. It looks to every side and sees itself from itself. Since it is infinite, he is ever incomprehensible. He is imperishable and has no likeness [to anything]. He is unchanging good. He is faultless. He is eternal. He is blessed. While he is not known, he ever knows himself. He is immeasurable. He is untraceable. He is perfect, having no defect. He is imperishability blessed. He is called 'Father of the Universe.' " . . .

Matthew said to him: "Lord, Savior, how was Man revealed?"

The perfect Savior said: "I want you to know that he who appeared before the universe in infinity, Self-grown, Self-constructed Father, being full of shining light and ineffable, in the beginning, when he decided to have his likeness become a great power, immediately the principle [or beginning] of that Light appeared as Immortal Androgynous Man, that through that Immortal Man they might attain their salvation and awake from forgetfulness through the interpreter who was sent, who is with you until the end of the poverty of the robbers.

"And his consort is the Great Sophia, who from the first was destined in him for union by Self-begotten Father, from Immortal Man, 'who appeared as First and divinity and kingdom,' for the Father, who is called 'Man, Self-Father,' revealed this. And he created a great aeon, whose name is Ogdoad, for his own majesty. . . .

"All who come into the world, like a drop from the Light, are sent by him to the world of Almighty, that they might be guarded by him. And the bond of his forgetfulness bound him by the will of Sophia, that the matter might be [revealed] through it to the whole world in poverty, concerning his [Almighty's] arrogance and blindness and the ignorance that he was named. But I came from the places above by the will of the great Light, [I] who escaped from that bond; I have cut off the work of the robbers; I have awakened that drop that was sent from Sophia, that it might bear much fruit through me and be perfected and not again be defective but be [joined] through me, the Great Savior, that his glory might be revealed, so that Sophia might also be justified in regard to that defect, that her sons might not again become defective but might attain honor and glory and go up to their Father and know the words of the masculine Light. And you were sent by the Son, who was sent that you might receive Light and remove yourselves from the forgetfulness of the authorities, and that it might not again come to appearance because of you, namely, the unclean rubbing that is from the fearful fire that came from their fleshly part. Tread upon their malicious intent." . . .

These are the things [the] blessed Savior [said,] [and he disappeared] from them. Then [all the disciples] were in [great, ineffable joy] in [the spirit from] that day on. [And his disciples] began to preach [the] Gospel of God, [the] eternal, imperishable [Spirit]. Amen.

What Was Lost Is Found

A Wider View of Christianity and Its Roots

An Interview with Elaine Pagels

Why do you think The Da Vinci Code *has captured the public's imagination?*

What I find interesting about Dan Brown's book is that it raises a very important question: if they—meaning the leaders of the church—suppressed so much of early Christian history, what else don't we know about it? What else is there to be known? As a historian, I think this is a really important question because the answer would mean a great deal. So I'd rather not say anything negative about his book. I simply am not an expert on it, but I'd like to say it raises an important question.

But what do we know about early Christianity and its roots now that we didn't a generation or so ago?

The earliest accounts we have about Jesus of Nazareth were written twenty years after his death at the earliest, and those are from letters. Then we have the New Testament Gospels, which were written maybe forty to seventy years after his death. So everything we have is from later accounts. These accounts are not neutral; they're either written by people devoted to Jesus or people hostile to Jesus, such as the Roman historian Suetonious, the Roman senator and historian Cassio-

---

Elaine Pagels is Harrington Spear Paine Professor of Religion at Princeton University and author of the bestselling *Beyond Belief* as well as *The Gnostic Gospels,* which won the National Book Critics Circle Award and the National Book Award.

dorus, and some polemical Jewish sources from late in the first century. So it's interesting that we have nothing except later accounts, either very positive or very negative.

Thanks to the Nag Hammadi discoveries in 1945, we now see that the early Christian movement was much wider and much more varied, and that the views of Jesus were much more wide ranging than we ever thought. This applies as well to the classical view of his disciples and, of particular interest at the moment, the later developing view that Mary Magdalene was a prostitute. But in the sources we have now, which include the *Gospels of Mary Magdalene, Thomas,* and *Philip,* we have early evidence that Mary was regarded not only as one of the women associated with the circle around Jesus, but was considered an important follower and disciple by many. We also know there were others.

Is there not a contradiction here? Would not the social and religious belief systems of the Judaic culture at the time militate against women playing an independent role as proselytizers?

In Jewish groups, it would have been very untypical to have women participating and learning and traveling with men. I'm picturing the circle around Jesus as a circle around an itinerant charismatic rabbi, and this group apparently did include women as well as men. That would have been unusual. Most rabbinic sources—which are a little later than this—thought it was not at all appropriate to teach women about the divine scriptures. And even among Greco-Roman circles, only the Epicurean philosophers and a couple of others had women students, but there were few of them. Much more often, it would be only men. Perhaps Mary's reputation of being a prostitute came about because the idea of a woman traveling, or simply spending time in the company of a group of men, would have been very unusual and obviously suspect.

Is it possible that she was closer to Jesus than the other disciples and privy to secret knowledge, as the Gospel of Mary suggests?

We don't know much detail, but yes, she must have had some important relationship to Jesus. There are some hints of that in the *Gospel of Mary,* where it is mentioned that he told her things that he didn't tell the others and that he had a special love for her. As to whether Jesus told her things he didn't tell others, we can't be sure, but there are hints of that. Whether it was a sexual relationship, I don't see the evidence in the sources I know. Dan Brown took a line from the *Gospel of Philip* that suggests Jesus loved Mary more than all the other disciples, and he read it as a sexual relationship. However, if you read the rest of the *Gospel of Philip,* many scholars think the sexual language there suggests a mystical union, not literal. It depicts Mary as a symbol of divine wisdom in some parts of the text and in other sections as the church, which is the bride of Christ. So she's understood to be Jesus's spiritual counterpart.

Might there be more documents waiting to be found that would shed further light on the relationship between Mary and Jesus, and between the orthodox tradition and this lost tradition? And, if so, why were some gospels preserved and not others?

There were probably countless people preserving copies of these texts. But because papyrus rots, except in the very driest parts of the world, like the part of Egypt where the Nag Hammadi texts were found, most of the copies would not have survived. As for why some Gospels were handed down through history and others hidden away, I wrote *The Gnostic Gospels* to try to figure that out.

I think as the orthodox tradition progressed and became more popular, some of its leaders felt they had to sort out what really were the right teachings of Jesus and what weren't. They were trying to consolidate an enormous number of people who were clustered in what is today Turkey, Africa, Spain, France, England, Italy, Egypt—what the Romans thought of as the known world. And some leaders, some bishops for example, were trying to say, well, let's choose the fundamental teachings on which we all agree. And then, let's look at all this other material, the mystical material, and just say this is irrelevant. We don't need it—it's misleading, it leads people to set up their own groups, which we don't want because we're bishops, after all. There's a more serious reason, as well. The Christian movement was also facing persecution and destruction by the Roman state, so it was trying to consolidate and unify. But we really don't have details about that process, so we have to try and reconstruct it. That's a hard thing to do, but that's what I try to do with my books.

What does that process of reconstruction lead you to believe about the differences between the way people worshipped under these discarded texts and those who followed the canonical texts of the New Testament?

I believe that the Nag Hammadi Gospels were written by people who felt that they had visions, revelations, and deeper understanding. A baptized Christian, in the middle of Egypt in the second century, might have needed a spiritual master who went beyond the orthodox, who said, "Yes, I can take you further. I can initiate you into the deeper mysteries, and you can receive the Holy Spirit so that you might have revelations of your own."

So this smaller group, dedicated to ecstatic prayer and visions, could have lead people away from allegiance to the local bishops, which the bishops wouldn't have liked because they thought having revelations and visions was threatening to the unity of the church. This problem remains: should a Catholic come forward today, describe a vision of the Virgin Mary, and say, "The Virgin Mary told me that women should be priests," he or she is certainly going to be called a heretic.

Yet Christianity could not have spread without revelation. The New Testament Gospels, particularly Luke, are full of dreams and revelations. The movement explodes in claims about visions and revelations. But later, these become problematic because leaders of the church responded, "Wait a minute, which are the right ones and which are the wrong ones?" And then standards of orthodoxy needed to be established. The texts that were found, like the *Gospel of Philip* and the *Gospel of Mary,* were discovered in Egypt in a monastery library. And it was a bishop who ordered the monks to destroy them.

Can you summarize the Gnostic texts for us?

Although we used to call these texts Gnostic texts, that term is often associated with a negative, dualistic view of the world that isn't found in these texts. So I don't use the term Gnosticism anymore or call the texts Gnostic. I prefer to look at them individually.

The *Gospel of Thomas* presents the idea that if you bring forth what is within you, what is within you will save you, but if you do not bring forth what is within you, what is within you will destroy you. And the idea behind that is, if you can bring forth something from within yourself, something intrinsic to human beings, it allows you to have access to God.

The *Gospel of Mary* says, in effect, seek the Son of Man within yourself; in other words, look within yourself to find the divine source rather than looking to Jesus the God Man. You can find the divine source through your own being, which comes from the same source as Jesus. It's more like a Buddhist teaching. This is heretical to priests, of course. A priest wants to say that the only access to God is to be found through the church. But these gospels imply that you can go off on your own and discover the divine within yourself. You might not need the church. You might not need a priest. You might just go meditate or have your own vision.

Is it possible that some of Christianity was influenced by mystery cults as Dan Brown suggests?

Yes. Dan Brown is right that some of the mystery cults, like the cult of the mother goddess, involved the mysteries of sexuality, death, and transcending death. But I don't see any evidence of those in the texts that we found. That's quite a different strain. There may well be, in Christian rituals, an influence of mystery cults, but I don't see sexual rituals there. I think it makes a good novel, I just don't know of any evidence.

Was this issue of sexuality central for early church leaders?

Yes, it certainly was an issue for Paul, just twenty years

after Jesus's death. He thought it is better to be celibate, as he was, for the sake of evangelizing the movement. Many people think he was widowed and had been married before. Peter was married and had children. That was, of course, normal for followers of Jesus because they were brought up in Jewish customs and that was understood to be a sacred value.

I think what happened is, these followers of Jesus, even the ones who weren't Jews, adopted Jewish attitudes about sexuality: it was meant for procreation, and any sexual relationship between a man and a woman might well end up with children. A sexual relationship between people of the same sex was absolutely regarded as an abomination by many Jews. Abortion was prohibited. So was killing infants, which was commonly done as birth control in the early centuries. So, since Christians were prohibited to kill babies or attempt abortions or even contraception, if they were going to devote themselves to the Kingdom and have a life that was free of the burdens of family and children and making money, then celibacy seemed to be required.

Coming back to today, what do you believe accounts for the widespread fascination with these spiritual issues in what might easily be called the age of rationality and skepticism?

First, I know for myself and for many others there is a tremendous hunger for spiritual understanding and a spiritual path. And that's true whether people are evangelical—I don't like the word *fundamentalists*—or Southern Baptists or Roman Catholic mystics or atheists. Many people really are exploring spiritual issues because, I think, these issues are a deep part of human life and we need them. Whether one believes that the world was created in six days or holds some other philosophic understanding, I think our heart, emotions, and attitudes towards other people are at the center of this tradition.

Do you think these texts and your work allow people who have trouble with their faith to say, "Oh, there is another dimension here?"

To me, that's very important because, I think, if you try to swallow Christian faith as it is often taught, it's indigestible. There is an element in it that, if you must take it all literally, causes most people to raise questions. Was Jesus really born from a virgin? What do we mean by the resurrection of the dead? So, yes, my work and what I try to do in my books is an invitation to say, "We can think about these things." We can look at them historically. We can look at the Bible, not as something that just descended from heaven in a cloud of gold, but a collection, laboriously assembled by countless people, with some very powerful truths in it. But that doesn't mean we have to take it all as if it were literally true and just simply try to swallow it. We can think about it, we can discuss it. As Jesus says, "Let the one who seeks not stop seeking until he finds. When he finds, he'll be troubled. When he's troubled, he'll be astonished." Jesus clearly invites us to a process of exploration—not simply a set of beliefs which we either accept or reject. We can hold to the elements we love about it, and say that for others maybe it's different. And with this new evidence, I think that's a remarkable opportunity.

4 The Early Days of Christianities

From the Many, One

Consolidation, or Cover-Up?

One form of Christianity . . . emerged as victorious from the conflicts of the second and third centuries. This one form of Christianity decided what was the "correct" Christian perspective; it decided who could exercise authority over Christian belief and practice; and it determined what forms of Christianity would be marginalized, set aside, destroyed. It also decided which books to canonize into scripture and which books to set aside as "heretical," teaching false ideas. . . .

Only twenty-seven of the early Christian books were finally included in the canon, copied by scribes through the ages, eventually translated into English, and now on bookshelves in virtually every home in America. Other books came to be rejected, scorned, maligned, attacked, burned, all but forgotten—lost.

—Bart D. Ehrman

In the beginning there was not one Christianity, but many. Sacred roots and twenty centuries of primacy in the Western world have led to the generally dominant view that modern Christianity evolved in a linear and direct way from the teachings of Jesus. The snapshot Western civilization has tended to see is a natural progression, starting with Jesus and followed by the preaching of the apostles as depicted in the New Testament, on through the establishment of the church by Peter, brought under the wing of Constantine and the Council of Nicea, and from there throughout the Roman Empire, Europe, and on into the modern world. If we think about debate, conflict, and heresy in Christian thought, our history and humanities classes tend to emphasize the comparatively recent experience of the Reformation.

Dan Brown's *The Da Vinci Code* wants to acquaint the reader with the lesser known, even "hidden" side of the story, the unanswered questions about the early history of Christianity:

- Who was Jesus?
- Who was Mary Magdalene?
- Why did people accept the notions of a virgin birth or of resurrection?
- Were Jesus and his fellow Jews seeking to define a different path for Judaism, or seeking to create a new religion?
- How credible are the four accepted gospels, when we know they were written many years after the facts they describe, and their accounts are sometimes at odds with each other?
- What can one make of all the other gospel-like accounts that we now know existed but did not find their way into the New Testament?
- What should we think about the fact that very little contemporaneous material survives from the lifetime of Jesus—when nothing has yet been found in his own

hand and what we do know of the gospel accounts has clearly been filtered and edited through the screen of the Roman and Greek translators?

Early Christian history proceeds to an untidy story punctuated by loose ends, unknowns, intrigues both political and personal, ironies, and considerable doses of what in today's political vernacular might be called "spin." As it turns out, the history of Christianity is primarily one of widely and sometimes wildly differing understandings of what correct Christian belief is, and considerable zeal in the identification and persecution of those thought not to believe correctly. These divergences, diversities, and differences may even go back to the very first moments of the Jesus movement. As we see throughout this book, the differences between Peter and others, the question of Mary Magdalene's role, and the inner questions and doubts of Jesus himself are all becoming far more apparent given today's scholarship, textual analysis, and archaeology than they were at any time in the last sixteen hundred years or so.

Scholars have long known that there is roughly a forty-year gap (maybe less, but maybe much more) between the death of Jesus and the writing of the first gospel. During that period the followers of Jesus were consolidating their beliefs through oral tradition, and deciding who Jesus was and what his life and death meant. Each gospel was an evangelist's telling of the story from a somewhat different point of view, based on the teller's own circumstances and audience. Eventually, four gospels and twenty-three other texts were canonized into a bible. This did not occur, however, until the sixth century.

As Deirdre Good points out in her lectures on Mary Magdalene and *The Da Vinci Code,* "Virtually everyone in the New Testament should be thought of as Jewish unless you can produce any evidence to suggest they are not." Most experts agree that Jesus was a Jew. New Testament accounts repeatedly describe his involvements in Jewish temple life—from his precocious understanding of the temple service as a child to his attack on the money changers in the temple during his maturity. In all cases, it is the traditional Jewish temple to which he relates, and which he is trying to induce to change according to his vision.

Indeed, there was so much ferment in Judaism in those days—different cults, sects, clans, tribes, prophets, false prophets, rabbis, teachers, the Greek-influenced, the Roman-influenced—that the Jesus movement may not have appeared as anything shockingly new or different when it first emerged. The Jewish communities scattered across Egypt, Turkey, Greece, Syria, Iraq, and elsewhere all had their own traditions of modified beliefs and influences drawn from their surrounding cultures. Judaism in those days was a big tent, even if under it things were often unruly, fractious, and bitterly—even fatally—divided.

It would certainly appear that for a long time after the death of Jesus his followers were not necessarily perceived as believers in a fundamentally different religion. What became Christianity was initially Jews preaching an increasingly different form of Judaism to other Jews. Sometimes called Nazareans by Jews and Christians by gentiles (non-Jews), some of the circles of Jesus's followers required that males be circumcised and that the Jewish ritual and dietary laws be followed, yet they professed belief that Jesus was the Son of God and the sole path to salvation—beliefs inconsistent with Jewish orthodoxy. Ebionites, described recently as "Christians still climbing out of their Jewish shell," insisted that to be part of their movement one had to be Jewish first.

Yet as Bart Ehrman, the contemporary expert on lost Christian beliefs and scriptures, argues, the Ebionites believed deeply in Jesus, but they saw him as "the Jewish Messiah sent from the Jewish God to the Jewish people in fulfillment of the Jewish scripture." The Ebionites believed that Jesus was a mortal man who was so righteous that God adopted him as His son and allowed his sacrifice to redeem humanity's sins.

Saul, a Greek Jew, was strongly opposed to the Nazareans, but on the road to Damascus he had a vision in which Jesus told him to spend the remainder of his life spreading the gospel to the gentiles. Saul changed his name to Paul. His beliefs differed in significant ways from those then emerging from the Jewish tradition: Paul felt that male converts should not have to be circumcised, and that following Jewish law was not necessary, thereby setting up one of the earliest Christian conflicts. Paul concentrated his efforts on converting gentiles, while others attempted to convert from within the Jewish community. Paul traveled widely and established Christian churches throughout the eastern Mediterranean. Even more zealous than the Paulines were the Marcionites, who sought to cast off their Jewish heritage completely, even to the point of looking on the Jewish concept of God as a God that had failed.

The apostles, and later their followers, went forth to spread the "good news" (gospels). The spread of Christianity was a protracted, complicated, and decidedly messy process that must be viewed within the context of the political world in the early centuries of this era. This was the time of the Roman Empire. As the empire spread geographically, it incorporated populations whose religious beliefs were primarily pagan and naturalistic, tied to Greek, Egyptian, Persian, and other mythologies. These existed side by side, with the state taking no side.

It was within this theological stew that Christianity arose and developed. Against the dominant polytheistic religions, Christianity and Judaism were monotheistic, teaching an entirely different relationship of man to God (as opposed to man to gods), and a decidedly different path to salvation. Along the way, many diverse interpretations of the Christian belief system arose, some borrowing elements from the surrounding pagan traditions and others simply having alternate interpretations of key doctrinal beliefs.

Christianity morphed from belief taught by itinerant evangelists to small communities of believers organized in local churches—each with its own leaders, writings, and beliefs—with no overarching authority or hierarchy. Slowly at first, then with increasing rapidity, a formal hierarchy came about, and with it a need for doctrinal uniformity. Bishops met in synods to declare what was doctrinally correct. Other views were declared "heresies" and were to be eradicated. In doing so, they chose to glorify certain gospel accounts that reinforced their version of Christendom's message—even to select those accounts to be included in the Bible and in what order—at the same time as they vigorously rejected as heretical anything seen as politically or textually deviating from their own self-declared mainstream. These people, including Irenaeus, Tertullian, and Eusebius, became the editors, so to speak, of the Bible. Reacting as they did to the severe repression of Christians they had witnessed, these church leaders developed their own biases, and have to be understood in their own context. Meanwhile, Gnostics and others set off on very different paths, believing themselves to be good followers of Jesus even while holding to a very different cosmology. Despite the growing formal power of the bishops and church leaders opposed to them, they persisted in their beliefs, often at great risk to their lives.

In the novel, Dan Brown makes a point of telling the reader (through a lecture by Leigh Teabing) of the extreme extension of the church's arguments against the heresies of this early era, which would be recycled a thousand years later in the *Malleus Maleficarum,* written in 1487 as the political platform of the Inquisition.

Perhaps it was inevitable that single-scripture Christianity would merge with single-power politics. To achieve primacy, the early church fathers believed they needed to turn Christianity into a force to unite and strengthen the empire, consistent with the empire's values, politics, and social and military infrastructure. Those who led the Roman Empire in this pursuit believed that a key task was to distill a core ideology and cosmology out of all the various ideas that made up the Christian message.

In 313 Emperor Constantine declared that it was "salutary and most proper" that "complete toleration" should be given by the Roman Empire to anyone who had "given up his mind either to the cult of the Christians" or any other similar cult. With this Edict of Milan, official persecution of Christianity and Christians was supposed to end. It is often said that Constantine converted to Christianity, but most scholars understand that this was not until very late in life. Possibly on his deathbed, possibly not at all.

Many historians believe Constantine's decision can best be explained as politically astute—a move that took into account the accumulating power of Christianity, and a way to put that power at his disposal. Moreover, it was a decision born of a fascinating mix of mystical, superstitious, military, and philosophical threads, in addition to the political impetus. As the historian Paul Johnson notes, Constantine was a "sun-worshipper, one of a number of late-pagan cults which had observances in common with Christians. Thus, the followers of Isis adored a Madonna nursing her holy child," and the followers of Mithras, many of whom were senior military men, celebrated their deity in much the same way Christians would celebrate Christ. Notes Johnson, "Constantine was almost certainly a Mithraic . . . Many Christians did not make a clear distinction between this sun cult and their own. They referred to Christ driving his chariot across the sky" and held a feast on December 25, considered the sun's birthday at winter solstice. Whatever the reality, this was a major turning point in Christian history. When the state became at least nominally Christian, the presiding bishops became judicial and administrative as well as scriptural authorities. Constantine and the church both gained power. Scholar Stringfellow Barr, in his book *The Mask of Jove,* sums it up this way: "Constantine . . . instinctively knew that the Christian polis, around which he had planned to rebuild [the Roman Empire,] must achieve a unity of spirit if his plans were to succeed."

A major thorn in Constantine's side was the ongoing controversy with the followers of Arius (Arians), who disputed the notion that Jesus was of the same substance as the Father. Only the Father was God, said Arius and his followers; Christ was not a deity. Constantine wanted the matter settled, and so in 325 convened the Council of Nicea, which declared Arianism a heresy. Heresies from the early church point of view had always been struggled against and denounced (see the Pagels essay in this chapter) and would continue to be—from the Sabellian heresy which said that the Father and the Son were different aspects of one Being rather than distinct persons, to the Inquisition and the Salem witch trials. Although the various shades of opinion of Arians and Donatists and other heretical groups are foggy to us today, the historical record is quite clear that Constantine stepped in and personally presided over the Council of Nicea, even crafting some of the language that came out of the meeting as the ultimate statement on the controversies.

What did and didn't happen at the Council of Nicea is one of the key subjects of debate between Dan Brown's *The Da Vinci Code* and what many religious practitioners and scholars believe. But Brown's version is highly compelling in this key sense: this was a power struggle over the intellectual infrastructure that would rule much of European politics and thought for the following thousand years. Nicea was not about truth or veracity of religious or moral vision. Ruling some ideas in and others out was fundamentally about politics and power. From Constantine at Nicea to Pope Gregory nearly three hundred years later (and much in between) it turns out, at least in retrospect, to have been largely about developing the intellectual and political infrastructure of Europe for the next thousand years. You might say it was about codification of the code—the Roman Empire's code.

In this chapter, two eminent scholars of religion provide perspective on this struggle of interpretation. Elaine Pagels looks at how the Word of God became the Word of man through the selection of which gospels to be included in the Bible. Bart Ehrman surveys the "other

Christianities" and the religious, political, and cultural implications of the church's victory and the Gnostics' loss. In addition, Rabbi Asher Jacobson discusses the Jewish roots of Christianity and the way Judaic history and symbolism are used in *The Da Vinci Code.*

A variety of other views are presented along the way. Among them is the theological and passionate cry of "foul" put forward by Timothy Freke and Peter Gandy. In common with some other postmodern commentators, Freke and Gandy see the deeply spiritual, mythical, poetic, romantic, goddess-cult, sacred feminine roots of Christianity being stamped out by these virulent antiheresy campaigns. They see the efforts to select the gospel truths and edit the rich history of Christian origins into an industrial-strength pabulum as the destruction of the feminine side of the continuum, a deracinating break with the collective unconscious and the collective past. "Some of the things that we put in Jesus's Word were actually words that were originally in the Goddess's mouth," they say. The chapter concludes with a brief essay by Colin Hansen, who outlines the prevailing Christian view that the Bible as we know it emerged from several centuries of composition and consolidation on its way to becoming authoritative; he scoffs at any Dan Brown–like notion that a "divine Jesus" could have emerged only after a "fourth-century power play."

What follows is a perspective on the history of Christianity that starts to peel the onion skin of time away from what Leigh Teabing tells Sophie Neveu was "the greatest cover-up in human history." Of course, it wasn't simply a cover-up—there was plenty of deep, heartfelt spirituality and belief as well. But to the degree there was debate, conflict, suppression of ideas, and rewriting of the early history of Christianity, that is a story which *has* been covered up and which *The Da Vinci Code* cracks open like Pandora's cryptex.

The Battle for Scripture and the Faiths We Didn't Get a Chance to Know

An Interview with Bart D. Ehrman

It is sometimes difficult to remember, but before *The Da Vinci Code* became a publishing phenomenon, few outside of academe seemed fascinated by the early days of Christianity. But in point of fact, alternate scriptures, lost gospels, and other mysterious aspects of the period were the subjects of deep academic scholarship long before there was a Dan Brown to mine this work for its pop culture value.

Among the leaders in this pioneering work at the crossroads of religion and history has been Bart D. Ehrman, chair of the Department of Religious Studies at the University of North Carolina at Chapel Hill. Ehrman is an authority on the life of Jesus and the propagation of his teachings in the first centuries of what came to be called Christianity, the subject of his popular book *Lost Christianities: The Battle for Scripture and the Faiths We Never Knew.* Here he talks about Christianity's most important alternative threads. Over time, these alternate sects came to be seen as a threat to the spreading orthodoxy. Competing ideas were, in effect, systematically declared to be heresy and then suppressed or marginalized by the church triumphant. Ehrman cites the example of the Gnostics, who believed that the goal of religion was to teach mankind how to escape this earth—a radically different concept from that espoused in standard Christian theology. He also discusses what he sees as one of the most radical shifts in any religion—how Christianity "shifted from being an other-worldly Jewish religion, in which the end of all time is at hand and people should not live for the values of their society . . . to being a this-worldly gentile religion."

Ehrman welcomes the newfound interest in alternate traditions and calls *The Da Vinci Code* "unusually intelligent for this genre." Still, as we can see from his "Ten Errors" list on pages 198–199, Ehrman has plenty of criticism of Dan Brown (which he elaborates in his own book-length analysis, *Truth and Fiction in* The Da Vinci Code). Professor Ehrman is in great demand as a speaker and television commentator.

An earlier version of this interview appeared in the hardcover edition of *Secrets of the Code*. It has been updated and significantly expanded for this edition.

Despite its errors on points of history you have pointed out here and elsewhere, doesn't The Da Vinci Code *play a positive role in expanding awareness of the number and significance of alternative, lost, or suppressed documents that emanate from the early Christian era?*

Absolutely. Not long ago I gave a public lecture about *The Da Vinci Code* in Charlotte, North Carolina, at the Myers Park Baptist Church. The bulk of my talk had to do with the forms of Christianity that did not "make it" from the early centuries—that is, the "lost" forms of Christianity, and the books they used. If I had given this talk five years ago, maybe a hundred people, at best, would have turned out. Instead, there were 450. *The Da Vinci Code* has opened enormous doors for me and others who are interested in the early history of Christianity, to take our message outside the walls of academia to a very interested public.

As a scholar who has specialized in early Christianity, you have done a great deal of research on what we call "alternate scriptures"—that is, hitherto lost or lesser-known scriptures and documents that give evidence of a wide variety of Christian schools of thought. What, to you, are the most interesting ideas and passages you have come across in the world of alternative scriptures?

There are so many intriguing passages in these writings that it is hard to do justice to them simply by making a list. But if I were to try to do so, the list would include the following:

(a) the stories of Jesus as a mischievous five-year-old who zaps his playmates when he finds them irritating, in the Infancy Gospel of Thomas;

(b) the secret sayings of Jesus of the Coptic Gospel of Thomas, especially his claim that only when we disrobe and trample our clothes like little children will we see the Kingdom of Heaven, and his injunction to us (in the shortest saying of the book) to "be passers-by";

(c) the "true" interpretations of the Hebrew Bible in the Letter of Barnabas, where we're told that the Mosaic law must be taken figuratively rather than literally, so that the commandment not to eat pork really means not to behave like pigs who make loud noises only when hungry (i.e., don't pray only when you're in need), that the commandment not to eat the weasel really means not to engage in oral sex, since the weasel conceives through its mouth, and the command to observe the Sabbath (the seventh day) means to realize that there will be a future millennium after the world exists for six thousand years (since a day equals a thousand years for God, and on the seventh day he rested)!

(d) the account of Jesus's crucifixion in the Coptic Apocalypse of Peter, where Peter sees Jesus being crucified but sees at the same time Jesus *above* the cross laughing at those who think they can really kill him;

(e) the narrative of Jesus's resurrection in the Gospel of Peter, where he is said to come out of his tomb taller than a skyscraper, with his head above the sky, while the cross emerges from the tomb behind him speaking to God in heaven. It doesn't get much better than this!

You have also brought to light ways in which Christian belief underwent change as this new theology and its body of documents moved from the Holy Land in the time of Jesus to become the de facto state religion of the Roman Empire several centuries later. What, in fact, are some of those changes? How drastic or trivial are these differences?

Christianity shifted from being an other-worldly Jewish religion, in which the end of all time is at hand and people should not live for the values of their society but should deny themselves in preparation for the coming Kingdom, to being a this-worldly gentile religion. The latter did not stress the imminent end of all things and taught instead that it is important to work with the world in order to convert the world, so that people could have life after they died. Some people would argue that the Christianity that ended up triumphing was a completely different religion from the one that started in Jerusalem after the death of Jesus—that it is, in fact, a different religion from that of Jesus himself! In this view of things, Christianity is less the religion that Jesus taught (the religion *of* Jesus) than the religion that proclaims Jesus (the religion *about* Jesus). I'd say these are fairly enormous differences.

The main focus of your work has been to uncover what you call "lost Christianities." Will you describe the most important of these and how they differed from each other?

The Ebionites, the Marcionites, and the Gnostics were all important sects within Christianity, and they were, indeed, very different from each other.

The Ebionites were Jewish Christians who emphasized the importance of being Jewish as well as Christian. The Marcionites were anti-Jewish and believed that all things Jewish actually belong to the god of the Old Testament, who was not the true God. The Gnostics held to the belief that there were a number of different gods.

All of these groups claimed to go back to Jesus, which means they probably originated soon after Jesus's death and resurrection, or within a few decades at least. For example, the Ebionites claim that their teachings were derived from James the Just, who was the brother of Jesus, and who better to know what Jesus taught than his own brother? And they may have been right, actually—they may have been propounding beliefs that James taught. Their faith did not spread widely, however, perhaps in part because their belief that people who were gentiles had to become Jewish to be Christian meant that men had to become circumcised, which means they probably didn't win too many converts.

You mentioned that the Ebionites emphasized the Jewishness of Christianity. How about the Marcionites?

The Marcionites were followers of the mid-second-century Greek philosopher and teacher Marcion, who had spent about five years in Rome working out his theological system. He believed the apostle Paul had the true insight into Christianity because Paul differentiated between the law and the gospel. Marcion pushed that view to an extreme, maintaining that if there is a separation between law and gospel they must have been given to humankind from two different gods—the god who gave the law is the god of the Old Testament, whereas the god who saved people from the law is the god of Jesus. Similarly, the wrathful god of the Old Testament is the god who created this world, and chose Israel and gave them his law, whereas the god of Jesus is the one who saves people from this god by dying for their sins.

Marcion had a huge following even after he was excommunicated (he may have been the first), going to Asia Minor, in modern-day Turkey, to establish churches. In truth, Marcionite Christianity was a real threat to the other forms—it almost took over Christianity as a whole.

How about the Gnostics?

All sorts of groups, very different from each other, are classified today by scholars as Gnostics. They were so different from each other that some scholars, like the historian Elaine Pagels, wonder whether we should even call them Gnostic anymore.

Where the Gnostics come from intellectually is difficult to determine. They appear to represent a kind of amalgam of a variety of different religions, including Judaism and Christianity and Greek philosophy, especially Platonic philosophy, and they appear to have taken elements of these various religions and philosophies and combined them together into a major religious system. We know that there was a full-blown Gnostic system in the second century, probably early-to mid-second century, which is right around the time of Marcion. It's hard to know if Gnosticism began in Alexandria or if it began in Palestine, or where exactly, but we have evidence of Gnostics in Syria and Egypt. Eventually they make their way to Rome.

The so-called Gnostic gospels, found near the Egyptian town of Nag Hammadi, have rightly gained a great deal of attention because of Dan Brown. What has been the most important implication of this find from your perspective?

The most important "discovery" of modern times has been that early Christianity was extremely diverse—far more diverse than previous scholars ever could have imagined. What we have learned from the Gnostic gospels is that there were groups of Christians who believed an enormous range of things that most people today would not even call Christian. For example, some believed that the world is a cosmic mistake, created by an inferior, lesser deity rather than by the Lord God Almighty; that Christ did not really suffer on the cross; that the way to eternal life is not through belief in Jesus's death but through understanding his secret teachings. These, and many many other beliefs, were held by people who considered themselves Christian, who claimed to be following the teachings of Jesus and his apostles, and who had books to *prove* it—books allegedly written by the apostles themselves. If nothing else, the discoveries of Nag Hammadi have opened our eyes to just how diverse the early Christians really were.

People who read the Gnostic gospels in English translation frequently come away very confused. The gospels are filled with ideas that are very foreign to mainstream Western religious thinking. Given that many different groups have been lumped under one rubric, that of "Gnostics," is there a single consistent body of thought expressed in these documents?

The books are confusing not only in English translation, but also in the Coptic originals! The authors of these books did not think like most of us. Many of them were very metaphysically and mythically oriented. They were not interested in setting out straightforward propositional truths, but were intrigued with the poetics of existence and the mysteries of this world and how we came to inhabit it.

Having said that, I think it does help to have a conceptual understanding of what the Gnostic systems involved, as I try to lay out in another of my books called *Lost Christianities.* In a nutshell, Gnostics believed that this world was not a good place, but was the result of a cosmic disaster. Some of us do not belong here, they said, but are spirits from the world above who have been trapped or imprisoned in these material bodies. The goal of the Gnostic religions is to teach us how to escape. We can escape the material trappings of this world by learning the secret knowledge (Greek: *gnosis*) of who we really are, where we came from, how we got here, and how we can return. Salvation then comes to those who learn the truth about themselves, and these Gnostic books—many of them very confusing, to be sure—are attempts to help us come to fuller self-knowledge. When we understand it, then we can be set free.

The attempt at fuller self-knowledge is surely a timeless aspiration. It existed before the time of Jesus, and it continues to exist in New Age spiritualists. So what would have made what the Gnostics believed in irrelevant? Why would they—and all the other early Christian sects—have died out?

Although there were a variety of historical and cultural reasons, most of these groups probably died out because they were attacked—successfully attacked, on theological grounds—and they weren't nearly as effective in their own propaganda campaigns. They failed to recruit new converts even while the orthodox groups created a strong structure, used letter campaigns and other means to propagate their views, and their rhetoric convinced people.

But what really secured the victory was that the Roman emperor Constantine converted to Christianity. Naturally, he converted to the kind of Christianity that was dominant at that time. Once Constantine converts to an orthodox form of Christianity, and once the state has power, and the state is Christian, then the state starts asserting its influence over Christianity. So by the end of the fourth century, there's actually legislation against heretics. So the empire that used to be completely anti-Christian becomes Christian. And it doesn't just become Christian, but also tries to dictate what shape Christianity ought to be.

The ramifications of this change of events are enormous, of course. It changed the entire way the Western world understands itself, and how people understand something. Think of the concept of guilt alone: if some other groups had won, things might have been completely different.

Is Dan Brown right when he suggests that the real "heretics" may be the Romans who turned a religion of the oppressed—in which women were given prominent roles and certain deeply antimaterialistic beliefs can be traced—into the state religion of the Roman Empire, which was characterized by hierarchy, patriarchy, and politics?

I think Dan Brown is on to something here, as he is often is, even though he gets almost all the historical facts wrong. It is not true to say that it was Constantine who once and for all altered the religion, turning it from a women-friendly to a patriarchal religion, who decided that Jesus would be God, who chose which books to include in the New Testament. None of these things was done by Constantine. They had already been done (or were later to be done, in the case of the formation of the canon) decades—well over a century, in fact—before Constantine ever came on the scene. But these shifts certainly did happen. Christianity started out giving a high role and authority to women, who were eventually oppressed and silenced. It started out as an other-worldly religion, and it became a religion that embraced the values and norms of the world. It started out in opposition to the state and all it stood for, and it came both to embrace and to be embraced by the state. Christianity at the end of the fourth century would have been virtually unrecognizable to Christians at the beginning of the first.

The history that most of us got in school in Western civilization classes suggested that all these theological and political arguments resolved themselves during the Council of Nicea, convened by the Roman emperor Constantine in 325. Is that view correct?

The debates didn't end, but shifted. By the time you get to the Council of Nicea, you just don't have large groups of Gnostics anymore, or Marcionites, or Ebionites. They're old history now. But it didn't stop the debates. They just became more refined, and more heated. As an example, the Council of Nicea was about a form of Christianity called Arianism, which by second- or third-century standards was completely orthodox. By the time you get to the fourth century, however, and the theologians have refined their beliefs, Arianism becomes a major heresy. These Arians believed Jesus must have been subservient to the Father; after all, he prays to the Father and does the Father's will. Therefore, he's a subordinate deity. But the Arians were defeated by the Christians who maintained that Christ is not a subordinate deity, but that he's been divine from eternity past, that he's always existed in relationship to God. And so Christ isn't a divine being who comes into existence—he's always been divine, and of the same substance as God the Father himself.

The shifts in theology weren't as important as another shift that took place when Constantine became a Christian. Now he, an authoritarian political leader, could decide what kind of Christianity was acceptable and what kind wasn't. Suddenly everything related to the church became a political issue as well as a religious one. Some people think that Constantine converted to Christianity precisely because he thought that the Christian church might be able to help unify the empire. Unlike paganism, which worshipped lots of different gods in lots of different ways, Christianity insisted on one god, and one way. That is why Constantine may have called the Council of Nicea. If the church was going to play the role of unifying the empire, the church itself must be unified. That is the when, why, and how it became a political issue.

Turning to another theme of The Da Vinci Code, *Dan Brown obviously believes that women, and Mary Magdalene in particular, had an important and very visible role among these sects. Is there evidence of this in the alternative gospels? Is there a discernible trend there about how women in the church were treated?*

Orthodox Christians weren't the only ones who oppressed women, insisting on their silence and submissiveness. You can find similar trends in other forms of Christianity as well. That being said, it is striking that some Gnostic groups were known for their emphasis on women and their view that the secret revelations that bring salvation could come to women as well as men. Witness the Gospel of Mary, the only gospel named for a woman to have survived antiquity, where the entire point is that Jesus revealed the truth to Mary Magdalene, and explicitly *not* to the male disciples!

You have also noted on several occasions that the alternative scriptures that have been found provide a tantalizing suggestion about the interesting documents that have not yet been found. What do you think might still turn up? What questions would you like to see illuminated, if documentary evidence were to be found? What about the things that are being found that are either fake or require a huge suspension of disbelief—the Ossuary of James, the Cave of St. John the Baptist, etc.? What do you think of the alleged seventeenth-century genealogy of Jesus that has received attention recently in Wales?

Most of these recent finds are either hoaxes or duds, in my opinion. But new gospels do turn up on occasion.

And some of them are spectacular. We know of the existence of numerous gospels from the early church that no modern scholar has laid eyes on. But that may change with the passing of time. One interesting, but highly fragmentary, gospel was published just six years ago: The Gospel of the Savior. It's in Coptic, and it contains a couple of intriguing scenes. In one, Jesus is transported to the throne room of God when he is praying in the Garden: "Let this cup pass from before me." Now he is given a face-to-face with God to make his petition! And later he comes back down to earth and starts speaking to the cross itself, telling the cross not to fear for soon he will mount up upon it. An intriguing piece, even if not widely known. And there is reason to think that even more spectacular finds will be made. Stay tuned!

Finally, what is your answer to the often-asked question about why The Da Vinci Code *has captured people's attention and held it so deeply?*

This is a question I get asked a lot. My view is this: *The Da Vinci Code* is not the kind of book people turn to, or should want to turn to, if what they are looking for is a great piece of English literature that will go down in history as a literary classic. If literary style is what you're after, read Jane Austen or Charlotte Brontë. But if you want a terrific page-turner, a fast-paced murder mystery that is unusually intelligent for this genre, with twists and turns in the plot that will keep you guessing—plot twists involving intriguing information about religion that you've never heard of before (most of it wrong, but that's not the point!), including important archaeological finds, conspiracy theories, and a Vatican cover-up—all of that is rolled up into one

Ten Errors of Religious Omission and Commission in *The Da Vinci Code*

1. Jesus's life was decidedly not "recorded by thousands of followers across the land." He did not have thousands of followers, let alone literate ones.

2. It is not true that eighty gospels "were considered for the New Testament." This makes it sound like there was a contest, entered by mail.

3. It is absolutely not true that Jesus was not considered divine until the Council of Nicea, that before that he was considered merely as "a mortal prophet." The vast majority of Christians by the early fourth century acknowledged him as divine.

4. Constantine did not commission a "new Bible" that omitted references to Jesus's human traits. For one thing, he did not commission a new Bible at all. For another, the books that were already included are full of references to his human traits (he gets hungry, tired, angry; he gets upset; he bleeds, he dies . . .).

5. The Dead Sea Scrolls were not "found in the 1950s." It was 1947. And the Nag Hammadi documents do not tell the Grail story at all; nor do they emphasize Jesus's human traits. Quite the contrary.

package here. No wonder that, after 132 weeks on the *New York Times* bestseller list, this book was still number two!

At the same time, as a historian, I have to say that you should *not* (NOT!) read this book for historical information about the beginnings of Christianity, the historical Jesus, his relationship with Mary Magdalene, our lost gospels, the question of how we got the canon of the New Testament, the issue of how Jesus came to

Ten Errors of Religious Omission and Commission in *The Da Vinci Code* *(continued)*

6. "Jewish decorum" in no way forbade "a Jewish man to be unmarried." In fact, most of the community behind the Dead Sea Scrolls were unmarried male celibates.

7. The Dead Sea Scrolls were not among "the earliest Christian records." They are Jewish, with nothing Christian in them.

8. We have no idea about the lineage of Mary Magdalene; nothing connects her with the "house of Benjamin." And even if she were, this would not make her a descendent of David.

9. Mary Magdalene was pregnant at the crucifixion?!? That's a good one.

10. The "Q" document is not a surviving source being hid by the Vatican, nor is it a book allegedly written by Jesus himself. It is a hypothetical document that scholars posit as having been available to Matthew and Luke—principally a collection of the sayings of Jesus. Roman Catholic scholars think the same thing of it as non-Catholics; there's nothing secretive about it.

—BART D. EHRMAN

be seen as God, the role of the emperor Constantine in the religion, and so on. For *that* kind of information, read the writings of historians who know something about it, rather than a novelist who doesn't.

The main thing to remember is that despite Brown's claims about "facts" at the beginning of the book, in actual fact even the so-called facts in this work of fiction are themselves part of the fiction. It's a novel, not history.

God's Word or Human Words?

BY ELAINE PAGELS

Within a century of Jesus' death, some of his most loyal followers had determined to exclude a wide range of Christian sources, to say nothing of borrowing from other religious traditions, although, as we have also seen, this often happened. But why, and in what circumstances, did these early church leaders believe that this was necessary for the movement to survive? And why did those who proclaimed Jesus the "only begotten son of God," as the Gospel of John declares, dominate later tradition, while other Christian visions, like that of Thomas, which encourages disciples to recognize themselves, as well as Jesus, as "children of God," were suppressed?

Traditionally, Christian theologians have declared that "the Holy Spirit guides the church into all truth"—a statement often taken to mean that what has survived must be right. Some historians of religion have rationalized this conviction by implying that in Christian history, as in the history of science, weak, false ideas die off early, while the strong and valid ones survive. The late Raymond Brown, a prominent New Testament scholar and Roman Catholic Sulpician priest, stated this perspective baldly: What orthodox Christians rejected was only "the rubbish of the second century"—and, he added, "it's still rubbish." But such polemics tell us nothing about how and why early church leaders laid down the fundamental principles of Christian teaching. To understand what happened we need

---

to look at the specific challenges—and dangers—that confronted believers during the critical years around 100 to 200 C.E., and how those who became the architects of Christian tradition dealt with these challenges. The African convert Tertullian, living in the port city of Carthage in North Africa about eighty years after the Gospels of John and Thomas were written, around the year 190 (or, as Tertullian and his contemporaries might have said, during the reign of Emperor Commodus), acknowledged that the Christian movement was attracting crowds of new members—and that outsiders were alarmed:

> The outcry is that the State is filled with Christians—that they are in the fields, in the cities, in the islands; and [outsiders] lament, as if for some calamity, that both men and women, of every age and condition, even high rank, are going over to profess Christian faith.

Tertullian ridiculed the non-Christian majority for their wild suspicions and denounced the magistrates for believing them:

> [We are called] monsters of evil, and accused of practicing a sacred ritual in which we kill a little child and eat it; in which, after the feast, we practice incest, while the dogs, our pimps, overturn the lights and give us the shameless darkness to gratify our lusts. *This is what people constantly charge,* yet you take no trouble to find out the truth. . . . Well, *you think the Christian is capable of every crime—an enemy of the gods, of the emperor, of the laws, of good morals, of all nature.*

Tertullian was distressed that throughout the empire, from his native city in Africa to Italy, Spain, Egypt, and

Asia Minor, and in the provinces from Germany to Gaul, Christians had become targets of sporadic outbreaks of violence. Roman magistrates often ignored these incidents and sometimes participated in them. In the city of Smyrna on the coast of Asia Minor, for example, crowds shouting, "Get the atheists!" lynched the convert Germanicus and demanded—successfully—that the authorities arrest and immediately kill Polycarp, a prominent bishop.

What outsiders saw depended considerably on which Christian groups they happened to encounter. Pliny, governor of Bithynia, in modern Turkey, trying to prevent groups from sheltering subversives, ordered his soldiers to arrest people accused as Christians. To gather information, his soldiers tortured two Christian women, both slaves, who revealed that members of this peculiar cult "met regularly before dawn on a certain day to sing a hymn to Christ as to a god." Though it had been rumored that they were eating human flesh and blood, Pliny found that they were actually eating only "ordinary, harmless food." He reported to the emperor Trajan that, although he found no evidence of actual crime, "I ordered them to be taken away and executed; for, whatever they admit to, I am convinced that their stubbornness and unshakable obstinacy should not go unpunished." But twenty years later in Rome, Rusticus, the city prefect, interrogated a group of five Christians who looked to him less like members of a cult than like a philosophy seminar. Justin Martyr the philosopher, arraigned along with his students, admitted to the prefect that he met with like-minded believers in his Roman apartment "above the baths of Timothy" to discuss "Christian philosophy." Nevertheless Rusticus, like Pliny, suspected treason. When

Justin and his pupils refused his order to sacrifice to the gods, he had them beaten, then beheaded.

Thirty years after Justin's death, another philosopher, named Celsus, who detested Christians, wrote a book called *The True Word,* which exposed their movement and accused some of them of acting like wild-eyed devotees of foreign gods such as Attis and Cybele, possessed by spirits. Others, Celsus charged, practiced incantations and spells, like magicians; still others followed what many Greeks and Romans saw as the barbaric, Oriental customs of the Jews. Celsus reported, too, that on large estates throughout the countryside Christian woolworkers, cobblers, and washerwomen, people who, he said, "ordinarily are afraid to speak in the presence of their superiors," nevertheless gathered the gullible—slaves, children, and "stupid women"—from the great houses into their workshops to hear how Jesus worked miracles and, after he died, rose from the grave. Among respectable citizens, Christians aroused the same suspicions of violence, promiscuity, and political extremism with which secretive cults are still regarded, especially by those who fear that their friends or relatives may be lured into them.

Despite the diverse forms of early Christianity—and perhaps because of them—the movement spread rapidly, so that by the end of the second century Christian groups were proliferating throughout the empire, despite attempts to stop them. Tertullian boasted to outsiders that "the more we are mown down by you, the more we multiply; the blood of Christians is seed!" Defiant rhetoric, however, could not solve the problem that he and other Christian leaders faced: How could they strengthen and unify this enormously diverse and widespread movement, so it could survive its enemies?

Tertullian's younger contemporary Irenaeus, often identified as bishop of Lyons, himself had experienced the hostility Tertullian was talking about, first in his native town of Smyrna (Izmir, in today's Turkey) and then in the rough provincial town of Lyons, in Gaul (now France). Irenaeus also witnessed the fractiousness that divided Christian groups. As a boy he had lived in the household of his teacher Polycarp, the venerable bishop of Smyrna, whom even his enemies called the teacher of Asia Minor. Although he knew that they were scattered in many small groups throughout the world, Irenaeus shared Polycarp's hope that Christians everywhere would come to see themselves as members of a single church they called catholic, which means "universal." To unify this worldwide community, Polycarp urged its members to reject all deviants. According to Irenaeus, Polycarp liked to tell how his own mentor, "John, the disciple of the Lord"—the same person whom tradition reveres as the author of the Gospel of John—once went to the public baths in Ephesus, but, seeing Cerinthus, whom he regarded as a heretic, John ran out of the bath house without bathing, exclaiming, "Let us flee, lest the bath house fall down; because Cerinthus, the enemy of the truth, is inside." When Irenaeus repeated this story, he added another to show how Polycarp himself treated heretics. When the influential but controversial Christian teacher Marcion confronted the bishop and asked him, "Do you recognize me?" Polycarp replied, "Yes, I recognize you—firstborn of Satan!"

Irenaeus says that he tells these stories to show "the horror that the apostles and their disciples had against even speaking with those who corrupt the truth." But his stories also show what troubled Irenaeus: that even two generations after the author of the Gospel of John qualified the claims of Peter Christians and confronted Thomas

Christians, the movement remained contentious and divided. Polycarp himself denounced people who, he charged, "bear the [Christian] name with evil deceit" because what they teach often differs from what he had learned from his own teachers. Irenaeus, in turn, believed that he practiced true Christianity, for he could link himself directly to the time of Jesus through Polycarp, who personally had heard Jesus' teaching from John himself, "the disciple of the Lord." Convinced that this disciple wrote the Gospel of John, Irenaeus was among the first to champion this gospel and link it forever to Mark, Matthew, and Luke. His contemporary Tatian, a brilliant Syrian student of Justin Martyr the philosopher, killed by Rusticus, took a different approach: he tried to unify the various gospels by rewriting all of them into a single text. Irenaeus left the texts intact but declared that only Matthew, Mark, Luke, and John *collectively*—and only these gospels *exclusively*—constitute the *whole* gospel, which he called the "four formed gospel." Only these four gospels, Irenaeus believed, were written by eyewitnesses to events through which God has sent salvation to humankind. This four gospel canon was to become a powerful weapon in Irenaeus's campaign to unify and consolidate the Christian movement during his lifetime, and it has remained a basis of orthodox teaching ever since. . . .

When Irenaeus met in Rome a childhood friend from Smyrna named Florinus, who like himself as a young man had studied with Polycarp, he was shocked to learn that his friend now had joined a group headed by Valentinus and Ptolemy—sophisticated theologians who, nevertheless, like the new prophets, often relied on dreams and revelations. Although they called themselves spiritual Christians, Irenaeus regarded them as dangerously deviant. Hoping to persuade his friend to reconsider, Irenaeus wrote a letter to warn him that "these views, Florinus, to put it mildly, are not sound; are not consonant with the church, and involve their devotees in the worst impiety, even heresy." Irenaeus was distressed to learn that an increasing number of educated Christians were moving in the same direction.

When he returned from Rome to Gaul, Irenaeus found his own community devastated; some thirty people had been brutally tortured and killed in the public arena on a day set aside to entertain the townspeople with this spectacle. With Bishop Pothinus dead, the remaining members of his group now looked to Irenaeus for leadership. Aware of the danger, he nevertheless agreed, determined to unify the survivors. But he saw that members of his own "flock" were splintered into various, often fractious groups—all of them claiming to be inspired by the holy spirit.

How could he sort out these conflicting claims and impose some kind of order? The task was enormous and perplexing. Irenaeus believed, certainly, that the holy spirit had initiated the Christian movement. From the time it began, a hundred years earlier, both Jesus and his followers claimed to have experienced outpourings of the holy spirit, dreams, visions, stories, sayings, ecstatic speech—many communicated orally, many others written down—reflecting the vitality and diversity of the movement. The New Testament gospels abound in visions, dreams, and revelations, like the one that Mark says initiated Jesus' public activity:

> In those days, Jesus came from Nazareth, and was baptized by John in the Jordan. And just as he was coming up out of the water, *he saw the heavens torn apart and the spirit*

> *descending like a dove upon him, and a voice came from heaven:* "You are my beloved son; with you I am well pleased."

Luke adds to his version of this story an account of Jesus' birth, in which a vision precedes every event in the drama, from the moments the angel Gabriel appeared to the aging priest Zacharias and later to Mary, to the night when "an angel of the Lord" appeared to shepherds to tell them of Jesus' birth, terrifying them with a sudden radiance that lighted up the nighttime sky. . . .

Irenaeus says that he tried hard, at a friend's request, to investigate Marcus's teaching in order to expose him as an interloper and a fraud. For by attracting disciples, performing initiations, and offering special teachings to "spiritual" Christians, Marcus's activity threatened Irenaeus's effort to unify all Christians in the area into a homogenous church. Irenaeus charged that Marcus was a magician, "the herald of Antichrist," a man whose made-up visions and pretense to spiritual power masked his true identity as Satan's own apostle. He ridiculed Marcus's claims to investigate "the deep things of God" and mocked him for urging initiates to seek revelations of their own:

> While they say such things as these about the creation, every one of them generates something new every day, according to his ability; for no one is considered "mature" [or "initiated"] among them who does not develop some enormous lies.

Irenaeus expresses dismay that many other teachers, too, within Christian communities "introduce an indescribable number of secret and illegitimate writings, which they themselves have forged, to bewilder the minds of foolish people, who are ignorant of the true scriptures." He quotes some of their writings, including part of a well known and influential text called the Secret Book of John (discovered among the so-called gnostic gospels at Nag Hammadi in 1945), and he refers to many others, including a Gospel of Truth (perhaps the one discovered at Nag Hammadi), which he attributes to Marcus's teacher, Valentinus, and even a Gospel of Judas. Irenaeus decided that stemming this flood of "secret writings" would be an essential first step toward limiting the proliferation of "revelations" that he suspected of being only delusional or, worse, demonically inspired.

Yet the discoveries at Nag Hammadi show how widespread was the attempt "to seek God"—not only among those who wrote such "secret writings" but among the many more who read, copied, and revered them, including the Egyptian monks who treasured them in their monastery library even two hundred years after Irenaeus had denounced them. But in 367 C.E., Athanasius, the zealous bishop of Alexandria—an admirer of Irenaeus—issued an Easter letter in which he demanded that Egyptian monks destroy all such writings, except for those he specifically listed as "acceptable," even "canonical"—a list that constitutes virtually all of our present "New Testament." But someone—perhaps monks at the monastery of St. Pachomius—gathered dozens of the books Athanasius wanted to burn, removed them from the monastery library, sealed them in a heavy, six-foot jar, and, intending to hide them, buried them on a nearby hillside near Nag Hammadi. There an Egyptian villager named Muhammad 'Alī stumbled upon them sixteen hundred years later.

Now that we can read for ourselves some of the writings that Irenaeus detested and Athanasius banned, we can see that many of them express the hope of receiving revelation, and encourage "those who seek for God." The author of the Secret Book of James, for example, *reinterprets* the opening scene we noted from the New Testament Acts, in which Luke tells how Jesus ascended . . .

But those who criticize such "proof from prophecy" suggest that Christians like Justin argue fallaciously—for example, by mistaking a misleading translation for a miracle. The author of the Gospel of Matthew, for example, apparently reading Isaiah's prophecy in Greek translation, took it to mean that "a virgin [*parthenos* in Greek] shall conceive." Justin himself acknowledges that Jewish interpreters, arguing with Jesus' followers, pointed out that what the prophet had actually written in the original Hebrew was simply that "a *young woman* [*almahl*] shall conceive and bear a son"—apparently predicting immediate events expected in the royal succession.

Yet Justin and Irenaeus, like many Christians to this day, remained unconvinced by such arguments, and believed instead that ancient prophecies predicted Jesus' birth, death, and resurrection, and that their divine inspiration has been proven by actual events. Unbelievers often find these proofs far-fetched, but for believers they demonstrate God's "history of salvation." Justin staked his life on this conviction, and believed that he had given up philosophical speculation for truth as empirically verifiable as that of the scientist whose experiments turn out as predicted.

Since Irenaeus saw the proof from prophecy as one way to resolve the problem of how to tell which prophecies—and which revelations—come from God, he added certain writings of "the apostles" to those of "the prophets," since he, like Justin, believed that together these constitute indispensable witnesses to truth. Like other Christians of their time, Justin and Irenaeus, when they spoke of "the Scriptures," had in mind primarily the Hebrew Bible: what we call the New Testament had not yet been assembled. Their conviction that God's truth is revealed in the events of salvation history provides the essential link between the Hebrew Bible and what Justin called "the apostles' memoirs," which we know as the gospels of the New Testament.

It was Irenaeus, so far as we can tell, who became the principal architect of what we call the four gospel canon, the framework that includes in the New Testament collection the gospels of Matthew, Mark, Luke, and John. First Irenaeus denounces various Christian groups that settle on only one gospel, like the Ebionite Christians, who, he says, use only Matthew, or followers of Marcion, who use only Luke. Equally mistaken, Irenaeus continues, are those who invoke many gospels. Certain Christians, he declared, "boast that they have more gospels than there really are . . . but really, they have no gospel which is not full of blasphemy." Irenaeus resolved to hack down the forest of "apocryphal and illegitimate" writings—like the Secret Book of James and the Gospel of Mary—and leave only four "pillars" standing. He boldly declared that "the gospel," which contains all truth, can be supported by only these four "pillars"—namely, the gospels attributed to Matthew, Mark, Luke, and John. To defend his choice, he declared that "it is not possible that there can be either more or fewer than four," for "just as there are four regions of the universe, and four principal winds," the church itself requires "only four pillars." Furthermore, just as the prophet Ezekiel envisioned God's throne borne up by four living creatures, so the divine Word of God is supported by this "four formed gospel." (Following his lead, Christians in later generations took the faces of these four "living creatures"—the lion, the bull, the eagle, and the man—as symbols of the four evangelists.) What makes these gospels trustworthy, he claimed, is that these authors, who he believed included Jesus' disciples Matthew and John, actually witnessed the events they related; similarly, he added, Mark and Luke, being followers of Peter and Paul, wrote down only what they had heard from the apostles themselves.

Few New Testament scholars today would agree with Irenaeus; we do not know who actually wrote these gospels, any more than we know who wrote the gospels of Thomas or Mary; all we know is that all of these "gospels" are attributed to disciples of Jesus. Nevertheless, as the next chapters will show, Irenaeus not only welded the Gospel of John to the far more widely quoted gospels of Matthew and Luke but praised John as the greatest gospel. For Irenaeus, John was not the *fourth* gospel, as Christians call it today, but the *first* and *foremost* of the gospels, because he believed that John alone understood who Jesus really is—God in human form. What God revealed in that extraordinary moment when he "became flesh" trumped any revelations received by mere human beings—even prophets and apostles, let alone the rest of us.

Irenaeus could not, of course, stop people from seeking revelation of divine truth—nor, as we have seen, did he intend to do so. After all, religious traditions survive through time only as their adherents relive and re-imagine them and, in the process, continually transform them. But, from his own time to the present, Irenaeus and his successors among church leaders did strive to compel all believers to subject themselves to the "fourfold gospel" and to what he called apostolic tradition. Henceforth all "revelations" endorsed by Christian leaders would have to agree with the gospels set forth in what would become the New Testament. Throughout the centuries, of course, these gospels have given rise to an extraordinary range of Christian art, music, poetry, theology, and legend. But even the church's most gifted saints, like Teresa of Avila and John of the Cross, would be careful not to transgress—much less transcend—these boundaries. To this day, many traditionally minded Christians continue to believe that whatever trespasses canonical guidelines must be "lies and wickedness" that come either from the evil of the human heart or from the devil.

Yet Irenaeus recognized that even banishing all "secret writings" and creating a canon of four gospel accounts could not, by itself, safeguard the Christian movement. What if some who read the "right" gospels read them in the wrong way—or in *many* wrong ways? What if Christians interpreted these same gospels to inspire—or, as the bishop might say, to spawn—new "heresies"? This is what happened in Irenaeus's congregation—and . . . he responded by working to construct what he called orthodox (literally, "straight-thinking") Christianity.

The Jesus Mysteries

BY TIMOTHY FREKE AND PETER GANDY

The traditional version of history bequeathed to us by the authorities of the Roman Church is that Christianity developed from the teachings of a Jewish Messiah and that Gnosticism was a later deviation. What would happen, we wondered, if the picture were reversed and Gnosticism viewed as the authentic Christianity, just as the Gnostics themselves claimed? Could it be that orthodox Christianity was a later deviation from Gnosticism and that Gnosticism was a synthesis of Judaism and the Pagan Mystery religion? This was the beginning of the Jesus Mysteries Thesis.

Boldly stated, the picture that emerged for us was as follows. We knew that most ancient Mediterranean cultures had adopted the ancient Mysteries, adapting them to their own national tastes and creating their own version of the myth of the dying and resurrecting godman. Perhaps some of the Jews had, likewise, adopted the Pagan Mysteries and created their own version of the Mysteries, which we now know as Gnosticism. Perhaps initiates of the Jewish Mysteries had adapted the potent symbolism of the Osiris–Dionysus myths into a myth of their own, the hero of which was the Jewish dying and resurrecting godman Jesus.

If this was so, then the Jesus story was not a biography at all but a consciously crafted vehicle for encoded spiritual teachings created by Jewish Gnostics. As in the Pagan Mysteries, initiation into the Inner Mysteries would reveal the myth's allegorical meaning. Perhaps those uninitiated into the Inner Mysteries had mistakenly come to regard the Jesus myth as historical fact and in this way Literalist Christianity had been created. Perhaps the Inner Mysteries of Christianity, which the Gnostics taught but which the Literalists denied existed, revealed that the Jesus story was not a factual account of God's one and only visit to planet Earth, but a mystical teaching story designed to help each one of us become a Christ.

The Jesus story does have all the hallmarks of a myth, so could it be that that is exactly what it is? After all, no one has read the newly discovered Gnostic gospels and taken their fantastic stories as literally true; they are readily seen as myths. It is only familiarity and cultural prejudice that prevent us from seeing the New Testament gospels in the same light. If those gospels had also been lost to us and only recently discovered, who would read these tales for the first time and believe they were historical accounts of a man born of a virgin, who had walked on water and returned from the dead? Why should we consider the stories of Osiris, Dionysus, Adonis, Attis, Mithras, and the other Pagan Mystery saviors as fables, yet come across essentially the same story told in a Jewish context and believe it to be the biography of a carpenter from Bethlehem?

We had both been raised as Christians and were surprised to find that, despite years of open-minded spiritual exploration, it still felt somehow dangerous to even dare think such thoughts. Early indoctrination reaches very deep. We were in effect saying that Jesus was a Pagan god and that Christianity was a heretical product of Paganism! It seemed outrageous. Yet this theory explained the similarities between the stories of Osiris, Dionysus, and Jesus Christ in a simple and elegant way. They are parts of one developing mythos.

The Jesus Mysteries Thesis answered many puzzling questions, yet it also opened up new dilemmas. Isn't there indisputable historical evidence for the existence of Jesus the man? And how could Gnosticism be the original Christianity when St. Paul, the earliest Christian we know about, is so vociferously anti-Gnostic? And is it really credible that such an insular and anti-Pagan people as the Jews could have adopted the Pagan Mysteries? And how could it have happened that a consciously created myth came to be believed as history? And if Gnosticism represents genuine Christianity, why was it Literalist Christianity that came to dominate the world as the most influential religion of all time? All of these difficult questions would have to be satisfactorily answered before we could wholeheartedly accept such a radical theory as the Jesus Mysteries Thesis.

The Great Cover-up

Our new account of the origins of Christianity only seemed improbable because it contradicted the received view. As we pushed farther with our research, the traditional picture began to unravel completely all around us. We found ourselves embroiled in a world of schism and power struggles, of forged documents and false identities, of letters that had been edited and added to, and of the wholesale destruction of historical evidence. We focused forensically on the few facts we could be confident of, as if we were detectives on the verge of cracking a sensational "whodunit," or perhaps more accurately as if we were uncovering an ancient and unacknowledged miscarriage of justice. For, time and again, when we critically examined what genuine evidence remained, we found that the history of Christianity bequeathed to us by the Roman Church was a gross distortion of the truth. Actually the evidence completely endorsed the Jesus Mysteries Thesis. It was becoming increasingly obvious that we had been deliberately deceived, that the Gnostics were indeed the original Christians, and that their anarchic mysticism had been hijacked by an authoritarian institution which had created from it a dogmatic religion and then brutally enforced the greatest cover-up in history.

The Jesus Mysteries

One of the major players in this cover-up operation was a character called Eusebius who, at the beginning of the fourth century, compiled from legends, fabrications, and his own imagination the only early history of Christianity that still exists today. All subsequent histories have been forced to base themselves on Eusebius's dubious claims, because there has been little other information to draw on. All those with a different perspective on Christianity were branded as heretics and eradicated. In this way falsehoods compiled in the fourth century have come down to us as established facts.

Eusebius was employed by the Roman Emperor Constantine, who made Christianity the state religion of the Empire and gave Literalist Christianity the power it needed to begin the final eradication of Paganism and Gnosticism. Constantine wanted "one God, one religion" to consolidate his claim of "one Empire, one Emperor." He oversaw the creation of the Nicene creed, the article of faith repeated in churches to this day, and Christians who refused to assent to this creed were banished from the Empire or otherwise silenced.

This "Christian" Emperor then returned home from Nicaea and had his wife suffocated and his son murdered. He deliberately remained un-baptized until his deathbed so that he could continue his atrocities and still receive forgiveness of sins and a guaranteed place in heaven by being baptized at the last moment. Although he had his "spin doctor" Eusebius compose a suitably obsequious biography for him, he was actually a monster just like many Roman Emperors before him. Is it really at all surprising that a "history" of the origins of Christianity created by an employee in the service of a Roman tyrant should turn out to be a pack of lies?

History is indeed written by the victors. The creation of an appropriate history has always been part of the arsenal of political manipulation.

The Da Vinci Code and Jewish Culture

An Interview with Rabbi Asher Jacobson

While *The Da Vinci Code* primarily concerns itself with matters of early Christian history and iconography, Dan Brown also makes mention from time to time of intriguing ideas relating to Judaism, its history, and its symbols. Late in *The Da Vinci Code* story, for example, Robert Langdon tells Sophie Neveu that the Star of David represents the intertwining of a pair of triangles, functioning as classic chalice and blade symbols, representing the sacred union of the male and the female, much like an Asian yin and yang symbol.

Perhaps, not surprisingly, given his role as a "symbologist," Langdon seems to have developed considerable background on the history of gender roles, sex and sexuality, language, and symbols among the Jewish people. At one point he talks about the notion of "Shekinah," a divine feminine force in ancient Jewish culture that many modern American Jews would no doubt say they had never heard of. In the scene at Château Villette, Langdon and Teabing emphasize how uncommon celibacy was among the Jews of two thousand years ago and how standard marriage was for rabbis and other leaders of that time period. They make this point in order to argue against the traditional church view, which presumes the celibacy of that charismatic Jewish leader called Jesus, as well as to emphasize the plausibility of Jesus' presumed marriage to Mary Magdalene.

Just as many Christian critics have pointed out numerous errors in the way *The Da Vinci Code* deals with early Christian history, a number of Jewish scholars have disputed the book's "facts" when dealing with ancient Jewish practices. Indeed, some Jewish leaders have been outraged by the book's suggestion that the Temple of Solomon in Jerusalem was, early in its history, the scene of sacred sexual rites. But other Jewish thinkers are more interested in the big picture of how Dan Brown weaves alternative themes taken from Judaism's own rich history of mysticism into the story. Thus one of the odder ripples in the slipstream of success spreading from *The Da Vinci Code* has been a revival of interest in Jewish mysticism.

Rabbi Asher Jacobson, an executive member of the Rabbinical Council of Canada who completed his rabbinical ordination at the Central Lubavitch Yeshiva in Brooklyn, New York, knows this well. These days more people attend his evening classes in Kabbalah, an aspect of Jewish mysticism, at the Chevra Kadisha B'nai Jacob Synagogue in Montreal than attend Saturday morning services. According to Rabbi Jacobson, *The Da Vinci Code* has unleashed an outpouring of interest among people—Jewish and Christian—eager to learn more. He now leads classes in Jewish iconology, mysticism, and numeric codes in the Hebrew alphabet, as well as teaching comparative religion and theology at Concordia University, Quebec. Unlike religious leaders who have condemned the novel, Rabbi Jacobson embraces it, believing that if the book has served as a springboard for people to search for spiritual knowledge, it has served a useful purpose. In this interview, Rabbi Jacobson clarifies and expounds on some of the points about Judaism discussed in *The Da Vinci Code.*

In the novel, the Star of David is said to be the symbolic fusion of the feminine and the masculine—the chalice and the blade. Is there any truth to this?

Interestingly, there is some merit to discussing the sacred union of male and female within Judaism. I must warn you, however, that when you enter into the mystical domain of Judaism—into Kabbalah, the esoteric or mystic doctrine of Judaism—you are going beyond historical fact. You are going into a teaching that is connected to the spirituality of life and of the world. In Jewish mysticism it is explained that the Star of David is the symbol of the world and of God. The arrow pointing downwards is God. God is seen as the male because God is the one that gives life. God is the creator, the father, the master. The world, the universe, everything of creation is compared to the female, for it receives. It receives life, it receives sustenance, it receives godliness.

This is similar to the chalice and the blade, although I think in the novel the roles are reversed with the downwards triangle being the feminine and the upwards triangle being the masculine. Also, you have to remember that the chalice and the blade is a Christian concept, so you won't find that specific symbolic expression in Judaism. But the idea of male and female is very much in line with the Star of David. The purpose of creation is to merge and combine both forces—to bring heaven down to earth and to elevate the earth to a level of godliness and of spirituality. This is what the Star of David expresses. As soon as I saw this in the book, my ears pricked up and I was impressed that Dan Brown had discovered it.

The book also says that in the early days of the Jewish faith there was a duality between a male divine force and a female divine force, the Shekinah force. What was Shekinah in ancient Judaism? Is Shekinah still a force in contemporary Judaism?

Shekinah means "the divine presence" and is seen as being feminine. Shekinah is a Hebrew word and in the

Hebrew language you have masculine and feminine words just as in French. Now, anything that ends with a letter *hey*—which would be *Shekinah*—is a feminine word. But this is not the only word connected with God which is feminine. The highest possible name of God—which according to Jewish law I cannot even pronounce—ends in a *hey.* It is spelt *yod, hey, vav,* and *hey.* It's the name of God that transcends and precedes all of creation.

Now that is very interesting because the question is always, is God male or female or both or none? But in Judaism, it is not insignificant that the highest name of God is expressed in the feminine. And it is the same with the Shekinah.

It is understood in the teachings of Kabbalah that the most elevated being in this world is the human being, but that the female comes from a higher source than the male. And that's why Kabbalah teaches that the female is more sensitive—because her soul is more connected; that's why she cries more, that's why she understands more.

The understanding in Judaism and Jewish law that women are not obliged to do as many things as men is not because women are weaker but because they are stronger. For instance, a man is obliged to place himself in a structured form of prayer. He needs to go to synagogue with a *minyan* (a quorum of ten or more adult male Jews) and *daven* (pray) there. That's how he fulfils the commandment of prayer. The female is not obliged to do that. She can pray however she wants in whatever context. That's because the understanding is that the male needs more of a structure, more guidance in his pursuit of spirituality, whereas the female intuitively has it already.

So rather than a duality, it's a superiority of the female over the male?

In a mystical sense, absolutely.

So what about in a real life sense? After all, The Da Vinci Code *is based on the characterization of an independent Jewish woman, Mary, who lived two thousand years ago.*

Throughout the generations in Jewish tradition, the idea of the female being superior was understood by some of our greatest thinkers and leaders. That is why we can be proud that in our past, many women were our leaders, judges, and our prophetesses: women like Penina Devora, Dina, Miriam, and women like Sarah, the first mother, of whom God says in the Bible to Abraham, "You need to listen to her voice" because Sarah, the first Jewish woman, was greater in prophesy than Abraham and had a better understanding of the spirituality of family dynamics.

This is why throughout Jewish history, women have been understood to be the very foundation and guide of the home. This notion has been etched in the national Jewish character, that the woman is the one that runs the show. Yes, males dominated in the leadership, but females had a tremendous role throughout our history. So for a woman two thousand years ago to have that type of power and influence is not that out of the ordinary in the Jewish tradition.

However, Judaism has always lived within the culture and the society around it. This idea of the female being superior to the male wasn't the understanding in the general society at that particular period of time. In the Roman times, women were second class for social, economic, and physical reasons. Society was based and shaped in a way that women were forced to rely on men for their sustenance, for their livelihood. In those days being a mother with children was considered to be the highest level of occupation that one could achieve. So I doubt that the Mary that we met in the novel could have been quite so independent as she is portrayed.

Well, what about the depiction of Jesus? Was a rabbi in those days expected to be married?

Well, here we have two very diverse approaches to sexuality and to marriage. In Christianity, the first woman is Eve. She is the one who enticed Adam to eat from the Tree of Knowledge. She brought evil into the world. It was the first sin. And women since then have been seen as the enticers. That's where we get the word evil from—Eve brought evil into the world. Thus, sexuality, and anything that has to do with enticing males, was seen throughout Christian history as a lower level of living. And that is why it's understood that committing yourself to a life of celibacy, a life before sin, is the ultimate spiritual way of life.

Judaism sees it from a completely different point of view. Eve is known as Hava, which in Hebrew means "the source of life." And she's the one who brings life into the world. She is seen as a tremendous woman, someone who gives birth to all of life. In Judaism, one of the greatest *mitzvahs* (commandments) that one can do is to get married. It is an obligation to get married and to find someone of the opposite sex with whom you can procreate and bring life into the world. Sexuality in Judaism was never seen as a descending level of being. It was seen as a holy act, a sanctified act.

In Judaism a marriage is not called a marriage, it's called *kiddushin,* which means you are sanctifying someone in an unselfish and godly relationship, and there are many mitzvahs that are associated with marriage. Jewish law would say to the eighteen-year-old male in those days: "You need to get married. It's a sin to live without marriage."

So would it make sense then that Jesus the rabbi would, as Dan Brown suggests, have been married?

Not necessarily, because there's one allowance that the Talmud gives for postponing marriage and that is for people who are dedicating their lives to the study of Torah. According to Jewish tradition, Jesus was a student of Rabbi Yehoshua ben Prachya. He was a student of this sage at a time when the Talmud was being written and he used to go to yeshiva and spend all day studying, debating and going over Jewish law. If this tradition is valid history, then it may not be so surprising that Jesus was not married.

What about the suggestion in The Da Vinci Code *that the marriage of Jesus and Mary was important because it represented a merger of the houses of David and Benjamin?*

In Jewish tradition there is a belief that the House of David would carry on the dynasty of the kingdom and would live on for eternity. There is a linkage in every generation to particular individuals connected to this bloodline, and it is believed that the messiah will come from this lineage. But marriage plays no part in this tradition. It's not required for someone from the House of David to be merged in any way with the tribe of Benjamin. Also, there is no evidence that Jesus or Mary were of these tribes. Jesus's lineage was never truly considered seriously and it is something that will be argued for many more years to come. As for Mary, we know very little about her at all.

What about the scene in the gospel account in which a woman called Mary washes the feet of Jesus and uses spikenard, an expensive unguent? Some analysts have even said this is an allusion to the Song of Solomon. Do you agree?

I have to say that I have never heard this before. What I can say is that if you look at the gospels most of them were written by Jewish people. Their knowledge of religion and faith was based on Jewish teaching and writings about people like David, Solomon, and Moses and the Torah. Everything they knew was contained within Jewish tradition. So it's not surprising that over and over you find the style, wording, and sentiments of the gospels are reflective of what is found in the Torah.

Specifically about the washing of feet, you'll find many references in the Torah: Abraham washing the feet of three angels that come to visit him, Moses's feet being washed by the daughters of Jethro. But within Jewish tradition there is not much attention focused on trying to find comparisons or insights between things that are written in the gospels and things that are found in the Tanakh (the books that comprise the Torah: "the prophets" and "the writings").

One of Dan Brown's most striking revelations is about the divine proportion, the number 1.618 (or PHI), which Langdon explains as being a "fundamental building block of nature" present in everything from honeybee populations to nautilus shell spirals. Does that number appear in Jewish tradition?

Well, that was one area where I felt that Dan Brown missed something. The number 1.618 is a very significant number in the Jewish community and I was surprised he didn't mention it along with the rest of his discussion on this topic. That number is a powerful force that symbolizes God's presence in this world in the Jewish tradition.

In the Torah there are 613 commandments and then there are five extra factors that bring you to 618. There are two opinions on what those factors are. Some say they are the five additional rabbinic commandments, which make 618. Others say that the 613 commandments that are performed by our five senses make 618. But we understand that this is the way in which God—the 1—permeates the world. God, the 1, enters into the world via the 618. When I saw 1.618 as the divine proportion, I thought this was very true from a Jewish religious perspective.

What about the Knights Templar? How are they perceived in Jewish history?

They're only really seen as extras. They enter the story after the destruction of the Temple in Jerusalem at a time when the Jews are dispersed. In the Jewish community the most we can say about them is that they did have a strong sense of spirituality and sensitivity seeing the Dome of the Rock as Solomon's Temple, but that's about it. As for the Holy Grail, well that is not something that enters into Judaism at all.

You get a larger attendance for classes in Kabbalah than you do for a Saturday service, and your talks on mysticism and numeric codes are very popular. What is it about these subjects that attracts people?

Throughout the generations religions were seen—and are still seen in many circles—as a set of laws: "thou shall" and "thou shall not." And it worked for many years. People were told that if they follow the laws they would go to heaven. If they didn't, then they would go to hell. Many observed religion out of fear and religion was transmitted to the masses through the context of persuasion. This approach to faith cannot truly be internalized and has been diminished through the development of science and our greater understanding of the world. It doesn't mean that people don't need faith. It just means that the mechanisms of transmission are not as effective as they used to be.

I live in Quebec, Canada, and Quebec was a Catholic province that was run by the church until forty years ago. Today there's been a turning away, in a sense. But people essentially are spiritual. They need faith. They need to be able to trust. They need something permanent in their life and they need something more than just the material world.

I think *The Da Vinci Code* is so appealing because it opened up people's eyes to the spirit of religion and the mysteries and underpinnings of all that goes on in religion. Dan Brown touched on many spiritual matters that are of much fascination to people. There's a reservoir of people that are wanting that type of spirituality; one that doesn't threaten them, one that doesn't shout at them, one that doesn't tell them that if they don't follow they are going to be damned. I think what a lot of people loved about the book is that they were not only reading a novel, they were learning about the world and about spiritual forces, and about topics like Kabbalah and the mystical tradition. All these things that are right in front of our eyes every day and we miss it.

But aren't you troubled by the way Dan Brown begins his book claiming that everything is true and then the story veers off into fact, fiction, truths, half-truths, etc?

In the teachings of Kabbalah, there is a saying that the words that you are learning can be healing for your soul or they can be poison. There is always a danger when you are entering into the unknown domain that it is possible to go off the wrong way and to misinterpret and to misunderstand.

What I find difficult about the book is that it speaks with absolute certainty. But I think it has to do that because Christianity has been speaking with near certainty for two thousand years. Perhaps the only way to get people to think is to speak with the same certainty and to create a balance.

I believe that people who are really searching won't take this book as the bible. If they have any sense of wisdom they will use it as a springboard to further their search. You hear about people reading this book and starting journeys in their life. That's a wonderful thing.

Breaking *The Da Vinci Code*

BY COLLIN HANSEN

We conclude this chapter by reminding ourselves of the "straight and narrow." The theological history depicted in *The Da Vinci Code* is stretched far, far beyond recognition and into destructive fiction, suggests Collin Hansen, an editorial resident with *Christian History* magazine with a background in both journalism and church history. What of Dan Brown's claim that all we were taught about early Christian history is false? Nonsense, says Hansen. Or the notion that somehow the New Testament was adopted by illegitimate means? Bunk as well.

Dan Brown's *The Da Vinci Code* has achieved coveted best-sellerdom, inspiring an ABC News special along the way, along with debates about the legitimacy of Western and Christian history.

While the ABC News feature focused on Brown's fascination with an alleged marriage between Jesus and Mary Magdalene, *The Da Vinci Code* contains many more (equally dubious) claims about Christianity's historic origins and theological development. The central claim Brown's novel makes about Christianity is that "almost everything our fathers taught us about Christ is false." Why? Because of a single meeting of bishops in AD 325, at the city of Nicea in modern-day Turkey. There, argues Brown, church leaders who wanted to consolidate their power base (he calls this, anachronistically, "the Vatican" or "the Roman Catholic church") created a divine Christ and an infallible Scripture—both of them novelties that had never before existed among Christians.

Brown is right that in the course of Christian history, few events loom larger than the Council of Nicea in 325. When the newly converted Roman emperor Constantine called bishops from around the world to present-day Turkey, the church had reached a theological crossroads. Led by an Alexandrian theologian named Arius, one school of thought argued that Jesus had undoubtedly been a remarkable leader, but he was not God in flesh. In *The Da Vinci Code,* Brown apparently adopts Arius as his representative for all pre-Nicene Christianity. Referring to the

Council of Nicea, Brown claims that "until that moment in history, Jesus was viewed by His followers as a mortal prophet—a great and powerful man, but a man nonetheless."

In reality, early Christians overwhelmingly worshipped Jesus Christ as their risen Savior and Lord. For example, Christians adopted the Greek word *kyrios,* meaning "divine," and applied it to Jesus from the earliest days of the church.

The Council of Nicea did not entirely end the controversy over Arius's teachings, nor did the gathering impose a foreign doctrine of Christ's divinity on the church. The participating bishops merely affirmed the historic and standard Christian beliefs, erecting a united front against future efforts to dilute Christ's gift of salvation.

With the Bible playing a central role in Christianity, the question of Scripture's historic validity bears tremendous implications. Brown claims that Constantine commissioned and bankrolled a staff to manipulate existing texts and thereby divinize the human Christ. Yet for a number of reasons, Brown's speculations fall flat. Brown correctly points out that "the Bible did not arrive by fax from heaven." Indeed, the Bible's composition and consolidation may appear a bit too human for the comfort of some Christians. But Brown overlooks the fact that the human process of canonization had progressed for centuries before Nicea, resulting in a nearly complete canon of Scripture before Nicea or even Constantine's legalization of Christianity in 313.

Ironically, the process of collecting and consolidating Scripture was launched when a rival sect produced its own quasi-biblical canon. Around 140 a Gnostic leader named Marcion began spreading a theory that the New and Old Testaments didn't share the same God. Marcion argued that the Old Testament's God represented law and wrath while the New Testament's God, represented by Christ, exemplified love. As a result Marcion rejected the Old Testament and the most overtly Jewish New Testament writings, including Matthew, Mark, Acts, and Hebrews. He manipulated other books to downplay their Jewish tendencies. Though in 144 the church in Rome declared his views heretical, Marcion's teaching sparked a new cult. Challenged by Marcion's threat, church leaders began to consider earnestly their own views on a definitive list of Scriptural books including both the Old and New Testaments.

By the time of Nicea, church leaders debated the legitimacy of only a few books that we accept today, chief among them Hebrews and Revelation, because their authorship remained in doubt. In fact, authorship was the most important consideration for those who worked to solidify the canon. Early church leaders considered letters and eyewitness accounts authoritative and binding only if they were written by an apostle or close disciple of an apostle. This way they could be assured of the documents' reliability. As pastors and preachers, they also observed which books did in fact build up the church—a good sign, they felt, that such books were inspired Scripture. The results speak for themselves: the books of today's Bible have allowed Christianity to spread, flourish, and endure worldwide.

5 Secret Societies

The secret things belong to the Lord, the things revealed are ours and our children's forever . . .

—DEUTERONOMY 29:29

Like a good spy thriller, the plot of *The Da Vinci Code* moves from one stunning secret to another—from one coded message to the next, from an ancient conspiracy to a modern one—exploring all the while some of the most fundamental secrets of the archaic past of human culture and even archaic areas of the brain itself, where primal myths and Jungian archetypes cavort and where secret fears, compulsions, and ancient traumas reside.

Dan Brown has said that Robert Ludlum is among his favorite writers, and you can see in *The Da Vinci Code* a touch of vintage Ludlum. Start with incredibly compelling, powerful secrets, throw an ordinary man (and a beautiful woman) into high-stakes action to figure out these secrets against the ticking clock of a threat to civilization, confront the characters with deep, dark secret societies no one thought still existed, bend their minds around conspiracies so intricate the reader can't ever really diagram the plot, and wrap it all into action fast-paced enough to make the reader forget the cardboard characters and the plot holes.

The role of secret societies in such plots—whether Ludlum, Le Carré, J. K. Rowling, J. R. R. Tolkien, or Dan Brown—is not to be understated. In this chapter we focus on three secret societies at work in the action of *The Da Vinci Code:* the Knights Templar, the Priory of Sion, and Opus Dei. Along the way, we consider various other secret rites and practices, from modern-day Gnostics celebrating *hieros gamos* rites in twenty-first-century New York to the plethora of secret societies that grew out of the Templar massacre in the fourteenth century.

As *The Da Vinci Code* points out, everyone loves a good conspiracy. Everyone finds it interesting to be let in on a mind-boggling secret. In the case of the three most prominent secret societies in *The Da Vinci Code*, each one is a fascinating world unto itself. The novel compresses the essence of these secret cultures into some easy-to-understand background material. But then it goes on to exaggerate greatly each one's power, influence, and history.

The Templars, for example, may have had some cultlike practices in medieval days that could be construed as sacred sex rites. Mary Magdalene may have figured more prominently in their culture than in contemporaneous Christianity. And they may well have found treasure in Jerusalem and built a nexus of power and influence. But it is extremely doubtful that they cared much for the theory of the sacred feminine or that they believed the Holy Grail had anything to do with Mary Magdalene's womb and the royal bloodline of the offspring she may or may not have had.

The Priory of Sion, while interesting to speculate about, may never have really existed as anything more than a minor political arm of the Templars during their heyday. As for the modern era, the idea of the Priory may be a complete canard in its twentieth-century incarnation. Leonardo da Vinci may well have been involved with secret sects, heretical philosophies, and unusual sexual practices—and his paintings may well have sought to pass on secret knowledge (or at least make insider jokes) to future generations. But it is highly unlikely that Leonardo served as a "grand master" of a functioning secret organization, while leaving not a single clue or bit of documentary evidence behind amid the tens of thousands of pages of notebooks he left to posterity. The same could be said about the other alleged grand masters. With all we know about the lives of Victor Hugo and Jean Cocteau, Newton and Debussy, don't you think there would be a scrap of corroborating evidence somewhere? And for an organization that is supposed to hold the sacred feminine in such high esteem (at least according to the novel), how come there are no prominent women on the list?

Opus Dei is certainly wealthy, powerful, and secretive. It may well be pledged to a religious philosophy and even a set of political goals that many find anathema. It may have a very interesting history of unexplained involvements with the CIA, the Vatican's finances, and right-wing death squads in Latin America's civil wars. But it is not dispatching albino monks to the streets of Paris to murder people over ancient religious secrets.

That is not to deny the concerns and fears some people may have about this or any other secretive group or conspiracy. Just the opposite is true: Dan Brown, like many novelists, exaggerates even to extremes and lets his imagination run wild for the express purpose of creating the right metaphors and the right thought provocations to rise above the clutter in this information- and entertainment-saturated world. His approach has had demonstrable success. He got our attention for secret societies and esoteric knowledge, which we had heard of, vaguely, but knew little about.

Welcome to the netherworld of *The Da Vinci Code*'s secret societies.

Recollections of a Gnostic Mass

By John Castro

I stand in a florescent-lit hallway, cold and apprehensive.

I'm not wearing any shoes.

A man dressed in black denim has just asked everyone gathered to remove our shoes to show respect for the temple we are about to enter. We comply. When we are finished, he asks us to wait for the ceremony to begin. While I wait, I listen. There are couples, groups of friends, people who seem to have known each other for years, greeting each other. I focus on a few conversations to pass the time.

An attractive young Hispanic woman, probably twenty-one or twenty-two, chatters on her cell phone: ". . . yeah, yeah, yeah. Three times. No, this is my third time. I'll be going minerval at the next initiation . . ."

A thin, muscular man with greased-back hair and a small goatee walks up the hall and joins the rest of us. He waits for a moment or two, spies a serious young woman with a pentacle medallion on a chain around her neck, and strikes up a conversation with her. "Ninety-three," he says.

"Ninety-three," she replies, smiling.

John Castro is a New York–based writer.

They begin talking to each other in low voices, heads bent.

"Man, I heard that *Jimmy Page* comes when he's in New York," says a heavy-metal enthusiast with a long ponytail, who appears to be in his thirties. His short, stocky friend nods with a weary nonchalance. I stand silently—I'm all alone here—and wait for admittance.

These are my recollections of a ceremony I attended in late 2002. I was an observer, and a surprisingly nervous participant, in a ritual hosted by the Ordo Templis Orientalis, an organization led for many years by Aleister Crowley. *The* Aleister Crowley—poet, magician, iconoclast, drug addict, and moral scourge of Great Britain, the esoteric magus who referred to himself as the "Great Beast 666."

Reading *The Da Vinci Code,* many of my memories of the event rose to the surface. These memories are almost two years old. I know that I missed details and may have remembered others incorrectly. Yet, like Sophie Neveu, my impressions of what I saw have remained intense and vivid.

The temple is in a small room. The walls are painted black, the room dimly lit by small scoop lamps hanging from the ceiling and dozens of candles at the base of an altar on the right side of the room. It's a large structure with three steps leading up to it and a stone slab carved with hieroglyphs at its summit. A long frame surrounds the altar, supporting an opened curtain.

Across the room from the altar is an oblong box, the height and width of a tall man, with a small curtain covering its front. Spaced at equal distances between the altar and the casket are two black boxes on the floor, each bearing an incense burner, books, and a mixing bowl.

On either side of this aisle are rows of chairs for the

congregation. We all enter slowly, awkwardly, about sixty of us in all, noisily placing our shoes, bags, and coats under our chairs.

I'm no longer cold. In fact, I'm beginning to sweat. By the time we're seated, we are packed in, the room filled to capacity, all of us feeling the heat of the candles and our fellow congregants. I am surprised by the number and variety of the worshippers—all ages, many different ethnicities, in fashions ranging from well-dressed yuppie to Dungeons and Dragons archetype.

A thin bearded man in a loose white robe stands facing the altar. He crosses himself at the forehead, chest, and shoulders; with each touch he speaks a word of what sounds like Hebrew.

He throws his arms forward, places his hands together, and begins slowly circumambulating the room with long steps. He breathes heavily, his face pinched, concentrating, staring past the walls of the temple. At four points in the room, he stops and intones a word or phrase—I can't guess what the language is—and dramatically draws the shape of a pentagram in the air.

When all four points have been inscribed with a pentagram, he faces the altar again. He recites the names of angels: Gabriel, Michael, Rafael, and Uriel . . . He crosses himself once more, turns to face the congregants, and spreads his arms wide, taking a deep breath. He holds it in, releases it slowly, then relaxes and smiles. Music, provided by a sitar player, winds its way through the dark air.

The bearded man in the white robe intones: "Do What Thou Wilt shall be the whole of the law."

The congregants respond: "Love is the Law, Love under Will."

The man recites what reminds me of a familiar element of the Catholic Mass—a list of beliefs reminiscent of the

Nicene Creed. In the middle of the creed is a line that gives me chills, although I don't know why:

> And I believe in the Serpent and the Lion, Mystery of Mystery, in His name BAPHOMET.

A woman dressed in blue and white slowly weaves her way down the aisle, eyes focused on the floor, followed by a man in black robes and a woman in white. She carries a sheathed sword at her side. She is a plump, attractive woman in her forties with dark red-brown hair. She stands before the oblong box and parts the curtain with her sword.

A stout young man steps out of the box, dressed in a white robe, bearing a long lance in front of him.

The woman sprinkles him with water that's been handed to her by one of her attendants. She then takes an incense burner on a chain and crosses it over him. They speak the whole time, the man with the lance proclaiming that he is not worthy to administer the rites, the woman enjoining him in a whispery voice to be pure in body and soul. She runs her open hands over his body, not touching him, then stands and drapes him in a red robe and places a crown on his head. He leans the lance forward, staring across at the altar.

She kneels and runs her hands up and down the shaft of the lance about a dozen times with open palms. Her air is reverent, quiet. "The Lord is among us!" she exclaims.

The congregation is now kneeling on the floor, arms in the air, hands clasped with the hands of our neighbors. A young woman with long blond hair is on my right and a balding African-American man with a salt-and-pepper beard to my left. All of the other congregants are in the same position, clasping hands. My arms begin to ache. I wonder if others are thinking of the intense pain in their arms and the ache in their backs. I long for sympathy, but find none—most of the congregants are staring at the altar or have their eyes closed in quiet worship. I try, surreptitiously, to lean against my chair, but it is fruitless; my neighbors will not sway. I try to focus on the altar instead.

The man with the lance is on the first step leading to the altar. The curtain is closed; a moment before the woman with the sword was sitting on the altar, but now she is hidden.

The man with the lance is speaking poetry to the woman behind the curtain; and after a moment, the woman responds in kind from behind the veil.

I can't focus. I'm starting to sweat, and the only thing I can think about besides the fire in my arms and back is that the perspiration from my arm, pressed against the arm of the woman to my right, is starting to dribble down her arm as well.

There's a naked woman on the altar.

We're standing again, staring up at her. The man with the lance has just parted the curtain, and there's the woman with the sword—stark naked, seated on the altar, facing us, with her legs hanging off the side. I try to take in the whole scene, but I keep averting my eyes.

A tiny voice in my head—the remnant of my Catholicism, made up of communion and confession and CCD classes every Wednesday after school—is starting to become louder, more insistent: *There's a naked woman on the altar. What the hell are you doing here?*

The man presents his lance to her. She takes it, kisses it perhaps a dozen times, and then presses it between her breasts. The man falls to his knees before her, throws his arms on the altar along the sides of her legs. Bent in adoration, he begins slowly kissing her knees and thighs.

When I was younger, I was terrified of botching communion. Which hand over which? What were the words I needed to say to the priest? I almost do it again tonight.

The congregants are filing through the rows of chairs and walking up the central aisle to the altar, where they receive the host from the naked priestess. They walk solemnly, slowly, with their arms crossed over their chests. I follow suit.

When I finally reach the altar, I focus on the naked woman's eyes; I don't want to embarrass her by staring. It doesn't matter. It's more my problem than hers, and I almost trip up the steps to the altar. Her eyes lock beatifically on mine, with a sweet look of utterly sincere welcome and comfort. It doesn't really feel like she's looking at me, which makes me feel better somehow. I take the host: sweet, chewy bread about the size of a quarter, and before I eat it, I say the same words that the other congregants have intoned, one by one:

"There is no part of me that is not of the gods."

The last part of the Mass that I remember is a poem, chanted by the congregation. It was written by Crowley, and I only remember a few lines:

> MEN: Glory to Thee from Gilded Tomb!
> WOMEN: Glory to Thee from Waiting Womb!
> MEN: Glory to Thee from earth unploughed!
> WOMEN: Glory to Thee from virgin vowed!

It was actually quite moving. The congregants knew it by heart; the semichoral effect was entrancing.

Now I am reflecting in retrospect on the connections to *The Da Vinci Code*.

There were obvious connections of subject matter: the mention of Baphomet; a link to the Knights Templar; ceremonial rituals echoing orthodox practices; deeper hints of a synthesis of many older Egyptian, Hebrew, and Greek traditions; echoes of Freemasonry and Rosicrucianism. Finally and most important, there was a willingness to place a woman at the center of the ceremony, and obvious, frank references to sexuality in the symbology of the event.

The Ordo Templis Orientalis is a secret society (although you can find a Web presence for it, including full texts of the Gnostic Mass). Like so many of the occult or esoteric societies that are mentioned in *The Da Vinci Code,* you have to be on the inside to really understand. While the trappings of the Mass might be related to the subjects in the book, I recognize that the "true" meaning of the Mass—the significance for the members themselves—is not for me to know. And it would never be, unless I joined and became a silent participant myself.

What I do know is that what I saw was a celebration of genuine belief and devotion from the congregation. When I recall my reaction to the event, I wonder: what unsettled reactions, what nervous bouts of laughter or discomfort did the first Christians inspire in Rome? And is this not always the way with every new god?

The Templar Revelation

By Lynn Picknett and Clive Prince

Lynn Picknett and Clive Prince are London-based writers, researchers, and lecturers on the paranormal, the occult, and historical and religious mysteries. Their book, *The Templar Revelation,* from which the following passage is excerpted, is one of the key books in *The Da Vinci Code's* bibliography and the original source of a number of the novel's theories about Leonardo, the Templars, and the Priory of Sion.

The names of Leonardo da Vinci and Jean Cocteau appear on the list of the Grand Masters of what claims to be one of Europe's oldest and most influential secret societies—the Prieuré de Sion, the Priory of Sion. Hugely controversial, its very existence has been called into question and therefore any of its alleged activities are frequently the subject of ridicule and their implications ignored. At first we sympathized with this kind of reaction, but our further investigations certainly revealed that the matter was not as simple as that.

The Priory of Sion first came to the attention of the English-speaking world as late as 1982, through the best-selling *The Holy Blood and the Holy Grail* by Michael Baigent, Richard Leigh and Henry Lincoln, although in its homeland of France reports of its existence gradually became public from the early 1960s. It is a quasi-Masonic or chivalric order with certain political ambitions and, it

---

seems, considerable behind-the-scenes power. Having said that, it is notoriously difficult to categorize the Priory, perhaps because there is something essentially chimerical about the whole operation. . . .

The underlying power of the Priory of Sion is at least partly due to the suggestion that its members are, and always have been, guardians of a great secret—one that, if made public, would shake the very foundations of both Church and State. The Priory of Sion, sometimes known as the Order of Sion or the Order of Our Lady of Sion as well as by other subsidiary titles, claims to have been founded in 1099, during the First Crusade—and even then this was just a matter of formalizing a group whose guardianship of this explosive knowledge already went back much further. They claimed to be behind the creation of the Knights Templar—that curious body of medieval soldier-monks of sinister reputation. The Priory and the Templars became, so it is claimed, virtually the same organization, presided over by the same Grand Master until they suffered a schism and went their separate ways in 1188. The Priory continued under the custodianship of a series of Grand Masters, including some of the most illustrious names in history such as Sir Isaac Newton, Sandro Filipepi (known as Botticelli), Robert Fludd, the English occult philosopher—and, of course, Leonardo da Vinci, who, it is alleged, presided over the Priory for the last nine years of his life. Among its more recent leaders were Victor Hugo, Claude Debussy—and the artist, writer, playwright and filmmaker Jean Cocteau. And although they were not Grand Masters, the Priory has, it is claimed, attracted other luminaries over the centuries such as Joan of Arc, Nostradamus (Michel de Notre Dame), and even Pope John XXIII.

Apart from such celebrities, the history of the Priory

of Sion allegedly involved some of the greatest royal and aristocratic families of Europe for generation after generation. These include the d'Anjous, the Habsburgs, the Sinclairs and the Montgomeries.

The reported aim of the Priory is to protect the descendants of the old Merovingian dynasty of kings in what is now France—who ruled from the fifth century until the assassination of Dagobert II in the late seventh century. But then, critics claim that the Priory of Sion has only existed since the 1950s and consists of a handful of mythomaniacs with no real power—royalists with unlimited delusions of grandeur.

So on the one hand we have the Priory's own claims for its pedigree and *raison d'être* and on the other the claim of its detractors. . . .

Any mystery connected with the Priory of Sion also involves those warrior-monks [the Templars], and so they are an intrinsic part of this investigation.

A third of all the Templars' European property was once found in the Languedoc, and its ruins only add to the savage beauty of the region. One of the more picturesque local legends has it that whenever 13 October falls on a Friday (the day and date of the Order's sudden and brutal suppression) strange lights appear in the ruins and dark figures can be seen moving among them. Unfortunately on the Fridays when we were in that area, we saw and heard nothing except the alarming snufflings of wild boars; but the story shows how much the Templars have become part of local legend.

The Templars have lived on in the memories of the local people, and those memories are by no means negative. Even in this century, the famous opera singer Emma Calvé, who came from Aveyron in the north of the Languedoc, recorded in her memoirs that the locals would say of an especially good-looking or intelligent boy, "He is a true son of the Temples."

The main facts concerning the Knights Templar are simple. Officially known as The Order of the Poor Knights of the Temple of Solomon, they were formed in 1118 by the French nobleman Hugues de Payens as knightly escorts for pilgrims to the Holy Land. Initially there were just nine of them, for the first nine years, then the Order opened up and soon it had established itself as a force to be reckoned with, not only in the Middle East, but also throughout Europe.

After the recognition of the Order, Hugues de Payens himself set out on a European trip, soliciting land and money from royalty and nobility. He visited England in 1129, when he founded the first Templar site in that country, on the site of what is now London's Holborn Underground Station.

Like all other monks, the knights were sworn to poverty, chastity and obedience but they were in the world and of it and pledged to use the sword if necessary against the enemies of Christ—and the image of the Templars became inseparably linked with the crusades that were mounted in order to drive the infidel out of Jerusalem, and to keep it Christian.

It was in 1128 that the Council of Troyes officially recognized the Templars as a religious and military order. The main protagonist behind this move was Bernard of Clairvaux, the head of the Cistercian Order, who was later canonized. But as Bamber Gascoigne writes in *The Christians:*

> He was aggressive, he was abusive . . . and he was a devious politician who was quite unscrupulous in the methods he used to bring down his enemies.

Bernard actually wrote the Templars' Rule—which was based on that of the Cistercians—and it was one of his protégés who, as Pope Innocent II, declared in 1139 that the Knights would be answerable only to the papacy from that time onwards. As both the Templars and the Cistercian Orders developed in parallel, one can discern a certain amount of deliberate co-ordination between them—for example, Hugues de Payens' lord, the Count of Champagne, donated to St Bernard the land in Clairvaux on which he built his monastic "empire." And significantly, André de Montbard, one of the nine founding knights, was Bernard's uncle. It has been suggested that the Templars and Cistercians were acting together according to a pre-arranged plan to take over Christendom, but this scheme never succeeded.

It is hard to exaggerate the prestige and financial power of the Templars when they were at the height of their influence in Europe. There was hardly a major centre of civilization where they did not have a preceptory—as, for example, the wide scatter of such place names as Temple Fortune and Temple Bar (London) and Temple Meads (Bristol) in England still shows. But as their empire spread, so their arrogance grew and began to poison their relations with both temporal and secular heads of state.

The Templars' wealth was partly a result of their Rule: all new members had to hand over their property to the Order, and they also gained a considerable fortune through massive donations of land and money from many kings and nobles. Their coffers were soon overflowing, not least because they had also amassed impressive financial astuteness, which had resulted in them becoming the first international bankers, upon whose judgement the credit ratings of others depended. It was a sure way of establishing themselves as a major power. In a short space of time their title of "Poor Knights" became a hollow sham, even though the rank and file might well have remained impecunious.

Besides their staggering wealth, the Templars were renowned for their skill and courage in battle—sometimes to the point of foolhardiness. They had specific rules to govern their conduct as fighters: for example, they were forbidden to surrender unless the odds against them were greater than three to one, and even then had to have their commander's approval. They were the Special Services of their day, an élite force with God—and money—on their side.

Despite their finest efforts, the Holy Land fell to the Saracens bit by bit until in 1291 the last Christian territory, the city of Acre, was in enemy hands. There was nothing for the Templars to do but to return to Europe and plot their eventual reconquest, but unfortunately by then the motivation for such a campaign had disappeared among the various kings who might have financed it. Their main reason for existing dwindled to nothing. Lacking employment, but still rich and arrogant, they were widely resented because they were exempt from taxation and their allegiance was to the Pope and to him alone.

So in 1307 came their inevitable fall from grace. The supremely powerful French king, Philip the Fair, began to orchestrate the downfall of the Templars with the connivance of the Pope, who was in his pocket anyway. Secret orders were issued to the king's aristocratic representatives and the Templars were rounded up on Friday 13 October 1307, arrested, tortured and burnt.

That, at least, is the story as told in most standard works on the subject. One is left with the idea that the entire Order met its horrible doom on that day long ago, and that the Templars were effectively wiped off the face of the earth forever. Yet that is nowhere near the truth.

For a start, relatively few Templars were actually executed, although most who were captured were "put to the question"—a well-worn euphemism for suffering excruciating torture. Relatively few faced the stake, although notably their Grand Master Jacques de Molay was slowly roasted to death on the Ile de la Cité, in the shadow of Notre-Dame Cathedral, in Paris. Of the thousands of others, only those who refused to confess, or recanted their confession, were killed. . . .

The accounts of Templar confessions are colourful, to say the least. We read of their having worshipped a cat or indulging in homosexual orgies as part of their knightly duties, or venerating a demon known as Baphomet and/or a severed head. They were also said to have trampled and spat upon the cross in an initiatory rite. . . .

This is hardly surprising—not many victims of torture manage to grit their teeth and refuse to agree with the words put in their mouths by their tormenters. But in this case there is more to the story than meets the eye. On the one hand, there have been suggestions that all the charges levelled against the Templars were trumped up by those envious of their wealth and exasperated by their power, and that they provided a good excuse for the French king to extricate himself from his current economic difficulty by seizing their wealth. On the other hand, although the charges may not have been strictly true, there is evidence that the Templars were up to something mysterious and perhaps "dark" in the occult sense. . . .

Much ink has been spilt on the debate over the charges made against the Templars, and their confessions. Had they actually committed the deeds to which they confessed, or did the Inquisitors invent the charges in advance and simply torture the knights until they agreed with them? (Some knights had testified that they had been told that Jesus was a "false prophet," for example.) It is impossible to say one way or the other conclusively. . . .

Certainly the Priory of Sion claims to have been the power behind the creation of the Knights Templar: if so, then this is one of the best-kept secrets of history. Yet it is said that the two Orders were virtually indistinguishable until their schism in 1188—after which they went their separate ways. If nothing else there does seem to have been some kind of conspiracy about the conception of the Templars. Common sense suggests that it would have taken more than just the original nine knights to protect and provide refuge for all the pilgrims who visited the Holy Land, especially for *nine years,* moreover, there is little evidence that they ever made much of a serious attempt to do so. . . .

Another mystery connected with their beginnings centres on the fact that there is evidence that the Order actually existed well before 1118, although why the date was falsified remains unclear. Many commentators have suggested that the first account of their creation—by William of Tyre and written a full fifty years after the event—was simply a cover story. (Although William was deeply hostile to the Templars, he was, presumably, recounting the story as he understood it.) But once again, just what it was covering up is a matter for speculation.

Hugues de Payens and his nine companions all came from either Champagne or the Languedoc . . . and it is quite apparent that they went to the Holy Land with a specific mission in mind. Perhaps, as has been suggested, they were searching for the Ark of the Covenant, or for other ancient treasure or documents that might lead them to it, or for some kind of secret knowledge which would give them mastery of people and their wealth. . . .

Holy Blood, Holy Grail

By Michael Baigent, Richard Leigh, and Henry Lincoln

Holy Blood, Holy Grail is the book that "started it all," in terms of the late twentieth century's interest in the intersecting secrets and conspiracies of the marriage of Jesus and Mary Magdalene, their supposed bloodline, the lost Gospels, the Templars, the Priory of Sion, Leonardo da Vinci, the *Dossiers Secrets,* the mystery of Rennes-le-Château and Abbé Saunière, etc. Baigent, Lincoln, and Leigh spent over ten years on their own kind of quest for the Holy Grail, delving deeply into the secretive history of early France in order to write *Holy Blood, Holy Grail,* which was published in the United Kingdom in 1982. Reading the book, one can almost see the places where Dan Brown might have highlighted something or put a Post-it on it, and said, "Aha! I've got to use that!"

However, as a number of articles in this volume point out, *Holy Blood, Holy Grail* has been seriously questioned in terms of its research, its methods, and its conclusions. Most academics with expertise in the fields the book touches upon find it either noncredible at best, or, at minimum, mistakenly supportive of the hoax that many experts believe the whole Priory of Sion to be.

Holy Blood, Holy Grail is definitely worth the reader's attention. Whether it is true or not, or how much of it might be true, we will

---

leave to each reader to judge. Let's just say Dan Brown had a good idea in weaving this fascinating material into a work of fiction.

The text that follows is just a sampling of the many fascinations to be found in the book. Much of the material is obscure and hard to follow without all the material that went before. Our aim here is to give readers a taste for this true Ur-text for *The Da Vinci Code.* If it interests you, get *Holy Blood, Holy Grail* and read the whole thing!

Granted, Guillaume [de Tyre] does provide us with certain basic information, and it is this information on which all subsequent accounts of the Templars, all explanation of their foundation, all narratives of their activities have been based. But because of Guillaume's vagueness and sketchiness, because of the time at which he was writing [1175–85], because of the dearth of documented sources, he constitutes a precarious basis on which to build a definitive picture. Guillaume's chronicles are certainly useful. But it is a mistake—and one to which many historians have succumbed—to regard them as unimpugnable and wholly accurate. Even Guillaume's dates, as Sir Steven Runciman stresses, "are confused and at times demonstrably wrong."[1]

According to Guillaume de Tyre the Order of the Poor Knights of Christ and the Temple of Solomon was founded in 1118. Its founder is said to be one Hugues de Payen, a nobleman from Champagne and vassal of the count of Champagne. One day Hugues, unsolicited, presented himself with eight comrades at the palace of Baudouin I, king of Jerusalem, whose elder brother, Godfroi de Bouillon, had captured the Holy City nineteen years earlier. Baudouin seems to have received them most cor-

1. Runciman, *History of the Crusades,* Vol. 2, p. 477.

dially, as did the patriarch of Jerusalem—the religious leader of the new kingdom and special emissary of the Pope.

The declared objective of the Templars, Guillaume de Tyre continues, was, "as far as their strength permitted, they should keep the roads and highways safe . . . with especial regard for the protection of pilgrims."[2] So worthy was this objective apparently that the king vacated an entire wing of the royal palace and placed it at the knights' disposal. And despite their declared oath of poverty the knights moved into this lavish accommodation. According to tradition their quarters were built on the foundations of the ancient temple of Solomon, and from this the fledgling order derived its name.

For nine years, Guillaume de Tyre tells us, the nine knights admitted no new candidates to their order. They were still supposed to be living in poverty—such poverty that official seals show two knights riding a single horse, implying not only brotherhood, but also a penury that precluded separate mounts. This style of seal is often regarded as the most famous and distinctive of Templar devices, descending from the first days of the order. However, it actually dates from a full century later, when the Templars were hardly poor—if, indeed, they ever were.

According to Guillaume de Tyre, writing a half century later, the Templars were established in 1118 and moved into the king's palace—presumably sallying out from there to protect pilgrims on the Holy Land's highways and byways. And yet there was at the time an official royal historian employed by the king. His name was Fulk de Chartres, and he was writing not fifty years after the or-

2. William of Tyre, *History of Deeds Done Beyond the Sea,* Vol. I, p. 525ff.

der's purported foundation, but during the very years in question. Curiously enough, Fulk de Chartres makes no mention whatever of Hugues de Payen, Hugues' companions, or anything even remotely connected with the Knights Templar. Indeed, there is a thunderous silence about Templar activities during the early days of their existence. Certainly there is no record anywhere—not even later—of their doing anything to protect pilgrims. And one cannot but wonder how so few men could hope to fulfill so mammoth a self-imposed task. Nine men to protect the pilgrims on all the thoroughfares of the Holy Land? Only nine? And *all* pilgrims? If this was their objective, one would surely expect them to welcome new recruits. Yet according to Guillaume de Tyre, they admitted no new candidates to the order for nine years.

Nonetheless, within a decade the Templars' fame seems to have spread back to Europe. Ecclesiastical authorities spoke highly of them and extolled their Christian undertaking. By 1128 or shortly thereafter, a tract lauding their virtues and qualities was issued by no less a person than Saint Bernard, abbot of Clairvaux and the age's chief spokesman for Christendom. Bernard's tract, "In Praise of the New Knighthood," declares the Templars to be the epitome and apotheosis of Christian values.

After nine years, in 1127, most of the nine knights returned to Europe and a triumphal welcome, orchestrated in large part by Saint Bernard. In January 1128 a Church council was convened at Troyes—court of the count of Champagne, Hugues de Payen's liege lord—at which Bernard was again the guiding spirit. At this council the Templars were officially recognized and incorporated as a religious-military order. Hugues de Payen was given the title of grand master. He and his subordinates were to be warrior-monks, soldier-mystics, combining the austere discipline of the cloister with a martial zeal tantamount to fanaticism—a "militia of Christ" as they were called at the time. And it was again Saint Bernard who helped to draw up, with an enthusiastic preface, the rule of conduct to which the knights would adhere—a rule based on that of the Cistercian monastic order, in which Bernard himself was a dominant influence.

The Templars were sworn to poverty, chastity, and obedience. They were obliged to cut their hair but forbidden to cut their beards, thus distinguishing themselves in an age when most men were cleanshaven. Diet, dress, and other aspects of daily life were stringently regulated in accordance with both monastic and military routines. All members of the order were obliged to wear white habits of surcoats and cloaks, and these soon evolved into the distinctive white mantle for which the Templars became famous. "It is granted to none to wear white habits, or to have white mantles, excepting the . . . Knights of Christ."[3] So stated the order's rule, which elaborated on the symbolic significance of this apparel: "To all the professed knights, both in winter and summer, we give, if they can be procured, white garments, that those who have cast behind them a dark life may know that they are to commend themselves to their creator by a pure and white life."[4]

In addition to these details the rule established a loose administrative hierarchy and apparatus. And behavior on the battlefield was strictly controlled. If captured, for instance, Templars were not allowed to ask for mercy or to ransom themselves; they were compelled to fight to the

3. Addison, *History of the Knights Templars*, p. 19.

4. Ibid.

death. Nor were they permitted to retreat unless the odds against them exceeded three to one.

In 1139, a papal bull was issued by Pope Innocent II—a former Cistercian monk at Clairvaux and protégé of Saint Bernard. According to this bull the Templars would owe allegiance to no secular or ecclesiastical power other than the Pope himself. In other words, they were rendered totally independent of all kings, princes, and prelates, and of all interference from both political and religious authorities. They had become, in effect, a law unto themselves, an autonomous international empire.

During the two decades following the Council of Troyes the order expanded with extraordinary rapidity and on an extraordinary scale. When Hugues de Payen visited England in late 1128, he was received with "great worship" by King Henry I. Throughout Europe younger sons of noble families flocked to enroll in the order's ranks, and vast donations—in money, goods, and land—were made from every quarter of Christendom. Hugues de Payen donated his own properties, and all new recruits were obliged to do likewise. On admission to the order a man was compelled to sign over all his possessions . . .

. . . Many of their [the Templars'] contemporaries shunned them, believing them to be in league with unclean powers. As early as 1208, at the beginning of the Albigensian Crusade, Pope Innocent III had admonished the Templars for unChristian behavior and referred explicitly to necromancy. On the other hand, there were individuals who praised them with extravagant enthusiasm. In the late twelfth century Wolfram von Eschenbach, greatest of medieval *minnesingers* or *romanciers,* paid a special visit to *Outremer* to witness the order in action. And when, be-

5. Wolfram von Eschenbach, *Parzival,* p. 251.

tween 1195 and 1220, Wolfram composed his epic romance *Parzival,* he conferred on the Templars a most exalted status. In Wolfram's poem the knights who guard the Holy Grail, the Grail castle, and the Grail family are Templars.[5]

After the Temple's demise, the mystique surrounding it persisted. The final recorded act in the order's history had been the burning of the last grand master, Jacques de Molay, in March 1314. As the smoke from the slow fire choked the life from his body, Jacques de Molay is said to have issued an imprecation from the flames. According to tradition he called his persecutors—Pope Clement and King Philippe—to join him and account for themselves before the court of God within the year. Within a month Pope Clement was dead, supposedly from a sudden onslaught of dysentery. By the end of the year Philippe was dead as well, from causes that remain obscure to this day. There is, of course, no need to look for supernatural explanations. The Templars possessed great expertise in the use of poisons. And there were certainly enough people about—refugee knights traveling incognito, sympathizers of the order, or relatives of persecuted brethren—to exact the appropriate vengeance. Nevertheless, the apparent fulfillment of the grand master's curse lent credence to belief in the order's occult powers. Nor did the curse end there. According to legend it was to cast a pall over the French royal line far into the future. And thus echoes of the Templars' supposed mystic power reverberated down the centuries.

By the eighteenth century various secret and semisecret confraternities were lauding the Templars as both precursors and mystical initiates. Many Freemasons of the period appropriated the Templars as their own antecedents. Certain Masonic "rites" or "observances" claimed direct lineal descent from the order as well as authorized custody of its arcane secrets. Some of these claims were patently preposterous. Others—resting, for example, on the order's possible survival in Scotland—may well have a core of validity, even if the attendant trappings are spurious.

By 1789 the legends surrounding the Templars had attained positively mythic proportions and their historical reality was obscured by an aura of obfuscation and romance. Knights Templar were regarded as occult adepts, illumined alchemists, magi and sages, master masons, and high initiates—veritable supermen endowed with an awesome arsenal of arcane power and knowledge. They were also regarded as heroes and martyrs, harbingers of the anticlerical spirit of the age; and many French Freemasons, in conspiring against Louis XVI, felt they were helping to implement Jacques de Molay's dying curse on the French line. When the king's head fell beneath the guillotine, an unknown man is reported to have leaped onto the scaffold. He dipped his hand in the monarch's blood, flung it out over the surrounding throng and cried, "Jacques de Molay, thou art avenged!"

Since the French Revolution the aura surrounding the Templars has not diminished. At least three contemporary organizations today call themselves Templars, claiming to possess a pedigree from 1314 and characters whose authenticity has never been established. Certain Masonic lodges have adopted the grade of "Templar" as well as rituals and appellations supposedly descended from the original order. Toward the end of the nineteenth century a sinister Order of the New Templars was established in Germany and Austria, employing the swastika as one of its emblems. Figures like H. P. Blavatsky, founder of Theosophy, and Rudolf Steiner, founder of Anthroposophy, spoke of an esoteric "wisdom tradition" running back through the Rosicrucians to the Cathars and Templars—who were purportedly repositories of more ancient secrets still. . . .

Of all the privately published documents deposited in the Bibliothèque Nationale, the most important is a compilation of papers entitled collectively *Dossiers secrets (Secret Dossiers).* Catalogued under Number 4∞ lm1 249, this compilation is now on microfiche. Until recently, however, it comprised a thin, nondescript volume, a species of folder with stiff covers that contained a loose assemblage of ostensibly unrelated items—news clippings, letters pasted to backing sheets, pamphlets, numerous genealogical trees, and the odd printed page apparently extracted from the body of some other work. Periodically some of the individual pages would be removed. At different times other pages would be freshly inserted. On certain pages additions and corrections would sometimes be made in a minuscule longhand. At a later date these pages would be replaced by new ones, printed and incorporating all previous emendations.

The bulk of the *Dossiers,* which consist of genealogical trees, is ascribed to one Henri Lobineau, whose name appears on the title page. Two additional items in the folder declare that Henri Lobineau is yet another pseudonym—derived perhaps from a street, the rue Lobineau, which runs outside Saint Sulpice in Paris—and that the genealogies are actually the work of a man named Leo Schidlof, an Austrian historian and antiquarian who purportedly lived in Switzerland and died in 1966. On the basis of this information we undertook to learn what we could about Leo Schidlof.

In 1978 we managed to locate Leo Schidlof's daughter, who was living in England. Her father, she said, was indeed Austrian. He was not a genealogist, a historian, or an antiquarian, however, but an expert and dealer in miniatures who had written two works on the subject. In 1948 he had settled in London, where he lived until his death in Vienna in 1966—the year and place specified in the *Dossiers secrets.*

Miss Schidlof vehemently maintained that her father had never had any interest in genealogies, the Merovingian dynasty, or mysterious goings-on in the south of France. And yet, she continued, certain people obviously believed he had. During the 1960s, for example, he had received numerous letters and telephone calls from unidentified individuals in both Europe and the United States who wished to meet with him and discuss matters of which he had no knowledge whatever. On his death in 1966 there was another barrage of messages, most of them inquiring about his papers.

Whatever the affair in which Miss Schidlof's father had become unwittingly embroiled, it seemed to have struck a sensitive chord with the American government. In 1946—a decade before the *Dossiers secrets* are said to have been compiled—Leo Schidlof applied for a visa to enter the United States. The application was refused on grounds of suspected espionage or some other form of clandestine activity. Eventually the matter seems to have been sorted out, the visa issued, and Leo Schidlof was admitted to the States. It may all have been a typical bureaucratic mix-up. But Miss Schidlof seemed to suspect that it was somehow connected with the arcane preoccupations so perplexingly ascribed to her father.

Miss Schidlof's story gave us pause. The refusal of an American visa might well have been more than coincidental, for there were among the papers in the *Dossiers secrets* references that linked the name Leo Schidlof with some sort of international espionage. In the meantime, however, a new pamphlet had appeared in Paris—which, during the months that followed, was confirmed by other sources. According to this pamphlet the elusive Henri Lobineau was not Leo Schidlof after all, but a French aristocrat of distinguished lineage, Comte Henri de Lénoncourt.

The question of Lobineau's real identity was not the only enigma associated with the *Dossiers secrets.* There was also an item that referred to "Leo Schidlof's leather briefcase." This briefcase supposedly contained a number of secret papers relating to Rennes-le-Château between 1600 and 1800. Shortly after Schidlof's death the briefcase was said to have passed into the hands of a courier, a certain Fakhar ul Islam—who, in February 1967, was to rendezvous in East Germany with an "agent delegated by Geneva" and entrust it to him. Before the transaction could be effected, however, Fakhar ul Islam was reportedly expelled from East Germany and returned to Paris "to await further orders." On February 20, 1967, his body was found on the railway tracks at Melun, having been hurled from the Paris-Geneva express. The briefcase had supposedly vanished.

We set out to check this lurid story as far as we could. A series of articles in French newspapers of February 21 did confirm most of it.[6] A decapitated body had indeed been found on the tracks at Melun. It was identified as that of a young Pakistani named Fakhar al-Islam. For reasons that remained obscure the dead man had been expelled from East Germany and was traveling from Paris to Geneva—engaged, it appeared, in some form of espionage. According to the newspaper reports the authori-

6. *Le Monde* (Feb. 21, 1967), p. 11; *Le Monde* (Feb. 22, 1967), p. 11; *Paris-Jour* (Feb. 21, 1967), no. 2315, p. 4.

ties suspected foul play and the affair was being investigated by the DST (Directory of Territorial Surveillance, or Counterespionage).

On the other hand, the newspapers made no mention of Leo Schidlof, a leather briefcase, or anything else that might connect the occurrence with the mystery of Rennes-le-Château. As a result we found ourselves confronted with a number of questions. On the one hand, it was possible that Fakhar ul Islam's death was linked with Rennes-le-Château—that the item in the *Dossiers secrets* in fact drew upon "inside information" inaccessible to the newspapers. On the other hand the item in the *Dossiers secrets* might have been deliberate and spurious mystification. One need only find any unexplained or suspicious death and ascribe it, after the fact, to one's own hobby horse. But if this were indeed the case, what was the purpose of the exercise? Why should someone deliberately try to create an atmosphere of sinister intrigue around Rennes-le-Château? What might be gained by the creation of such an atmosphere? And who might gain from it?

These questions perplexed us all the more because Fakhar ul Islam's death was not, apparently, an isolated occurrence. Less than a month later another privately printed work was deposited in the Bibliothèque Nationale. It was called *Le Serpent rouge (The Red Serpent)* and dated, symbolically and significantly enough, January 17. Its title page ascribed it to three authors—Pierre Feugère, Louis Saint-Maxent, and Gaston de Koker.

Le Serpent rouge is a singular work. It contains one Merovingian genealogy and two maps of France in Merovingian times, along with a cursory commentary. It also contains a ground plan of Saint Sulpice in Paris, which delineates the chapels of the church's various saints. But the bulk of the text consists of thirteen short prose poems of impressive literary quality—many of them reminiscent of the work of Rimbaud. Each of these prose poems is no more than a paragraph long, and each corresponds to a sign of the zodiac—a zodiac of thirteen signs, with the thirteenth, Ophiuchus or the Serpent Holder, inserted between Scorpio and Sagittarius.

Narrated in the first person, the thirteen prose poems are a type of symbolic or allegorical pilgrimage, commencing with Aquarius and ending with Capricorn—which, as the text explicitly states, presides over January 17. In the otherwise cryptic text there are familiar references—to the Blanchefort family, to the decorations in the church as Rennes-le-Château, to some of Saunière's inscriptions there, to Poussin and the painting of *Les Bergers d'Arcadie,* to the motto on the tomb: "Et in Arcadia Ego." At one point there is mention of a red snake, "cited in the parchments," uncoiling across the centuries—an explicit allusion, it would seem, to a bloodline or a lineage. And for the astrological sign of Leo there is an enigmatic paragraph worth quoting in its entirety:

> From she whom I desire to liberate, there wafts towards me the fragrance of the perfume which impregnates the Sepulchre. Formerly, some named her isis, queen of all sources benevolent. come unto me all ye who suffer and are afflicted and i shall give ye rest. To others, she is magdalene, of the celebrated vase filled with healing balm. The initiated know her true name: notre dame des cross.[7]

The implications of this paragraph are extremely interesting. Isis, of course, is the Egyptian mother goddess, patroness of mysteries—the "White Queen" in her

7. FeugËre, Saint-Maxent, and Koker, *Le Serpent rouge,* p. 4.

benevolent aspects, the "Black Queen" in her malevolent ones. Numerous writers on mythology, anthropology, psychology, and theology have traced the cult of the mother goddess from pagan times to the Christian epoch. And according to these writers she is said to have survived under Christianity in the guise of the Virgin Mary—the Queen of Heaven, as Saint Bernard called her, a designation applied in the Old Testament to the mother goddess Astarte, the Phoenician equivalent of Isis. But according to the text in *Le Serpent rouge* the mother goddess of Christianity would not appear to be the Virgin. On the contrary, she would appear to be the Magdalen—to whom the church at Rennes-le-Château is dedicated and to whom Saunière consecrated his tower. . . .

The Grand Masters and the Underground Stream

In the *Dossiers secrets* the following individuals are listed as successive grand masters of the Prieuré de Sion—or, to use the official term, *Nautonnier,* an old French word that means "navigator" or "helmsman":

Jean de Gisors	1188–1220
Marie de Saint-Clair	1220–1266
Guillaume de Gisors	1266–1307
Edouard de Bar	1307–1336
Jeanne de Bar	1336–1351
Jean de Saint-Clair	1351–1366
Blanche d'Evreux	1366–1398
Nicolas Flamel	1398–1418
René d'Anjou	1418–1480
Iolande de Bar	1480–1483
Sandro Filipepi	1483–1510
Leonardo da Vinci	1510–1519

Connétable de Bourbon	1519–1527
Ferdinand de Gonzague	1527–1575
Louis de Nevers	1575–1595
Robert Fludd	1595–1637
J. Valentin Andrea	1637–1654
Robert Boyle	1654–1691
Isaac Newton	1691–1727
Charles Radclyffe	1727–1746
Charles de Lorraine	1746–1780
Maximilian de Lorraine	1780–1801
Charles Nodier	1801–1844
Victor Hugo	1844–1885
Claude Debussy	1885–1918
Jean Cocteau	1918–[8]

When we first saw this list, it immediately provoked our skepticism. On the one hand it includes a number of names which one would automatically expect to find on such a list—names of famous individuals associated with the "occult" and "esoteric." On the other hand it includes a number of illustrious and improbable names—individuals whom, in certain cases, we could not imagine presiding over a secret society. At the same time many of these latter names are precisely the kind that twentieth-century organizations have often attempted to appropriate for themselves, thus establishing a species of spurious "pedigree." There are, for example, lists published by amorc, the modern "Rosicrucians" based in California, which include virtually every important figure in Western history and culture whose values, even if only tangentially, happened to coincide with the order's own. An often haphazard overlap or convergence of attitudes is misconstrued

8. Henri Lobineau, *Dossiers secrets,* planche no. 4, Ordre de Sion.

as something tantamount to "initiated membership." And thus one is told that Dante, Shakespeare, Goethe, and innumerable others were "Rosicrucians"—implying that they were card-carrying members who paid their dues regularly.

Our initial attitude toward the above list was equally cynical. Again, there are the predictable names—names associated with the "occult" and "esoteric." Nicolas Flamel, for instance, is perhaps the most famous and well-documented of medieval alchemists. Robert Fludd, seventeenth-century philosopher, was an exponent of Hermetic thought and other arcane subjects. Johann Valentin Andrea, German contemporary of Fludd, composed, among other things, some of the works that spawned the myth of the fabulous Christian Rosenkreuz. And there are also names like Leonardo da Vinci and Sandro Filipepi, who is better known as Botticelli. There are names of distinguished scientists, like Robert Boyle and Sir Issac Newton. During the last two centuries the Prieuré de Sion's grand masters alleged to have included such important literary and cultural figures as Victor Hugo, Claude Debussy, and Jean Cocteau.

By including such names the list in the *Dossiers secrets* could not but appear suspect. It was almost inconceivable that some of the individuals cited had presided over a secret society—still more, a secret society devoted to "occult" and "esoteric" interests. Boyle and Newton, for example, are hardly names that people in the twentieth century associate with the "occult" and "esoteric." And though Hugo, Debussy, and Cocteau were immersed in such matters, they would seem to be too well known, too well researched and documented, to have exercised a "grand mastership" over a secret order. Not, at any rate, without some word of it somehow leaking out.

On the other hand, the distinguished names are not the only names on the list. Most of the other names belong to high-ranking European nobles, many of whom are extremely obscure—unfamiliar not only to the general reader, but even to the professional historian. There is Guillaume de Gisors, for instance, who in 1306 is said to have organized the Prieuré de Sion into an "Hermetic Freemasonry." And there is Guillaume's grandfather, Jean de Gisors, who is said to have been Sion's first independent grand master, assuming his position after the "cutting of the elm" and the separation from the Temple in 1188. There is no question that Jean de Gisors existed historically. He was born in 1133 and died in 1220. He is mentioned in charters and was at least nominal lord of the famous fortress in Normandy where meetings traditionally convened between English and French kings took place [sic], as did the cutting of the elm in 1188. Jean seems to have been an extremely powerful and wealthy landowner and, until 1193, a vassal of the king of England. He is also known to have possessed property in England, in Sussex, and the manor of Titchfield in Hampshire.[9] According to the *Dossiers secrets,* he met Thomas à Becket at Gisors in 1169—though there is no indication of the purpose of this meeting. We were able to confirm that Becket was indeed at Gisors in 1169,[10] and it is therefore probable that he had some contact with the lord of the fortress; but we could find no record of any actual encounter between the two men.

In short, Jean de Gisors, apart from a few bland details, proved virtually untraceable. He seemed to have left no

---

9. Loyd, *Origins of Anglo-Norman Families,* p. 45ff. And Powicke, *Loss of Normandy,* p. 340.

10. Roger de Hoveden, *Annals,* Vol. I, p. 322.

mark whatever on history, save his existence and his title. We could find no indication of what he did—what might have constituted his claim to fame or have warranted his assumption of Sion's grand mastership. If the list of Sion's purported grand masters was authentic, what, we wondered, did Jean do to earn his place on it? And if the list were a latter-day fabrication, why should someone so obscure be included at all?

There seemed to us only one possible explanation, which did not really explain very much in fact. Like the other aristocratic names on the list of Sion's grand masters, Jean de Gisors appeared in the complicated genealogies that figured elsewhere in the "Prieuré documents." Together with those other elusive nobles he apparently belonged to the same dense forest of family trees—ultimately descended, supposedly, from the Merovingian dynasty. It thus seemed evident to us that the Prieuré de Sion—to a significant extent at least—was a domestic affair. In some way the order appeared to be intimately associated with a bloodline and a lineage. And it was their connection with this bloodline or lineage that perhaps accounted for the various titled names on the list of grand masters.

From the list quoted above it would seem that Sion's grand mastership has recurrently shifted between two essentially distinct groups of individuals. On the one hand, there are the figures of monumental stature who—through esoterica, the arts, or the sciences—have produced some impact on Western tradition, history, and culture. On the other hand, there are members of a specific and interlinked network of families—noble and sometimes royal. In some degree this curious juxtaposition imparted plausibility to the list. If one merely wished to "concoct a pedigree," there would be no point in including so many unknown or long-forgotten aristocrats. There would be no point, for instance, in including a man like Charles de Lorraine—Austrian field marshal in the eighteenth century, brother-in-law to the Empress Maria Theresa, who proved himself signally inept on the battlefield and was trounced in one engagement after another by Frederick the Great of Prussia.

In this respect, at least, the Prieuré de Sion would seem to be both modest and realistic. It does not claim to have functioned under the auspices of unqualified geniuses, superhuman "masters," illumined "initiates," saints, sages, or immortals. On the contrary, it acknowledges its grand masters to have been fallible human beings, a representative cross section of humanity—a few geniuses, a few notables, a few "average specimens," a few nonentities, even a few fools.

Why, we could not but wonder, would a forged or fabricated list include such a spectrum? If one wishes to contrive a list of grand masters, why not make all the names on it illustrious? If one wishes to concoct a pedigree that includes Leonardo, Newton, and Victor Hugo, why not also include Dante, Michelangelo, Goethe, and Tolstoi—instead of obscure people like Edouard de Bar and Maximilian de Lorraine? Why, moreover, were there so many "lesser lights" on the list? Why a relatively minor writer like Charles Nodier, rather than contemporaries like Byron or Pushkin? Why an apparent "eccentric" like Cocteau rather than men of such international prestige as André Gide or Albert Camus? And why the omission of individuals like Poussin, whose connection with the mystery had already been established? Such questions nagged at us and argued that the list warranted some consideration before we dismissed it as an arrant fraud.

We therefore embarked on a lengthy and detailed study of the grand masters—their biographies, activities, and accomplishments. In conducting this study we tried, as far as we could, to subject each name on the list to certain critical questions:

1) Was there any personal contact, direct or indirect, between each alleged grand master, his immediate predecessor, and his immediate successor?
2) Was there any affiliation, by blood or otherwise, between each alleged grand master and the families who figured in the genealogies of the "Prieuré documents"—with any of the families of purported Merovingian descent, and especially the ducal house of Lorraine?
3) Was each alleged grand master in any way connected with Rennes-le-Château, Gisors, Stenay, Saint Sulpice, or any of the other sites that had recurred in the course of our previous investigation?
4) If Sion defined itself as a "Hermetic Freemasonry," did each alleged grand master display a predisposition toward Hermetic thought or an involvement with secret societies?

Although information on the alleged grand masters before 1400 was difficult, sometimes impossible to obtain, our investigation of the later figures produced some astonishing results and consistency. Many of them were associated, in one way or another, with one or more of the sites that seemed to be relevant—Rennes-le-Château, Gisors, Stenay, or Saint Sulpice. Most of the names on the list were either allied by blood to the house of Lorraine or associated with it in some other fashion; even Robert Fludd, for example, served as tutor to the sons of Henry of Lorraine. From Nicolas Flamel on, every name on the list, without exception, was steeped in Hermetic thought and often also associated with secret societies—even men whom one would not readily associate with such things, like Boyle and Newton. And with only one exception each alleged grand master had some contact—sometimes direct, sometimes through close mutual friends—with those who preceded and succeeded him. . . .

The Opus Dei Debate

Pulling his shades, he stripped naked and knelt in the center of his room. Looking down, he examined the spiked cilice belt clamped around his thigh. All true followers of The Way wore this device . . .

—The Da Vinci Code

Some Opus Dei members make limited use of the cilice and discipline, types of mortification that have always had a place in the Catholic tradition because of their symbolic reference to Christ's Passion . . . [and] it simply is not possible to injure oneself with them as the novel depicts. Moreover, their use is motivated by love of God and desire to unite oneself with Jesus Christ, not guilt, self-hatred, or self-punishment.

—Statement by Opus Dei

In some ways, the real villain of *The Da Vinci Code* is not Sir

Leigh Teabing, or even the murderous albino monk, Silas—any more than the real hero is Robert Langdon, or Sophie Neveu. Instead, the "enemy" is Opus Dei, representing the constrictive worship of a single man, Jesus, while the hero is the symbolic union of male and female—the holy grail of "sacred marriage."

In targeting Opus Dei, Brown chose a villain that is in fact a secret society, one which the public knows little about, other than to be generally mistrustful of it. Opus Dei often appears to outsiders as some kind of strange cult, conspiring under the cover of the church, God, and Jesus. Without a doubt, it is the most controversial Catholic organization in the world. Founded in Spain in 1928 by Saint Josemaria Escrivá, Opus Dei is quite small, with only 85,000 members worldwide. "In terms of influence, however, it is enormous," writes Craig Offman in "Thank You, Lord, May I Have Another?" a questioning look at the organization. "The group has accumulated billions of dollars in assets," adds Offman, "and has converted many public figures." Among those tied to Opus Dei are a series of influential judges and senators, including Antonin Scalia, Clarence Thomas, Robert Bork, and Republican senators Rick Santorum and Sam Brownback. Opus Dei points out that many of these individuals are not members.

Opus Dei disputes the negative image of it painted by *The Da Vinci Code* and critics like Offman. It sees itself as a defender of the true faith against the corruption of modern life, and in no way cultlike. It is a profound religious institution, its members say, which "condemns immoral behavior, including murder, lying, stealing, and generally injuring people. . . . Its spiritual education and counseling help members to be more ethical rather than less so."

Yet its critics, even within the mainstream Catholic

Church, persist in their concern, if not fear. "It is a powerful, even dangerous, cultlike organization that uses secrecy and manipulation to advance its agenda," wrote Father James Martin, SJ, in his article analyzing Opus Dei in the national Catholic magazine *America*. What makes it even more powerful is that it is the only Catholic organization designated a "personal prelature" of the pope—which means that it has a direct pipeline into the Vatican and is not subject to the normal archdiocese structure that is second nature to most Catholics.

The list of questions about Opus Dei is a long one. Perhaps the most comprehensive exploration of it appears in *Opus Dei,* a new book by John L. Allen Jr., the highly respected Vatican analyst for CNN, as well as the Vatican correspondent for the *National Catholic Reporter.* Among the questions listed by Allen that are typically asked about the organization are "Is it true that men and women are segregated, and if so, why? Did Opus Dei bail out the Vatican Bank? Do members whip themselves and, if so, why? Is Opus Dei a secret society? Is Opus Dei a right-wing political force? Does Opus Dei intentionally target young and impressionable recruits?" Allen, who was given access by Opus Dei to its centers, devotes considerable space in his book to examining each one, as even-handedly as possible.

And yet, both in Allen's book and in the two perspectives we offer here, clear answers may remain in the eye of the beholder. Escrivá, Opus Dei's, founder, is a saint and revered by many. But to his critics, writes Allen, he was "vain, often controlling, and somewhat paranoid, with an explosive temper." Allen found that the women with whom he spoke see their segregation, as well their traditional duties of cooking and cleaning, as a way of serving God. Still, Allen writes, "There is admittedly something strange about an organization in the twenty-first century that would have a whole class of members devoted to domestic service, and that this class would be composed exclusively of women." Then there are the recent scandals that have added to Opus Dei's image problem, including the unmasking of Opus Dei member Robert Hanssen as a double agent.

So what does Opus Dei make of all of this criticism? To judge from Fr. C. John McClosky III, the head of the Catholic Information Center who is cited in Craig Offman's article, Opus Dei is a bulwark against the storm of secularism. "When you see contraception, abortion, divorce, pornography, active homosexuality from a Catholic point of view, they are deadly," McClosky told Offman. "They cause enormous harm to souls who are involved in any of those activities, and also to a culture."

We conclude this section on Opus Dei with the organization's own rebuttal to Dan Brown's book in a "frequently asked questions" format. Any claims about its strange, much less villainous ways are completely unfounded, maintains Opus Dei. The organization believes its mission is to do good works, and has no idea why it is so often targeted for criticism as conspiratorial, cultlike, violent, masochistic, or power-seeking.

Craig Offman is a frequent contributor to the *Financial Times,* and has also written feature articles for *Salon, Wired,* and *Time.* This article originally appeared in the December 2003 issue of *GQ.* Used by permission.

Thank You Lord, May I Have Another?

By Craig Offman

Pope John Paul II left three major legacies: He helped remove the Communists from power in Eastern Europe, mended relations with the Jewish community and, closer to home, granted unparalleled power to the orthodox lay organization known as Opus Dei. Not since the Jesuits were founded five centuries ago has the Vatican seen such controversy over a new group, and the pope, a conservative, has been one of its most tireless advocates. Founded by the Spanish priest Josemaria Escrivá de Balaguer y Albas in 1928, this young and wealthy group has a modern message with a fierce traditional spin: Sanctify your everyday life and you can be a saint.

Opus Dei is small, with only 85,000 members worldwide. In terms of influence, however, it is enormous. The group has accumulated billions of dollars in assets and has converted many public figures. Most important, Opus Dei has enjoyed access to the pope, who in 1982 granted it the status of "personal prelature." This means that, unlike any other Catholic group, Opus Dei doesn't have to report to the local archbishop. A floating diocese, it answers only to the Vatican.

To critics, Opus Dei represents an elitist, radical and cultish group that deliberately cultivates an aura of mystery. Its lavish centers and residences located in posh neighborhoods across the world seldom identify themselves as Catholic or even religious. No outsider knows the sources of its immense wealth. Members rarely announce themselves as such. They keep their internal publications under lock and key. They even have a secret greeting: *Pax, in aeternum*. They have their own vernacular. And then there is their long flirtation with fascism to consider. In Europe and Latin America, where Opus Dei's presence is stronger than in the United States, Catholics with long memories cite the fact that several Opus Dei members served in various juntas, from Franco's in Spain to Pinochet's in Chile.

In the United States, Opus Dei is still relatively tiny, with only 3,000 members. But for a group that could barely fill a high school auditorium, it has considerable cultural clout. Some of the country's best-known conservatives have been pegged as Opus Dei sympathizers or friends: Antonin Scalia, Clarence Thomas, Robert Bork, Republican senators Rick Santorum and Sam Brownback, former Information Awarenesss Office director John M. Poindexter, and TV pundits Lawrence Kudlow and Robert Novak.

Many Americans first heard about the Work when they picked up the best-selling thriller *The Da Vinci Code* or when they came across the group's name after FBI mole and Opus Dei member Robert Hanssen was arrested in 2001 for selling secrets to the Russians. Late last year, another follower, Tyco counsel Mark Belnick, gave the Work a black eye when he was charged with embezzling millions. Though he was eventually acquitted, his connection to the group remained the focus of intense speculation.

Responding to recent controversies, Opus Dei is trying to improve its image. In 2002 it opened a $47 million, seventeen-story national headquarters in the middle of Manhattan, and to some people's surprise, journalists are allowed inside. The building has separate entrances for men and women, and segregated parking. Inside, it's all mahogany and marble, with six dinning rooms, six opulent chapels, and numerous bedrooms and living rooms. Massive wooden bookcases line almost every wall, and

Sharon Clasen has a small voice and apologizes too much. She's not someone you'd think would pick a fight with a group like Opus Dei. But those people made her suffer. It's been years since she left the group and she's still suffering. Still wounded. Still angry. They threatened her with hell. She had to confront them. Make them answer to her for once. For a long time after she left, Sharon didn't talk about Opus Dei. If she'd learned one thing in her six years in the church, it was this: You never air the group's dirty laundry. Opus Dei is too powerful—entrenched in the media, the government, the Supreme Court. The group could make life hard for you. But Sharon had no job to risk. Opus Dei couldn't take away her kids. So she posted her memoir online: "My Nightmarish Experience in Opus Dei." Expecting the worst, expecting catharsis. Neither came.

Sharon first encountered Opus Dei—or "met the Work," as members say—when she was a freshman at Boston College in 1981. Yeah, looking back, she was probably a little gullible, a little earnest, looking for direction. Opus Dei offered her a room at Bayridge, their lavish single-sex residence designed by Louis Comfort Tiffany, on leafy Commonwealth Avenue. Rent was reasonable, religious supervision free. She decided to try it.

In no time, Sharon's devotion to the group was fierce. After three years, a senior member pulled Sharon aside and told her that God had "chosen" her. She could be a core member. Sharon jumped at the chance and became what is known as a "numerary." A nun, just about. She made commitments to chastity and to poverty. She didn't have to wear a habit, but she couldn't wear pants either. Her spiritual director came by and tossed out things she thought Sharon didn't need.

(*continues*)

(*continued*)

There were so many obligations. For two hours each day, Sharon had to wear a cilice—a barbed thigh chain that left puncture marks in her skin. Once a week, she submitted to the "discipline"—a long, macramé-like rope she used to whip herself. She took cold showers, slept on bed boards, and went without a pillow once a week. She wasn't supposed to see her family. Opus Dei was her family now, she was told. No outside friendships. No photos of anybody but Josemaria Escrivá, the name that members called "the Founder." Or "the Father." Like he was God.

Sharon had no money of her own. She was required to turn over her will and all her paychecks to the Work. Even presents had to be relinquished.

Things came to a head about the time when her spiritual director forbade her to go to her best friend's wedding. Sharon snapped. This was against her conscience, her closest friends, her better judgment. Enough already. She was in the wedding party. She went all right, and had a great time too. And afterward she realized that she didn't want to be married to God anymore. She wanted to marry a man, have a family. She wanted out. But what would happen to her soul? Opus Dei told her that God was calling her and that she had made a commitment to Him for life:

the shelves are cluttered with donkeys, the Founder's favorite animal. There are small photos of the Founder—and of almost no one else—everywhere. Opus Dei wants to make this center a religious sanctum for holy Catholics with day jobs.

But even the most sympathetic journalists can't undo the PR damage caused by Dan Brown's *The Da Vinci Code,*

Leave Opus Dei and you're abandoning God. You're paving your own path to damnation.

She wrote a letter to the Opus Dei leadership and asked permission to leave.

Four months later, she was free. She moved out and got a place of her own. Got a new job. One night during that time, she was coming out of work and her spiritual director was there. Just standing outside the building, waiting for her. The spiritual director wasn't menacing or rude, but Sharon told her to get lost. Undeterred, the director followed her into the North Station subway. So many questions: What was Sharon doing about her daily rituals? Was she still praying? Would she reconsider Opus Dei? Sharon couldn't shake her. She told her she had an interview and had to get off at the next stop. The director followed her out onto the platform, uttering words that have tortured Sharon ever since.

"I'm worried about the salvation of your soul," the director said.

"Are you saying that I'm going to hell?" Sharon asked.

The director didn't say anything. Sharon asked her again, this time at the top of her lungs. "Are you telling me that I'm going to hell?"

Sixteen years later, she still doesn't know.

—CRAIG OFFMAN

in which the Work is depicted as a stealthy, unswervingly loyal and murderous extension of the Vatican—in effect, the pope's secret police. The film version, directed by Ron Howard, is expected to minimize Opus Dei's role following complaints that the novel demonizes the group. But regardless of how it is portrayed on screen, real-life enemies still abound.

"We'd love it if the Work was put out of business," says Dianne DiNicola, executive director of the Opus Dei Awareness Network, a principal source for *The Da Vinci Code*. The mother of a former numerary, DiNicola runs the network out of her home in Pittsfield, Massachusetts. Like many parents of former members, she believes Opus Dei used mind-control techniques that gutted her daughter's personality. "Opus Dei is based on manipulation and deception," DiNicola says. "It is a cancer on our Church."

THE MOST VISIBLE Opus Dei official in the United States, Father C. John McCloskey III, belies the nefarious image of Opus Dei. He's anything but subtle. "I don't know about this whole *secretive* thing," he says. "I can't find anything I do on a daily, weekly or monthly basis that I haven't read about. Except for my squash game."

A former Wall Street executive, McCloskey runs the Catholic Information Center in Washington and has converted many major Republican players to Catholicism, including Brownback, Kudlow and Novak, as well as influential conservative publisher Alfred Regnery and even the former abortionist Bernard Nathanson. A galvanizing speaker with an occasional flash of wicked humor, McCloskey is a news program fixture when Catholic controversies arise. Some members say that his eloquence elevates the group's image. Others complain that he's grown too big; the Founder didn't ever want one member to become ubiquitous.

Core members like McCloskey are called numeraries. They live in single-sex Opus Dei centers and represent 30 percent of the official membership. (When critics allege that all of Opus Dei is a cult, they are usually referring to the lifestyle of these core members.) Supernumeraries, on the other hand, represent about 70 percent of the membership. They live at home, raise families, participate in such rituals as daily Mass or meditation, and contribute a percentage of their income to the Work. The most casual Opus Dei associate is called a cooperator: a person who prays for the Work or donates money to it.

Cooperators are not considered members, and McCloskey says that very few of the famous people he counsels belong officially to the organization. "Some of them may be cooperators, but that's a very loose term," McCloskey says. "It's like signing up for a Web site and getting on the spam list." Typically, cooperators give money to Opus Dei because they like its message; former members say that cooperators want to attach themselves to the Work because of its elitist aura. The Work doesn't publish a list of cooperators, but if it did, prominent names from the Republican establishment would be on it.

McCloskey says people don't understand Opus Dei because they don't understand Catholicism. In his opinion, most Opus Dei members are only doing what good Catholics should be doing every day: praying and bringing people closer to God.

While some orders, such as the Jesuits, have abandoned the orthodox teachings of the Church, Opus Dei has remained the faithful son mimicking the father. For example, "culture of death" is an epithet that Pope John Paul II often used to describe the United States and Europe; McCloskey uses the same damning terminology. "When you see contraception, abortion, divorce, pornography, active homosexuality from a Catholic point of view, they are deadly," he says. "They cause enormous harm to souls who are involved in any of those activities, and also to a culture. That's what I mean by the 'culture of death.'" As far as Opus Dei is concerned, liberalism and tolerance lead to one thing: the extinction of Catholicism. "We've had the whole thing with homosexuality, gay marriages, abortions, et cetera, et cetera, et cetera," he says. "People could say, 'We're being tolerant.' That's not being tolerant. That's *revolutionary*."

In response to criticism that its practice of self-mortification is too traditional, McCloskey insists that many Catholic groups still practice self-mortification and that Opus Dei's whips and barbs are minor compared to other, more secular forms of self-punishment. "I see people jogging on a summer morning in D.C.," he says, "and that looks more uncomfortable to me."

You don't find Opus Dei. They find you. If you're a young guy, you might meet the Work on a college campus. If you're a devout Catholic, you may have a friend in the Work who invites you to a retreat or to volunteer at one of its centers for the underprivileged. If you're the son of a supernumerary, you don't have much choice: Your parents probably sent you to an Opus Dei school or to one of their recreation centers, where an Opus Dei priest took your confession.

If you're a very spiritual Catholic, once-a-week Mass won't slake your soul's thirst. Some people say that you could go to a parish. But you'll have a hard time finding people there who'll struggle with you. If you're serious about God, you don't neglect your soul for days on end; it is a finely tuned instrument that requires constant attention. Opus Dei helps you refine it until it sings.

Your new Opus Dei friends will draw you closer. They share your interests, ask you about them and promote them. You'll go to more meditations, attend more weekend retreats. Your new Opus Dei friends will tell you that it's possible to lead both a holy and an ordinary life. Even your most menial tasks can turn into something holy. Getting a coffee, talking on the phone with a friend—any small act of charity becomes an offering to God. Everything is a prayer. They also remind you that it is every Catholic's sacred duty to bring people closer to God. Opus Dei members don't freely admit it, but they call the courtship process "fishing." There's even an Opus Dei song about it: "La Pesca Submarina." This kind of fishing is hardly recreational. It's run like a bureaucracy. Members must have lists of ten to fifteen candidates, three of whom should be close to seeking a vocation, or divine calling. A former member gave me a form that fishers fill out to assess the virtues of a female candidate. "Does she have devotion to our father? Understand our ideal? The big picture? Family? Is there love, respect, service, serenity, tension, drinking/drug problems?"

If Opus Dei thinks you're a candidate to be a numerary, a director will tell you, "I think you have a vocation," and you will accept. "You feel that if you say no," says former numerary Mariano Curat, "you're denying God." You'll be a plainclothes monk with a day job and no money of your own—an eternal contract with the possibility of a postmortem promotion. You work for God. You're literally doing *His Work.* Opus Dei.

You begin your "plan of life." Your day starts at dawn, when you jump from bed and kiss the ground. You get ready in silence until 7 a.m., at which time you have a half-hour meditation, a half-hour Mass, then a silent breakfast. After a morning at your job, you have an afternoon prayer and another prayer time in the evening. You wear your cilice. You repeat the Holy Rosary, followed by another half hour of silent prayer. You then turn in for the night, but not before sprinkling holy water on your bed. If you're good, you get weekend excursions or even trips to Rome. You're likely involved in good works. You're counseling others. Once a year, you go on a weekend retreat, where leaders may spell out some of your future responsibilities. Every year, you renew your commitment. If you want to leave, you can—Opus Dei says that the door is always open—but not without turning your back on God.

After six and a half years, you "make your fidelity"—or your lifelong commitment to God. Your priest and spiritual director call you in and give you a ring. You're on the road to salvation.

When it comes to the issues that divide American Catholics, Opus Dei's positions are firmly in the conservative camp—no female priests, birth control or gay rights. "In the English-speaking world, Opus Dei has become the lightning rod for the broader cultural wars in the Church," says John L. Allen, the Vatican correspondent for the *National Catholic Reporter* and author of the book *Opus Dei*.

Facing a declining membership in the States and a bruised public image, the Catholic Church is at a critical juncture. With fewer priests and a growing number of secularized, liberal Catholics, there aren't as many people to carry on and follow the faith. And if the Church can't find enough priests, who will look after the flock? Liberals suggest turning to women or to married men. But traditionalists (including the pope) insist that only men who uphold traditional values can instill them in others. If the Church ever gets to the point where it can't get a priest to look after a parish, orthodox lay groups like Opus Dei may function as the second wave of the priesthood. Who knows? In ten years, you could be taking Communion from an Opus Dei numerary.

Opus Dei members feel as though their dissidents have grossly misrepresented them. Most members are happy, they maintain, but if you speak to one of these poor people, you'd think everyone was heading for the door. They aren't. The fraction of people who leave with rancor is small but mighty: It's 125 anti-apostles fighting 85,000 believers. The anti-apostles are getting all the attention, and the believers are painfully aware of it. Some members admit that mistakes have been made, and reforms are under way. The minimum age for new members has been raised to eighteen, for instance. But overwhelmingly, the attitude remains that the dissidents, not the organization, are at fault.

When confronted with the complaints, current members simply compare these departures to defections. They've seen the Web sites. They've read the stories. And they just call it bad PR. "Any organization is going to have disgruntled people leaving it," says Father McCloskey. "Like David Brock leaving the Republican Party and writing a book about how awful it was. People are trying to justify themselves."

Current and former members compare the problem to divorce. Once Opus Dei tells you that you have a vocation, that's it. You're married for life. Good Catholics don't divorce their wives, and they don't divorce God. Opus Dei says the door is open, that you can leave at any time, but then again, God called you. Can you forget that?

As Opus Dei gathers momentum in the next decades, it may also become victim of its most effective tactic: zeal. The former members didn't belong to the group for nothing. They are obsessive, articulate and intelligent. They are still slightly leery of this pagan world. They come by all these qualities honestly. They may have left Opus Dei, but Opus Dei will never leave them.

Opus Dei Responds to *The Da Vinci Code*

Many readers are intrigued by the claims about Christian history and theology presented in *The Da Vinci Code.* We would like to remind them that *The Da Vinci Code* is a work of fiction, and it is not a reliable source of information on these matters.

The book has raised public interest in the origins of the Bible and of central Christian doctrines such as the divinity of Jesus Christ. Readers who do further research will discover that assertions made in *The Da Vinci Code* about Jesus Christ, Mary Magdalene, and Church history lack support among reputable scholars. By way of example, the book popularizes the idea that the fourth-century Roman emperor Constantine invented the doctrine of the divinity of Christ for political reasons. The historical evidence, however, clearly shows that the New Testament and the very earliest Christian writings manifest Christian belief in the divinity of Christ.

We also want to point out that *The Da Vinci Code*'s depiction of Opus Dei is inaccurate, both in the overall impression and in many details, and it would be irresponsible to form any opinion of Opus Dei based on reading *The Da Vinci Code.*

Opus Dei and Monks

Throughout *The Da Vinci Code,* Opus Dei members are

presented as monks (or, rather, caricatures of monks). In fact there are no monks in Opus Dei. Opus Dei is a Catholic institution for lay people and diocesan priests, not a monastic order.

Opus Dei's approach to living the faith does not involve withdrawing from the world like those called to the monastic life. Rather, Opus Dei helps people grow closer to God *in and through* their ordinary secular activities.

"Numerary" members of Opus Dei—a minority—choose a vocation of celibacy in order to be available to organize the activities of Opus Dei. They do not, however, take vows, wear robes, sleep on straw mats, spend all their time in prayer and corporal mortification, or in any other way live like *The Da Vinci Code*'s depiction of its monk character. In contrast to those called to the monastic life, numeraries have regular secular professional work.

In fact, *The Da Vinci Code* gets Opus Dei's nature 180 degrees backwards. Monastic orders are for people who have a vocation to seek holiness by withdrawing from the secular world; Opus Dei is for people who have a vocation to live their Christian faith in the middle of secular society.

Opus Dei and Crime

In *The Da Vinci Code,* Opus Dei members are falsely depicted as murdering, lying, drugging people, and otherwise acting unethically, thinking that it is justified for the sake of God, the Church, or Opus Dei.

Opus Dei is a Catholic institution and adheres to Catholic doctrine, which clearly condemns immoral behavior, including murder, lying, stealing, and generally injuring people. The Catholic Church teaches that one should never do evil, even for a good purpose.

Opus Dei's mission is to help people integrate their faith and the activities of their daily life, and so its spiritual education and counseling help members to be more ethical rather than less so.

Opus Dei and Corporal Mortification

The Da Vinci Code makes it appear that Opus Dei members practice bloody mortifications. In fact, though history indicates that some Catholic saints have done so, Opus Dei members do not do this.

The Catholic Church advises people to practice mortification. The mystery of Jesus Christ's Passion shows that voluntary sacrifice has a transcendent value and can bring spiritual benefits to others. Voluntary sacrifice also brings personal spiritual benefits, enabling one to resist the inclination to sin. For these reasons, the Church prescribes fasting on certain days and recommends that the faithful practice other sorts of mortification as well. Mortification is by no means the centerpiece of the Christian life, but nobody can grow closer to God without it: "There is no holiness without renunciation and spiritual battle" (*Catechism of the Catholic Church,* n. 2015).

In the area of mortification, Opus Dei emphasizes small sacrifices rather than extraordinary ones, in keeping with its spirit of integrating faith with secular life. For example, Opus Dei members try to make small sacrifices such as persevering at their work when tired, occasionally passing up some small pleasure, or giving help to those in need.

Some Opus Dei members also make limited use of the cilice and discipline, types of mortification that have always had a place in the Catholic tradition because of their symbolic reference to Christ's Passion. The Church teaches that people should take reasonable care of their physical health, and anyone with experience in this matter knows that these practices do not injure one's health in any way. *The Da Vinci Code*'s description of the cilice and discipline is greatly exaggerated and distorted: it is simply not possible to injure oneself with them as the novel depicts. Moreover, their use is motivated by love of God and desire to unite oneself with Jesus Christ, not guilt, self-hatred or self-punishment.

Opus Dei and Cult Allegations

In various places, *The Da Vinci Code* describes Opus Dei as a "sect" or a "cult." The fact is that Opus Dei is a fully integrated part of the Catholic Church and has no doctrines or practices except those of the Church. There is no definition or theory—whether academic or popular—that provides a basis for applying the pejorative terms "sect" or "cult" to Opus Dei.

Opus Dei is a Catholic institution that seeks to help people integrate their faith and the activities of their daily life. As a personal prelature (an organizational structure of the Catholic Church), it complements the work of local Catholic parishes by providing people with additional spiritual education and guidance.

Opus Dei was founded in Spain in 1928 by a Catholic priest, St. Josemaría Escrivá, and began to grow with the support of the local bishops there. It received final approval from the Vatican in 1950 and began growing in many countries around the world. Today Opus Dei has roughly 83,000 lay members (3,000 in the United States) and 2,000 priests. Several million people around the world participate in its programs and activities, which are conducted in more than sixty countries.

Opus Dei proposes to people to give their lives to

God, following a special path of service within the Catholic Church. One's life can only be given freely, through a decision coming from the heart, not from external pressure: pressure is both wrong and ineffective. Opus Dei always respects the freedom of conscience of its members, prospective members, and everyone else it deals with.

As a manifestation of its beliefs about the importance of freedom, Opus Dei has specific safeguards to ensure that decisions to join are free and fully informed. For example, nobody can make a permanent membership commitment in Opus Dei without first having completed more than six years of systematic and comprehensive instruction as to what membership entails. Additionally, no one can make a temporary commitment before age eighteen, nor a commitment to permanent membership before age twenty-three.

Opus Dei and Women

The Da Vinci Code says about Opus Dei's U.S. headquarters: "Men enter the building through the main doors on Lexington Avenue. Women enter through a side street." This is inaccurate. People, whether male or female, use the doors leading to whichever section of the building they are visiting. The building is divided into separate sections, for the straightforward reason that one section includes a residence for celibate women and another for celibate men. But these sections are not sex-restricted, and it is the women's not the men's section that fronts on Lexington Avenue, the opposite of what is said in the book. (Note: The book sometimes also inaccurately calls the building Opus Dei's "world headquarters.")

The Da Vinci Code also suggests that women Opus Dei members are "forced to clean the men's residence halls for no pay" and are otherwise accorded lower status than men.

This is not true. Opus Dei, like the Church in general, teaches that women and men are of equal dignity and value, and all of its practices are in accord with that belief. Women members of Opus Dei can be found in all sorts of professions, those which society views as prestigious and those which society today tends to undervalue, such as homemaking or domestic work. Opus Dei teaches that any kind of honest work done with love of God is of equal value.

Some women numerary members of Opus Dei have freely chosen to make a profession of taking care of Opus Dei's centers, both women's and men's. They also run conference centers where activities of cultural and spiritual formation are held. These women are professionally trained and are paid for their services, which include interior decorating, catering, and other highly skilled work. The millions of people who attend retreats or other spiritual formation activities at Opus Dei centers can attest to their professionalism. *The Da Vinci Code*'s insinuation that their work lacks dignity and value is demeaning to these women.

Opus Dei and the Vatican Bank

The Da Vinci Code says that Opus Dei was made a personal prelature as a reward for "bailing out" the Vatican bank.

Neither Opus Dei nor any of its members helped "bail out" the Vatican bank. The Church's authorities made Opus Dei a personal prelature in 1982 because they recognized that this new canonical category was a good fit for Opus Dei's mission and structure.

In any event, the personal prelature status is nothing

special: it is simply one of several canonical categories the Church has for designating an institution that carries out special pastoral activities. Personal prelature status in no way implies some special favor of the Pope or that Opus Dei members are removed from the authority of their local bishops.

The Canonization of Opus Dei's Founder

The Da Vinci Code suggests that the Church bent its canonization rules to put Opus Dei's founder on the "fast track" to being named a saint.

The canonization of St. Josemaría Escrivá in 2002 came twenty-seven years after his death (not twenty, as the book says). It was one of the first to be processed after the 1983 Code of Canon Law streamlined the procedures for canonization, and so it moved more quickly than was typical before. Mother Teresa is on pace to be canonized even more quickly, having been beatified just six years after her death (Escrivá was beatified in seventeen years). Even under the old procedures, the canonization of St. Therése of Lisieux made it through the process in twenty-seven years, roughly the same as Escrivá's.

6 The Mystery of Codes, Symbols, and Other Clues to the Hidden Past

Nothing is hidden that shall not be made clear;
nothing is secret that shall not be made manifest.
—LUKE 8:17

In the 1997 movie *Conspiracy Theory,* Mel Gibson plays the part of paranoid New York cabbie and conspiracy buff Jerry Fletcher, who clips articles from the *New York Times* which he believes contain coded information about the secret plans of NASA, the UN—and even Oliver Stone—to destroy America. Similarly, in *A Beautiful Mind,* mathematician and schizophrenic John Nash searches for coded messages he is sure the Soviets have hidden in *Life* magazine and the *New York Times.* (We will let you, the reader, decide if there is a hidden message in the selection of those two examples, since Mel Gibson's *The Passion of the Christ* is so often compared as a counterpoint to *The Da Vinci Code,* and since Ron Howard and most of his team that worked on *A Beautiful Mind* are the same team that has created *The Da Vinci Code* film.)

One does not need to reach for these extremes to recognize how ubiquitous and powerful the search for the "hidden" has become a preoccupation in our everyday reality. Without them, business and finance would grind to a halt, our military and government could not function effectively or defend the nation against its enemies, and no citizen could shop online or get cash from an ATM. The secrecy of coded messages is now a daily front-page issue, whether as admonishments to keep one's social security or PIN number safe from prying eyes, or debates over who may copy the software code that defines digital music and images.

Symbols and coded messages can unlock secrets profound and profane, their interpretation reliant on a priestly class of religious, social, and political thought leaders—including Harvard symbology professors. We encounter a profusion of such symbols daily, from the cars we drive and the colleges we attend to the sacred objects used in churches or New Age conclaves. And as *The Da Vinci Code* so successfully conveys, in the art we behold and the literature we read. The more we understand symbols, the novel seems to tell us, the closer we can come to fathoming the deepest mysteries of man and God.

In this chapter we explore various perspectives on both codes and symbols as they relate to *The Da Vinci Code*. We begin with art historian Diane Apostolos-Cappadona, who turns her attention to Leonardo's use of symbolism in his paintings. Then Gwen Kinkead brings us up to date on the grail-like hunt for the earliest relics of Christianity and direct knowledge of Jesus. Before *The Da Vinci Code*, many such findings would scarcely make a ripple in the public consciousness, but since the publication of the novel they have become the subject of front-page articles and TV specials, often with captivating introductory prose suggesting a real-life da Vinci code.

We conclude with a visit to Rosslyn Chapel, the alternate "cathedral of codes" and symbols which, for Robert Langdon and a strange assemblage of his real-life counterparts, may hold the secret of the Holy Grail.

The "Symbology" of *The Da Vinci Code*

An Interview with Diane Apostolos-Cappadona

Although, as she points out below, Diane Apostolos-Cappadona never heard the word *symbologist* (Robert Langdon's alleged field of expertise at Harvard) until she read Dan Brown's work, she is about as close as one can get to being a real-life professional symbologist.

An expert on symbolism in religious art, she is adjunct professor of Religious Art and Cultural History at the Center for Muslim-Christian Understanding as well as adjunct professor and core faculty in Art and Culture in the Liberal Studies Program, at Georgetown University. She also regularly lectures on the theme of the "Truth of *The Da Vinci Code*."

What is the importance of symbols in Christianity—and in religion in general?

Symbols are a form of communication. However, this is a form of communication that is multileveled, or multilayered, and in that there is no equal, one-for-one exchange. This is what makes them both fascinating and difficult, or confusing. Symbols operate on a variety of levels: they do such "simple things" as teach the ideas or the history of a faith or tradition, teach the stories of religious or societal traditions, teach religious doctrine, and explain how one is to gesture and posture and stand during liturgical services. They tell you about communicating with members of your community, and how to identify yourself within that community. There is the further understanding that symbols—and this principle is at work for all world religions, not specifically Christianity—are a way of communicating an embodied identity of knowledge and an embodied identity of who this community is. So symbolism and symbols are an integral part of the socialization process.

Do the meanings of symbols tend to change over time?

Yes, the meanings of symbols can change because of shifts in theology, doctrine, art styles, politics, and economic situations. For example, enormous changes in symbolism occurred during the Reformation, which was a complex umbrella of economic, political, and social transformations, as well as a religious revolution. This is the problem with symbols, and simultaneously the fascination; it's never as simple as a red light means stop and a green light means go.

What's a Christian symbol that's changed over time?

The fish has had multiple connections and meanings, from the Last Supper to the risen Christ. The fish was found in original depictions of the Last Supper. The fish had many meanings in early Christianity; then, it basically disappeared from the Christian consciousness . . . only to return in the late twentieth century when the *ichthyus* was retrieved, or rediscovered, as a symbol. It, not the cross, was the first symbol of Christian identity. The cross didn't become an identifying and visual symbol until the fourth or fifth centuries. The fish, from the Greek *ichthys,* as it is transliterated into English, is related as an anagram of the earliest prayer of the Christian tradition. Taking the first letter of each word from the prayer "Jesus Christ, Son of God and Savior," the Greek letters spell ICHTHYS—that is, the fish. There were several connections in the Hebrew and Christian scriptures between the fish and the Messiah. For example, there was the verbal connection to the "fishers of men," and further connections with relation to water, fish, fishing, and boats in early Christianity.

What symbols historically have been connected to Mary Magdalene?

The most important one is the unguent jar, which relates to her being the anointer and connects her symbolically, if not metaphorically, to the other women anointers in the scripture, including the women who anointed the feet and the head of Jesus before the crucifixion. The female anointer who cared for—that is, washed, anointed, and dressed—the body of the deceased was a common practice in Mediterranean cultures. These anointers were always women. It was taboo for men to wash and anoint the dead. Women were considered "unclean," so for them to wash and anoint the dead was not inappropriate; this may be a negative reading for women. However, you could relate this activity to a Jungian reading—that every man has three women in his life: his mother, his wife, and his daughter. Each woman initiates him into a different part of his life—and one of the functions of the daughter, ultimately, was to purify and anoint her parents' bodies after death. Then again, there are all of those wonderful legends about the Magdalene's unguent jar over the centuries. My favorite story related to the unguent jar is from the *Arabic Gospel of the Infancy of the Savior* [Chapter 5]. Mary of Magdala buys a jar of unguents to anoint the body of Jesus of Nazareth. Her purchase turns out to be the jar that was put on the shelf after the birth of this child named Jesus, and which contained within the nard his umbilical cord. So that the anointing of his body becomes profoundly symbolic: making him whole again and reconnecting him to his mother at the end of his life.

What about the pentacle, which is used as an important symbol in The Da Vinci Code?

The pentacle has five sides. The symbolic meaning is related to numbering, numerology, and the significance of the number five. In Christianity, five is the number of the wounds of the crucified Jesus (his two hands, his two feet, and his pierced side). Five relates fundamentally to the concept of "the human"—two arms, two legs, and a head. Numbers have meanings. There are mystical numbers, normally odd numbers, and therefore indivisible. Seven, for example, is the number of fulfillment; there are seven days in the creation story. Three is a mystical number and so forth: three, five, and seven.

What about the rose, another important symbol in The Da Vinci Code?

I have problems with the descriptions of the rose as a symbol in *The Da Vinci Code.* I don't interpret the rose the same way that Dan Brown does, especially with relation to his discussions of genitalia. He suggests that the rose has always been a premier symbol of female sexuality. My guess is that he learned this from reading a series of symbol dictionaries. However, I don't think this is the meaning of the rose in Western Christianity. In classical Mediterranean cultures, the rose was the flower sacred to Venus or Aphrodite, which is how Brown may have made a connection to female sexuality. Venus or Aphrodite signified much more, however, than simple sex and sexuality. She was about romantic love, and love on a variety of levels, not just sexual intercourse. As a sign of romantic love, the color of the rose becomes important. The early color symbolism of the rose was simpler than it is today with such an array of hues available at florists. For early and medieval Christians, there were only four colors for roses: white signified innocent love or pure love; pink, first love; red, true love; and yellow, which meant "forget it, it's over."

However, what is important about the rose and its relationship to Mary is the thorn. The popular understanding—and it's a legendary, not a scriptural, understanding—is that the roses, and rosebushes, had no thorns in the Garden of Eden. Thereby, whenever you saw a rosebush positioned near Mary, and especially a presentation of Mary and the Child, it was a sign of Paradise, for it was Mary who began the process of our reentry into Paradise, the place where the roses had no thorns. The rose, then, became a symbol and a signifier, if you will, of Mary's role in human salvation. Her rose was a sign of grace; so the rose window was created to glorify Mary the Mother, not Mary Magdalene.

Roses were related to a variety of female saints, but Mary Magdalene was not one of them.

Then there's the fleur-de-lis, which plays a prominent role in Dan Brown's book . . .

The fleur-de-lis is both a symbol of France and the city of Florence. It's a lily—a flower that in Christianity signifies the trinity. According to tradition, King Clovis—whose baptism made him the first Christian king of France—initiated the use of the fleur-de-lis as the sign of purification for both his own personal spirituality (that is, when he was baptized) and the purification of France. It became the emblem of French royalty, and later an attribute of many French saints, including Charlemagne. It's important in *The Da Vinci Code* because the key shaped in a fleur-de-lis would connect to the purification of France.

In some instances, like this one, Dan Brown uses symbols very well. Those are the elements that make *The Da Vinci Code* both believable to someone who has symbolic knowledge and absolutely fascinating to those who don't have any idea what these signs were about. The fleur-de-lis connects visually to the lily, which in turn has multiple meanings in Christianity, particularly in relation to women, from purity to innocence to royalty. The beauty of the lily's fragrance pleases the senses. It was sacred traditionally to the virgin and mother goddesses throughout the Mediterranean world prior to Christianity. Then, it became a significant symbol for Mary. There was a popular tradition that the lily sprang up from the tears Eve shed as she was expelled from the Garden of Eden. Weave all of those meanings together, add the relevance of this symbol to French history, and Brown has a powerful symbol to use. Although I suspect he uses it because the fleur-de-lis is the symbol of France.

That raises the question of Mary Magdalene's alleged French connection.

There are several legends and traditions about the Magdalene being the missionary to France, the patroness of France, saving France, Christianizing France, spending her last days in France, and being buried in France. You have your choice; you can go to the Dominicans or the Benedictines, to Vézelay or Aix-en-Provence. You have that whole tradition, even down to the making of madeleine cookies, which used to be served only on the twenty-second of July—that is, her feast day on the Roman calendar. These lemon-flavored, fan-shaped cookies signify both her geographic location in the south of France and the pious legends of her penitence in the desert. For if Mary Magdalene did live in Sainte Baume for thirty years (or fifty years, depending on which legend you're reading), she was reputed to have eaten no food. Rather, she survived on the fragrance of the lemon trees and the sacred food that she received every day when she was elevated for communion. Now, why any person in her right mind would go to the south of France for thirty or fifty years and not eat anything has always escaped me. . . .

Do you believe that the Holy Grail is a metaphor or a real object . . . or both?

I believe that there has been—and always will be—a perpetual mythology about the Holy Grail. Further, there is a history of an understanding that the Grail was a true object, a physical object that could be touched, to which Christians would have had great devotion, and which for some reason disappeared. According to certain legends and popular traditions, the Grail disappears and then reappears in England, reputedly brought there by Joseph of Arimathea. The place in England where the Grail reappears is at the site we would identify as Camelot. Of course, the important principle is that the concept of the Grail is a metaphor for the spiritual quest. So to be honest, I suppose my answer is that it's both—both a metaphor and a real object.

There was a *Newsweek* article ["The Bible's Lost Stories," 12/08/03] with a small sidebar, "Decoding *The Da Vinci Code,*" which included images of the Last Supper and one of the Chalice of the Abbé Suger now in the National Gallery of Art in Washington, DC. The alabaster part of that chalice was believed to be the Holy Grail. Abbé Suger had it encased in the gold and bejeweled fashion that we have today, and it was used at the first mass that he celebrated at the Cathedral of Saint-Denis in Paris, the first Gothic cathedral. The building of this cathedral was, of course, during the period of the Crusades and the pilgrimages to the Holy Land, when devout Christians brought back as many major relics as possible. The chalice has been tested—carbon-dated—and it's from the appropriate time period. However, I think of the Holy Grail more as a metaphor because the reality of history is that when Jesus of Nazareth and his followers had this meal together, they were not in a position, financially or otherwise, to have had this very elaborate tableware and other objects. If they were, would they have used a chalice? Or would they have used something that was more like a glass or a pitcher or a small urn?

The *San Graal* is a very important metaphor in nineteenth-century pre-Raphaelite painting and literature, with the revival of Dante and the Arthurian romances. The Grail is found in a variety of literary, musical, and dramatic productions, from the Ring Cycle by Wagner to *The Lord of the Rings,* in both book and movie formats. It is the same story over and over again: this quest for spiritual salvation. The tangible object being sought takes a variety of shapes, so that in these operas and the Tolkien works, it is a ring rather than a cup. In that way it's a metaphor.

What about the idea put forth in The Da Vinci Code *that the Holy Grail is actually Mary Magdalene?*

That's a very Jungian reading of Mary Magdalene—women as receivers and containers, women as vessels. But historically this is a connection that is older than Jung. You find this symbolism in classical mythologies. There are a variety of metaphors here. The mysterious connection in terms of sexual intercourse is the one that matters most. Women receive the male during sexual intercourse. They thereby conceive a child and hold that child in their sacred vessel, and then expel the child from their sacred vessel. I suppose one can make an argument for Mary Magdalene as the *San Graal* if one is a Jungian. However, I have my own way of reading symbols, so for me it doesn't work. I think Mary Magdalene has sacramental importance, but that's not her primary importance. Who she is is a mystery, and that's what makes her great to write about. I think in the year 3000 people will argue just as much about who she is or who she was as they do right now. By that I don't mean arguing about a prostitute or a woman of means or a poor woman or a sexual woman; I mean how she is in Christianity perhaps the one mirror of all aspects of humanity. The one thing she isn't is a mother or a wife, as far as we know.

What is the significance of Jesus appearing first to Mary Magdalene after the resurrection?

Well, I don't think it was because they were lovers or, for that matter, possibly married as Dan Brown suggests. Rather, I think it was because she signified the witness—the one for whom seeing is enough to believe. This is as a parallel to Thomas, who had to touch the wounds and physically feel the body of Jesus—that is, the empirical evidence—before he would believe that Jesus had been resurrected. I think there are ways of reading scripture that argue for Jesus being very feminist. One way is that it is the women who continue to believe in him, who are faithful to him unto his death and provide the rituals of his death, his dying, his mourning, his burial; and it is the women who still come and who are not afraid. To me, the principle is that they represent that part of humanity that never loses faith, that never loses hope, the people for whom to see is enough to understand. To me it is empowering of women and of the feminine. Intuition is more important to me than reason. The Mary Magdalenes of this world trust their intuition, the Thomases do not.

How accurate do you find Dan Brown's portrayal of Saint-Sulpice church in Paris—where a pivotal scene of the novel takes place—and its iconography?

There is a reality that Christianity built churches, basilicas, and cathedrals on the sites of earlier religious buildings. There are churches throughout Rome, Athens, and France built on the sites of temples to Mithras, Athena, and other prior gods and goddesses. The most obvious is the church in Rome called Santa Maria Sopra Minerva—Mary over Minerva. However, the connection usually is more than architectural; that is, Mary's church is built over the church of Minerva because there is a connection between Mary and Minerva as goddesses of wisdom.

For me, to propose that Saint-Sulpice is built over a temple or shrine to Isis makes no sense, because Isis connects to Mary the Mother more than she connects to Mary Magdalene. If parts of *The Da Vinci Code* were more about Mary the Mother, I might recognize the connection with Isis. For example, the Black Madonna cult relates Mary the Mother and Isis; so that the majority of the churches with black Madonnas were built on sites of earlier Isis shrines. So, yes, there is this whole tradition in Christianity.

In The Da Vinci Code, *Dan Brown's hero is a so-called symbologist. Is there such a thing, or such an academic discipline?*

The study of religious symbols is usually identified as iconography or religious art, not symbology. The first time I ever saw the word *symbology,* in fact, was in Dan Brown's *Angels & Demons;* I read his first book in this series of "Robert Langdon mysteries" first.

If such a term, *symbology,* were used as an academic or disciplinary title, it is part of what I do. I'm not a purebred academic in the sense that I research and study in an interdisciplinary or multidisciplinary fashion. I work with the arts, with art history, with cultural history, with the history of religion, with theology, with gender studies, and with world religions, so I don't have a pure academic discipline. However, I don't know of anybody who identifies him- or herself as a symbologist, and there is no formal academic study by that name that I know of. There may well be now because Brown's book has taken off.

Secrets of Sand and Stone

The Da Vinci Code *and New Archeological Finds*

GWEN KINKEAD

When Robert Langdon peers at the cryptex left by the murdered Jacques Saunière to guide his granddaughter, Sophie, to the true secrets of the Holy Grail, the past swims into view. Through the object in his hand, Langdon is connected to the dawn of Christianity, the crucifixion of Christ, and the legend that the mysterious Knights Templar unearthed the Holy Grail from the ruins of the Temple of King Solomon in Jerusalem and transported it to . . . who knows where? That moment electrifies Langdon. Suddenly the secrets of the life of Jesus and his apostles—including Mary Magdalene, known even in the accepted gospels as the "apostle to the apostles"—seem within his grasp.

Biblical archeologists have searched for years, of

Gwen Kinkead, an award-winning journalist, has contributed to the *New Yorker* and the *New York Times*. In 1980 she co-won the prestigious George Polk Award for cultural reporting.

course, for direct knowledge about Jesus. Since the publication of *The Da Vinci Code,* however, the hunt has become almost a global media spectator sport. Today, early Christianity is "hot" and with it, the study of bones, artifacts, documents, and miscellaneous detritus lost in the ruins of history. Still, the lack of *any* physical remains proving conclusively that Jesus actually walked this earth grieves, confounds, perplexes, and fascinates many people.

The search for everything having to do with the life of Jesus is alive and well at historic sites from Jerusalem to Rome, and in places as far afield as Tibetan libraries (some people think Jesus spent some of his "missing years" not accounted for in the gospels traveling to India or Tibet), to the Egyptian desert where the Gnostic Gospels were found in 1945, to the underground vaults below Rosslyn Chapel in Scotland where the climax of *The Da Vinci Code* takes place.

Today's hunt includes professional and amateur archeologists, intellectual sleuths, forensic detectives, and armchair theorists, among others. Most of those on the hunt are brilliant and devoted people of academic and spiritual integrity. Some are twenty-first-century adventurers using high-tech tools to explore under water, in caves, and under desert sands. A few, unfortunately, are the perpetrators of hoaxes and frauds.

Since the publication of *The Da Vinci Code,* archeological finds that normally might not have even appeared in daily newspapers and magazines have become the subject of front-page articles and TV specials, often with captivating introductory prose suggesting a real-life *Da Vinci Code.* Sorting out fact and fiction in *The Da Vinci Code* is hard enough; in the real world of archeology and ancient document analysis, it is even more difficult. There are two tombs of Jesus promoted in Jerusalem, for example—the

Church of the Holy Sepulcher and the Garden Tomb—and each one is itself disputed. Some scholars attribute the dearth of artifacts of Jesus, Mary and Joseph, the apostles, and Mary Magdalene to early Christianity's rigorous asceticism. Jesus counseled a simple life and, at least in the very early days, his followers lived simply and did not have many material objects to leave behind nor DNA fingerprints for modern forensic experts to find. Others explain the absence of evidence by saying the Bible is simply a collection of legends and morality plays, and that the individuals described did not actually lead real lives, so it is no wonder we cannot find evidence of them today.

Nevertheless, while the search for the historical Jesus has yielded little fruit as yet, some intriguing bits of crumbly text, foundations of homes, old bones, papyri, and other documents have surfaced that have allowed contemporary archeologists to piece together an increasingly detailed picture of the Holy Land at the time of Jesus. The picture emerging is of a fractious community of Jews, pagans, gentiles, and Christians, fringe prophets and messianic sects whose leaders expounded an intellectual, theological and cosmological stew of ideas, all jostling together under harsh Roman rule.

Some recently found pieces of the past seem to confirm certain stories in the Bible. For instance, the Temple of Solomon, the magnificent center of Judaism in Jerusalem three thousand years ago, is described in the Old Testament as having golden walls around the Ark of the Covenant. The Temple was burned down in 586 BC by Nebuchadnezzar, king of the invading Babylonians. The sole object thought (at least until recently) to have escaped the fire is a tiny 1 1/2"-high carved ivory pomegranate, now in the Israel Museum. It was treasured as much as the Dead Sea Scrolls, both because of its exceptional beauty and because it was presumed to be the only evidence of the existence of Solomon's fabled temple.

Just before the birth of Jesus, Herod the Great, king of Judea, rebuilt the Temple to a size estimated to be twenty-four football fields in length. Here, the contemporaries of Jesus worshipped; this is where, presumably, Jesus overturned the tables of the moneylenders for defiling the sacred spot. This enormous structure was razed by the Romans in AD 70 when they destroyed Jerusalem during the first Jewish uprising. But Herod's Temple is known to have actually existed—excavations in the 1970s revealed several of Herod's great gates and ramparts, as well as a monumental staircase. A part of its western wall (known by some as the Wailing Wall) remains standing today and is considered holy by Jews as a remnant of the Temple. Several "burnt houses" nearby were also discovered, containing charred body parts and scorched stone pottery. These have been dated by coins to AD 69, also seeming to confirm the fateful fire.

Successive waves of conquerors after the Roman destruction of the Temple in AD 70 occupied the Temple Mount, and crowned it with mosques, churches and palaces. As Dan Brown correctly writes in *The Da Vinci Code,* the Knights Templar occupied it after conquering Jerusalem in the first Crusade in 1099, adding an altar and a cross and reconstructing subterranean vaults as stables. Whether they also dug up secrets—as Robert Langdon and many present-day occult writers seem to think they did—about the Holy Grail, Mary Magdalene, or anything else of interest is, of course, another question altogether. Dan Brown's novel implies that they did, but there is no historical or archeological evidence to support this.

More Secrets of Sand and Stone

In addition to the archeological finds discussed in the foregoing, some other recent archeological finds from biblical times that are piquing international curiosity in light of *The Da Vinci Code* include:

- A tenth-century public building uncovered in 2005 in east Jerusalem is claimed by archeologist Eilat Mazar to be the famous palace of the biblical King David.

  Not likely, other archeologists say, while agreeing the find is impressive. As a report in the *New York Times* on the find noted, Mazar's work "has been sponsored by a conservative Israeli research institute and financed by an American Jewish investment banker who would like to prove that Jerusalem was indeed the capital of the Jewish kingdom described in the Bible...But...(even her critics)...acknowledge that what she has uncovered is rare and important: a major public building from around the 10th century BC, with pottery shards that date to the time of David and Solomon and a government seal of an official mentioned in the book of Jeremiah."
- "Jesus Boat": This 26-foot-long first-century wooden boat found in mud in the 1980s at the Sea of Galilee is remarkable for being presumably the type of fisherman's boat in which Peter and Andrew plied their trade. Perhaps also it's the sort of boat Jesus and his disciples traveled in on the Sea of Galilee. Several ancient bronze coins and iron nails overturned by a tractor stuck in the mud suggested the site, empty of water after a long drought.
- Mosaics of fish and another bearing the name of Jesus in ancient Greek were the first clues that, under the

(*continues*)

More Secrets of Sand and Stone (*continued*)

floor of a prison in northern Galilee, there might be an ancient church. The 2005 find at Megiddo Prison near the biblical site of Armageddon could be third- or fourth-century AD. An inscription on the floor reads for "the God Jesus Christ as a memorial." If this was, indeed, a Christian church, and if the dating is accurate, it would be the oldest Christian church ever unearthed in the Holy Land, and one of the oldest anywhere in the world. The dating, however, is in dispute because Christianity was outlawed until the middle of the fourth century and some experts think it unlikely that Christians would have openly declared themselves under those circumstances.

- The earliest known monk cells have been found beneath an older church in Zafarana, an Egyptian desert town about a hundred miles southeast of Cairo. Here, it is believed, St. Anthony went to live in a cave in the mountains around AD 270, making it the birthplace of Christian monastic life. The others who followed built their cells of bricks and plaster in the ravines of the same mountains. "Forgive me, Savior. Forgive me, Lord," one wrote in Coptic. The 2005 find was reported in the *New York Times* this way:

  "Men have retreated to the desert for centuries in search of God, drawn by the quiet and the isolation, by a feeling of divine presence in the barren landscape. The Rev. Maximous Elantony was one of those men drawn to the desert in search of a relationship with God. But he could hardly believe it when he recently helped to discover some of the earliest physical evidence of

(*continues*)

More Secrets of Sand and Stone (*continued*)

Christians who made that quest as well." The finds encompass what Egyptian antiquity officials say are the "oldest monastic cells ever discovered, dating to the fourth century. They are so well preserved it is as if someone just lifted off the roof." The *Times* account went on to quote Father Maximous: "When you live in a quiet place, like a cell, and you are not busy with anything but God, you start to hear yourself and to see yourself. . . . We only want to be busy with God, to hear God, to see God."

These monk's cells coexisted in time with the period when the Gnostic Gospels—found at a different location in Egypt—were probably being written in Coptic. Further research may help determine whether the monks who occupied the cells in Zafarana had cosmological inclinations that leaned in the direction of the Gnostics, or whether they subscribed to the more mainstream Christian beliefs of the time.

- Meanwhile, at Deir al-Surian, another Coptic monastery in the western Egyptian desert, a treasure trove of manuscripts, some up to fifteen thousand years old, was discovered in 2005. The work of translating and interpreting has just begun, but any time new document caches are found, excitement runs high that some of the lost or missing scriptures that scholars have been searching for will be found.
- Ancient Canaanites may have been polytheistic worshippers of a pair of deities—El, the forerunner of the

(*continues*)

More Secrets of Sand and Stone (*continued*)

Hebraic Yahweh, and Asherah, a female goddess figure. Asherah was very popular, to judge by the number of village and home shrines to her that have been found in the Holy Land, some with food offerings, says respected biblical scholar and archeologist William G. Dever in a new book, *Did God Have a Wife?* Dan Brown makes the argument in *The Da Vinci Code* that there were goddesses before there were gods and that ancient Judaism as well as early Christianity incorporated influences of the "sacred feminine" from throughout the eastern Mediterranean and the Near East. Scholars have noted that there are more than forty references to Asherah in the Old Testament. Indeed, a sign of the strength of this goddess cult may be the number of those references that are devoted to praising those who took measures to stamp out worship of her.

"Asherah was buried long ago by the Establishment," Dever was quoted as saying in *Archaeology* magazine. "Now, archaeology has excavated her." The article went on to note: "Dever is quite certain that he knows who the Asherah of ancient Israel and of the biblical texts is—she is the wife or consort of Yahweh, the one god of Israel."

This is such a controversial subject that Dever says he has received death threats. Sounds like a chapter out of *The Da Vinci Code,* only this is real archeology and real life.

—Gwen Kinkead

Illegal and legal excavations on the site are always a source of disputes between the three major religious communities who worship at or nearby the Temple Mount. The area is now home not only to key sites of Jewish and Christian history, but also to one of the holiest mosques in Islam. Access and control of the Temple Mount and surrounding area remains a world political and military hot button, just as it was in the time of the Crusades nine hundred years ago. Under the circumstances of highly politicized and constricted excavations, it is not surprising to learn that debate rages over how to interpret what has already been found, as well as what might be found in the future.

The most recent find to parallel the plot of *The Da Vinci Code* comes not from the Temple Mount but from the far western edge of Europe—Wales to be specific. There, in the spring of 2005, an enormous seventeenth-century manuscript turned up with the intriguing title *The Genealogy of Jesus Christ*. The 596-page handwritten document details the family tree of every figure in the Bible. Apparently, it was donated to Llandovery College in Wales by that institution's founder, Thomas Philips, in 1851, but had not been seen for at least the last seventy years.

The UK media dubbed it a find out of the plot of *The Da Vinci Code*. Indeed, British press reports quoted Peter Hogan, warden of Llandovery College, who rediscovered the *Genealogy* in the National Library of Wales, as calling on Dan Brown to help analyze the find. "I think Mr. Brown would be interested," Hogan was quoted as saying. "If he would like to take a look at it he'd be more than welcome." Hogan has continued to have trouble locating the right expertise to authenticate, value, and interpret the work.

The text may be almost four centuries old, but details

about its author—one William Spenser—or why he created it are unknown. Curiously, it has a good deal to say about Mary Magdalene, but much of its commentary about her has been crossed out. In addition to the media's general willingness to liken virtually any current document or relic discovery to *The Da Vinci Code,* Hogan had a particular reason to suggest Dan Brown might be interested in *The Genealogy of Jesus Christ.* At first blush, descriptions of the *Genealogy* sound a lot like the so-called *Dossiers Secrets,* which figure prominently in the plot of *The Da Vinci Code* and are bound up with the various myths woven together by Dan Brown about the bloodline of Jesus and Mary Magdalene and the Priory of Sion.

As demonstrated elsewhere in *Secrets of the Code,* the *Dossiers Secrets* and the Priory of Sion itself are almost certainly part and parcel of a mid-twentieth-century hoax, perpetrated by the Frenchman Pierre Plantard, who imagined himself as the modern grand master of the Priory of Sion. Plantard tried to convince the world that he had inherited a tradition that went back to Jesus and Mary Magdalene and their offspring, and continued through the Merovingian kings (the first kings of France), the Knights Templar, Leonardo da Vinci, and a variety of famous European intellectuals and artists up to the present day. Plantard and his colleagues wrote up much of this mythic history in the form of genealogies and lists of grand masters, which they then deposited in the French national library. Later, these documents would inspire the imagination of serious researchers and novelists alike, eventually giving impetus to a variety of books ranging from *Holy Blood, Holy Grail* in 1982 to *The Da Vinci Code* in 2003.

Unlike the *Dossiers Secrets,* which turned out to be part of an elaborate hoax, as of this writing the Welsh *Genealogy of Jesus Christ* appears to be a genuine seventeenth-century document. (See further commentary about the *Genealogy*, pages 316–318.)

Another enigmatic glimpse into Jesus's teachings comes from a pile of blackened papyri thrown out in a rubbish heap thousands of years ago in lower Egypt, in a vanished city called Oxyrhynchus. The 400,000 manuscripts and fragments found there were brought to Oxford University in England over a century ago, and have been carefully scrutinized, documented, and slowly published ever since. The work is incredibly meticulous and painstaking because of the condition of the papyri. Even after more than a century of study, at least 50,000 "very rich" and "substantial" pieces remain to be published, including five fragments of the Gospel of St. John, according to the Oxford collection's curator, Nikolaos Gonis. Some of the texts are literary, including a few with enormous significance for academics—lost plays of Sophocles, lost poems of Sappho, and lost histories. Some shed interesting light on the way people lived more than two millennia ago, including records of payments for hexes, real estate transactions, and even love potions and sex manuals.

In this fascinating mix there are early versions of biblical works, including fragments of gospel-like accounts that did not make it into the standard New Testament we know today. New technology is making it easier to read the texts and some new insights into the early Christian world may still be found. A few of the fragments that have been published to date offer some clues to a Jesus different in some ways than the one presented in the standard version of the New Testament.

Fragment #840, for example, dates from the fourth century and is a polemic on a water ritual, according to the Harvard Divinity School's François Bovon, who has published articles about the find. In Fragment #840, Jesus enters Herod's Temple and is accosted by a high priest who asks why he has not first purified himself in a bath. In an English translation of the Greek original, with lacunae bracketed, Jesus replies that he and his disciples have bathed in "waters of li[fe] [eternal co]ming from . . ." This passage shows a Jesus free of certain orthodox rituals, argues Bovon. "Jesus is defending a spiritual purity and these priests condemn Jesus because he didn't go through the ritual purifications in the pool of David." The one-page parchment, he says, "is very important and very interesting for the history of Christianity at its dawn. It is probably a second-century vision of Jesus."

Some scholars believe more lost gospels will be discovered in the Middle East, noting that the two most important document finds of modern times—the Gnostic Gospels in Egypt in 1945 and the Dead Sea Scrolls in Israel in 1947—each reshaped what we know about the world of the Holy Land two thousand years ago. Scores, if not hundreds, of gospels or documents that told the story of the life of Jesus circulated after his death, but comparatively few survived the antiheretic purges of the church in the third and fourth centuries. "We know of the existence of numerous gospels from the early church that no modern scholar has laid eyes on. That may change with the passing of time," says Bart D. Erhman, an authority on the New Testament and a professor at the University of North Carolina at Chapel Hill. (See page 185 for an interview with Ehrman, containing his observations about *The Da Vinci Code* and the possibility of finding other lost scriptures).

Recently, two fragments did sift out of the sands. Archeologist Hanan Eshel of Tel Aviv's Bar Ilan University has spent decades rappelling into limestone cliff caves over the Dead Sea looking for "refuge caves" where Jews

The Curious Case of the *Genealogy of Jesus Christ*

The man with white cotton gloves lifted a thick, musty, old leather-bound book he'd just removed from a vault onto an enormous mahogany desk in his room overlooking green playing fields at a boarding school in Wales, and opened it to page 1. "The Geneology of Jesus Christ, by William Spenser," it said, in handwritten letters on thin old vellum.

Ted Williams, the bursar of Llandovery College, carefully turned another page. Here, a firm hand in black ink began to tell the relationship of every character in the Old and New Testaments to one another. Certain urgent points were inscribed in red ink, as were some of the drawings of family trees that illustrated the web of relations.

When I had interviewed Peter Hogan, the college warden, about the *Genealogy* for the foregoing essay on archeological finds in the wake of *The Da Vinci Code,* he had mentioned at one point that Mary Magdalene was referred to in the text as a widow. The editors of *Secrets of the Code* had been particularly interested in this reference, especially since they are aware of Dan Brown's fascination with the traditional Masonic reference to "the widow's son," a reference that Brown embedded in coded form into the dust jacket flaps of the original hardcover *Da Vinci Code.* My editors had asked me to go back to find out a little more about what this curious seventeenth-century book had to say about Mary Magdalene in particular.

"She was one of many women ministering into Christ of their substances," Williams read aloud. He explained that Mary Magdalene is most often described in the book as "an earthly being who was with Jesus in a sort of matter-of-fact way, which is in itself rather controversial." She is por-

(*continues*)

The *Genealogy of Jesus Christ* (*continued*)

trayed as "a friend, possibly his wife," he says. Even if the *Genealogy* suggests the possibility of a husband-and-wife relationship between Jesus and Mary, it wouldn't be proof positive of anything, since that marriage, if it happened, occurred two thousand years ago, and the *Genealogy* is only at most five hundred years old. Nevertheless, if it speaks about Jesus and Mary as husband and wife, it would be one of only a very small number of in-print old document references to this idea that so captivated Dan Brown and, in turn, has so captivated millions of his readers.

Williams notes that about half the references to Mary have been crossed out. But it is possible, he says, to make out the references underneath the crossed-out passages. This is work for scholars and old document experts. But all the publicity about the *Genealogy* has seemed to suggest that there are some new and unusual ideas about the lives of the early Christians contained in this volume.

Llandovery's Peter Hogan, who found the mysterious book while poking around the archives of the National Library of Wales, reports that "as soon as we uncovered it, there was quite a lot of interest in its remarks on Mary Magdalene. The text says she was wealthy, a widow, and one of seven women who supported Jesus in his ministry. The Bible doesn't say she's a widow. That's what is so interesting about this." In addition, Hogan notes that the manuscript "has some very interesting pieces of information about Jesus Christ," but he declined to reveal these. "We need to find a religious historian to flick through every page and tell us its significance," Williams adds. "It's four hundred years old, maybe five hundred years old."

(*continues*)

The *Genealogy of Jesus Christ* (*continued*)

Who was William Spenser, the *Genealogy*'s author? No one knows. The book was donated to the college by Llandovery's founder in the nineteenth century. A century later, it was put away for safekeeping in a library vault, where it remained until Hogan rediscovered it in 2005. Could this volume of biographical descriptions of biblical figures be a hoax? Wrapping it back up carefully in a box in bubble wrap, Williams said he doubted it. This was only the book's second airing in half a century. He felt he had answered my questions and now he was on his way to smoke a cigar by the playing fields where cricket bats resounded. Then it was back to the vault for the *Genealogy* until a scholar materialized who could help the Welsh school understand the mysteries of this unusual book in context.

—Gwen Kinkead

hid from the Romans in AD 135 during an uprising. When a Bedouin showed Eshel two scraps of brown leather with writing on them that had been robbed from a cave, Eshel recognized these as sections of the Book of Leviticus from an ancient Torah. With money from his university, he bought them for three thousand dollars and gave them to Israel's Antiquities Authority for authentication. "This time we were very lucky," Eshel says. "Unlike the tribe that found the Dead Sea Scrolls, this tribe did not have the connections and sophistication to smuggle these out of the country and get the crazy prices on the open market." The find has been hailed as one of the most important in half a century. But it also landed Eshel in trouble: he was arrested briefly under suspicion of illegally dealing in antiquities, a misunders⁺anding he says he hopes will be resolved soon.

The black market in antiquities is so overheated that, just before publication of *The Da Vinci Code,* a storm of excitement broke out around the world when a stone ossuary, or burial box, was presented in 2002 in Washington, DC, by the *Biblical Archaeological Review,* a popular publication about archeology. It was inscribed "James son of Joseph brother of Jesus." Legend now seemed fact. Here seemed to be actual evidence that James, the brother of Jesus Christ, had actually lived—and died. The ossuary was immediately dubbed the most important Christian discovery ever by newspapers, magazines, and websites the world over.

The box belonged to an Israeli collector, Oded Golan. A year earlier, Golan had introduced another amazing relic, a black stone tablet describing ninth century BC repairs to Solomon's Temple. For a stone to materialize from the vanished Temple was as extraordinary as the sudden appearance of the ossuary of James, brother of Jesus.

Though the antiquity of the box and the tablet were not questioned—both passed scientific tests by Israeli authorities who examined their patinas and confirmed they were old and undisturbed—scholars questioned their inscriptions. A fierce debate broke out between promoters of the ossuary, including *Biblical Archaeology Review* editor Hershel Shanks, and dissenting academics.

Epigrapher Kyle McCarter said the phrase "brother of Jesus" on the ossuary appeared to have been written by a different, cruder hand. James Strange, a leading biblical archeologist at the University of South Florida, notes that the inscription lacks an honorific. "If it were Christian, we'd expect an honorific like 'Jesus Our Lord.' It makes me skeptical it had anything to do with *the* James and *the* Jesus." Scholar Rochelle Altman argued that both inscriptions were inauthentic. The one on the tablet mixed seventh century BC Aramaic and Phoenician letters with modern Hebrew square script and was a forgery, she claimed. Other Israeli experts argued just the opposite. Since both objects came from the black market, not authorized excavations, authentication was essential. The Israel Museum was rumored to be ready to purchase the stone tablet for four million dollars if its authenticity could be confirmed.

Unknown to the public, the Israeli police were investigating Golan, having heard rumors of a forger who, when drunk, boasted of his skills. Months after the James ossuary appeared in Washington, DC, police raided Golan's apartment looking for the stone tablet. They returned in the summer of 2003 and found the ossuary on the top of a toilet. They also found tools for forgery, like dental drills, as well as rocks and dirt from many archeological sites.

Golan and his co-conspirators were arrested and went on trial in the fall of 2005 in Jerusalem. They were charged with faking relics over the last twenty years—including the Solomon Temple stone tablet, the James ossuary, and even the famous ivory pomegranate in the Israel Museum, which the museum now acknowledges is probably a modern forged inscription on a genuinely ancient object. Golan, however, denies any guilt. The legal process could last several years.

If these pieces are proven to be forgeries, they will be at least remembered as technically innovative forgeries, created by performing new incisions into genuinely ancient relics. Experts speculate the forger ground up calcium carbonate with hot water and poured the mixture on the stone tablet after it had been incised, creating a patina that appeared uniform inside and outside the inscription.

Whatever the outcome of the trial, however, the field of biblical archeology is under a cloud. Entire collections will have to be reevaluated. Anything inscribed from the first or second century is now highly suspect. There are suspicions about other new finds, as well. A subterranean pool with a smooth stone for feet by its edge and a niche for oil that was discovered in Israel a few years ago was announced by its discoverers to be the Cave of St. John the Baptist where, according to tradition, he baptized his followers. The fiery saint was born in the village of Ein Kerem, the site where he baptized Jesus. A member of a local kibbutz found the cave in the late 1990s, hidden by trees and bushes and choked with soil. Archeologist Shimon Gibson supervised the dig, clearing out layers of earth and finding about 250,000 shards of pottery. At the time, newspapers excitedly hailed the find as "the connecting link between Jewish and Christian baptism." Gibson's own book on the find is subtitled *The Stunning Archeological Discovery that Has Redefined Christian History.*

However, a number of Gibson's colleagues think *Newsweek* put it well when the magazine referred to his "stupefyingly audacious leap to the conclusion" that this particular cave was the baptismal cave of St. John. "It's pure fiction. It's not archeology," said a senior member of the Israeli Antiquities Authority team.

One of the least controversial finds, on the other hand, is the Pool of Siloam, which is described in ancient texts as a gathering place for pilgrims entering Jerusalem and a main water reservoir for the city's residents two thousand years ago. In the Bible, Jesus is said to heal a blind man at this pool.

During repairs to a sewer main at the southern end of Old Jerusalem in 2004, the Pool of Siloam appears to have been rediscovered. It was dated by coins dropped on the steps leading down to the reservoir that depict a king who ruled Jerusalem in 103–76 BC and others from 60–70 AD. "The moment that we revealed and discovered this, we were 100 percent sure it was the Siloam Pool," said archeologist Eli Shukron at the time. "We know today that the Siloam Pool is connected to the Temple Mount. There is a road that connects the two elements." According to a news account of the find, Stephen Pean, a Bible scholar, said the pool's waters were considered so pristine it was believed they could purify even a leper. Pean said Jesus likely chose to cure the blind man using the purest water available, because people with any disabilities were barred from the temple. "The whole point is that people will not only be healed physically but also healed spiritually," he said. "This discovery helps bring the gospel alive in the context of Jewish practice."

Another intriguing and important discovery has thus far not met with much dispute: the burial box of Joseph Caiaphas, the high priest of Herod's Temple who, according to scriptural accounts, delivered Jesus to Pontius Pilate for crucifixion. This ornate limestone ossuary was found by accident in 1990 when a bulldozer bashed in the top of a tomb in an ancient Jewish cemetery in Jerusalem. Archaeologists called to the scene found twelve ossuaries containing the remains of sixty-three people. One of these was inscribed with the name "Joseph son of (or, of the family of) Caiaphas," the full name of the high priest who is described in biblical as well as early historical accounts as the man who arrested Jesus. Inside the ossuary were the remains of a sixty-year-old male. The lack of dispute about this particular find has led at least one expert to declare, "This remarkable discovery has, for the first time, provided us with the physical remains of an individual named in the Bible."

With no trace of the Holy Grail in the Holy Land, could it turn up in Rosslyn Chapel in Scotland? In *The Da Vinci Code* a variety of legends are mentioned, suggesting that the Knights Templar brought the Holy Grail from the Temple of Solomon and buried it in Rosslyn's underground vaults. (Even in the novel, however, the suggestion is made that while the Holy Grail may have once been at Rosslyn, it has been moved—perhaps to an underground location beneath the Louvre in Paris!) Rosslyn's trustees have, in the past, allowed for underground imaging tests to be done, which suggested that there are, indeed, underground chambers and possibly objects in them. But so far, no full-fledged archeological excavation has been permitted.

If not Rosslyn, could the Holy Grail also have a connection to a mysterious monument in Staffordshire, England? Called Shepherd's Monument, the stone gate decorates the garden of the estate of the Lords of Lichfield. It displays a carving of a famous painting—*Les Bergers d'Arcadie* (The Shepherds of Arcadia) by Nicolas Poussin. It also presents a line of code that reads like this:

D OUOSVAVV M

Charles Darwin and Charles Dickens tried to read the code and failed—as did many other ordinary people and luminaries over the years. Rumors have long suggested that the monument held the key to the Grail's location because Poussin (1594–1665) was believed to be a leading figure in the baroque era's version of the Knights Templar, and a painter with a variety of occult beliefs that he expressed in coded messages in some of his works. (It is a Poussin painting that is critical to understanding the legend of Rennes-le-Château, the Ur myth for the story of the Priory of Sion and for *The Da Vinci Code* itself.)

Recently, the Lichfield estate held a contest for international codebreakers. The British intelligence codebreaking center, Bletchley Park, which deciphered Hitler's Enigma code in World War II, sent two World War II veteran cryptologists, Oliver and Sheila Lawn, both now in their eighties, to work on the Lichfield code contest. Reviewing entries, Sheila Lawn sided with those who believed the code is a love poem from a Lichfield lord to his wife, each letter corresponding to a line of Latin verse. Oliver Lawn, however, preferred a different solution to the code. He opined that it was a message from the Priory of Sion: "Jesus H Defy," which means "Jesus (as Deity) Defy"—or in other words, resist or defy the Christian tenet that Jesus was divine. The Priory of Sion is said in some accounts to believe Jesus was an earthly prophet, not a divine one.

Bletchley Park says these two rival interpretations are the most cogent possibilities. If Mr. Lawn is correct, the strange monument is a fascinating echo of *The Da Vinci Code* and perhaps one that looks forward to Dan Brown's next novel, *The Solomon Key,* which the author has said will be about the Masonic Order. The carving was commissioned in 1748 by a Lichfield ancestor who may have been associated with Freemasonry and perhaps even belonged to a group resembling the Priory of Sion. If so, the monument could mark the spot where secret society members met to discuss their heretical beliefs. The message had to be encrypted, or so the argument goes, because the Church of England viewed these secret societies as dangerous and persecuted its members.

Will Dan Brown put the Shepherd's Monument or any of these other finds and documents, real or hoaxes, in his next novel? We'll just have to wait for *The Solomon Key* to find out. But since many of the discoverers and commentators on today's finds are putting Dan Brown in their stories, it wouldn't be too far-fetched to expect the novelist to return the compliment next time around.

In Search of the Holy Grail at the Rosslyn Chapel

BY DIANE MACLEAN

No publication in the world has been as uniquely tuned to *The Da Vinci Code* phenomenon as the *Scotsman,* a daily newspaper that bills itself as "Scotland's national newspaper." The reason is not hard to fathom: Rosslyn Chapel, the critical landmark fifteenth-century church where the climax of *The Da Vinci Code* takes place, is in its backyard. The range of stories is fascinating—from its coverage of *The Da Vinci Code* movie star Tom Hanks coming to the town, to interviews with the Sinclair family (who have inherited Rosslyn's care from their ancestors, who built it), to the newly discovered code in the ceiling stones that when solved turns out to be a musical composition.

Of course, there are the tourists—a veritable explosion of them. Before the novel only a handful of tourists visited Rosslyn. Now that the novel has popularized the legend that Rosslyn may be the place where the Holy Grail resides, tens of thousands of searchers and

---

Diane Maclean is a correspondent for the *Scotsman* (Edinburgh). Reprinted with permission from The Scotsman Publications Ltd.

seekers are descending on this curious "Cathedral of the Codes." Among these are the so-called Grail questers—an often remarkable cast of characters who seek to explain, or learn about, the chapel's transcendent meaning. And, as Diane Maclean reports, if you thought it was difficult to separate fact from fiction already. . . .

It is the hottest day of the year so far in Scotland and crowds escape the melting heat in the dark, hallowed vaults of Rosslyn Chapel. Copies of *The Da Vinci Code* are clutched in sweaty hands. Tourists take photos "to show the folks back home," while others admire the architecture. Beside the south door of the chapel is a group looking intently at what is described as a Templar gravestone. They are here in search of the grail.

The Holy Grail made its first appearance in a twelfth-century romance by Chrétien de Troyes. The story grew legs with Wolfram von Eschenbach's thirteenth-century epic poem *Parsifal* where, for the first time, the Knights Templar entered the frame.

"Grail questing" has reached fever pitch since Dan Brown's 2003 bestseller, which culminates in Rosslyn. A weekend workshop at nearby Newbattle Abbey College offers enlightenment to grail aficionados. Their guest speakers number a Knight Templar, a Freemason, and a member of the mysterious Saunière Society. I joined a group of the curious for the experience.

After the tour of Rosslyn we gather in the crypt at Newbattle. Everyone has read Brown's book and virtually everything else that has ever been written about the grail. We are here to learn the truth, but as one member of a secret society after another promises to reveal their mysteries, the truth seems slipperier than an oil slick. Why else do secret societies call themselves secret?

Archie Shields, a flesh-and-blood Knight Templar, sets the scene by describing a contemporary Templar. Shields concedes the society is governed by initiation, rites, and secrecy. Amid his failure to elaborate on these matters, we cannot judge what its connection is to the original Templars. Instead, he focuses on the present-day Christian interpretation the Templars have of the grail. "The grail is about life and knowledge," he says. "It is about our journey, and hoping that in the end God finds in our favor and we reach heaven."

Next up is Jim Munro, grand master Freemason. He is knowledgeable about Rosslyn and disputes claims that there are Templar graves in the chapel. At this news we feel hope leaving by a side door, as if the links among the Templars, grail, and Rosslyn are evaporating in the heat of the midday sun. The atmosphere perks up as Munro then reveals he never travels without his crystal and found something intriguing when he dowsed the church. "There is a very powerful ley line running through the north side of Rosslyn. If you follow it, it runs to Temple [or Balantrodoch]—where the Knights Templars lived—and then all the way on to Jerusalem."

Galvanized by this more esoteric information (although unable to see quite how it fits in with the grail), we await expectantly to hear from John Millar of the Saunière Society. Set up originally to promote the work of Henry Lincoln, a coauthor of *Holy Blood, Holy Grail,* which started the holy bloodline theory, the society now investigates the unexplained. Millar's interpretation of the grail is the most cryptic we have heard so far.

"It is something very special with strange properties that requires exploration," he begins. Like many involved in the "grail quest" he is hard to pin down, and his explanation involves a five-thousand-year-old book, *The Epic of Gilgamesh,* thought to be the oldest on earth.

"Through history there have been recorded accounts of strange devices," he continues. "Herodotus, the Mahabharata, even the Bible mentions them. These accounts convince me that there is something rather strange out there." Finally he cuts to the chase and offers his own insight to the grail. Derived in part from Plato, Millar's theory focuses on the idea of a cyclical universe: "At periodic intervals our civilization has been destroyed and slowly rebuilds again in a cycle, and the grail must be something that survives when we implode and destroy, forming a link between our old civilizations and the new."

We are now warming to our subject and coffee-break chat is dominated by contradictory theories. Most believe that the grail is Christ's bloodline, but as talk veers off into conspiracy theories and the "murder" of Princess Diana, it is hard to keep focused. George and Linda Scott from the American town of Roswell, New Mexico [itself one of the epicenters of world-class conspiracy theories, owing to its close association with UFOs and aliens—ed.], came to the course to satiate their obsession for Brown's book and satisfy a desire to get the truth. They are also both looking for something to replace organized religion, which they consider too fundamental. Linda, who is in her fifties, has breast cancer, so the quest for knowledge has been brought into sharp focus. "I think your whole life is a quest," she says. "When you have to confront your mortality this close, you want to know that life has had a meaning."

The course doesn't present any answers as to whether the grail is in us or hidden in a chapel pillar, but it does end with one tantalizing item. "A number of years ago an American lady came on a course here," says Millar. "I told

Rosslyn Chapel: The Cathedral of Codes and Symbols

Saunière's clues lead Robert Langdon and Sophie Neveu to the Rosslyn Chapel in Scotland near the end of *The Da Vinci Code.* When the pair arrives at the chapel to search for the Grail, they discover that the meaning of the legend is more complicated than they previously imagined.

Rosslyn Chapel is a real place, with a fascinating history. Work on the chapel—also known as the Cathedral of Codes—began in 1446 at the behest of Sir William St. Clair, or Sinclair, a hereditary grand master of the Scottish Masons and a reputed descendent of the Merovingian bloodline. Sir William exercised personal control over the chapel's construction, which halted shortly after his death in 1484. Only the choir—the part of the church occupied by the choir and the clergy, where services are performed—is completed.

The chapel is replete with religious imagery that has become a touchstone for endless speculation by esoteric writers, Grail enthusiasts, and conspiracy theorists. It is no wonder Dan Brown set the next to the last scene in *The Da Vinci Code* in this chapel, much worshipped by occultists the world over.

Rosslyn is reputed to be an approximate copy of the design of the ancient Temple of Solomon and is adorned with innumerable carvings, including Judaic, Celtic, Norse, Templar, and Masonic symbols, in addition to mainstream Christian images. The many different signs and symbols from many cultures, certainly a unique architectural rendering for its time, gives Rosslyn Chapel its nickname as the "Cathedral of Codes."

(*continues*)

Rosslyn Chapel:
The Cathedral of Codes and Symbols (*continued*)

Curators at Rosslyn Chapel are fond of pointing out a code scrawled on the walls of the crypt, a code supposedly left by the masons. Legend has it that the code indicates the presence of a great secret or a hidden treasure within the chapel walls, but so far no one has been able to decipher its meaning.

Technology may, in the end, solve many of the chapel's mysteries. In January 2003, the grand herald of the local branch of the Scottish Knights Templar—the self-proclaimed successors to the warrior monks who fled to Scotland in the fourteenth century to avoid religious persecution—announced that the Knights were using new scanning technology "capable of taking readings from the ground up to a mile deep." They hope to discover ancient vaults beneath the chapel that contain the reputed Rosslyn treasure.

her about the Templars and everything, and she was extremely interested, even asked me to cowrite a novel with her." Nothing came of the proposed collaboration, but Millar was delighted to see her return the next year. "She came back, and she brought her novelist husband with her," he recalls. Millar does not remember the surname of the couple, but he can clearly remember being introduced to her husband—Dan. To this day he is convinced that the man he told all his secrets to was the author Dan Brown. So, you see, we may not have found the grail, but we might have found the genesis for the world's most talked about book.

Anagram Fun

Solving and decoding anagrams is a critical task for Robert Langdon and Sophie Neveu in *The Da Vinci Code*. Fortunately, they are both good at it. But if you read the book and wonder what you would have done if put in their position, relax! You could have used anagram software on any conventional laptop while dashing through the Louvre. Using a program called Anagram Genius, we produced thousands of anagram alternatives for each of the following phrases. We are sharing only a random small sample below.

Our heroic couple has to decode the anagram O, Draconian devil! Oh, lame saint! (It turns out, of course, to be: Leonardo da Vinci! The Mona Lisa!) But it could have been any one of thousands of phrases:

An odd, snootier Machiavellian.
Honored idea man vacillations.
Ovations and dire melancholia.
A dishonored, mean vacillation.
Avid and snootier melancholia.
Sainthood and lovelier maniac.
Vanities or an odd melancholia.
Oh Man! Anti-social and evildoer.
Valiant homicide as a Londoner.
Lame vile, Draconian sainthood.
Homicidal Satan on an evildoer.
Ovational, disharmonic, leaden.
I am a harlot's ideal on connived.
Oh! Innovate cordial ladies' man.
I am a violent, odd, inane scholar.

(*continues*)

Anagram Fun (*continued*)

Just in case you were wondering, rearranging the letters of *Mona Lisa* by themselves yields these code names for the most famous painting in history:

A man's oil.
Somalian.
Lion as am.
Sol mania.
O! Snail am.
I a salmon.
O! Animals.

Later, our cryptographer–symbologist team has to decode the phrase "So dark the con of man." Our anagram finder suggests these, among many others:

Shock mad afternoon.
Craft damn hooknose.
Fat 'n' handsome crook.
Fame and shock or not.
Chats of naked moron.
Oh! Comfort and snake.

And then one wonders whether some of the other phrases called out in the book are anagrams for anything.

(*continues*)

Anagram Fun (*continued*)

For example, there is the much-mulled-over scrawl, "P.S. Find Robert Langdon." If this was intended to be an anagram, some of the results might be:

Forbidden, strong plan.
Finest bold, grand porn.
Finer, top, grand blonds.
Bold, sporting fan nerd.

When Sophie leaves the scene of her grandfather's *hieros gamos* rite, she runs home, packs her things, and leaves a note on the table: "I was there. Don't try to find me." Is this an anagram for anything? It could be any one of the following expressions of Sophie's real feelings about her experience:

Now mystified rotten hatred.
Worthy of strident dementia.
Stonyhearted if modern twit.
Tormented if sainted worthy.
Witty and thorniest freedom.
Fiery, hot, tarted disownment.

All anagrams generated using Anagram Geniustm version 9, www.anagramgenius.com.

7 *Sfumato*

Leonardo and His Secrets

Wisdom is the daughter of experience.
—Leonardo da Vinci

Leonardo da Vinci is the disciple of experience.
—Leonardo da Vinci

Leonardo da Vinci hovers over *The Da Vinci Code* from its opening pages set in the Louvre's Grand Gallery to its closing scene at the museum's La Pyramìde Inversée. He is everywhere in Dan Brown's novel, looking over the shoulder of the plot with the Mona Lisa eyes that gaze out from the cover. Did Leonardo integrate a secret coded message into *The Last Supper?* And if he did, was it about Mary Magdalene and her marriage to Jesus? Or was it more generally about women and sexuality? Was it a heretical in-joke? Was it a secret gay message? Or was it something even more obscure to us today about the relative importance of John the Evangelist and Jesus Christ?

Was Leonardo a secret devotee of the Templars and possibly a grand master of the Priory of Sion? Did he know anything about the Holy Grail beyond what other sophisticated Renaissance men knew? Did he believe the Holy Grail was not literally a chalice but the metaphorical or real womb of Mary Magdalene? Did he believe in the cult of the sacred feminine? (The aphorisms quoted above suggest he ascribed a feminine character to wisdom and knowledge, much as the Gnostics did.)

Why did he write in codes? Who was the Mona Lisa—or was it actually a self-portrait? What happened toward the end of his life when he moved to France? Why did this greatest of all painters paint so few paintings? Where did he get his insights into physics, anatomy, medicine, the theory of evolution, chaos theory, aviation, and other subjects on which his thinking was hundreds of years ahead of the world's leading-edge thinkers and inventors?

There are many mysteries about Leonardo, and food for many more thrillers and flights of postmodern imagination to come long after *The Da Vinci Code* has become an answer to a trivia game question.

In the commentaries presented here, we have tried to illustrate two basic schools of thought. The mainstream view, held by most Leonardo scholars and art historians, suggests that while there are innumerable mysteries and questions in the life and work of Leonardo, there is no evidence to support conclusions as far afield as that the John character in *The Last Supper* is really Mary Magdalene, or that Leonardo presided over the Priory of Sion, or that he was leaving coded messages behind in his artworks to be interpreted in later eras.

The other view—well expressed here by Lynn Picknett and Clive Prince, and documented much more extensively in their books—is certainly much more interesting, even if the evidence is thin. Their view offers fascinating answers to some of what the more established experts can only point to as a long list of questions. This type of thinking about Leonardo may turn out to have little basis in fact. But it may have a lot to offer metaphorically and conceptually. Reading Picknett and Prince, you can see the wheels turning in Dan Brown's mind as he says to himself, "Now, what if I took a bit of this thread and a bit of that, and wove a plot together like this . . ."

Finally, we have brought readers up to date on all the new "finds" and theories related to the artist that have come to the public's attention since the publication of *The Da Vinci Code,* including the continuing debate over the *Mona Lisa, The Last Supper,* and a surprising, newly found painting—a seminude Mary Magdalene unseen for fifty years and which one of the world's leading Leonardo scholars now thinks may be the work of the grand—er—the master himself.

The Secret Code of Leonardo da Vinci

BY LYNN PICKNETT AND CLIVE PRINCE

As noted previously, Lynn Picknett and Clive Prince's several books on topics ranging from Mary Magdalene to Leonardo da Vinci to the Templars figured prominently in Dan Brown's research for *The Da Vinci Code* and are referred to in Brown's bibliography. Although most mainstream academic experts and scholars disagree with them, seeing little or no evidence for their interpretations of the symbols in Leonardo's work, there is no denying they have had some intriguing, unique ideas and made some fascinating connections that have challenged the status quo of academic debate over many of these issues. The excerpt that follows is a perfect example.

To begin our story proper we have to return to Leonardo's *Last Supper* and look at it with new eyes. This is

---

not the time to view it in the context of the familiar art-historical assumptions. This is the moment when it is appropriate to see it as a complete newcomer to this most familiar of scenes would see it, to let the scales of preconception fall from one's eyes and, perhaps for the first time, really look at it.

The central figure is, of course, that of Jesus, whom Leonardo referred to as "the Redeemer" in his notes for the work. (Even so, the reader is warned against making any of the obvious assumptions here.) He looks contemplatively downwards and slightly to his left, hands outstretched on the table before him as if presenting some gift to the viewer. As this is the Last Supper at which, so the New Testament tells us, Jesus initiated the sacrament of the bread and wine, urging his followers to partake of them as his "flesh" and "blood," one might reasonably expect some chalice or cup of wine to be set before him, to be encompassed by that gesture. After all, for Christians this meal came immediately before Jesus' "Passion" in the garden of Gethsemane when he fervently prayed that "this cup pass from me"—another allusion to the wine/blood imagery—and also before his death by crucifixion when his holy blood was spilled on behalf of all mankind. Yet there is no wine in front of Jesus (and a mere token amount on the whole table). Could it be that those spread hands are making what, according to the artists, is essentially an empty gesture?

In the light of the missing wine, perhaps it is also no accident that of all the bread on the table very little is actually broken. As Jesus himself identified the bread with his own body which was to be broken in the supreme sacrifice, is some subtle message being conveyed about the true nature of Jesus' suffering?

This, however, is merely the tip of the iceberg of the

unorthodoxy depicted in this painting. In the biblical account it is the young St John—known as "the Beloved"—who was physically so close to Jesus on this occasion as to be leaning "on his bosom." Yet Leonardo's representation of this young person does not as required by the biblical "stage directions" so recline, but instead leans exaggeratedly away from the Redeemer, head almost coquettishly tilted to the right. Even where this one character is concerned this is by no means all, for newcomers to the painting might be forgiven for harbouring curious uncertainties about the so-called St John. For while it is true that the artist's own predilections tended to represent the epitome of male beauty as somewhat effeminate, *surely this is a woman we are looking at.* Everything about "him" is startlingly feminine. Aged and weathered though the fresco may be, one can still make out the tiny, graceful hands, the pretty, elfin features, the distinctly female bosom and the gold necklace. This woman, for surely it is such, is also wearing garments that mark her out as being special. They are the mirror image of the Redeemer's: where one wears a blue robe and a red cloak, the other wears a red robe and a blue cloak in the identical style. No one else at the table wears clothes that mirror those of Jesus in this way. But then no one else at the table is a woman.

Central to the overall composition is the shape that Jesus and this woman make together—a giant, spreadeagled "M," almost as if they were literally joined at the hip but had suffered a falling out, or even grown apart. To our knowledge no academic has referred to this feminine character as anything other than "St John," and the M shape has also passed them by. Leonardo was, we have discovered in our researches, an excellent psychologist who amused himself by presenting the patrons who had given him standard religious commissions with highly unorthodox images, knowing that people will view the most startling heresy with equanimity because they usually only see what they expect to see. If you are commissioned to paint a standard Christian scene and present the public with something that looks superficially like it, they will never question its dubious symbolism. Yet Leonardo must have hoped that perhaps others who shared his unusual interpretation of the New Testament message would recognize his version, or that someone, somewhere, some objective observer, would one day seize on the image of this mysterious woman linked with the letter "M" and ask the obvious questions. Who was this "M" and why was she so important? Why would Leonardo risk his reputation—even his life in those days of the flaming pyre—to include her in this crucial Christian scene?

Whoever she is, her own fate appears to be less than secure, for a hand cuts across her gracefully bent neck in what seems to be a threatening gesture. The Redeemer, too, is menaced by an upright forefinger positively thrust into his face with obvious vehemence. Both Jesus and "M" appear totally oblivious to these threats, each apparently lost in the world of their own thoughts, each in their own way serene and composed. But it is as if secret symbols are being employed, not only to warn Jesus and his female companion of their separate fates, but also to instruct (or perhaps remind) the observer of some information which it would otherwise be dangerous to make public. Is Leonardo using this painting to convey some private belief which it would have been little short of insane to share with a wider audience in any obvious fashion? And could it be that this belief might have a message for many more than his immediate circle, perhaps even for us today?

Let us look further at this astonishing work. To the observer's right of the fresco a tall bearded man bends almost double to speak to the last disciple at the table. In doing so he has turned his back completely on the Redeemer. It is this disciple—St Thaddeus or St Jude—whose model is acknowledged to be Leonardo himself. Nothing that Renaissance painters ever depicted was accidental or included merely to be pretty, and this particular exemplar of the time and the profession was known to be a stickler for the visual *double entendre.* (His preoccupation with using the right model for the various disciples can be detected in his wry suggestion that the irritating Prior of the Santa Maria Monastery himself sit for the character of Judas!) So why did Leonardo paint himself looking so obviously away from Jesus?

There is more. An anomalous hand points a dagger at a disciple's stomach one person away from "M." By no stretch of the imagination could the hand belong to anyone sitting at that table because it is physically impossible for those nearby to have twisted round to get the dagger in that position. However, what is truly amazing about this disembodied hand is not so much that it exists, but that in all our reading about Leonardo we have come across only a couple of references to it, and they show a curious reluctance to find anything unusual about it. Like the St John who is really a woman, nothing could be more obvious—and more bizarre—once it is pointed out, yet usually it is completely blanked out by the observer's eye and mind simply because it is so extraordinary and so outrageous.

We have often heard it said that Leonardo was a pious Christian whose religious paintings reflected the depth of his faith. As we have seen so far, at least one of them includes highly dubious imagery in terms of Christian orthodoxy, and our further research, as we shall see, reveals that nothing could be further from the truth than the idea that Leonardo was a true believer—a believer, that is, in any accepted, or acceptable, form of Christianity. Already, the curious and anomalous features in just one of his works seem to indicate that he was tying to tell us of another layer of meaning in that familiar biblical scene, of another world of belief beyond the accepted outline of the image frozen on that fifteenth century mural near Milan.

Whatever those heterodox inclusions may mean, they were, it cannot be stressed too much, totally at variance with orthodox Christianity. This itself is hardly news to many of today's materialist/rationalists, for to them Leonardo was the first real scientist, a man who had no time for superstitions or religion in any form, who was the very antithesis of the mystic or the occultist. Yet they, too, have failed to see what is plainly set out before their eyes. To paint the Last Supper without significant amounts of wine is like painting the critical moment of a coronation without the crown: it either misses the point completely or is making quite another one, to the extent that it marks the painter out as nothing less than an out and out heretic, someone who did possess religious beliefs, but ones which were at odds, perhaps even at war, with those of Christian orthodoxy. And Leonardo's other works, we have discovered, underline his own specific heretical obsessions through carefully applied and consistent imagery, something that would not happen if the artist were an atheist merely engaged in earning his living. These uncalled for inclusions and symbols are also much, much more than the skeptic's satirical response to such a commission—they are not just the equivalent of sticking a red nose on St Peter, for example. What we are looking at in *The Last Supper* and his other works is the secret code of Leonardo da Vinci, which we believe has a startling relevance to the world today.

Picknett and Prince then go on to discuss their thoughts about another painting by Leonardo, the *Madonna of the Rocks,* also sometimes known as *Virgin of the Rocks.* This painting also figures prominently in the plot of *The Da Vinci Code.* After Sophie Neveu deciphers the anagram "So dark the con of man" and realizes its unscrambled letters spell out "Madonna of the Rocks," she finds the key to the Swiss bank's vault hidden behind this painting. This bit of coded message decrypting affords Robert Langdon the opportunity to explain ideas to Sophie about the painting—ideas that are clearly drawn from the writings of Picknett and Prince, such as the passage that follows.

This apparent reversal of the usual roles of Jesus and John can also be seen on one of the two versions of Leonardo's *Virgin of the Rocks.* Art historians have never satisfactorily explained why there should be two, but one is currently exhibited in the National Gallery in London, and the other—to us by far the more interesting—is in the Louvre in Paris.

The original commission was from an organization known as the Confraternity of the Immaculate Conception, and was for a single painting to be the centrepiece of a triptych for the altar of their chapel in the church of San Francesco Grand in Milan. (The other two paintings for the triptych were to be by other artists.) The contract, dated 25 April 1483, still exists, and sheds interesting light on the expected work—and on what the members of the confraternity actually received. In it they carefully specified the shape and dimensions of the painting they wanted—a necessity, for the frame for the triptych already existed. Oddly, both of Leonardo's finished versions meet these specifications, although why he did two of them is unknown. We may, however, hazard a guess about these divergent interpretations which has little to do with perfectionism and more with an awareness of their explosive potential.

The contract also specified the theme of the painting. It was to portray an event not found in the Gospels but long present in Christian legend. This was the story of how, during the Flight into Egypt, Joseph, Mary, and the baby Jesus had sheltered in a desert cave, where they met the infant John the Baptist who was protected by the archangel Uriel. The point of this legend is that it allowed an escape from one of the more obvious and embarrassing questions raised by the Gospel story of Jesus' baptism. Why should a supposedly sinless Jesus require baptism at all, given that the ritual is a symbolic gesture of having one's sins washed away and of one's commitment to future godliness? Why should the Son of God himself have submitted to what was clearly an act of authority on the part of the Baptist?

This legend tells how, at this remarkably fortuitous meeting of the two holy infants, Jesus conferred on his cousin John the authority to baptize him when they were both adults. For several reasons this seems to us to be a most ironic commission for the confraternity to give Leonardo, but equally one might suspect that he would have delighted in receiving it—and in making the interpretation, at least in one of the versions, very much his own.

In the style of the day, the members of the confraternity had specified a lavish and ornate painting, complete with lashings of gold leaf and a flurry of cherubs and ghostly Old Testament prophets to fill out the space. What they got in the end was quite different, to such an extent that relations between them and the artist became acrimonious, culminating in a lawsuit that dragged on for twenty years.

Leonardo chose to represent the scene as realistically as possible, with no extraneous characters—there were to be no fat cherubs or shadowy prophets of doom for him. In fact, the *dramatis personae* have been perhaps excessively whittled down, for although this scene supposedly depicts the flight into Egypt of the Holy Family, Joseph does not appear in it at all.

The Louvre version, which was the earlier, shows a blue-robed Virgin with a protective arm around one child, the other infant being grouped with Uriel. Curiously, the two children are identical, but odder still, it is the child with the angel who is blessing the other, and Mary's child who is kneeling in subservience. This has led art historians to assume that, for some reason, Leonardo chose to pose the child John with Mary. After all, there are no labels with which to identify the individuals, and surely the child who has the authority to bless must be Jesus.

There are, however, other ways to interpret this picture, ways that not only suggest strong subliminal and highly unorthodox messages, but also reinforce the codes used in Leonardo's other works. Perhaps the similarity of the two children here suggests that Leonardo was deliberately fudging their identity for his own purposes. And, while Mary is protectively embracing the child generally accepted as being John with her left hand, her right is stretched out above the head of "Jesus" in what seems to be a gesture of downright hostility. This is what [art historian] Serge Bramly describes as "reminiscent of an eagle's talons." Uriel is pointing across to Mary's child, but is also, significantly, looking enigmatically out at the observer—that is, resolutely away from the virgin and child. While it may be easier and more acceptable to interpret this gesture as an indication of the one who is to be the Messiah, there are other possible meanings.

What if the child with Mary, in the Louvre version of *The Virgin of the Rocks,* is Jesus—as one might logically expect—and the youngster with Uriel is John? Remember that in this case it is John who is blessing Jesus with the latter submitting to his authority. Uriel, as John's special protector, is avoiding even looking at Jesus. And Mary, protecting her son, is casting a threatening hand high above the head of the baby John. Several inches directly below her outstretched palm the pointing hand of Uriel cuts straight across, as if the two gestures are encompassing some cryptic clue. It is as if Leonardo is indicating that some object, some significant—but invisible—thing ought to fill the space between them. In the context it is by no means fanciful to understand that Mary's outstretched fingers are meant to look as if they were placed on the crown of an invisible head, while Uriel's pointing forefinger cuts across the space precisely where the neck would be. This phantom head floats just above the child who is with Uriel. . . . So this child *is* effectively labeled after all, for which of the two of them was to die by beheading? And if this is truly John the Baptist, it is he who is shown to be giving the blessing, to be the superior one.

Yet when we turn to the much later National Gallery version, we find that all the elements needed to make these heretical deductions are missing—but those elements only. The two children are quite different in appearance, and the one with Mary bears the traditional long-stemmed cross of the Baptist (although it is true that this may have been added by a later artist). Here Mary's right hand is still outstretched above the other child, but this time there is no suggestion of a threat. Uriel no longer points, nor looks away from the scene. It is as if Leonardo is inviting us to "spot the difference"—daring us to draw our own conclusions from the anomalous details.

This kind of examination of Leonardo's work reveals a plethora of provocative and disturbing undercurrents. There does seem to be a repetition, using several ingenious subliminal symbols and signals of the John the Baptist theme. Time and time again he, and images denoting him, are elevated above the figure of Jesus. . . .

There is something driven about this insistence, not least in the very intricacy of the images that Leonardo used, and indeed, in the risk he took in presenting even such clever and subliminal heresy to the world. Perhaps, as we have already hinted, the reason he finished so little of his work was not so much that he was a perfectionist, but more that he was only too aware of what might happen to him if anyone of note saw through the thin layer of orthodoxy to the outright "blasphemy" that lay just under the surface. Perhaps even the intellectual and physical giant that was Leonardo was a little wary of falling foul of the authorities—once was quite enough for him.

However, there was surely no need for him to put his head on the block by working such heretical messages into his paintings unless he had a passionate belief in them. As we have already seen, far from being the atheistic materialist beloved of many moderns, Leonardo was deeply, seriously committed to a system of belief that ran totally counter to what was then, and still is now, mainstream Christianity. It was what many would choose to call the "occult."

To most people today that is a word that has immediate and less than positive connotations. It is taken to mean black magic, or the cavortings of depraved charlatans—or both. In fact the word "occult" simply means "hidden" and is commonly used in astronomy, such as in the description of one heavenly body "occulting," or eclipsing, another. Where Leonardo was concerned, one might agree that while there were indeed elements in his life and beliefs that smacked of sinister rites and magical practices, it is also true that what he sought was, above and beyond anything else, knowledge. Most of what he sought had, however, been effectively "occulted" by society—and by one omnipresent and powerful organization in particular. Throughout most of Europe at that time the Church frowned upon any scientific experimentation and took drastic steps to silence those who made their unorthodox or particularly individual views public.

However, Florence—where Leonardo was born and brought up, and at whose court his career really began—was a flourishing centre for a new wave of knowledge. This, astonishingly enough, was due entirely to this city being a haven for large numbers of influential occultists and magicians. Leonardo's first patrons, the de Medici family who ruled Florence, actively encouraged occult scholarship and even sponsored researchers to look for, and translate, specific lost manuscripts.

This fascination with the arcane was not the Renaissance equivalent of today's newspaper horoscopes. Although there were inevitably areas of investigation that would seem to us naive or downright superstitious, there were also many more which represented a serious attempt to understand the universe and man's place within it. The magician, however, sought to go a little further, and discover how to control the forces of nature. Seen in this light perhaps it is not so remarkable that Leonardo of all people was, as we believe, an active participant in the occult culture of his time and place. And the distinguished historian Dame Frances Yates has even suggested that the whole key to Leonardo's far-ranging genius might have lain in contemporary ideas of magic.

The details of the precise philosophies so prevalent in this Florentine occult movement can be found in our previous book, but briefly, the lynchpin of all the groups of the day was hermeticism, which takes its name from Hermes Trismegistus, the great, if legendary, Egyptian magus whose books presented a coherent magical system. By far the most important part of hermetic thinking was the idea that man was in some way literally divine—a concept that was in itself so threatening to the Church's hold on the hearts and minds of its flock as to be deemed anathema.

Hermetic principles were certainly demonstrated in Leonardo's life and work, but at first glance there would seem to be a glaring discrepancy between these sophisticated philosophical and cosmological ideas and heretical notions which nevertheless upheld the importance of biblical figures. (We must stress that the heterodox beliefs of Leonardo and his circle were not merely the result of a reaction against a corrupt and credulous Church. As history has shown, there was indeed a strong, and certainly not undercover, reaction to the Church of Rome—the whole Protestant movement. But had Leonardo been alive today we would not find him worshipping in *that* kind of church either.)

However, there is a great deal of evidence that hermeticists could also be outright heretics. Giordano Bruno

(1548–1600), the fanatical preacher of hermeticism, proclaimed that his beliefs came from an ancient Egyptian religion that preceded Christianity—and which eclipsed it in importance.

Part of this flourishing occult world—but still too wary of the Church's disapproval to be anything other than an underground movement—were the alchemists. Again they are a group which suffers from a modern preconception. Today they are derided as fools who wasted their lives trying vainly to turn base metal into gold; in fact this image was a useful smokescreen for the serious alchemists who were more concerned with proper scientific experimentation—but also with personal transformation and its implicit total control of one's own fate. Again, it is not difficult to see that someone as hungry for knowledge as Leonardo would be part of that movement, perhaps even a prime mover in it. While there is no direct evidence for his involvement, he was known to consort with committed occultists of all shades, and our own research into his faking of the Turin Shroud suggests strongly that the image was the direct result of his own "alchemical" experiments.

Put simply: it is highly unlikely that Leonardo would have been unfamiliar with any system of knowledge that was available in his day, but at the same time, given the risks involved in being openly part of them, it is equally unlikely that he would commit any evidence of this to paper. Yet as we have seen, the symbols and images he repeatedly used in his so-called Christian paintings were hardly those which, had they realized their true nature, would have been appreciated by the Church authorities.

Even so, a fascination with hermeticism might seem, superficially at least, to be almost at the opposite end of the scale to a preoccupation with John the Baptist—and the putative significance of the woman "M." In fact, it was this discrepancy which puzzled us to such an extent that we delved further. Of course it could be argued that what all this endless raising of forefingers means is that one Renaissance genius was obsessed with John the Baptist. But was it possible that a deeper significance lay behind Leonardo's own personal belief? Was the message that can be read into his paintings in some way actually *true?*

Certainly the Maestro has long been acknowledged in occult circles as being the possessor of secret knowledge. When we began researching his part in the Turin Shroud we came across many rumours among such people to the effect not only that he had a hand in its creation, but also that he was a known magus of some renown. There is even a nineteenth-century Parisian poster advertising the Salon of the Rose + Cross—a meeting-place for artistically minded occultists—that depicts Leonardo as Keeper of the Holy Grail (which in such circles can be taken to be shorthand for Keeper of the Mysteries). Again, rumours and artistic licence do not in themselves add up to much, but, taken together with all the indications listed above, they certainly whetted our appetite to know more about the unknown Leonardo.

So far we had isolated the major strand of what appeared to be Leonardo's obsession: John the Baptist. While it was only natural that he would receive commissions to paint or sculpt that saint while living in Florence—a place that was dedicated to John—it is a fact that when left to himself, Leonardo chose to do so. After all, the last painting he was to work on before his death in 1519—which was not commissioned by anyone, but painted for his own reasons—was of John the Baptist. Perhaps he wanted the image to look at as he lay dying. And even when he had been paid to paint an orthodox

Christian scene, he always, if he could get away with it, emphasized the role of the Baptist in it.

As we have seen, his images of John are elaborately concocted to convey a specific message, even if it is grasped imperfectly and subliminally. John is certainly depicted as important—but then he was the forerunner, herald, and blood relative of Jesus, so it is only natural that his role should be recognized in this way. Yet Leonardo is not telling us that the Baptist was, like everyone else, inferior to Jesus. In his *Virgin of the Rocks* the angel is, arguably, pointing to *John,* who is blessing Jesus and not vice versa. In the *Adoration of the Magi* the healthy, normal-looking people are worshipping the elevated roots of the carob tree—John's tree—and not the colourless Virgin and child. And the "John gesture," that upraised righthand forefinger, is thrust into Jesus' face at *The Last Supper* in what is clearly no loving or supportive manner; at the very least, it seems to be saying in a bluntly threatening manner, "Remember John." And that least known of Leonardo's works, the Shroud of Turin, bears the same kind of symbolism, with its image of an apparently severed head being placed "over" a classically crucified body. The overwhelming evidence is that, to Leonardo at least, John the Baptist was actually superior to Jesus.

All this might make Leonardo appear to have been a voice crying in the wilderness. After all, many great minds have been eccentric, to say the least. Perhaps this was yet another area of his life in which he stood outside the conventions of his day, unappreciated and alone. But we were also aware, even at the outset of our research in the late 1980s, that evidence—albeit of a highly controversial nature—had emerged in recent years that linked him with a sinister and powerful secret society. This group, which allegedly existed many centuries before Leonardo, involved some of the most influential individuals and families in European history, and—according to some sources—it still exists today. Not only, it is said, were members of the aristocracy prime movers in this organization, but also some of today's most eminent figures in political and economic life keep it alive for their own particular aims. . . .

Trying to Make Sense of Leonardo's "Faded Smudge"

An Interview with Denise Budd

Is anything known about Leonardo that would suggest he was a member of the Priory of Sion or similar secret society?

There's no real evidence at all that Leonardo da Vinci was a member of the Priory of Sion or any other secret organization. The documents that Dan Brown relied upon heavily were discovered, apparently, in the Bibliothèque Nationale in Paris in the 1960s, and they appear to be twentieth-century forgeries.

Besides sometimes writing backwards, did Leonardo use codes or coding?

There is evidence of codes in some of his writing; one example is the so-called Ligny memorandum, in which

---

Denise Budd is a Columbia University Ph.D. whose doctoral dissertation on Leonardo da Vinci focused on a reinterpretation of the documentary evidence from the first half of his career.

he interspersed names and places in scrambled letters. And he may have worked as a spy when he was a military engineer for Cesare Borgia. But the backwards writing is not a particularly difficult code to crack. That was a function of Leonardo's left-handedness.

Leonardo is known for peppering his works with symbolism and, some say, heretical ideas, in his Virgin of the Rocks *paintings, for example. Do you agree?*

No, I don't. The *Virgin of the Rocks* was a religious commission for the Confraternity of the Immaculate Conception for the church of San Francesco Grande in Milan—not for nuns, as Brown says. Leonardo da Vinci got the commission in 1483. There were some complex legal issues regarding it and its copy, including issues of payment for Leonardo and his associate, Ambrogio de Predis. One of the reasons that Dan Brown argues that the painting is heretical is because he misreads the work, confusing the figure of St. John the Baptist with Christ, and vice versa. The composition shows Mary—with her hand suspended over her son, creating a dominant axis—embracing Christ's cousin St. John, who kneels in reverence. The Baptist is the first to recognize Christ's divinity, which he does in the womb, so this composition falls completely within the norms of tradition.

With the added element of the angel Uriel, Leonardo is actually combining two separate moments: this scene from Christ's infancy, with the scene when the Baptist (who is living as a baby hermit with the angel Uriel, according to an apocryphal text) visits the holy family on the flight into Egypt. Leonardo guides us through the composition by the play of hands, which relate the figures to one another. Presumably, the subject would have been worked out with the confraternity, and it would have played an important role in establishing the iconography, which likely refers to the issue of Mary's immaculate conception, which was not yet a matter of settled church doctrine. During the Renaissance, an artist was not generally given free rein on important commissions. There would have been specific guidelines. And presumably, Leonardo worked within that framework.

Can you comment on Leonardo's hypothesized homosexuality? How might his sexuality have played into his style of painting?

While there is rarely evidence for a person's sexuality in this age, here is what we know: he was accused twice, anonymously, of sodomy in Florence in 1476, while he was living with the painter Verrocchio. The same accusation included a member of the Medici clan, which certainly could suggest political motivation. The charges were dropped. Leonardo did not marry, which was the case for a whole litany of Renaissance artists, from Leonardo to Michelangelo, to Donatello, Brunelleschi, della Robbia, and others. Leonardo's presumed homosexuality stems primarily from later sixteenth-century sources, written after his death, as well as from his penchant for young and often not very talented workshop assistants, who, rather than leaving after their traditional period in the workshop, stayed on for many, many years. Was he a homosexual? Probably. But I do not think it had anything to do with his manner of painting. His women, portraits aside, are among the most beautiful of the period.

In one of the drawings in his notebooks, there's an anatomical study of intercourse. His comment is that the members on the page are so unappealing that if people didn't have beautiful faces the human race would die out. However, his works do not really give us any clues about his sexuality, nor would you expect them to.

What about Dan Brown's thesis about The Last Supper?

There is no disembodied hand as Dan Brown suggests. The hand with the knife—which is the hand Dan Brown says "threatens Mary Magdalene"—that's Peter's hand. And Peter's not threatening Mary Magdalene nor trying to suppress the feminine side of the church. Peter is holding the knife, which is a premonition of the violent reaction he will have during the arrest of Christ, when he cuts off the ear of the Roman soldier. So that is a fairly standard iconographic tool.

Dan Brown uses the absence of a chalice as an introductory point to bring Mary Magdalene into the picture. Yet if you look at the picture, you'll see that Christ's hands are spread out on the table. His right hand is reaching toward a piece of bread, and his left hand is actually, quite clearly, reaching toward a cup of wine. And that's the hand that's pointed down. The institution of the Eucharist is clearly presented in the bread and the wine. Now it's not a chalice per se, like a chalice in your modern church practice, but there's a cup of wine. It's what you would expect to see at the Last Supper.

And what about the idea that the painting depicts Mary Magdalene instead of John the Baptist?

As far as the Magdalene, clearly there is no dispute. That figure is St. John the Evangelist. St. John is Christ's favorite and he is always shown by Christ's side. The major difference between Leonardo's *Last Supper* and earlier Florentine examples of the scene is that Leonardo put Judas among the disciples, not on the other side of the table. But the figure of John is always by Christ's side, he is always beardless and he's always beautiful. And in some instances, he is so innocent that while Christ is making the announcement that he will be betrayed, John actually sleeps. A perfect example of this "feminine" characterization of John is in Raphael's *Crucifixion* in the London National Gallery, painted around 1500.

A second point that must be mentioned is the atrocious state of the *Last Supper,* which makes it patently unreliable to examine for any reason other than basic composition, which, presumably, it retains. It was called a wreck only twenty years after its completion, while da Vinci was still alive, and has again and again been called barely visible. In the sixteenth century, Vasari called it a "faded smudge." It was restored in 1726, 1770; hung in a room that was used for a barracks for Napoleon's troops in 1799 and as a stable; damaged in a flood of 1800; a door was cut through the bottom of it; there was an attempt to remove it from the wall in 1821; it was restored in 1854–55, 1907–8, 1924, 1947–48, 1951–54, and all throughout the 1980s and 1990s. There is not enough of any of the faces left to make any serious determinations. Christ's face, for example, is a completely modern repainting.

"No, I do not believe there is a woman in *The Last Supper* . . ."

An Interview with Diane Apostolos-Cappadona

As you know, some people, including Dan Brown, seem to see all sorts of things in The Last Supper *that traditional art historians and scholars do not. What do you see when you look at this painting?*

What Leonardo presents us with in his painting of *The Last Supper* is what he does primarily throughout all of his art—the humanizing of art. This is one of his biggest appeals. From my way of reading Christian art, this painting is iconographically important because Leonardo changes the focus of the iconography. Historically, the earlier carvings and sculptures on cathedral exteriors and interiors, on liturgical vestments, and in paintings, sculptures, and manuscript illuminations of the Last Supper, the artist emphasizes either the identification of the traitor, which is the most important moment for most people, or the Institution of the Eucharist, which is liturgically the importance of *The Last Supper.*

What Leonardo does is portray the announcement, "I am going to be betrayed," and the aftermath of that moment. The disciples are in shock. They look at each other, pointing with exaggerated gestures as if to say, "It can't be me, it must be you, but who could it be, how could it be any of us?" And Jesus is saying, not only, "I know I will be betrayed," but also, "I know which of you is going to do it."

What Some People See in *The Last Supper*

1. A knife hangs in the air seemingly tinged with symbolic meaning as it is disassociated from the rest of the image.
2. *The Da Vinci Code* suggests that the character to Jesus' right, generally thought to be John, is really female, not male, and is Leonardo's vision of Mary Magdalene, sitting in the most important place next to Jesus.
3. Peter's hand, slicing through the air in a menacing way in "Mary Magdalene's" direction, could be a gesture reinforcing Peter's rivalry with Mary Magdalene for control of Jesus' movement after his death and Peter's jealousy over the important place in the movement Jesus may have given to Mary.
4. The 45-degree angled space between Jesus and "Mary Magdalene" suggests a V—said in *The Da Vinci Code* to be the archetypal symbol of the chalice, the vagina, the womb, and female sexuality.

Scala/Art Resource

5. The line that outlines Jesus and "Mary Magdalene" traces the shape of an M. According to another argument advanced by *The Da Vinci Code* this M could connote either Mary Magdalene or matrimony.
6. The garments worn by Jesus and "Mary" are mirror images of each other's red and blue fabrics.
7. The blue color denotes spiritual love, fidelity, and truth. Red and blue are seen as the royal colors, in this case possibly suggesting the "royal blood" theme and the alignment of the royal House of Benjamin (from which Mary is said to be descended) and the House of David (from which Jesus is said to be descended).
8. There is no central chalice or wine goblet in the *Last Supper* despite the popular preconception that there is. Instead, each person at the table has a small glass cup of his/her own.

In the larger context of Leonardo's oeuvre, gestures are humanizing as well as symbolic. In this particular painting, the gestures signify surprise, disbelief, accusation, and awe or wonder. This is what is important in this painting. The Jesus figure is set off in a particular way because the others are stunned. He is both the announcer and the betrayed.

What do you think, specifically, about The Da Vinci Code*'s supposition that the "John" character is really Mary Magdalene?*

Initially, my response was this is a very interesting interpretation, to say that there was a woman at the table. It fits nicely with feminist theology or the post-feminist era of theology. However, that doesn't make it true.

If you look at the history of the Last Supper in Christian art, you see the figure of Jesus, sometimes seated at the center of a table, other times at an end of a table. The table may be round, square, or rectangular depending upon contemporary cultural and social customs as much as for artistic spacing. Simultaneously, you see regularly the figure of John the Evangelist (also known as John the Divine, or John the Beloved Disciple) in closest proximity to Jesus. There is a tradition of John being seen in our eyes—our late-twentieth century/early-twenty-first century eyes—as soft, feminine, and youthful.

However, if you look carefully at the Leonardo painting, you will notice other disciples who do not have beards or who could be construed as possessing feminine features. However, from my work in gender studies, I would caution that gender is a culturally and socially conditioned concept. What you and I accept today as being masculine or feminine is most likely not what would have been accepted in Florence or Milan during the fifteenth century. If you look carefully at Christian art, in particular at the depictions of male and female bodies, faces, and gestures, then the *Last Supper* is not such an extraordinary presentation!

Can you be more specific?

If you look at the history of angels in Renaissance art contemporary to Leonardo, or in other Leonardo paintings, these angelic bodies are intended to be masculine. Yet I have students who become quite upset when I project slides of medieval and Renaissance paintings with depictions of angels. In despair, the students ask, "But why does he have long hair? Why does he have curls? His face is sort of preadolescent." We have to stop and to consider, what is our preconception of gender?

No, I do not believe that there is a woman in the *Last Supper* and I do not believe in any way that it's Mary Magdalene. I think that the *V* that's there—the one Dan Brown defines as a symbol of femininity—is there, first of all, to emphasize the Christ figure and to emphasize the reality of the perspective within that fresco.

What role does artistic form and perspective play in this?

Perspective is extraordinarily important in Renaissance art generally, and in Leonardo's art in particular. The apostles are all grouped into triangular formations. For example, there is the triangle composed of the so-called Mary Magdalene–John figure, the graybearded figure behind [who is Judas], and the foreground figure [who is Peter]. Dan Brown has omitted any discussion of pyramidal composition in Leonardo's oeuvre, of the four triangular groupings which are important to form the compositional balance for the central triangular figure who is Jesus. Centrally positioned, Jesus is in a pyramidal posture, and it is this pyramidal composition that is one of Leonardo's great gifts to Western art.

Today, we see the *Last Supper* within the shrine of a museum atmosphere; however, the work was created on a wall, in a refectory where the monks ate. They either looked up at it or at the painting of the crucifixion on the opposite wall depending on what was being said and what meal it was, and what prayers were being recited. So the painting functioned differently, at different days of the liturgical calendar. Dan Brown ignores totally that original monastic context.

New Discoveries about the "Grand Master" Himself

Leonardo since The Da Vinci Code

BY CATHLEEN MCGUIGAN

The Botticelli Code? The Michelangelo Code? The Raphael Code? Hmm, they just don't have the right ring. Leonardo da Vinci was the old master Dan Brown

---

Cathleen McGuigan is a senior editor and national arts correspondent of *Newsweek*. Her articles have appeared in *Smithsonian* and *Art News,* among other publications. She is also an adjunct professor of journalism at Columbia University.

shrewdly tapped to jump-start his thriller about the secrets of art and dark religious mysteries. Of the great High Renaissance painters, Leonardo was the true Renaissance man. Not only was he the original multitasker—diving into the worlds of art, architecture, engineering, natural science, weaponry—but he connects so well to the modern sensibility. Though Brown's novel treats him as the historical figure of the late fifteenth and early sixteenth centuries that he was, you can picture Leonardo quite at home in the twenty-first century—a brilliant, ambitious, inventive genius embracing new technologies and scientific advances, patronized by the rich and powerful, lionized by the media, a global traveler trailed by a posse of gorgeous young men.

The man who painted the *Mona Lisa*—and designed an airplane four hundred years before the Wright brothers—has long captured the public imagination. But with the runaway success of *The Da Vinci Code,* fascination with Leonardo has soared. Flocks of tourists now crowd the little Scottish town of Rosslyn, where the trail of clues in Dan Brown's novel ends, or rush off the beaten track of Paris to see the church of St. Sulpice, the site of one murder, all in search of Leonardo. (Or rather they're looking for "Da Vinci," as Brown incorrectly refers to him, from the title of the book to numerous references in the text. In fact, "Vinci" was his Tuscan hometown, not his last name. Art historians usually refer to him simply as "Leonardo," with the first syllable pronounced "lay.")

The few museums fortunate enough to own a Leonardo are even more jammed than usual. The Château du Clos Lucé in the Loire valley, where the artist died, has become a magnet for tourism. So has the town of Vinci, where conservative religious critics of the Dan Brown novel put on a mock "trial" of the controversial contentions in *The Da Vinci Code* in 2005. At least two important scholarly biographies of Leonardo have been published since the bestselling novel came out, and there are dozens of new monographs, pop culture books and even children's books. Many new exhibitions are also planned. In 2006, Universal Leonardo, a program spearheaded by Oxford professor Martin Kemp, is promoting museum shows from Munich to Budapest to London to exploit the vast collections of the artist's amazing drawings and notes. Kemp's exhibition at London's Victoria and Albert Museum will attempt to show how Leonardo's mind worked, using models and computer animation of some of his astonishing ideas and inventions.

Both new biographies of the artist have won high praise. Charles Nicholl's *Leonardo da Vinci: Flights of the Mind* is an exhaustively researched narrative of Leonardo's life and times, from his illegitimate birth in 1452, to his long career spent mostly in Florence and Milan, to his last years in Rome and then France, where he died in 1519. Delving into his notebooks and other documents, Nicholl creates a portrait of a genius often unappreciated during his own life—one who struggled to complete artistic commissions while observing the natural world around him in minute detail, drawing everything from the human heart to a nautilus shell. Oxford's Kemp, author of *Leonardo* and one of the foremost Leonardo scholars today, is trained in both science and art history. His fascinating, concise take on the artist is a different sort of biography, organized thematically rather than chronologically. Kemp weaves together the scientific and artistic impulses of his subject to try to get inside that amazing mind.

Meanwhile, there's been a surge in students at universities pursuing art history, which at least one British professor links explicitly to the popularity of *The Da Vinci Code.* The book has clearly sparked an animated curiosity in Leonardo's art and life that goes far beyond the usual academic circles.

Leonardo has done equally well of late on the popular front. Although he already had a Teenage Mutant Ninja Turtle named after him in the 1980s, marketers riding the coattails of *The Da Vinci Code* are now seriously cashing in. For the kids, there's a board game called Da Vinci's Challenge, with the goal of creating symbols out of geometric pieces, and a book called *Who Can Crack the Leonardo da Vinci Code?* Television news and documentary programs have weighed in with all manner of specials, such as the History Channel's *Da Vinci and the Code He Lived By.* Several video and cell phone games have been developed to accompany the release of the movie version of *The Da Vinci Code,* as well as a variety of licensed and unlicensed tie-in products. You can even buy a custom-made cryptex with your own personal code embedded. The item resembles the one central to the plot of *The Da Vinci Code,* although it is not clear Leonardo actually ever designed such a cryptex.

But let's get back to his art. Leonardo's reputation as one of the greatest artists who ever lived is based on less than two dozen surviving paintings. And so the possibility of finding a previously unknown work by Leonardo stirs enormous excitement. In the fall of 2005 a leading Leonardo scholar, Carlo Pedretti, curated an exhibition in Ancona, Italy, that included a painting of Mary Magdalene that used to be attributed to a Leonardo pupil, Giampietrino. Yet Pedretti thinks that Leonardo may have had a major role in the creation of this painting. "Because of the very high quality, I am inclined to believe that it is much more than a supervision of the student by the master," he says. "I can't say for sure yet, but this is my position, and I am prepared to follow up with the whole process of laboratory verification."

Pedretti discovered the little-known painting in a private collection in Switzerland, along with a version of *The Virgin of the Rocks.* (Two other versions of that subject by Leonardo exist. One hangs in the Louvre in Paris and the other in the National Gallery in London. These two paintings also figure prominently in *The Da Vinci Code.*) The Mary Magdalene painting hadn't been shown in public in more than fifty years. Like the *Mona Lisa,* it was painted on a wooden panel (but even smaller, only twenty-three by eighteen inches). This small masterpiece depicts a beautifully voluptuous young woman, her reddish blond hair tumbling over white shoulders, her rich scarlet robe open to expose her breasts, her hands clutching a gauzy veil across her belly.

If this picture is indeed an authentic Leonardo, it would be the only time the artist painted Mary Magdalene—unless you believe what *The Da Vinci Code* says about *The Last Supper,* which is that the effeminate youth seated at the right hand of Jesus isn't the apostle John, but instead Mary Magdalene. One of the many controversial themes of the novel, of course, maintains that Mary Magdalene wasn't a repentant ex-prostitute but a wealthy patron of Jesus who became his wife and mother of his secret child—an exemplar of the "sacred feminine" whose real role and contributions were later scrubbed from church doctrine. Ironically, one of the only serious Leonardo scholars even to consider the possibility that the John figure in *The Last Supper* could be a woman is Carlo Pedretti, though his statements have been ambiguous. In any event, it's puzzling to think that Leonardo would promote the unorthodox view of Mary Magdalene as Jesus's wife when he painted *The Last Supper* in 1498—and then turn around and depict her some fifteen or so years later as the iconic temptress in this voluptuously beautiful rendering.

So how can Pedretti determine if this stunning painting really is by Leonardo? The kind of laboratory exam he refers to is actually mentioned in *The Da Vinci Code,* in a brief passage about a real art analyst in Florence today, Maurizio Seracini. Seracini uses infrared reflectography to see what's sketched on white primer beneath a painting's layers of pigment. Because Leonardo's drawing is so exquisitely distinctive, it's "easy" to identify, according to Pedretti. Martin Kemp agrees. Kemp used this technique to authenticate the Lansdowne Madonna and the similar *Madonna with the Yarnwinder* (which, in another plot twist, was stolen from the Duke of Buccleuch in Scotland in 2003 and, as of this writing, has yet to be recovered). Though some other scholars still question the quality of those two Madonnas, Kemp points out that "the technical analysis shows clearly that Leonardo participated" in both paintings—meaning his studio assistants did a lot of the work. "There was probably a category of picture," says Kemp, "which he and the lads were working on, basically."

The notion that Leonardo didn't have the only hand in what we take to be Leonardo paintings might sound shocking, but the old master-apprentice system is hardly a secret. (Young Leonardo himself is said to have painted one of the angels in *The Baptism of Christ* [c. 1476] by his teacher, Andrea del Verrocchio, which today hangs in the Uffizi in Florence.) But whether others' additions to paintings subvert the artist's original intentions is a serious concern, one that *The Da Vinci Code* takes up with the cameo appearance of the real-life analyst Seracini and his investigation into Leonardo's great unfinished *Adoration of the Magi*. Using infrared reflectography, Seracini finds that the underdrawing is clearly Leonardo's, but he believes that the surface was painted by obviously lesser artists who altered, in part, the original design.

In real life, Seracini's painstaking, four-year-long technical study wrapped up in 2005, after *The Da Vinci Code* had already been on the bestseller list for two years. His ultimate findings are fascinating. A tour de force of complex composition, the *Adoration of the Magi* shows the Madonna and child calmly at the center, surrounded by a tumult of teeming, twisting figures that emerge from the shadows, wide-eyed drama in their faces. Some of Leonardo's first ideas, Seracini discovered, never appeared on the surface. Hidden underneath the pigment is the suggestion of a pagan or Egyptian temple, rather than the more classical ruins we actually see, with a violent battle scene sketched in a distant corner of the picture. What these findings mean will surely fire up a new round of interpretive debate.

Elsewhere in Florence, excitement is brewing over whether faded frescoes on the upper floors of Santissima Annunziata Monastery could be by Leonardo and his pupils, who may have worked in those very rooms at one point. While most scholars are skeptical of this potential "find," there is keen interest in Seracini's latest project. It is nothing less than a hunt for the most famous "lost Leonardo" of all—the epic painting of the Battle of Anghiari. Originally commissioned as a fresco in the Palazzo Vecchio in Florence, it was legendary for years after Leonardo's death, known through drawings and copies. Rubens was inspired around 1605 to make a beautiful grisaille (a painting in gray and soft tints) of the action-packed central scene. The Rubens version now hangs in the Louvre. Powerful fragmentary sketches from

Leonardo's own notebooks also survive, particularly of a soldier's twisted face, his mouth open in a scream. According to the sixteenth-century Florentine artist and writer Giorgio Vasari, Leonardo abandoned the painting out of frustration with his own experiments in combining fresco and oil paint. Decades after Leonardo's death, Vasari himself was commissioned to modify the same room for the Medicis: he built a new interior, with his own paintings depicting military glory on the walls. But Seracini has found a surprising gap behind one of those walls, just under a tiny green flag in Vasari's painting carrying the words "*Cerva, trova*" (Seek and you shall find). Vasari left that clue for us, Seracini believes, and took care not to destroy Leonardo's unfinished masterpiece beneath it.

But if Seracini gets behind that wall, what will he actually find of Leonardo's work after five hundred years? Not much, worries Professor Kemp. "If you think about a painting in an experimental oil medium, sealed up with all the changes in temperature and humidity," he says, "I rather fear the chance of anything still adhering to the wall, given what happened to *The Last Supper.*" Right, just look at the history of that masterpiece. When Leonardo painted *The Last Supper* on the refectory wall in the convent of Santa Maria delle Grazie in Milan, he again fiddled with his own formulas for paint. In a true fresco, the pigment was mixed with wet plaster on a wall—a technique that really sticks—but it dried too fast for him. So he used egg tempera and oil paint on dry plaster—and the colors started flaking off in no time. Over the centuries, *The Last Supper* received a lot of patching and several makeovers—Jesus even grew a red beard at one point. Then in 1977 Italian experts began a painstaking, radical restoration. The results, unveiled in 1999, have been controversial: every fleck of non-Leonardo paint was removed. Though the original Leonardo parts now look brighter, big patches of the piece are gone—or rather, they've been repainted lightly in watercolor to recreate the overall composition. Many of the faces—including that of Jesus—have little left by the master's hand.

Still, that isn't stopping hordes of *Da Vinci Code* pilgrims from zipping over to Milan (be forewarned: to see *The Last Supper* in its delicate condition you need a reservation, which can take months to score). As much as the new art fans may wish to see Jesus, many of them are most interested in checking out that guy—or gal—at his right hand. We know that Leonardo didn't paint the figure of the apostle John with a beard: his girlish softness is a typical Renaissance depiction of the teen apostle, a favorite of Jesus. To emphasize the youthfulness of the John character, a variety of classical artists have shown him as beardless or sometimes even asleep on Christ's chest at the Last Supper scene. But the guides at Santa Maria delle Grazie are getting used to being peppered by tourist questions about the figure's sex, and they've developed a stock answer: "You'd have to raise the tunic to know for sure."

A big part of Dan Brown's thesis is that Leonardo secretly held to centuries-old heretical religious ideas. But there's no evidence of that, according to Kemp. "He believed absolutely in a supreme creator, that someone had designed all these wonders in the world," says the scholar. "He had no real room for humbug. He thought the sacred books revealed truths but were not susceptible to reason." Kemp is adamant that Leonardo's works aren't filled with coded messages.

Which brings us to Leonardo's most enduring masterpiece, the *Mona Lisa.* She's his real mystery figure. And it's not just because of her famously enigmatic smile: no one is entirely sure who she is. Begun in 1503, the painting is most widely believed to be a portrait commission of Lisa Gherardini, wife of the Florentine merchant Francesco del Giocondo (hence the French name for the painting, *La Joconde*). But if it is Lisa, she never got her picture. "A painting is never finished," Leonardo once said, "it is just abandoned." But this is one painting he could never let go. He carried it with him for the rest of his life. In 1516 he took it to France, where he worked under the patronage of King Francis I until his death three years later. Over the years he continued to work on the painting—which is perhaps how the *Mona Lisa* came to be less a portrait and more a vision of an ideal. The entire painting was carefully built up of the thinnest layers, creating the *sfumato,* or mysterious atmosphere that was one of Leonardo's brilliant painterly achievements.

In *The Da Vinci Code,* Robert Langdon tells his students at Harvard that the artist painted his own features into that famous face, making the *Mona Lisa* a deliberate portrait of androgyny. One bit of evidence the fictional Langdon gives is that "Mona Lisa" is an anagram of Amon and Isis, the Egyptian god and goddess of fertility. In fact, Leonardo never gave the painting a name. It was Vasari who first called it the *Mona Lisa,* decades after Leonardo's death, with "Mona" serving not as a first name, but as a contraction for the Italian honorific "madonna," rather like an English version of "ma'am" or "Mrs."

Over the years, other people have popped up with their own ideas about who the Mona Lisa really is. Most recently a German writer living in Australia, Maike Vogt-Lüerssen, claimed her research proved that the *Mona Lisa* was actually Isabella of Aragon, who married into the family of Leonardo's patron, the Duke of Milan. Okay—

that's one theory. But then Vogt-Lüerssen got carried away. She speculated that the unhappily wed Isabella and Leonardo were in love, perhaps secretly married after her husband's death, and that her son was their son and became the model for the beautiful boy apostle John in *The Last Supper.* Did you get that? One small problem: Leonardo is less likely than Jesus ever to have married, since most scholars are relatively certain that Leonardo's sexual preference was for the lads, not the ladies. Still, it is an interesting speculative theory—akin to the speculations in *The Da Vinci Code* itself.

Since the spring of 2005, the *Mona Lisa* has had pride of place in the Louvre, in a new, roomier gallery that replaced her cramped old spot in those opening scenes of *The Da Vinci Code.* She has a brightly lit wall all to herself, where she smiles calmly through nonglare bullet-proof glass at the fifteen hundred people who troop by her each hour (that's twenty thousand a day, six million a year). A Japanese company paid six million dollars for the gallery's renovation, as the Japanese are among the *Mona Lisa*'s biggest fans.

There is apparently some archetypal human impulse to attempt to decode the mystery of the *Mona Lisa.* The French art historian who is the curator of the *Mona Lisa,* Cécile Scaillierez, told the *Wall Street Journal* recently that she regularly receives fan letters with new theories about the painting. A numerologist, for example, recently offered a theory that connected the painting's dimensions to Leonardo's birth date. "Everybody has a discovery," Scaillierez says.

Of course, now the *Mona Lisa* has more fans than ever. And behind her smile is Leonardo himself, whose amazing mind and work spark our curiosity across the centuries.

8 The Dan Brown Revelations

Langdon is the man I wish I were.
Langdon is cooler than I am.
—Dan Brown

If we knew as much about Dan Brown as the man through whom he has chosen to live vicariously, we wouldn't, in truth, know very much. From *Angels & Demons* and *The Da Vinci Code* we know that Robert Langdon is a Phillips Exeter Academy graduate, a respected Harvard professor renowned for his ability to crack codes and explain symbols, and that he is attracted to highly intelligent women of some accomplishment. There is not much more when it comes to revealing Dan Brown himself. From his publisher's PR material, or the scant background information he provided during interviews in the days when he was still giving them, we essentially learn that he is a graduate of Phillips Exeter Academy and Amherst, where he had several influential teachers, that he wrote three novels prior to *The Da Vinci Code* that achieved only modest success, that he has a strong preference for a quiet, ordinary New England life, a penchant for detailed research, and a writing discipline that includes hanging upside down in his gravity boots.

If you are David Shugarts, you want to know much more. And his dogged, careful research has paid big dividends, as readers will find when they dig into his groundbreaking mini-bio in this chapter. It is the first serious attempt to answer the question, What made Dan Brown Dan Brown? We begin our quest to know Dan Brown better, however, through a rare interview given when he began promoting *The Da Vinci Code*. We also find out how a person who has a joint major in English and Spanish makes use of Latin in his novels.

We conclude with another "first." Again our indefatigable investigative reporter and code-cracking ace, Dave Shugarts, has been at work, this time turning his attention to the clues Dan Brown has "hidden in plain sight" about his next novel, the much awaited sequel to *The Da Vinci Code,* which will probably be titled *The Solomon Key.* You will get a very good sense here of Dave's work to "reverse engineer" the writing mind of Dan Brown. To find out even more, you will want to get Dave's full-length book on this subject, *Secrets of the Widow's Son*.

A Collision of Indiana Jones and Joseph Campbell

Craig McDonald Interviews Dan Brown

Craig McDonald hosts a website devoted to interviews with interesting authors (www.modestyarbos.com). As *Secrets of the Code* was researched, we found this to be one of the more revealing interviews with Dan Brown as writer that we came across.

You taught English at Exeter. What were some of the books you used in your teaching?

I taught both [literature and writing]. We'd teach books like *The Iliad* and *The Odyssey, Of Mice and Men.* You know, anything by Shakespeare. Anything by Dostoyevsky. The classics.

How long did it take you to sell your first novel?

You know, I got exceptionally lucky. My book sold in twenty days. The first editor who saw it bought it. Part of it had to do with the fact that it was an exceptionally commercial topic at that time. That being national security and civilian privacy. Electronic code-breaking. E-mail . . . National Security Agency [NSA]. It was a piece of fiction that had actual ties to the real world.

Would you write Digital Fortress *differently if you were doing it in a post-9/11 world and with some of the controversies stemming from Homeland Security?*

I don't think so. You know what's funny is when I first started writing that book and I learned about NSA, I thought, "Oh my God, this is a *huge* invasion of privacy." I contacted a former NSA cryptographer and said, "You know what you guys are doing? This scanning e-mail and cell phones—this is an invasion of privacy." This guy responded in a brilliant way. He faxed me the transcript of a Senate Judiciary hearing where the then-director of the FBI, Louis Freeh, testified that in one year alone—I believe the year was 1994—the NSA's ability to infiltrate civilian communication had thwarted the downing of two US commercial airliners and a chemical weapons attack on US soil. What was funny, was, I must have done 150 different radio interviews after *Digital Fortress* came out and we'd get these callers who would call in and say, "I can't believe you're supporting the National Security Agency—it's basically *Brave New World.*" And then, after September 11, people would call in and say, "I don't care what NSA needs. If they want to put a streaming video camera in my bedroom, that's fine. Whatever they need to stop this, it's fine." The entire feeling about national security, as a priority, shifted. Now, the question is, "Have we gone too far?" and we'll just bounce back and forth, I'm sure.

Given the subject matter, and its potential to offend some on a religious level, how do you account for The Da Vinci Code *selling in such vast quantities?*

I did a lot of research for this novel, and I really got the sense that people were ready for this story. It was the type of thing that people were just ready to hear. As far as my surprise with the success: I'm surprised with the level of success—the fact that this book is just breaking all records and we just found out it went back to number one on every list in the country, next week. I should say that when the book came out, I was a little bit nervous about the response. The response from priests, nuns—all sorts of people in the church—for the most part, has been overwhelmingly positive. There have been a few people for whom the book was shocking and was upsetting, but less than one percent.

Robert Langdon appears in your second and fourth novels. There have been some statements issued that you intend to focus on him as a series character. A number of crime and thriller writers launch a series, then rue the fact that they can no longer follow their muse in other directions. Why are you moving the other way?

Langdon is a character who has my own interests. I am fascinated with ancient mysteries. Art history. Codes. You spend a year, a year and a half writing a book, you better be darn sure your hero is involved in subject matter you are excited about. As excited as I was about NASA and meteors or the National Security Agency, my passions really do lie with ancient mysteries and codes and that sort of thing.

Have you always had that interest in the covert?

I have. I grew up on the East Coast, right in New England, sort of in the heart of prep schools and Ivy League colleges with all of their little fraternities and eating clubs and secret societies and all of that. I had associations early on with people from the National Security Agency. Secrets, I think, interest everybody and the concept of secret societies—especially after I visited the Vatican—just really captured my imagination.

Ah yes, your famously touted "audience with the pope."

A lot of people have had an audience with the pope. It basically means that you are in his presence and that's just a very sort of arcane and silly way to put it. I was in a room with a group of other people and that's about the extent of it.

You were also purportedly afforded some unusual access to the Vatican grounds. . . .

That's true. I have a very good friend who has a connection, extremely high, in the Vatican. The parts of the Vatican that we saw—such as the Necropolis . . . currently, something like eleven people a day are allowed in to see the Necropolis. That was probably the most secure area that we saw that was absolutely really really memorable and special. The Vatican archives—only three Americans in history have been allowed inside. I was not one of them. Two were cardinals and one was a professor of religious studies, I think, at the University of Florida. All of the descriptions were accurate. But I was not allowed inside the secret archives myself. I was allowed inside the Vatican library and the Vatican archives, but not the Vatican secret archives.

Think you might still be afforded that access after Angels & Demons *and* The Da Vinci Code?

Chances are slim.

There was a statement somewhere to the effect that you're in possession of something like a dozen rough outlines for future Robert Langdon novels.

I am. Chances are I won't get to write them all.

Given the plot complexity of the novels, I assume you must write to a pretty structured outline.

Oh my, yeah. The outline to *The Da Vinci Code* was over one hundred pages. The stories are very intricate and plot-driven. They have a lot of twists, a lot of codes. A lot of surprises. You can't write those freehand—those come from careful planning.

You've indicated you spend about a year and a half on a book's composition. How much of that time is committed to research?

About half.

You've taken on some fairly powerful entities in your books—the Catholic Church . . . the Masons . . . various alleged secret societies and government agencies. Are you starting to have any fears for your own safety?

I really am not. I work very hard to portray these organizations in a fair and even light and I think I've succeeded. Certainly, with respect to Opus Dei, as I say in the book, there are those for whom Opus Dei has been a wonderful addition to their lives. And there are those for whom Opus Dei has been a nightmare, and I talk about both.

Do you think these Langdon books would have been written if you weren't married to an art historian?

My wife is an enormous influence—her knowledge and her passion for the subject matter certainly buoys the process when it bogs down. Writing a book is incredibly hard. I would not wish it on my worst enemy. There are definitely days when it helps to have somebody around—especially in the case of *The Da Vinci Code*—who understands art and da Vinci and is passionate about it and can say, "You know, let's go take a walk and talk about why we got into this in the first place—what's so exciting about da Vinci and what he believed." So I'm very fortunate on that front.

Returning a little bit to September 11, 2001, I read an interview that you gave in 1998 and it's particularly prescient, now, looking back on it. You were commenting on projects that were under way to monitor U.S. citizens for the reason specifically of preventing terrorist attacks, and you said, "The threat is very real. . . . Americans hate to admit it, but we have a lot of enemies; we are a ripe target for terrorism and yet have one of the lowest rates of successful domestic terrorist attacks on earth." Such an attack was on your radar a bit before it was on most peoples' radar. Why?

I think because of my shock, well, you probably read the story about the guys who showed up at the campus of Phillips Exeter from the Secret Service.

Yes, you had a student who had written something in an e-mail and they came to investigate the student.

Right. That really was my first encounter with the National Security Agency. The more I read about them, the more upset I got. And I couldn't believe that essentially highly trained American civilians would be working on projects to snoop other civilians. It made no sense to me, until I started to dig deeper and realized why it's happening and why no matter what we say and what we want, it will continue to happen. And ending up getting lists of terrorist attacks that never happened because of NSA. I started to sense, "*Oh my God,* we are under attack, almost daily, and just never hear about it." It's important to remember about terrorists that their job is not necessarily to kill people, it's to create terror. In the event that there is a bomb under the White House, or, say, a bomb in New York City that NSA is able to stop with three seconds left, they will make that bomb disappear and hope nobody ever found out about it, because whether or not the bomb goes off, the second you know it almost went off, it's *almost just as scary.* So there is a lot of protecting our ignorance/innocence.

Looking at the dates, you were touring immediately after September 11 for Deception Point, *I take it?*

Yes.

What was that like?

It was awful. It was a tough time. I was working on *Da Vinci Code* on the morning of September 11. I have an office where I have no telephone, no e-mail, no nothing, where I go just to be totally alone. My wife walked over and just said, "Something terrible is happening" and I instantly knew that it had finally happened. For a couple of months after that, it was very hard to be motivated to write fiction. It felt totally unimportant. With so much going on in the world, how can you afford to allow yourself the luxury of moving fictional characters around in a fictional landscape—you know, how are you helping your country doing that? As it turns out, you *are*—at some point you're giving people release from the pain of reality and some recreation. It's just hard to remember that.

You have a background in music. Have you thought of using any musical themes or elements in your novels?

I have. One of my future novels focuses on a famous composer and his associations with a secret society, all factual.

There have been some mentions that your next book after The Da Vinci Code *is going to be set in Washington, D.C.*

That's correct.

And, something about Freemasons . . . ?

Yep . . . Are you hoping I will say more? [laughing]

I thought I would leave some ellipses dangling there and maybe you would fill 'em in . . . but I guess not.

That's about all I'm allowed to say.

You do get a sense of readership through your readings and signings?

You know, that has been the most *gratifying* aspect of tour—to look out at these bookstores and see men, women, and *a lot* of teenagers. Kids have really reacted—especially to *Da Vinci Code* and *Angels & Demons.* It's sort of like a more mature Harry Potter, I guess, is what a lot of kids are feeling. It has some of those ancient mystery elements that people like in Harry Potter.

That comparison is made in some of the press materials from your publisher.

The first time I heard the analogy was Janet Maslin in the *New York Times,* who wrote an absolutely glowing review. People called and said, "Is Janet Maslin your mother, because she never says stuff like that." She invoked the holy name of Harry Potter and I believe she was first. I don't read fiction, except occasionally to blurb somebody's novel if I'm asked by my editor. That's the other thing—I'll get novels almost daily saying, "Wouldn't you love to read this and put a blurb on it?" I have not read Harry Potter, but in my mind, anything that gets kids that excited about reading has got to be really good. I think it's just fantastic.

Any of the books been optioned for film yet?

All kinds of interest. Because Langdon is a series character, I'm hesitant to sell the film rights. One of the beauties of the reading experience is that everybody pictures Langdon in his or her perfect way. The second you slap a character [in a script]—no matter how you describe Langdon or any other character—they picture Ben Affleck or Hugh Jackman or whoever it happens to be, you know? So, I'm hesitant. Also, Hollywood has a way of taking a story like this and turning it into a car chase through Paris with machine guns and karate chops. So, I'm very hesitant, and yet I'm talking to a few specific individuals who are the kinds of people who could make this a *smart* movie, and that's the only way I would sell, is if I had exceptional amounts of control.

In Search of Dan Brown

By David A. Shugarts

Since the first publication of *Secrets of the Code* in April 2004, the Secrets editorial team has been inundated with questions about *The Da Vinci Code* and its underlying issues of antiquity, history, theology, art, architecture, cryptography, etc. Amid all the debates and controversies about what really happened at the Council of Nicea seventeen hundred years ago, or what the real meaning of Jesus "kissing Mary frequently on the M . . ." may be, or what Leonardo was really trying to communicate in *The Last Supper,* one set of questions asked at almost every forum where the Secrets editors have spoken is, Who is Dan Brown, really? Where did he get his ideas? How did he burst so suddenly on the scene as the author of the world's bestselling novel? Is he anti-Christian? Does he have a religious agenda or is he just trying to sell books?

To try to develop answers to those questions, investigative reporter David A. Shugarts spared no effort to look into the intriguing person that is Dan Brown. Shugarts will be known to *Secrets* readers as Dan Brown's "fact-checker" and "code-breaker." In *Secrets of the Code* as well as *Secrets of Angels & Demons,* Shugarts analyzed the contents of Dan Brown's novels and uncovered dozens of mistakes and plot flaws in the text. He also cracked the code embedded on *The Da Vinci Code* dust jacket, which led to our 2005 book-length volume by Shugarts, *Secrets of the Widow's Son,* addressing the themes and mysteries from history that will likely be found in Dan Brown's sequel to *The Da Vinci Code* (*The Solomon Key*) long before Brown even publishes it. For a taste of Shugarts's other forensic work into the mind of Dan Brown, see pages 452 and 574 in this edition of *Secrets of the Code.*

For now, however, we invite you to go on a fascinating tour with Shugarts as he walks the streets of Exeter, New Hampshire, and explores other chapters of Dan Brown's life story. To Shugarts, certain things about Brown just don't add up—and he is still at work on teasing out the answers to some of his questions. As Shugarts points out, this exclusive tour of Dan Brown's past is still very much a work in progress, awaiting, among other things, an opportunity for an interview with the novelist himself. At the time we went to press, Brown remained enigmatically aloof from the normal media circus of interviews and publicity, refusing to either give interviews or to allow the media to cover his small handful of public appearances.

For about a year now, I have tried to get a handle on how Dan Brown developed as a writer, based on the biographical facts that can be collected.

What emerges is an enigmatic transformation, from an unknown musician and writer who had experienced precious little success and a lot of failure, to a novelist whose success is beyond all reckoning in the history of publishing. Perhaps the most salient point is that Dan Brown the man still clings to the same home stomping grounds and attempts quiet anonymity, even though his name is now a household word in the more than forty countries where *The Da Vinci Code* has been published. His hero, Robert Langdon, roams the world's great cities and great themes of religion and history, while Dan Brown sits and writes in solitude in a loft in his hometown, going only on occasional research trips abroad.

Whereas the record suggests that Brown once craved fame and recognition, now he has an excess of it. At his only pre-announced public appearance in 2005—a speech at a benefit dinner in Manchester, New Hampshire—he was escorted by an armed guard and left immediately after his talk.

Dan Brown hasn't sat for an interview since sales of *The Da Vinci Code* ascended like a rocket in 2003. So it's not easy to know the inner Dan Brown, although I have tried to come up with some reasonable guesses based on the facts. I have gone to Exeter, his hometown. I have visited the schools he attended. I have sat in seats he occupied, looked at sights he saw as a young person, some of which he continues to gaze at today.

I have also chased his thoughts down through the canyons and over the mountains of history and philosophy. It has been wonderfully exhilarating. In writing *Secrets of the Widow's Son,* an attempt to anticipate Dan Brown's next novel, I zoomed through time and space like a video game sprite, always searching for a glimpse of the same thematic vistas that Dan Brown must be seeing.

At the outset, I must give sincere thanks to Dan Brown for two things: his book led me into a journey that itself is certainly the most fulfilling intellectual work I have done and, if I ever finish my own novel, it will be because he gives hope to an ordinary guy sitting at a blank screen. (Indeed, I believe we are beginning to witness the torrential flows of creative works generated by the "Dan Brown effect" in the current crop of novels, television series, and movies.)

But journalists covering Dan Brown have caught on

that he is not exactly a reliable source for his own biographical information. Among other things, he tends to slip about dates. For instance:

> Daniel Gerhard Brown was born June 22, 1964, in Exeter, New Hampshire.

When he gave his talk in October of 2005 in nearby Manchester, he was introduced as a lifelong New Hampshire boy, and he largely agreed with that introduction, but said, "I have lived a couple of years in Spain and a couple in California and the rest in New Hampshire. I'm forty years old, so you do the math." Then, doing the math himself, he admitted, "Well, actually I'm forty-one."

This isn't the only mistake of its kind, as we will see, and it leads some to wonder why Dan Brown is keeping himself hidden from view. Is it mere shyness? Is it because parts of his career are fairly embarrassing? Or is it because his success with *The Da Vinci Code* is somehow bound up with a few personal myths about himself, which his editors, agents, and spinmeisters now don't want to see questioned?

Here is a fundamental question that has kept me on this hunt for many months: How did an otherwise undistinguished writer suddenly deliver *The Da Vinci Code,* the world's bestselling book? Was it luck, or skill? Was it his lifelong destiny, or a sudden serendipity?

What I have found so far is that there is little or no evidence to indicate from Dan Brown's first thirty or so years of life that in his late thirties he would be even modestly successful as a creative person in either of his two chosen pursuits—music or books. In fact, well into his early thirties, Brown lacked success and seemed to lack clear direction in life as well. What he made of himself after that is truly amazing. Hindsight allows for looking back and seeing little hints of what was to come, but they seem to be few and far between.

In 1998, with the publication of *Digital Fortress,* his first novel, Dan Brown at thirty-four made his first bliplike appearance on the radar screen of American action-adventure novels. What was the event that caused his transformation from a guy who wanted to write books to actual novelist? Dan Brown's own description is found in answer to one of the frequently asked questions (FAQs) on his website:

> In 1994, while vacationing in Tahiti, I found an old copy of Sydney Sheldon's *Doomsday Conspiracy* on the beach. I read the first page . . . and then the next . . . and then the next. Several hours later, I finished the book and thought, "Hey, I can do that." Upon my return, I began work on my first novel—*Digital Fortress*—which was published in 1996.

This may seem like a huge digression, but we need to fact-check Dan Brown here, and I'm not talking about the typo that remains on his high-visibility website where he misspells the *Doomsday* author's first name, which is correctly spelled *Sidney.* Another small point caught my notice here. Brown's mention of the date makes it seem like a neatly packaged, two-year effort to produce his first novel. That's partly because he fails to remember that the year of his vacation in Tahiti was *1993.* And it is because he remembers the publication date as 1996.

We can be reasonably certain he's wrong about the Tahiti date because I spoke with one of the other eight people who were loosely associated with Dan and his future wife, Blythe Newlon, as the only Americans at the Tahitian resort. In the scrapbook that she keeps, Kay

Borden, of Marietta, Georgia, has the plane ticket for her flight on April 9, 1993. On a website page, Mrs. Borden displays snapshots of a young-looking Dan and Blythe.

But, according to Brown's own statements in a different interview, *Digital Fortress* was actually triggered by an event that occurred on the Exeter Academy campus in the spring of 1995. As he relates it, some Secret Service agents showed up on campus to arrest a student for an allegedly threatening email message. He had opined that President Clinton "ought to be shot." I have searched, but so far not found any press account of this event.

Also, Dan Brown did not copyright *Digital Fortress* in 1996, but in *1998,* the year of its first publication by Thomas Dunne Books, an imprint of St. Martin's Press. To be fair, publication of a book often takes a year or more from delivery of the completed manuscript to actual publication.

One of Dan Brown's favorite sayings is that history is "written by the victors," or in other words, history gets rewritten by whomever gets control of the pen or the word processor. It's ironic, but it appears that, with little errors and other inaccuracies, Brown seems to rewrite his own history rather regularly.

The Local Boy

In order to understand Dan Brown as a writer, it is absolutely essential to visit Exeter, New Hampshire.

Exeter is a truly charming New England town situated not far from Boston and Portsmouth. It's considered part of the Seacoast area, even though it is about ten miles inland. Several different roads out of Exeter will lead you easily to the resort towns on the Atlantic beaches, such as Seabrook, Hampton and Rye.

Exeter is one of those old New England mill towns that lost a lot of jobs as factories closed over the years. Undoubtedly, some of the suffering was eased by the presence of the renowned Phillips Exeter Academy, which owns a large part of the central town and provides a significant number of jobs, in addition to the intellectual and cultural benefits it brings to the area.

Exeter is compact. Practically everything is within walking distance of everything else. The main streets come down to Water Street, whose eighteenth-century shops line the Squamscott River. Dan Brown said of it in 1996, "I've returned to this small town of Exeter. I'm learning to appreciate the silence of the woods, the clarity of the air and the bareness of winter."

It's also the kind of town where they say "ayup" and "nope" as their long answers to a question. As I wandered around the town of Exeter and the Academy on several visits, I was treated politely by everyone. But whether it was because they know Dan Brown personally, or just think of any outsider as potential trouble, the townspeople button their lips if you ask about Brown. They often ask, "Did Dan Brown authorize you to write about him?" When I told them my work was independent and unauthorized, they tended to become stereotype laconic New Englanders. Eventually, though, I did find a few who would talk, even in Exeter.

It was here, in the early 1960s, that a young couple, Richard and Connie Brown, settled and started a family. Richard had been hired as an Academy math teacher, and Connie would make the quintessential faculty wife. But more than that, she had skills as an organist, and the pair also found a home as co-choir directors at Christ Church, Exeter's Episcopalian church. Connie would remain as the church's organist for many years. Was it nature or nurture? Math—more specifically Richard Brown's specialty, geometry—church, and music would become several of the biggest influences on Dan Brown.

Initially, the Browns lived in the Academy dorms, as was the custom—new faculty are expected to superintend the dorms for their first ten years at the school. This is where Dan Brown spent his earliest years. Two years after his birth, Valerie Jo Brown was born (1966). The third and last of the Brown children, Gregory, arrived in 1974.

An interesting ballet began around 1963 involving not people, but houses. A couple named John and Miriam LeBaron lived on Pine Street, within a couple of blocks of the Academy campus. They had many acres of land behind their house, stretching all the way to the Little River. They decided to move the house to an area in the rear of their property, spinning it around in the process to afford a view of the river. The rearrangement made it possible to sell off the rest of their land, and the buyer was Christ Episcopal Church, which was looking for a place to build a new house of worship, having worn out the former structure on Elliot Street.

This not only gave the church a site for a Pine Street address, but also a parking lot in the rear, and land left over. It allowed for the creation of a new road, Nelson Drive, which would eventually yield building lots for several more houses beyond the LeBarons. One of these lots, which had originally been designated for a rectory, was sold to Connie and Dick Brown, and they also chose to have an existing house moved onto the lot, rather than building anew (this according to the recollection of Mrs. LeBaron). Around 1975 (based on a deed of that year), they settled in at 7 Nelson Drive, on the rim of a cul-de-sac.

(It was almost a mystical experience for me to find the Browns' church. Within a small sector of town, there are about six or seven churches, all cozy and welcoming. For some inexplicable reason, the Cross of St. George attracted my eye, and I drove into the Pine Street entrance of Christ Church to inquire. Yes, out of the multiple churches I could have tried, I had found the right one on the first try. As I drove out the back lot, I was again surprised to find myself on the Browns' little road, Nelson Drive.)

The Brown homestead's location is important for quite a number of reasons. It is within easy walking distance of the Academy campus, as well as all the public schools and downtown Exeter. Moreover, if Connie and Dick, or the children, wanted to be a part of a church event, they could be there in about a minute. At Christ Church, Dan Brown went to Sunday school, to church camp, and sang in the choir. To say that Dan Brown grew up in the shadow of the church would not be an overstatement.

Over the years Dick Brown became a stalwart of the Exeter Academy faculty and eventually was named head of the mathematics department. Dick Brown also became a very accomplished author of math textbooks. For the space of about thirty years, he was constantly writing or editing or contributing to various textbooks, some of which remain in use today.

Dick Brown enjoyed appearing in local musical productions. In fact, when Dan was a junior at the Academy, his father starred in the Exeter Players production of *The Pirates of Penzance.* As the classic Major-General in the Gilbert and Sullivan operetta, math teacher Brown sang, "I'm very well acquainted too with matters mathematical. I understand equations, both the simple and quadratical . . . I am the very model of a modern Major-General."

Dan Brown, on the other hand, was not a stand-out musician at Exeter Academy, although he had an excellent voice and could be a part of any choir he wished to join. According to his former principal, Dr. Stephen Kurtz, Dan Brown and his classmate William "Chip" Beckett did put together a play that was performed to some success. But in an interview, Dr. Kurtz could not recall details of the production.

The Browns took full advantage of the great side-benefit for faculty, the opportunity to send their children through the prep school at greatly reduced fees. All three Brown children went through the Academy when their turns came. Dan graduated in 1982, Valerie in 1985, and Greg in 1993.

Dan Brown sometimes mentions to Exeter Academy students that he once lived in the dorms, which is a true statement, because he was a child when his parents were living in and supervising the dorm. But, by the time he was actually a student at the Academy, he was living at Nelson Drive and his status was "day student." The gulf at any prep school between "day students" who live in town and "residential" students who live in the dorms while their parents are far away in Boston or New York is substantial. It usually reflects class and status issues that are often revealed, however subtly, in student attitudes about themselves and toward others. Dan Brown was apparently somewhat on the edge of student society. He was a friendly, somewhat ordinary fellow who got along well with his schoolmates, and never particularly excelled beyond the achievements of the expected standards of excellence at a place like Exeter Academy, known for its bright, talented young people—then and now.

Although I searched the student publications looking for it, I could find no instance of Dan Brown stepping out as a writer. He did play squash for the varsity team, and he was among twelve students selected to be proctors at the library, assigned to patrol and enforce the rules.

In sum, Dan Brown did not appear to be headed for a career as a writer nor even a "creative type." He was simply a guy who went through the Academy. However, this raises a good question: Is it possible to get through the Academy and not be marked for future distinction? How much of an effect can the school have on an "average" student there?

Now, that's one mighty good question! In my search for the answer, I found a lot of information and food for thought. One former school official said to me, "I hope Dan remembers that he really owes it all to Exeter Academy."

Changes

By the time Dan Brown had slipped the bonds of the town of Exeter's elementary school system and entered the hallowed halls of the Academy in 1978, the prep school had put in place a number of systematic changes that were almost certain to leave an impression on him.

Although it may appear slow to act sometimes, Exeter Academy has shown the ability to morph itself in changing times. All of the social problems of the wider society in the past fifty years have had some expression in the changes that have occurred at the Academy, from dealing with racism and civil rights, to gender equality, to environmental issues.

Three Latin text elements of the Academy seal translate into English as "the end depends upon the beginning," "by the grace of God," and "not for oneself." The latter (*non sibi*) is taken to mean that knowledge is to be gained not only for the improvement of the individual, but also to be useful for the wider society.

Exeter Academy was founded as a boys' school in 1781, and it would remain a male bastion for 189 years. By the way, Paul Revere fashioned the first seal for the Academy in 1782. The list of illustrious graduates is too long to cite, but it includes Arthur Schlesinger Jr., David Eisenhower, Pierre DuPont III, Adolph Coors III, Senator Jay Rockefeller of West Virginia, and the late Senator H. John Heinz of Pennsylvania. The current Director of National Intelligence, John Negroponte, is a graduate. U.S. President Franklin Pierce was an Exeter Academy graduate. President Abraham Lincoln sent his son to Exeter, as did President Ulysses S. Grant. So in an American culture that is generally uninterested in history, Dan Brown didn't have to look too far to be surrounded by it and to develop a certain appreciation for it.

The first female faculty member was hired in 1968. The school's student body remained all-male until 1970 when a transitional period began, starting with the admission of a handful of female students and culminating in full inclusion a few years later. Strides were later made in adding female teachers and elevating them to management positions. By the time Dan Brown arrived, Exeter Academy, a one-time bastion of the male power elite, was fully coed.

Dan Brown's time at the Academy came in the late 1970s and early 1980s, as Exeter made a serious effort to be sensitive to women's issues and to be more inclusive of sexual preferences and points of view. Surely, living through this time of change, some of this rubbed off on Dan Brown and may have been part of his interest in entertaining themes of feminism in his novels.

Religion in School

The Academy's founder, John Phillips, had set down a religious aspect of the school's foundation, and chapel services were a part of the school's regimen. But in the early 1960s (just a few years after the Brown family had settled in at Christ Church), a change took place at the Academy that would have reverberations much later. The principal, Richard W. Day, met an Episcopalian priest, Rev. Edward S. Gleason (at the actual dedication of the new Christ Church building on Pine Street), and soon hired him as the school's minister. As such, he was to oversee services that were Congregational, rather than Episcopalian, but this was not the big change. Principal Day charged Rev. Gleason with transforming the school's church attendance policy from compulsory to voluntary.

Gleason innovated. He started by enlisting the students themselves. He made certain students "deacons" of the Phillips Church, and with them he created special worship services, crafted to be relevant to the student congregation. It largely worked, and students continued to attend services at Phillips Church, even though not required. To this day, they keep coming to services. They are there because they want to be.

The tone was set, and over the years, Phillips Church began to be even more open to diverse kinds of worship. By the time Dan Brown was an Academy student, the structure was the place of worship for Quakers, Jews, and Buddhists as well as Congregationalists and other Christian denominations.

What had been set in motion continued after Dan Brown left the Academy. In 2003, after a renovation, the Phillips Church reopened with an evening of prayer and celebration led by the peace activist Rev. William Sloan Coffin, to the sounds of chamber music and African drums. The evening's readings included a traditional Zulu prayer, a Shanti mantra read in Sanskrit, a meditation on world peace by a Buddhist monk, the Lord's Prayer read in Aramaic by an Exeter Academy senior, and selections from the Quran and the Old Testament read by Academy students in Arabic, English, and Hebrew. It might have been a religious service designed for its cross-cultural symbolism by Robert Langdon himself.

It seems to me the inevitable conclusion to be drawn here is that Dan Brown was steeped in principles of religious tolerance. The contrast between his early experiences of diversity and tolerance at Exeter Academy and the world beginning to swing toward all sorts of religious fundamentalism right around the time he graduated may have prompted his selection of religious themes to include in *Angels & Demons* and *The Da Vinci Code,* and may also explain how deeply he was shocked by the religious furor these novels sparked.

A Temple of Knowledge

After a long and legendary search for an architect, in 1965 the Academy hired the famed Louis I. Kahn to design the school's new library. It took six more years to complete it, but in November of 1971 the faculty and students physically carried some 60,000 books into their new library. It now holds more than 140,000 books, eclipsing anyone's expectations of a high school library. It is a library worthy of a very good small college.

There is no way to overestimate the presence that this structure has on campus, even though it is "hidden in plain sight." It is a truly magnificent building and thoroughly modern, but it tends to blend into the campus without a murmur. The brick outer construction colors it the same as the many brick campus buildings of neo-Georgian style. The library was given the 25 Year Award by the American Institute of Architects in 1997, and in 2005 it was among twelve buildings selected for a series of U.S. Postal Service commemorative stamps called Masterworks of American Architecture.

The library is the hub of the Academy community, and a true temple of knowledge. Outwardly, it looks like a cube. One of its main characteristics is the transmission of natural light into the structure, made possible by a kind of open lattice of outer walls, an inner sanctum admitting light through giant circular holes, and a giant skylight.

Before I saw this building, I had been sensitized to a number of strong symbols relating to Freemasonry, a study I had taken up to be able to understand and explain many themes in Dan Brown's works. Freemason history and symbolism make multiple appearances in both *Angels & Demons* and *The Da Vinci Code,* and are expected to form the context for Dan Brown's much-awaited next novel, *The Solomon Key.* I had learned to notice two of the shapes revered by the Masons, the circle and the square. In addition, *The Da Vinci Code* begins with the dead Louvre curator laid out like the Vitruvian Man, the image made famous by the Leonardo drawing that fits the human proportions to both a circle and a square.

I have now visited this building several times, roaming the same stacks and floors that Dan Brown himself once patrolled as a proctor, sitting in chairs that he sat in, looking at the same views and angles. Perhaps I am overly sensitized, but I do not see how a person could look around and *not* see unmistakable symbolic references to the Vitruvian Man and the ancient symbols of circle and square.

In addition, the view upward from the central atrium reveals an equal-armed cross. All of this is by design.

The architect Louis Kahn could, himself, have been an influence in the formation of a Dan Brown character. Although Jewish by birth and culture, Kahn is seen in architectural history as something of a pantheistic mystic. He actively sought to work into his buildings elements of sacred geometry, Kabbalistic traditions, classical Greek and Roman allusions, archetypal forms and shapes, and the spiritual essence of religions as various as Buddhism and Islam. Dan Brown's Robert Langdon often sees the male and female symbols of blade and chalice appearing in surprising places in art and architecture. These symbols are in obvious evidence in the work of Louis Kahn as well.

I do not think the young Dan Brown, Exeter Academy student, conceived much of the detail of his novels in his high school library. But years later, when the character of Robert Langdon begins to speak about symbolism "hidden in plain sight," it surely must have occurred to Brown that he had been immersed in a system of ancient symbolism, right at the Academy library. (Brown still maintains an office in Exeter where he does some of his writing, and he often strolls over to the library, so he gets a regular dose of the symbolism.)

Famous Writers' School?

Exeter Academy has a long list of distinguished alumni, and a tradition of celebrating those alums that have become authors. Other eras featured Daniel Webster, Booth Tarkington, and John Agee, but some of the famous and relatively recent ones are Gore Vidal (1943), George Plimpton (1944), John Knowles (1945), Peter Benchley

(1957), John Irving (1961), Joyce Maynard (1971)—and, of course, Dan Brown (1982).

The living writers are often brought back to the campus for various celebrations and awards, or to give inspiring mentoring-type talks to the students. Thus, in Dan Brown's days as a student, he was offered the opportunity to sit in for lectures by Vidal, Plimpton, and Irving. In fact, all three visited Exeter Academy in the spring semester of his junior year, and good accounts of most of these sessions were published in the school's paper, the *Exonian,* or the local newspaper, the *Exeter News-Letter.*

Irving, author of *The World According to Garp* and *The Cider House Rules,* was (like Dan Brown) the son of an Exeter faculty member, or what in Exeter slang is called a "fac-brat." Irving admitted that it took him five years to get through the Academy, since he failed math and Latin. He told the students he didn't mind staying around for an extra year, since he was "happy here," having friends both in the school and in the town. He later went to the University of Pittsburgh, but became disillusioned with the English program there and left to join the Writer's Workshop in Iowa. In 1989 Irving wrote the acclaimed *A Prayer for Owen Meany.* The book takes place in "Gravesend, New Hampshire," which is instantly recognizable as Exeter.

Plimpton was hailed as a returning Exeter Academy alumnus even though he admitted that his many pranks got him expelled from the Academy with three months remaining in his senior year. (In fact, there was at least one faculty member who had to be kept in the shadows to avoid a violent confrontation when Plimpton came to visit.) Plimpton, in various essays, described some of his misdeeds, such as stealing a rhinoceros head from one of the lounges. Plimpton admitted he was a disappointment to his family, who had been graduating from the Academy for three generations. Indeed, the name Plimpton was attached to various Exeter Academy playing fields and land that had been donated by his grandfather.

When Plimpton spoke at Exeter Academy during its two-hundredth-year festivities in 1981, he related some of the adventures of his early days as a "participatory journalist." Plimpton was known in literary circles as one of the founding editors of the *Paris Review.* But he was probably best known by the public for the book *Paper Lion,* describing how he played out the average fan's fantasy by training for and eventually suiting up for a Detroit Lions game as a quarterback.

But for the students, Plimpton related the story of how he accidentally got started in "participatory journalism." He said when he was at Harvard and trying to get a writing position on that school's famous *Lampoon,* he offered to cover the Boston Marathon. The editor told him the only way he would be given the post was if he actually ran in the marathon, to get a first-person story. Plimpton took public transportation to a spot a few blocks from the finish line, burst out of the crowd, and sprinted alongside the race leader—who nonetheless beat Plimpton to the line. (Later, in 1981, the famous Rosie Ruiz attempted a repeat of Plimpton's stunt at the New York Marathon, and was promptly discovered.)

In Plimpton's amusing tales of his participatory journalistic adventures, it is not hard to see the general idea of "Everyman" thrust into extraordinary circumstances that runs through all four of Dan Brown's novels. It is also not that much of a stretch from George Plimpton as the Lions quarterback to Dan Brown playing academic iconographer and symbologist through his Robert Langdon character. Just as Plimpton inserted himself into the real-life mauling of NFL football, Brown has inserted himself into the real-life debates about church history, religion vs. science, etc.

Gore Vidal, a precocious writer who penned his first novel at age nineteen, is famous for many books challenging American sexual mores, and he developed a series of historical novels, such as *Burr, 1876,* and *Lincoln*. According to the *Exonian,* he told students that his methods of weaving fact and fiction were absolutely legitimate, a form of moral instruction that had ancient traditions.

"Literature began as a record, real or imagined, of gods and heroes," Vidal said, stressing that "fiction and fact" were mingled in most of the ancients' accounts. Answering questions from students, Vidal argued that "we ought to make history the basis of education." He said the Big Bang theory and the story of the Garden of Eden should be taught to six-year-olds. Asked about Christianity, he said, "It's not one of my all-time favorites." He called it "hard to defend" and "primitive." But he said the chief fault of Christianity is its "proselytizing" in asserting that "all other religions are false."

We don't know what Dan Brown thought at the time Gore Vidal gave that talk at Exeter Academy, but we can see echoes of most of the ideas quoted above in Brown's novels.

The open atmosphere that could entertain these ideas is just one aspect of Exeter Academy. An important part of the teaching environment is a concept called the Harkness Table, wherein just twelve students and one teacher come together around an oval table. This promotes a collegial approach, where students often seize the discussion and direct their own learning.

In addition to the regular appearance on the campus of famous literary alumni, an aspect of the Exeter Academy curriculum seemed tailored to preparing its grads to be writers. This was an assignment for juniors ("uppers") called "reporter at large." The students were asked to write an English term paper depicting a character in a career setting based on an interview. Thus, for example, the student might create an interview with "a Saudi Arabian national executioner, a Hare Krishna follower or a hog farmer," according to the *Exonian*. Students considered this a very challenging assignment, but at least one English teacher said it was the opportunity for students to "start to believe in themselves as writers."

Dan Brown himself has high praise for a ninth-grade English teacher at the Academy, Jack Heath. In response to a *Boston Globe* call for memories of great teachers, Brown recalled, "I wrote my first essay about the Grand Canyon, describing with inexhaustible prolixity the subtle hues and fissures of the limestone. Mr. Heath returned the essay doused in red pen. He had deleted 90 percent of my adjectives and given me a C-.

"At the top of the page were three words: 'Simpler is better.'

"By the end of the semester, I was barely making a C+. On the last day, I asked Mr. Heath if he had any parting advice.

"He nodded: 'Simpler is better.' "

I recently contacted Jack Heath and asked him about this. He acknowledged that the story is "probably true" and he is grateful for the compliment, but said he doesn't feel he had much to do with Dan Brown's development as a writer. Nevertheless, those who have attempted to dissect Dan Brown's writing style to discern the reasons his books are so widely read almost all point out the simplicity of the actual prose, the short, active sentences, and the sparse description. His ability to tackle as many big ideas as he does in such simple, active prose passages suggests he did indeed learn the lesson Jack Heath tried to teach.

The Piper's Price

Outstanding as the education at Exeter Academy is, and diverse as its student population has become today, there can be no doubt about the main reason families spend $33,000 for a year of this experience today—or spent a similarly hefty $7,000 a year in Dan Brown's day. Indeed, the biggest secret hiding in plain sight at the Academy is the real Purpose for being there. The Purpose becomes stark and graphic every spring, when the *Exonian* publishes a small table of data headed "Where the Class of 1982 Will Go to College." The table fairly shouts to the student: "Your Purpose is to get into an Ivy League college!"

Exeter students are so focused on the college quest that they have a special slang term, *college suck*. This is defined as "the cynical term for those clubs, activities, and leadership positions that one acquires, not because of genuine interest, but in order to pad one's resume for college applications."

There are eight Ivy League schools (Brown, Columbia, Cornell, Dartmouth, Harvard, Princeton, University of Pennsylvania, Yale). There is also a gaggle of schools known as the "Little Ivy League" (such as Amherst or Wesleyan) and some others known as the "Seven Sisters" (Barnard, Bryn Mawr, Mount Holyoke, Radcliffe, Smith, Vassar, and Wellesley). Together these schools represent arguably the pinnacle of prestige in American colleges (or, at least, eastern U.S. prestige). Across America, any high school would be proud to have one or two graduates accepted to Harvard or Yale, one or two more at the Little Ivies or the Seven Sisters.

In Dan Brown's class of about 312 Exies, fully one hundred made it into Ivy League, and sixty-eight more into Little Ivy or Seven Sister colleges. In other words, half the Exeter Academy class made it into the top one percent of the country's colleges. There were twenty going to Harvard, twenty-three to Yale, sixteen to Dartmouth, and eleven to Princeton. (If you want the proper reaction to these statistics, just show them to any high school guidance counselor. But before you do, refresh yourself on first-aid procedures for people who have fainted.)

Dan Brown didn't get into Harvard, but he did achieve something almost as good: he got into Amherst College, one of ten Exies that year to do so.

Amherst

Situated only a couple of hours' drive away from Exeter, Amherst College was surely a comfortable fit for the freshman Dan Brown. Almost identical to the physical situation at Exeter Academy, the college owns a big parcel of the town, as well as being an enclave within it. And it is a compact campus so that, again, everything is a short walk from everything else. Its enrollment is about the same as at Exeter Academy. And like the Academy, Amherst is an outstanding institution; unlike it, however, Amherst is not quite at the absolute top of reputation and prestige.

In a 2004 report on the Amherst admissions procedure, the *Jim Lehrer Newshour* gave a detailed look at how Amherst selects its incoming freshmen, winnowing some 5,400 applications down to 1,034 acceptances. Those candidates then decide whether Amherst will be their choice, or perhaps another marginally more outstanding, more prestigious school where they may also have been accepted. In 2004 this process netted about 400 freshmen—meaning that some 600 very bright students went to other schools. What schools? "Harvard, Yale, Princeton, Stanford, Swarthmore, Williams, Dartmouth, Duke, Columbia," an admissions officer rattled off without hesitation. "Those are the schools that we compete with."

As all fans of Dan Brown's novels know, the hero Robert Langdon is a graduate of Exeter Academy who went on to become a Harvard professor. Dan Brown has also admitted that Langdon is an expression of who he would like to be (except that "Langdon is cooler than I am"). It seems to me that all the facts align: as fans have suspected, I think Dan Brown is a Harvard wannabe, even though Amherst is, of course, one of the finest schools in the country, and nothing to be ashamed of either.

In making Langdon's pedigree from Harvard, rather than Amherst or another smaller, more intriguing academic center, Brown reveals another technique he uses frequently. He takes something obscure and makes it as recognizable as possible. Arguably, the key historical character he describes in *Angels & Demons* has more in common with Giordano Bruno than with Galileo. But he makes Galileo the centerpiece of the novel, since Bruno is so much less well known. Similarly, if you were looking for a fifteenth-century master painter who placed symbolic coded messages in his paintings and belonged to a secret occult society that may have worshipped the sacred feminine, you would be looking more at Hieronymus Bosch than Leonardo da Vinci. But if you called a book *The Bosch Code,* readers might think it was about the well-known fictional LA detective, Harry Bosch. Despite the similarities between Langdon and Brown, Langdon could not be from Amherst—he needed to be from Harvard.

I visited Amherst and made a search of the various student publications in the archives from Dan Brown's years there. Similar to my experience at Exeter Academy, I could find no evidence that Dan Brown stepped out in public with his writing. He pursued a combined major of English and Spanish, and it's my unconfirmed guess that he spent his junior year abroad in Spain. (*Digital Fortress* is set partly in Seville, Spain, and relies in a few places on certain architectural details and place descriptions that Brown could have observed as a student there.)

After he became a published author with his first few novels, Dan Brown was interviewed by an *Amherst Student* reporter for an article in October 2001. As he looked back on his Amherst education, he recalled a freshman course called Introduction to Liberal Arts, also dubbed "Music and Words." According to the *Student*, "In that class he learned to incorporate his two seemingly disparate talents and create one unique sound. This introductory course set the stage for his successful Hollywood musical career." (As we will explore shortly, although he had talent, Dan Brown did not have what most people would call a "successful Hollywood music career.")

The *Student* article went on to say:

> Brown didn't always have a natural passion for writing. It wasn't until he attended a writing class taught by Alan Lelchunk, a visiting professor and novelist, that he felt comfortable writing. The class helped him to improve his compositional skills, which gave him the confidence to eventually write novels.
>
> This class, he claims, was the one that sparked his passion for writing. Only at Amherst could he have had the

opportunity to study alongside a writer who, in Brown's words, was "actually doing it." He felt empowered by the class and his new mentor. Unique interactions like this are what captivated Brown and why he feels eternally grateful towards his alma mater.

Of course, I went looking for Alan "Lelchunk" and I found Alan *Lelchuk* (the correct spelling), now an adjunct professor at Dartmouth College where he teaches Jewish studies as well as creative writing. Dr. Lelchuk in 2003 was awarded a Fulbright Scholarship to study in Russia. He is the author of some six novels, starting with *American Mischief* in 1973. Lelchuk himself was friends with, and encouraged in writing by, the famed novelist Philip Roth (author of such classics of modern literature as *Goodbye, Columbus* and *Portnoy's Complaint*).

Dr. Lelchuk told me that his Amherst class was very "literary in content, and at a high level," so that it would have taken a committed student to get through the course. He had "some very fine writers" who were in it around the same time as Dan Brown, including the critically acclaimed David Foster Wallace, author of *Infinite Jest* and *Brief Interviews with Hideous Men*. Thus, there were writers who were "good talkers in class." In such a context, Dan Brown was not particularly memorable. Lelchuk said Brown was "a nice guy, pleasant and quiet. He was not one of the talkers."

I discussed with Lelchuk the content of the course Dan Brown took with him at Amherst. Apparently, it included short stories by classic writers, including Anton Chekhov, Isaak Babel, John Updike, Guy de Maupassant, Flannery O'Connor, Grace Paley, Milan Kundera, and Yukio Mishima. When I asked whether this seemed to hold any portents for the kind of pop fiction that Dan Brown would later write, he couldn't think of any. It was never part of Lelchuk's purpose to try to prepare a student for commercial success, he said. Lelchuk wasn't even aware of Dan Brown's success until he got a surprise copy of *The Da Vinci Code* in the mail with a thank-you note from Brown. (Until I told him about it, he also wasn't aware of just how much credit Dan Brown had given him in the *Amherst Student* interview.)

Part of the course involved individual conferences about the students' work and it was during these sessions that Lelchuk would offer some criticism, as well as lots of encouragement. He always hoped that this was beneficial to the student, he said, but it wasn't always possible to see an effect. Lelchuk said, in sum, "You never can tell when a quiet student is absorbing a great deal."

The reference to David Foster Wallace being one of the active talkers in the class, while Dan Brown was in the camp of the quiet, may be highly instructive. Some post-modern critics believe Wallace is the most brilliant literary figure on the contemporary scene; some have compared his role in late-twentieth-century literature to James Joyce's in the early twentieth century. Whether one buys the comparison to Joyce or not, Wallace's novels, like Joyce's, are masterly synthetic mixtures of many ideas from many different intellectual disciplines, and from low culture as well as high culture. One can imagine a smart, hard-working, well-intentioned, perfectly decent Dan Brown feeling utterly intimidated by the brilliance of a David Foster Wallace. But like the fable of the Tortoise and the Hare, Dan Brown watches and learns what these searing intellects are doing in the literary world, and then mass-produces it for the readership of the masses. Thus the ordinary well-educated person trying to read Wallace may experience a déjà vu of their challenging experiences trying to read Joyce. Dan Brown, on the other hand, mixes the same range of ideas from similar sources, but without (or as some critics would say, with the opposite of) the literary flair of a Wallace or a Joyce. By the same token, of course, Brown's novelistic mélanges are gripping page-turners, easy to read and highly accessible to understand.

Fraternal Experiences

On the Dan Brown website (danbrown.com), one of the frequently asked questions (FAQs) pages eventually came to include this Q and A with Dan Brown:

> Q: You seem to have a fascination with secret societies. Can you comment?
>
> A: My interest in secret societies is the product of many experiences, some I can discuss, others I cannot. Certainly my research of organizations like NSA, the Vatican, NRO, and Opus Dei continues to fuel my intrigue. At a more fundamental level, though, my interest sparks from growing up in New England, surrounded by the clandestine clubs of Ivy League universities, the Masonic lodges of our Founding Fathers, and the hidden hallways of early government power. New England has a long tradition of elite private clubs, fraternities, and secrecy. On that theme, the next Robert Langdon novel (already in progress) is set deep within the oldest fraternity in history . . . the enigmatic brotherhood of the Masons.

This seems to be a hint by Dan Brown that he has some firsthand knowledge, based on secret societies he encountered in his upbringing and schooling. I have made contact with Freemasons at various levels and have not found any evidence that Dan or his father was a member of the Freemasons. But I did find that he was a member of a fraternity, if perhaps only briefly.

Dan Brown was initiated into the Psi Upsilon fraternity at Amherst on October 1, 1983 (as was confirmed to me by a national spokesman for the fraternity). This would have been at the start of his sophomore year. Unfortunately for new fraternity members, it was the year that Amherst abolished the sanctioned fraternity system, a year of turmoil.

At Amherst, the fraternity system once ruled supreme and you were not really a success at the all-male college unless you belonged to a fraternity. Boy, did that change!

Throughout the 1970s, the Ivy and Little Ivy schools transformed from all-male or all-female to coed (just like Exeter Academy). Amherst made the switch in 1976 after some 156 years of being male-only.

Newly admitted women at Amherst began to demand the same privileges as any student. Since fraternity housing was a form of privilege, they demanded entrance into the fraternities. Some of these brotherhoods dug in their heels, partly because they had been chartered from their very origins as men-only. But other fraternities accepted women. Psi Upsilon, for instance, found nothing in its charter to prohibit women, so it began to admit them.

However, as Amherst entered the 1980s, the trend was definitely toward taking over the fraternity housing—ostensibly for such reasons as safety and health standards—and the die was cast. In 1983 the college banned fraternity activities on campus. Again there was a split in behavior. Some fraternities went underground and tried to continue as they were, while others, such as Psi Upsilon, adhered to the rules and moved their activities off-campus. Today Psi Upsilon is an active, coed society with a chapter house off-campus.

But, during that special year (1983–84) and for a few years beyond, "some members stuck it out and abided by the new and difficult rules, while others simply walked away," said a spokesman for Psi Upsilon. It is not possible in the fraternity's records to determine which choice Dan Brown made, he said.

It is interesting that the "Greek" fraternity system in America grew up around two basic kinds of social affiliations. On the one hand, some of the oldest fraternities were begun as literary societies, where the members sought secrecy so that they could share their poetry or stories (some of which may be assumed to have been risqué or taboo). On the other hand, there were the many brotherhoods who fashioned themselves in imitation of the Freemasons, right down to the symbolism, rituals, and regalia.

Psi Upsilon is one of the earliest fraternities, stemming from a group of writers, not Freemason imitators. This cuts two ways for Dan Brown. It has a kind of auspiciousness to it, for a fellow who would later become a world-famous writer. But for a writer who would later name Freemasonry as his field of deep research, it doesn't give him much of a leg up. Not only was his contact with fraternities minimal, but he had no firsthand opportunity to absorb the rituals and symbolism of Freemasonry, not even through a derivative version of it.

Extracurriculars

In addition to his Psi Upsilon membership, some of Brown's other activities at Amherst included playing on the varsity squash team and being a member of the famed Amherst College Glee Club.

Dan Brown tends to like individual, noncontact sports. He has played some soccer, but his stated games of choice are squash and tennis. His love of squash comes out in at least a couple of his novels, although he makes the signature hero, Robert Langdon, out to be an ardent swimmer and water polo player.

Singing and music were a deep pursuit for Dan Brown in college. One of the biggest events of his college life was a two-month world tour in the summer of 1983 with the glee club. This would introduce Brown, however fleetingly, to the great capitals and buildings of Europe and elsewhere.

The then Amherst choirmaster, a legend to all his singers wherever he went, Bruce G. McInnes, recently retired after a forty-year career devoted to singing groups at Yale, Amherst, and churches in Wisconsin and New York City. It was his policy to take his singing groups on tours and he worked out the spectacular 1983 tour, taking the glee club to about thirteen stops around the world.

Web sleuths in the blogosphere have unearthed some of the promotional statements about Dan Brown that surfaced later during his attempt to get attention for his musical work. One of these says:

> Dan's live performance experience includes a world tour with the renown [sic] ACGC and appearances in such venues as Notre Dame Cathedral (Paris), St. Marco's Cathedral (Venice), St. Stephen's (Vienna), the Acropolis (Athens), and the American Embassies in Delhi, Tokyo, Taipei, Hong Kong, and Seoul. He's also performed as a solo piano/vocalist at The Rojo y Negro in Spain and in

Hollywood at the National Academy of Songwriters Acoustic Underground.

The "ACGC" acronym would seem to be a way to conceal the fact that his live performance experience in these world historic settings came as a member of the Amherst College Glee Club. By not spelling it out, the acronym sounds like ACGC might be a musical group you should have heard of.

Dr. McInnes told me that he recalls Dan Brown very clearly as a "pleasant fellow with a big smile" who faithfully showed up for the glee club during his entire college career. "I don't recall him ever auditioning for a solo, though," McInnes said. He said that when Brown arrived at Amherst, the quality of the Exeter Academy choir program was already known to him. McInnes knew he could expect good preparation from its singers who went on to Amherst, so Brown easily made it into the glee club. Because so many singers arrive with baritone voices and a group needs tenors and basses, he said, it is common practice to assign some singers to these other sections. Thus Dan Brown was in the bass section in the ACGC.

The former members of McInnes's choirs simply revere him: some years ago they put together a group, the Mastersingers USA, whose sole function each year is to meet and sing during an intense three-day weekend. "These are all guys who were bitten by the [singing] bug," McInnes said. "It gives them a chance to step outside their normal lives and do something that they love." Additionally, they then go on a tour abroad every two or three years. In recent years the Mastersingers won top honors at a large international singing competition in Wales.

As with lots of people who helped him along the way, Dan Brown takes time to keep in touch with Dr.

McInnes. During the most recent tour in the summer of 2005, Dr. McInnes said he heard from Brown, who was expressing hopes of meeting the choir (and, no doubt, singing with them) in Barcelona, Spain, but the dates didn't work out. However, Brown may show up at the next Mastersingers gathering, McInnes said.

Confessions of This Writer

I should confess a number of odd coincidences about myself that apply to Amherst. In early 1966, as a college student, I visited Amherst to see an old high school buddy, and to check in with a couple of girls we knew at Smith and Mount Holyoke. While at Amherst, I was treated very well by the members of Psi Upsilon, what would later be Dan Brown's fraternity, in the old and grand chapter house just at the edge of campus. The brothers there loaned me an ideal make-out room, with a crackling fire, in which to entertain my date. (I never got past first base, but I never forgot the experience.)

Moreover, my buddy (or his roommate, perhaps) was a member of the glee club and he told me that, since I had been part of the high school chorus, I could just step up into the back risers at a rehearsal. So I did, singing merrily along with the ACGC in my clunky baritone. My only saving grace was that I could sight-read the music. But it was very memorable because the practice hall was a special building at Amherst called the Octagon House. The choirmaster, the very same Bruce McInnes who led Dan Brown years later, stopped the rehearsal at one point because the room was getting too stuffy, and commanded that we all run once around the outside of the building in the crisp winter air.

Also, like Dan Brown, I spent part of my college career

playing piano in practice rooms (and as the background noise at fraternity cocktail parties). I am not trying to compare myself musically to Dan Brown— since he was a very competent keyboard artist and I was a ham-handed klutz—but I can say for sure that I know what it is to pursue music for its own sake, to commune with it in solitude.

Bottom line: I can say that I socialized with Dan Brown's fraternity brothers, and sang in a "live performance" with his glee club!

Post-Graduation

Dan Brown wound up a college graduate in 1986 and didn't really have a career to embark on. He certainly did not declare himself a fiction writer. Music was most attractive to him. It appears that he reacted by not choosing a career, playing music locally for about a year, and going off to Spain again in the summer of 1987. Later that year he moved to California, which he viewed as a land of promise for a musician.

Luckily for people who want to keep track, Dan Brown made regular contributions to the Class of 1986 section of *Amherst Magazine,* the alumni publication, checking in at least every couple of years. It gives an almost running record of what he considered his triumphs at any given time.

In the spring of 1988, this is the entry: "Dan Brown is still living in California working his way into the music world dodging strange people and ideas. He supports himself by working as a counselor for 'The Millionaires Club,' a well-to-do private club for singles. He sends his phone number to anyone wishing to vacation in Southern California . . ."

But later that year, an entry said: "Dan Brown has come back East after a few years in Los Angeles and is working on a record we'll get to hear in September."

Two years passed, and in the summer of 1991 the *Amherst Magazine* entry read: "Dan Brown was featured in an article in the *Portsmouth Herald,* detailing his singing musical career. Dan is back in Hollywood, where he has gained the support of the National Academy of Songwriters, a non-profit organization dedicated to promoting talented songwriters. NAS has promoted such notables as Billy Joel, Prince, Phil Collins, Carole King and Neil Diamond. Dan's tape, *Perspective,* has been distributed to New England record stores, and another tape of children's music, *SynthAnimals,* is selling briskly."

Then, in the spring of 1993, came this entry: "Dan Brown's debut album was recently released on DGB Records. Dan was discovered by Hollywood producer Barry Fasman, who is now backing Dan with his own resources. The *Portsmouth Press* ran a feature article on Dan in November [1992], chronicling a visit to his hometown. Dan is currently teaching English literature at the Beverly Hills (90210) Preparatory School."

To recap these events, Dan Brown had been attempting to break into the Hollywood music scene for upward of four years, in at least two separate sojourns in California. It was on the second attempt, around 1991, that he hooked up with the National Academy of Songwriters (NAS).

This means that his earlier attempts at music production, both audio cassettes—*Perspective,* copyrighted in 1990 and *SynthAnimals,* in 1989—were self-produced, although undoubtedly with help from friends. One such friend was Chip Beckett, who had been a day student at Exeter Academy and graduated from Harvard in 1986.

Chip Beckett collaborated with Dan Brown on a number of music projects, including an earlier pair of cassettes called *Piropo Collected Works,* in 1986–87. Dan Brown had also been collaborating with an Amherst classmate, Jas Paley, during his early postgraduate years. *SynthAnimals* was remarkable because it was a series of electronic music sounds that imitated animals, intended for children. But, although Brown probably got some local shops to hawk his wares, it is safe to say that Brown remained the prototypical struggling musician. The tapes never got any real distribution and are nearly impossible to find today.

But the benefit of the early tapes is that in 1991 he could parlay them into an introduction to the NAS. This eventually led him to Barry Fasman, a skilled music director, arranger, engineer, and musician, who could help Dan Brown get all the way to a professional-sounding production.

Also, at the NAS Brown met a woman named Blythe Newlon, at the time serving as director of artist development. She would eventually become his wife. He was twenty-seven, she thirty-nine.

The outcome of all this was the audio production *Dan Brown,* created in 1992 and copyrighted in early 1993. Setting aside everything he had done before, it was his "debut" album, and it contained ten songs. At the time, the record label that bore Brown's initials, DGB Records, had a Hollywood address, but this would soon change to Exeter.

Let's Check the Charts

Through the miracle of eBay, I was able to obtain a copy of the *Dan Brown* album on tape and CD, and I will always treasure my CD copy of it, with its unbroken shrink-wrap and a little sticker showing it was probably bought in a benefit sale to help a local Exeter charity. (Even at that time, it appears, Dan Brown was doing his part for local causes.)

Here is what I can tell you about the album: Dan Brown has a great voice, great diction, sings on key, with great breathing and good expression. His keyboard musicianship is competent, and he had very skilled studio musicians accompanying him.

But . . . most of his songs are just not memorable. Of the first eight songs, if you heard them and then closed your eyes, you probably would not remember any of the lines or any of the tunes. The genre has been described as "accessible New Age," and I guess that's true, but I would say more like "pseudo-Barry Manilow."

I think there are two clear problems. One is that Dan Brown's voice is excellent, but doesn't have anything to make it unique. The other problem is that the lyrics are too general. In fact, in all ten songs I only counted two capitalized words (both in the last song, "Kuhlstihl and Kampuchea"). Otherwise, the rest of the songs can be characterized by grand-sounding titles but flat, disappointing lyrics, as in this snatch from "Birth of a King":

> He stands alone
> Outside your castle window
> He's traveled far
> From distant shores
> And from your throne
> You watch him kneel in silence
> And lay a flower at your door

The only real signs of departure from mundane lyrics are two songs, "976-LOVE," which is about phone sex using 900-numbers, and "Sweet Pleasure in Pain," which is open to interpretation, but probably relates to sadomasochism. As far as I can tell, "976-LOVE" is in *praise* of phone sex, by the way.

In the liner notes, Dan Brown gives special thanks "to Blythe Newlon and The National Academy of Songwriters for their belief and support." He then adds: "This album is dedicated to my parents for their unending generosity and love. Thank you both." This is among many examples of heart-felt thank-yous to his parents and family.

Sometime in 1993, Dan Brown moved back to Exeter permanently. An *Amherst* entry in early 1994 says so, but does not mention Blythe. However, a couple of activities were in motion. One was that Dan Brown and NAS did their best to promote his debut album, and Blythe was quoted in the materials in high praise of his work:

When the National Academy of Songwriters first heard Dan Brown's music, we paired him immediately with one of the most respected producers in pop music today, British Record Producer of the Year, Barry Fasman. No expense was spared in the recording of this album. The tracks were cut in some of the nation's finest studios with some of the most accomplished musicians living today. When the lights came up on tracking day, the all-star cast standing ready to play was awesome. The band included Michael Jackson's sax player, Madonna's bass player, and the Doobie Brothers' drummer, just to name a few. When the dust settled, they had recorded an album we believe will be remembered as one of the strongest independently released projects in quite some time. All of the synthesizer programming and arranging was done by Barry Fasman, whose arranging credits include Billy Joel, Diana Ross, Fame, and Air Supply. We believe Dan Brown is an artist destined to become a major talent and that this original pressing of his debut album could very well become a collector's item. Treat yourself.

—Director of Artist Development,
The National Academy of Songwriters

Notably, though, Dan Brown would look back on this time and, in at least one interview, refer to Blythe as his "music agent," not merely a staff member at NAS.

The second activity, begun in about 1993 and carrying into 1994, was the production of Dan Brown's other CD, with a title that was now a definite harbinger of things to come: *Angels & Demons.* Yes, the CD bore the same title as the novel he published in 2000, and which bears a close structural and intellectual resemblance to *The Da Vinci Code,* published three years later. What's more, Dan Brown had found the artist who is now famous for creating ambigrams, John Langdon, who brilliantly created an ambigram of the words "Angels & Demons" for the CD liner. Brown thanked "the ingenious John Langdon for attempting and accomplishing the impossible."

According to a recent article in the Philadelphia *City Paper,* the real-life John Langdon had released a book of ambigrams in 1992 called *WordPlay* and it was Dick Brown who first corresponded with him, then called him one day and asked whether Langdon could help his son with a project—which turned out to be the CD liner artwork. Years later, Brown would work John Langdon's specially created ambigrams into a pivotal role in the novel *Angels & Demons.*

Mention is made of some West Coast studio work on the *Angels & Demons* music CD in 1994, but mainly the production is East Coast, with local musicians, including Brown's old buddy from Exeter, Chip Beckett. (If you ever listen to this album, you will also hear the voice of Blythe as a back-up singer in some cuts.)

The *Angels & Demons* album is a vast improvement over the eponymous *Dan Brown* album, but it suffers from the same two basic problems: the unmemorable voice and the lowercase lyrics.

However, there are touches and hints of things that will eventually seem to have foretold Brown's novels. The general themes are grand ideas like chivalry, honoring one's forefathers, or asking, "Where are the heroes?"

There is a song, "All I Believe," which will no doubt fuel the fires of all the people who have accused Dan Brown of being antireligious. It is actually clearly intended to be a love song, with the chorus "I don't need a preacher to save me / from demons who deceive / Just you / You're all I believe." However, it does contain these lines as the opening:

> There's no god above
> There's no fire below
> There's no perfect truth
> No place we all go
> There are no angels in heaven
> And no guarantees
> There's just you
> You're all I believe

Among the songs there is, again, one special cut that contains practically all the proper nouns of the whole album. It is called "Dover Beach," and I would say it is the pained lament of a bare-naked heart for a lost love. This paints a view from a lonely beach within sight of the Isles of Shoals, but also of "the lights of Kensington Green."

It was easy enough to visit the real-life place on the New Hampshire coast where I could see the Isles of Shoals. It has been frequented over the years by poets and artists (the American Impressionist Childe Hassam painted one of his most famous works here). The Isles of Shoals area is bound up with numerous romantic legends about shipwrecks, treasure, and pirates.

Since the description was specific enough, I went looking for the Dover Beach in question. Using a combination of town maps and nautical charts, it was easy enough to find the town of Dover, as well as Dover Point. If you left Dan Brown's house and went south a few miles, you would arrive at the little village of Kensington. Both of these are within about eight miles of the Atlantic beach, but you cannot see all of these landmarks from one spot.

Thus I am convinced a "Dover Beach" does not actually exist by that name, but is an amalgamation of several spots that Dan Brown knew. I consider this a good thing. As I see it, here is a case where artistic license was used by Dan Brown in a very appropriate way.

The *Angels & Demons* album now had DGB Records located in Exeter, at what would be Dan Brown's digs for about ten years, an apartment on Chestnut Avenue in a converted brick mill along the Squamscott River—again, within easy walking distance of practically everything in Exeter. According to at least one account, Brown did a lot of his local commuting by bicycle.

The album liner thanks a string of unusual entities, such as "Macintosh Computers." It contains a special note of thanks to "Blythe Newlon . . . tireless co-writer, co-producer, second engineer, significant other, and therapist."

Teaching Days

At times in his life, Dan Brown has been a teacher. From the evidence, I would say it is something he turned to in order to make ends meet, not as a true vocation. Sometimes he taught English and other times, Spanish. During the early to mid-1990s, he taught in Exeter and at nearby Stratham.

Later on, history would be rewritten a bit to make it seem logical that Dan Brown would teach English and later write novels. For instance, many of the publicity materials issued about Dan Brown feature this statement: "He is a graduate of Amherst College and Phillips Exeter Academy, where he spent time as an English teacher before turning his efforts fully to writing." Strictly speaking, this is a true statement, but I think it is crafted to lead the reader to believe that Dan Brown was on the faculty of Phillips Exeter Academy. In fact, however, he was occasionally a part-time teacher there, and was never elevated to a faculty position.

To put it more bluntly, I don't find any evidence that Dan Brown held a full-time job for any continuous period of more than a couple of years, from the time he graduated from college in 1986 to about 1996, when he could certainly say he was engaged in the trade of novel writing. Many writers have worn their poverty-stricken hungry days as a badge of honor, but it doesn't appear that Dan Brown would see it that way. My hunch is that this is because he had certain appearances to maintain. Neither the Protestant ethic of Exeter Academy nor the ambitions of its bright, talented, elite students tend to favor drifting from coast to coast, trying one's hand at music and writing, and never demonstrating tangible success.

A Hint of a Book

In the spring of 1994, the *Amherst* entry says, "Dan Brown is living in Exeter writing a book about the difference between men. For example, those who wear boxer shorts versus those who wear briefs . . ."

This was certainly a signal of something significant, since it was the first time that Dan Brown publicly told his classmates about any aspirations to write books. The book that would eventually emerge in 1995 was *187 Men to Avoid,* written by Dan, but under the pseudonym "Danielle Brown." It is a small paperback of humor, with a one-liner on each page. Those to avoid include "Men who stir-fry" or "Men who own hamsters." A friend of mine argues that this gimmicky book, which at the time was Brown's entry-level effort to get his foot in the publishing door, is actually important to Dan Brown's development: out of the negative space of men to avoid, Robert Langdon was sculpted, possessing exactly zero of the unfortunate 187 characteristics. I'm not so sure, but there may be something to this idea.

But what about "Men who join Mensa"?

Mensa

In some of Dan Brown's pieces intended to promote his music, there is a mention that he was a member of Mensa, a society for people with high intelligence. Mensa International's headquarters in the U.S. confirms that Dan Brown was once a member. Other materials make it clear that he did not continue his membership for very long.

Mensa membership is open to people who can demonstrate that their IQ is within the top two percent of a given population. According to the organization,

> Mensa was founded in England in 1946 by Roland Berrill, a barrister, and Dr. Lance Ware, a scientist and lawyer. They had the idea of forming a society for bright people, the only qualification for membership of which was a high IQ. The original aims were, as they are today, to create a society that is non-political and free from all racial or religious distinctions. Mensa has three stated purposes: to identify and foster human intelligence for the benefit of humanity, to encourage research in the nature, characteristics and uses of intelligence, and to promote stimulating intellectual and social opportunities for its members.

The organization explains the word *mensa* as follows: "The word 'table' in Latin. The name stands for a round-table society, where race, color, creed, national origin, age, politics, educational or social background are irrelevant."

I don't think that it would be any stretch to suppose that Dan Brown would find this music to his ears, echoing the aims of the traditional Harkness Table at Exeter Academy, where small groups of students were encouraged to lead the discussion in directions that would most benefit their self-education. It also vaguely suggests Exeter's atmosphere of religious tolerance (plus overtones of Freemasonry). Most of all, it demonstrates his strivings to be among intelligent people discussing big ideas—not exactly what he was on track to accomplish with *187 Men to Avoid*. Nonetheless, he did not remain a Mensa member.

Receding Hairlines

Unchastened by a lack of public acclaim for *187 Men*, Brown in 1998 released *The Bald Book,* another bit of silliness, intended to cheer up men who are losing their hair.

This was put out with Blythe Brown's name on the cover, but the copyright is registered to Dan Brown as the author.

Dan Brown did not brag about either humor book in his newsletter entries intended to keep his former classmates posted on his activities. The main news they had of him in this period was in the fall of 1996, when the entry read: "Among other engagements in the news are Dan Brown and Blythe Newlon. The two are living happily in Exeter, NH, where Dan is writing music and books and Blythe is a dental hygienist." Would it be too much of a leap to assume that with Dan Brown maxing out his credit cards to get his CDs recorded and pressed, and with his books generating only small sales at best, that Blythe—the older woman who would turn him on to art, Europe, and the spirit of the sacred feminine—was supporting his effort to find himself creatively by working in a dental office?

Several cynical bloggers have questioned the claim that appears in Dan Brown publicity materials that one of his songs, "Peace in Our Time," was played at the 1996 Olympics in Atlanta, Georgia. Blog sleuths expressed doubts that Dan Brown ever wrote such a song, noting it wasn't on the official CD released after the Olympics.

Well, the blogosphere was wrong. The *Angels & Demons* CD does contain the song "Peace in Our Time." It is exactly the kind of general anthem about peace that you might imagine. And I have found an explanation that fits it into the Olympics. It turns out that Wei Wei, a very famous female singer in China, sang it during one of the Olympic events, according to Dan Brown. Now, I wasn't able to confirm whether it was the women's archery or the men's three-meter diving, so the only way to research it further would be to listen to all sixteen days (and nights) of 1996 Olympic tapes for some 271 events.

The Butterfly Emerges

Well, there you have it. An Exeter Academy education, followed by an Amherst education and about ten years of trying, and both the music and writing careers of Dan Brown looked like scripts for the movie *Titanic*. In fact, at long last, Dan Brown himself admitted the music thing wasn't working. Having his song played at the Olympics "was a real thrill, and quite honestly about all I have to show for my grueling four-year music stint in Hollywood is the fact that my three CDs received plenty of critical success but turned out to be bona fide commercial duds," Brown wrote to his classmates.

But it was now the fall of 1997, and without even mentioning his humor books, he could point to something big and successful: "After my last CD, I decided to take a year off and try my hand at writing a novel (a logical change of gears, I know). I wrote the novel, sent it out, and damn if the first publisher who read it didn't buy it." The book was *Digital Fortress*. Like the boom of a cannon, it announced a new writer was launching his assault on the publishing world.

And Now, Back to Sidney

But to return (at last) to Sidney Sheldon's novel and its effect on Dan Brown: I do believe he is telling the truth when he says that it gave him the chutzpah to write a novel (after a suitable gestation period). I think Sheldon's *Doomsday Conspiracy* is so important that Dan Brown should mark his life in two divisions: BS (before Sheldon) and AS (after Sheldon).

What you should also know (and please, confirm it for yourself) is that *Doomsday* is in the running for one of the worst novels of its type ever foisted on the public. It was written half a century after Sheldon had established a name for himself in a career that would see him on bestseller lists with numerous trashy novels and on multiple movie and TV credits as screenwriter. *Doomsday,* released in 1991, was Sheldon's eleventh novel. His tenth, *Memories of Midnight,* was a sequel to a 1974 novel, *The Other Side of Midnight,* which had held the record in that era for longevity on the *New York Times* bestseller list (52 weeks). Of course, *The Da Vinci Code* blew away that record, and anything remotely close (it had been on the list for 141 weeks at press time).

Doomsday's plot is embarrassingly predictable. A U.S. Navy intelligence officer is dispatched on a beyond-top-secret mission to identify the witnesses to a "balloon crash" in the Swiss Alps. As he pursues the mission, he realizes that the puppet-masters who dispatched him are killing the witnesses as quickly as he identifies them. Also, the "balloon" was really a UFO and the conspiracy is an international effort to cover up the fact that aliens have arrived. Early in the novel we learn that there are some ten witnesses. We are then forced to endure ten iterations of the hero, Robert Bellamy, locating a witness, followed by a nefarious sanctioned assassin cleaning up behind. To do this, Bellamy hops around Europe and America using an unlimited government credit card. It becomes a running gag, where the only question is whether the next victim will be strangled, shot, or burned to death. But (in perfect hindsight, of course) there were things that Dan Brown could learn from *Doomsday.* Primarily, a plot can be driven forward with a combination of keeping the chapters short and always looking for some way to leave an impending development hanging—commonly known as the *cliffhanger.*

Anyone who looks at Dan Brown's works can see that he learned Sheldon's lesson very well. In fact, *The Da Vinci Code* is one of the best examples anywhere of these techniques and it puts Sheldon to shame. Dan Brown was already good at it with *Digital Fortress,* though, and has been improving on it with each successive novel. All of his novels have at least 100 chapters, and one has 137 (*Angels & Demons*). The brevity of the chapters keeps giving contemporary readers the positive reinforcement of having completed a chapter of a book—an experience most of us have all too rarely these days. Meanwhile, the cliffhangers at the end of the chapters and the intercutting of the action taking place in several different story lines keeps the reader pushing on to attain the next short chapter, and the next . . .

Sheldon put a twist in the end of *Doomsday* to reveal that the hero's superior officer and mentor throughout most of the book was actually the spooky figure known as Janus (the two-faced Roman god) who had been one of the evil puppet-masters. Dan Brown paid attention to this, and essentially all of his plots so far have come up to some kind of very similar revelation that the chief bad guy, portrayed throughout the book as evil incarnate, turns out not to be the source of the evil conspiracy, while another character, groomed carefully so as not to arouse much suspicion, is unmasked in the end as the evil and nefarious villain. Sir Leigh Teabing has this part in *The Da Vinci Code,* and the Camerlengo has it in *Angels & Demons.* In *Angels & Demons,* the head honcho of the evil Illuminati conspiracy is even named Janus, just like in the

Sheldon novel. Moreover, *Angels & Demons*—and *The Da Vinci Code* to a degree—features a variety of murders performed in different homicidal styles, just like *Doomsday.*

But while Brown may have learned a lot about plotting and structure from Sheldon, he put a lot more work into the research part of his novels than Sheldon ever did. The legend of *Digital Fortress* has it that when he was writing the book, Dan Brown put out feelers through Internet newsgroups and got responses from two anonymous former National Security Agency cryptographers, giving him inside information about the world of codes and the computers that crack them. He thanks the two as part of his acknowledgments.

Quite courageously for a first novelist writing in the action-adventure genre, Brown created a female heroine to carry the load. Susan Fletcher has the superintelligence of a top cryptographer, the mental toughness to keep cool and process information under extreme pressure, and even some action-hero physical skills. In a nice twist, her boyfriend gets sent to Seville, Spain, to pursue some of the clues of the mystery, and they only reunite after the main drama has been resolved. Like *The Da Vinci Code* and *Angels & Demons,* most of the action of *Digital Fortress* takes place in a twenty-four-hour day. It is set in a reasonably exotic, cultured European setting, and features a ticking time bomb of a plot-driver on which the future of Western civilization depends. All three books pair up a brainy, beautiful math/science female heroine with a professorial humanist hero. Together, the two have to somehow crack codes and figure out the mind of the evil genius threatening the world. As indicated before, in each case the evil villain turns out to be secretly controlled by a kindly figure presented earlier in the story as a well-loved positive character whom the reader is fooled into believing is on the side of the angels.

Dan Brown pioneered all of this in *Digital Fortress,* all the while using Sidney Sheldon's short chapter technique, including one with only four paragraphs, occupying less than half a page of text! Within the plot of the novel, he introduced the code method known as the "Caesar's box," using it to good effect, and also gave his readers a good indoctrination into basic cryptography techniques. He then cleverly fashioned a string of numbers printed without explanation on the last page of the book, which could be used with the first letters of each chapter to spell out a message, again using a Caesar's box: "We are watching you." This coding became a "Dan Brown thing," used in several of his novels.

Some of the codes are relatively difficult, but when it matters within a plot, Dan Brown makes a good adjustment that rewards the average reader with the illusion that he or she is participating in code-breaking. In *Digital Fortress,* there is a moment when the entire action of the plot necessitates the decrypting of a five-letter code, which turns out to be the name of the heroine, Susan. In *The Da Vinci Code,* of course, much of the plot hangs on decrypting the cryptex, which ultimately turns out to have been programmed with five-letter codes—one is a play on the Greek word for wisdom (Sophia) and the heroine's name, Sophie; the other makes reference to Newton's apple.

While Brown did far more research than Sidney Sheldon would have ever thought necessary to support a potboiler, *Digital Fortress* also commenced Brown's troubling mix of realism gleaned from serious research, plot flaws based on insufficient or sloppy research, and outright fiction masquerading as factual, researched information. Some of the computer equipment and procedures in *Digital Fortress* didn't match reality and were somewhat stylized, leaving little hints that the author didn't really visit an NSA cryptography center. Also, his scenes in Seville were probably created from time-dimmed recollection. (According to one account, the mayor of Seville said he wanted to invite Brown to visit the city for the first time!)

One very significant difference between Sidney Sheldon and Dan Brown is how they deal with sex. Sheldon is completely explicit about sex acts, which are frequent and utterly gratuitous in his novels. Brown, on the other hand, despite the relationships of love that develop between his characters, almost never depicts an actual sex act, but merely hints that one will take place, off-camera, so to speak. But *Digital Fortress* does have at least one scene that is explicit, and it is also the only one of Brown's novels to feature a good slathering of swear words, including the F-word.

Pouring on the Coals

Although there were surely rounds of revisions, by 1997 Dan Brown had proved in *Digital Fortress* that he could write a novel, and it was time to set his sights on his next projects. It was also a time of change for him in Exeter: his father retired from the math department after some thirty-five years. Dick and Connie Brown had a picture-perfect retirement house on the shore of a lake in upstate New Hampshire, so they sold the Nelson Drive homestead.

It was time for Dan and Blythe to get married, and they did it with great panache and romance. According to a college classmate who attended, the August 1997 afternoon found the guests on Connie and Dick's lawn, assembled in chairs facing the lake, with no wedding party in view. A small chamber music ensemble stopped playing. Then they heard the faint sounds of a bagpipe, and from the lake there arrived a Boston Whaler (driven by younger brother Greg Brown) towing a barge. On the barge, which was adorned with boughs, were Dan, Blythe, a minister, and the bagpiper in full Scottish regalia. They alighted onshore and the ceremony began. "There was not a dry eye in the house, least of all Dan's!" said the Amherst alumni reporter. The newlyweds spent their honeymoon in Quebec City, one of the oldest and most romantic cities in North America, and one of the only places on the continent that approximates the architectural beauty or historic intrigue of any of the sites in which Brown would set a novel, such as Seville, Paris, or Rome.

By early 1998, *Digital Fortress* could be called a hit, going into its third printing. Dan Brown also hinted to his classmates that a movie of it might be in the works (so far, it hasn't happened, but it is probably coming after *The Da Vinci Code* movie and the *Angels & Demons* movie). And by mid-1998, Brown was justifiably crowing: "On the book front, *Digital Fortress* has sold through four printings, and Simon & Schuster just bought the rights to my next two novels. Off we go! And I always thought I was going to be a rock star. At least now I don't have to wear spandex."

The next book was *Angels & Demons.* In it he would take the character prototype he had developed in *Digital Fortress* and build upon it to invent Robert Langdon. Brown would eventually speak about a trilogy of Robert Langdon stories (including *The Da Vinci Code* and the anticipated *Solomon Key*). In many, many respects, *Angels &*

Demons reads like a rough draft for *The Da Vinci Code,* incorporating major secrets from history that powerful people want to keep quiet, big issues of science vs. religion, secret societies (including Templars, Illuminati, and Freemasons), lost manuscripts, famous characters from history, coded messages, art and architectural symbolism, improbable chases through the tourist centers of major European cities, and many other shared allusions and literary devices.

In due course, Brown announced to his classmates in the summer of 1999 that he had finished *Angels & Demons* and that it would be released the following February. With a wink to classmates, Dan Brown talked about having had to do a "research trip/tax write-off" to Rome for the book. In a winter 2000 report, Dan talked of continued success for *Digital Fortress,* the arrival of *Angels & Demons,* and "Blythe is doing great . . . very into her Renaissance painting and sculpture (our place smells like oil paint and marble dust) and she continues to amaze me every day with some new artistic talent." In the spring of 2000, he checked in again and it was clear that he was working hard on something new: "I'd really love to tell you that Blythe and I are doing cool things like bungee jumping in Thailand, but lately life has been one long blur of typing, editing, and black coffee." By the fall of 2000, *Angels & Demons* had shot to bestseller position.

Angels & Demons opens with a statement very similar to the one that opens *The Da Vinci Code,* suggesting that all the major elements of the story are factual. It is not clear when this brainstorm for how to start a novel that is a mishmash of fact and fiction occurred to Dan Brown, but the power of suggestion has worked wonders for creating reader credibility (or perhaps I should say gullibility). *Angels & Demons* introduced the Langdon character, and, in doing so, signaled two key things about Brown's future as a novelist: a new kind of attractive action hero had been born, who is no action hero at all, but a Harvard symbology professor, and a putative genre of "fact-based fiction," richly layered with references to art, architecture, and alternative history, had been created as context.

It is ironic that in *Angels & Demons* Dan Brown played fast and loose with the Vatican's procedures for papal succession and many other matters of Vatican history. He suggested that an Illuminati conspiracy could seize control of the Catholic Church, and dredged up the twenty-year-old conspiracy theory that Pope John Paul I had been murdered by poison. Yet apparently, this was all so "over the top"—especially in a plot involving an antimatter bomb set on the burial remains of St. Peter, poised to blow up the entire Vatican—that the Catholic Church came out with no particular reaction to *Angels & Demons.* When huge acclaim followed *The Da Vinci Code,* though, the church denounced it through an Italian cardinal who called it "a pack of lies." (For more on the church reactions, see page 500.)

In the spring of 2001, a classmate reported that Dan and Blythe had visited him during the winter:

> Dan is feverishly researching and writing his next book. He gave the lie to the notion that writers set their own schedules and don't have bosses. Dan and Blythe spend hours every day researching and Dan writes into the night and has some very hard deadlines set by unsympathetic editors at Simon & Schuster. No extensions allowed unless you are Stephen King or John Grisham.

It seems apparent that all this intense activity was to produce *Deception Point,* released in 2001. The novel has a

Sidney Brown/Dan Sheldon plot, in the sense that an evil puppet-master, disguised as a good guy, lurks and manipulates things until the big revelation scene at the end. There is a he-she pair of central characters, the heroine doing the bulk of the thinking and some of the brawling, and the hero generally in the role of physical and moral support. The novel is also populated by a rather rich cast of characters who dance around a central conspiracy. Because the secret has to do with an asteroid of mysterious composition, government agencies like NASA and the National Reconnaissance Office are involved, along with helicopters, hi-tech ultrasonic airplanes, and a black-ops Delta Force with their own specialized war toys. Although it is an action tale, it does have secrets and codes and requires some brain work by the protagonists. But it is quite different from a Langdon tale, as in *Angels & Demons* or *The Da Vinci Code.* Some of the action is set in the frozen north, and some in government corridors in Washington, DC. Naturally, the White House is also implicated.

For a novel that followed *Angels & Demons,* there is a puzzling aspect of *Deception Point,* in that it involves lots of military equipment, mercenaries, and the like, with plenty of shooting and very James Bond–like predicaments for the hero and heroine. Langdon novels tend to be more cerebral. *Deception Point* has no dedication page. Why? Maybe this doesn't seem significant, but it will keep me wondering until I arrive at an answer. And, despite now-frequent updates for his college classmates in *Amherst,* Brown never even mentioned this novel's title to them. He merely jumped from talk of his second novel (*Angels & Demons*) to his fourth novel (*The Da Vinci Code*) without explanation.

In the summer of 2001 (I think indicating that his delivery of *Deception Point* had satisfied his contract), *Amherst* reported, "Dan has recently switched from publisher Simon and Schuster to Doubleday," following the path of his editor, Jason Kaufman. Frankly, even if Brown whacked out *Deception Point* merely in order to get clear of an option clause for his next book in a Simon & Schuster contract, it actually has a pretty clever plot, lots of action, and a fairly nifty conspiracy and sci-fi mystery involving an extraterrestrial artifact (again putting to shame Sheldon's *Doomsday*). I think it is very noticeable that in *Angels & Demons* and *The Da Vinci Code,* Brown retained the male-female pairing of main characters, but both women (Vittoria in *Angels & Demons* and Sophie in *The Da Vinci Code*) were made far less imposing than either heroine in *Digital Fortress* and *Deception Point*.

Brown held a two-edged sword when he picked Arctic Circle scenes for a lot of the action in *Deception Point*. On the one hand, it meant that he was hardly likely to do any first-person research, so he could not speak with any authority about life in the far north. But, on the other hand, no one in his audience could, either. When he brought the action down to Washington, DC, he kept events generally within the bounds of the major tourist areas (thus keeping his on-location research to a minimum). Although there are indications that Dan Brown was already beginning to hear from fans and critics telling him about technical errors and plot flaws, he didn't see a need to do more accurate research, even as he began to write "fact-based" novels.

"Real" Novels

In *Deception Point* Brown added an author's note that proclaimed the Delta Force, National Reconnaissance Office, and Space Frontier Foundation all exist and "all technologies described in this novel exist." In a foreshadowing of the debates over his future books, the truth is that his depictions of certain technological elements in *Deception Point* were riddled with errors, despite the opening statement. And not only were Brown's two Langdon novels based on history and conspiracy legends, but they each had a page in the front pronouncing as "fact" certain parts having to do with art, architecture, the Illuminati, the Priory of Sion, and so on.

Moreover, in those final days when Brown still found it necessary to sit for interviews to promote *The Da Vinci Code,* he continued to insist that it was based on fact. He once famously said that if he were to rewrite *The Da Vinci Code* as nonfiction, he wouldn't change a thing. On other occasions he implied that all of its content about Jesus, Mary Magdalene, the Holy Grail, etc. was factual, because the only relevant story he could not pin down was that Jesus did not die on the cross, but took a potion to endure the pain and was revived three days later. Since he could not confirm this story—told in books like the *Passover Plot* and alluded to in *Holy Blood, Holy Grail*—he did not use it. He made this point in several interviews and talks, as if to emphasize that he had been able to document everything else as factual. Since he was now also toying with some fundamental tenets of Christianity, it caused an uproar.

Why did Dan Brown bring on the burden of having to defend his assertions as true? It is actually part of a recognizable tradition almost as old as literature. In recent times there has been a propensity for certain bestselling novelists to support their ideas with facts. But during the heyday of the Hellenistic era when the Library of Alexandria served as the center of a great literary community spanning numerous cultures, there was a legendary debate between two camps. The older tradition held that a writer should employ poetry and prose to convey factual knowledge to the next generation. Thus the writer of an epic tale of adventure would stop to catalog the flowers along the way, or explain how to harvest grapes. The newer writers felt that it was okay for literature merely to entertain, in the moment, and could skip the task of educating the audience. You could just drink the wine, stupid.

Although thoroughly American, a classic adhering to the older tradition is *Moby Dick* by Herman Melville. Imitating ancient Greek writers, Melville gave the reader a complete indoctrination into the whaling trade, detailing everything that goes into hunting, killing and processing whales. *Moby Dick* tends to drive modern students to tears as they plow through hundreds of boring pages, trying to get to the action scene where Ahab, the Pequod, and the white whale finally duke it out.

In 1922 T. S. Eliot published *The Waste Land,* a poem that students find inscrutable, but critics and scholars love. Like a Dan Brown novel, it contained a large collection of one-line references from a vast number of historic periods, countries, religions, cultures, and languages. There are snatches of German, Italian, and Hindu, as well as allusions to Greek and Indian myths, all mixed up together. Unique among great poems, it was published with numerous footnotes. It is fair to say that appreciating the poem fully requires the help of the footnotes. Eliot (though really just intending to enhance the experience of the poem) had set a standard for a kind of "fact-based poetry" that others would find impossible to imitate.

But in Brown's era, some of the biggies are Tom Clancy and Michael Crichton. Clancy came out with a series of nonfiction books in the 1980s giving insider-styled details of tanks, planes, and submarines, so that the audience can assume he knows a lot about the war toys in, say, *The Hunt for Red October.* Clancy even became a public figure in the Reagan years, commenting on defense policy and military preparedness as a result of his acclaim as a detail-oriented Cold War novelist.

Michael Crichton on several occasions went so far as to cite detailed technical references in his novels, explaining aspects of biotechnology and cloning in *Jurassic Park* and nanotechnology in *Prey.* Crichton was among the early pioneers in the use of nonfiction bibliographies in the back of his books. As early as *Rising Sun,* he included a long bibliography of scholarly and public policy books having to do with the Japanese economy and Japanese investment in the United States—the issues that formed the backdrop and context for his otherwise pedestrian action-adventure novel. When Dan Brown sought to bolster the perception of a factual basis for *The Da Vinci Code,* he put a bibliography on his website. Brown did this in 2003 and in an interview made it clear that he considered it innovative, even though Michael Crichton's bibliographies came more than a decade earlier.

Dan Brown went to Paris to be able to write about the city with some authority, but in *The Da Vinci Code* he failed to depict simple elements like routes to the Louvre and the American Embassy correctly. He got the direction of one-way streets wrong, timetables and train stations were in error, Château Villette's location was misplaced. The Louvre's now-famous bathroom, where Robert and Sophie spend so many pages of novel, has no window and only liquid soap. The tracking dot, so key to *The Da Vinci Code*'s plot, could not have been embedded in a nonexistent bar of soap, nor could it have been hurled out the nonexistent window. *Angels & Demons* is littered with similar errors about Rome. In fact, it seems as though the in-depth, meticulous research claimed by Brown and praised so highly by some of the initial rave reviewers of his books is rather deeply flawed.

Both *Angels & Demons* and *The Da Vinci Code* are dedicated to Blythe, whom Brown has given a great deal of credit, stressing her invaluable help as a co-researcher. By implication, Blythe may be the one who came up with certain references, especially in the areas of her interest: art, architecture, and perhaps the occult. In one published account reprinted in Chapter 6, the suggestion has been made that it was possibly Blythe who first became interested in Rosslyn Chapel and then took her novelist husband there to see what she had seen the following year. In various promotional materials or press accounts, you will sometimes see Blythe referred to as an "art historian," although in more recent references Brown tends to call her simply an "art history buff."

Brown's plot flaws, technical howlers, and general fast-and-loose approach to calling anything that comes out of research—even from dubious sources—a "fact" raises a series of interesting questions. Obviously, no novelist writing fiction has any obligation to be factual. This includes novelists who have the temerity to publish an opening note suggesting everything in their book is based on fact. Indeed, even those who proclaim in television interviews and with straight faces that they wouldn't have changed a thing if they had written nonfiction are fully protected under the fundamental right of a fiction writer to make stuff up.

But why all this pretense of fact and research without the more common authorial note—that fact, fiction, and speculation have been uniquely combined in the imagination of the novelist? What about the disclaimer "Any resemblance to real people, places, and historical incidents is purely coincidental"? Did he not know, when he was writing *Angels & Demons* and *The Da Vinci Code,* what kind of a fishbowl he would later be in, and therefore thought there would be no problem mixing established fact with speculation and imagination? Is it just a marketing ploy to create more interest and credibility for the books? Is it a deliberately Machiavellian manipulation that plays on reader gullibility about conspiracy theory and how far powerful people in our society would go to cover up important secrets? Did he ever believe that the story told in *Holy Blood, Holy Grail* and other occult and New Age tales about the Priory of Sion, its history of grand masters, and the secret about the royal bloodline of Jesus and Mary they kept was based on anything more than myth, legend, archetype—and the hoax of Pierre Plantard?

Of course it isn't the technical details that have been the biggest source of questions about how Dan Brown sees the bright line between fact and fiction. The overwhelming majority of his critics are people of religious faith and belief who have attacked his version of religious history and theology. For many of us, however, there is no obvious winner in the question of who is more factual in their rendering of the life of Jesus—those who believe that the Bible is entirely factual, or Dan Brown who says he believes his rendering is entirely factual.

Dan Brown has big and important things to say. He urges us to consider very interesting and important speculations about religious history and what might have really happened millennia ago—between Jesus and Mary, among the Gnostics, among the alchemists, or with the Knights Templar. He introduces extremely significant philosophical debates about the source material for

Christian belief and whether modern followers of Jesus know or understand that their Bible was edited by Roman emperors, most of whom were probably more interested in developing a state religion than what Jesus may actually have said. He urges us to understand the signs and symbols, the artworks, and classic texts that have come down to us from the ancients. He comes at us over and over again with provocative thoughts about the sacred feminine, gods and goddesses, the place of sexuality in the human experience, the origins of spiritual thinking, and the arguments between science and religion.

In his handful of public appearances he gives a powerful, if now standardized stump speech, on how he sees fusing the common interests of religion and science and the need to oppose religious extremism and the antiscientific bent our culture is taking. He is about to raise the same kind of provocative questions he did about early Christianity in *The Da Vinci Code* as he takes us into the world of early American history with his next book. And as he moves on from Jesus to George Washington, he will undoubtedly have many new intellectual provocations for us. The reality is that Dan Brown—whether he was ever a full-time faculty member of Exeter Academy or not; whether history judges him as a great novelist or a "pop schlockmeister" or something in between—is an important teacher to millions of readers, posing critical questions of our time and encouraging people to go questing for their own answers.

Now that he has had such success, now that no one can question his influence as a cultural force in our society, will he be able to come down off the clever marketing and positioning of his past novels and acknowledge that he is serving up his own home-cooked stew of fact and fiction? A dead giveaway will be what, if anything, he puts on the "Fact" page of his as yet unpublished new book, *The Solomon Key.* He could just skip that page, or, better yet, point out he has created his own version of history—interesting, speculative, plausible, but not necessarily fact.

Publishing company accountants are now processing royalty checks. Not only *The Da Vinci Code,* but all of Brown's prior novels have been republished and have ended up on bestseller lists in the United States and all over the world. Brown's agent recently up-negotiated the contract for his next books. Soon *The Da Vinci Code* movie will be generating a torrent of cash flow, complete with licensed video games and other products, not to mention all the other books being turned into movies over the next few years. Even *187 Men to Avoid* trades at a huge premium on eBay. Dan Brown's ship currently has waves of money pouring in over the gunwales. He can afford any car, house, or vacation he likes. There is no research trip he can't afford, nor any "research vacation" he could take that would have any appreciable effect as a tax write-off.

Nonetheless, he has chosen to remain in the Exeter vicinity and cling to a relatively simple, quiet life. He maintains a writing loft in Exeter. He claims that he hasn't had a good start to a writing day unless he has arisen by 4 a.m. He stays fit with sports, such as tennis, and takes frequent breaks from his desk, sometimes to hang upside down in gravity boots to get the stimulation of additional blood flowing to the brain.

The Browns have purchased two properties not far from Exeter. I have visited the addresses, and it appears to me that they are living in one home, a comfortable-looking house of quiet grandeur, while they are razing the house on their other parcel to make way for something nice—and secluded—in the trees. What I find very obvious, in the context of the town they chose, is that they avoided any temptation to snap up an ostentatious, highly visible address, even though there are prime candidates available.

Dan and Blythe—and even Dan's parents—took some time off in the summer of 2005 to be movie-groupies and watch Tom Hanks and Ron Howard on location as they hammered out *The Da Vinci Code* movie. In obvious response to rumors that some of the most provoking references to Opus Dei and religious matters have been sanitized in order to keep potential Catholic audiences on board, Brown told his dinner audience that the movie will reflect the book. "It will be as though you have seen the book itself," Brown promised.

In honor of his father, Dan recently joined with siblings Valerie and Greg to endow a $2.2 million fund at Exeter, earmarked for computers and other high-tech equipment for students. In announcing the gift, he said, "My dad's contribution to education through teaching and textbooks is a powerful legacy. My sister, brother, and I want to honor our father's contribution to the Academy, and his lasting impact on the thousands of students whom he taught." Dan Brown is fond of mentioning how his love of codes began when his father and mother used to hide the holiday presents and then give coded clues to the kids. In *The Da Vinci Code,* this is exactly what Sophie Neveu does as a child, decoding messages from her grandfather.

Brown has also "given back" in the form of time that he spends at the Academy, meeting with current students as well as prospective students and their parents. He occasionally turns up unannounced at town of Exeter benefit events as well. A recent local story in the Exeter papers tells how Dan is living the simple life and maintaining his relationship in the Big Brother program. For more than three years, while his fame went through the roof and his free time dwindled, Dan Brown has made a point of fulfilling his pledge to be a Big Brother. He has been taking a twelve-year-old local boy, "Colby," to the Exeter Academy library, to baseball and football games, "boogie boarding" at the beach, and even to a paintball session. Brown uses his language fluency to help tutor Colby in Spanish.

And he passes a torch: "Dan even sends Colby coded messages in the mail. His mother, Cheryl, even wondered jokingly if they were supposed to go to the library to figure them out," said the *Portsmouth Herald*.

The Latin Etymology of *The Da Vinci Code*

BY DAVID D. BURSTEIN

Popular modern works of epic fiction ranging from the *Harry Potter* series to *The Da Vinci Code* often feature a rich use of language, including references to ancient languages and interesting word play. Dan Brown has a few special interests in using some real Latin words in *The Da Vinci Code*. First, he obviously loves words and wordplay and he knows very well how much of our English language is based on Latin. Second, he is a former teacher at Exeter, one of the country's top private high schools. And third, since *The Da Vinci Code* itself is centered on debates within

---

David D. Burstein is a high school Latin student, writer, actor, and filmmaker. He is currently working on a bipartisan public service documentary, *I'm 18 in '08*, to encourage young people to vote and become involved in politics.

and without the Catholic Church, Latin words and allusions are particularly relevant.

Latin is considered a dead language. But Brown makes it very much alive and present in his contemporary novel (along with bits of Greek, French, and smatterings of other languages). For some items, the reader needs only an ordinary Latin dictionary: Opus Dei ("God's Work"), or *crux gemmata* ("jeweled cross"). However, other words and phrases are more subject to interpretation.

Everyone's favorite Albino assassin-monk, Silas, is a devout Catholic and member of Opus Dei. He can be remembered by his skin color (as a character in Homer who is consistently recalled by the same epithet, Brown often refers to Silas as "the Albino monk"). But his more significant character trait is as a penitent. The word *penitent* (*paenitit* in Latin) comes from *paeān,* referring to "praise from the gods." Like the real-life members of Opus Dei, Silas believes the way to praise God is to suffer pain himself. Interestingly, the word for *cloak* in Latin, *paenula,* comes from the same root as *penitent*. This seems to suggest the characteristic cloak that a monk wears comes from this root as well. The painful self-discipline belt that Silas wears is called a cilice, which may come from the Latin word *cicātrīx,* which means "scar." And of course the intention of the belt is to cause physical pain (likely leaving a scar) to repent for sins. But the more interesting connection is how close *cilice* and *chalice* are. Chalice, of course, is another word for the Holy Grail—a key concept in a book that is all about defining the Holy Grail and searching for it. Chalice . . . cilice . . . Silas: although the "Teacher" is the mastermind, Silas is doing all the murdering and other grunt work on this hunt for the Holy Grail.

Silas is the character in the book who invokes the most Latin in the course of the day. When he is flagellating himself he says, "*Castīgo corpus meum.*" In Latin, this means "castigate" (or "correct" or "punish") my body. This is a logical, ritualistic comment for a religious penitent. However, it's intriguing that *castīgo,* which means "punish" or "correct," is the root of *castitās,* which means "chastity" or "virginity." This of course ties into the purity of Jesus and the Virgin Mary. It also connects to another of the central dramas of the book: whether Jesus Christ and Mary Magdalene had a sexual relationship and, if they did, how it was viewed by their contemporaries and should be viewed in retrospect by following generations. If Brown's theory is true, Jesus was not as pure as is historically imagined and *castīgo corpus meum* could be another wink at this issue.

"O Draconian Devil! Oh Lame Saint!" is one of the clues a dying and bleeding old man can come up with in the last fifteen minutes of his life to point Robert Langdon and Sophie Neveu on the first step of their hunt for the Holy Grail. These exclamations are an anagram for *Leonardo da Vinci! The Mona Lisa!,* where the next clue turns out to be hidden. An interesting part of this anagram is the word *draconian,* used to mean measures that are very strict or severe. Actually, Draco was no ruthless barbarian. He was, in fact, an early Athenian lawmaker. He emphasized creating laws and writing them down—along with the consequences for breaking them. But the law came first and it is Draco's real contribution to Greco-Roman civilization. Although he did enforce laws strictly, it is interesting that this word has become so associated with evil and ruthlessness. Langdon even suggests that these words are Saunière's violent attack on the church, emphasizing both *Draconian* and *devil.*

When Langdon and Sophie mull over the mysterious key they now possess and assume it is related to the Priory of Sion, Landgon is intrigued that the cross is the equal-armed square type of cross. As a symbologist, this object in his hand gives him an opportunity to discuss the history and etymology of the Christian cross. Langdon points out that *cross* and *crucifix* are derived from the Latin word *cruciāre,* which means "to torture." A word with a similar root, *cruor,* means "blood."

The Da Vinci Code is full of anagrams, several of which come to light through Saunière's last messages to Sophie Neveu and Robert Langdon. Brown, who is obviously an anagram devotee, refers to *ars magna,* which in Latin means "great art" and is considered part of the sacred symbolism of Roman culture. In fact, it is from rearranging the letters of *ars magna* that we get the English word *anagrams.*

Through the years, *heretic* has always been thought to mean something very negative. In fact, the word *heretic,* which Dan Brown relates to the Latin *haereticus,* means "choice." Those who chose not to believe in the standardized set of Gospels—the documents and principles that the Roman emperor Constantine sought to enforce at the Council of Nicea and afterward—became known as heretics, meaning they had made a "choice" to take a different road. Soon, they would be abused, attacked, and tortured for having made this choice, but at the outset, to call them heretics might have been like calling them *choosers* or *pro-choice.*

Brown also includes a meditation on the meaning of the word *pagan.* Some people today assume the word *pagan* was always a religious word, referring to a devil-worshipping deviant opposed to Christianity. Brown suggests that "Pagans were literally unindoctrinated country folk who clung to the old, rural religions of nature worship." The word comes from the Latin *pāgānus,* which means "country dwellers." The peasants of the Roman Empire's countryside would prove to be late converts to Christianity, continuing to practice their old Greco-Roman rites and worship their many gods and goddesses. Over time *pagan,* originally a benign word like *heretic,* became tinged with connotations of evil and devil worship.

The same association with the evil nature of country dwellers arises in the word *villain,* according to yet another etymological discussion in *The Da Vinci Code.* The word *villa* is Latin for "country house." These country houses were the homes of country dwellers or pagans. According to Brown, the church feared those who lived in the rural *villes.* As a result, "the word for a villager—'vilain'—came to mean a wicked soul." But Dan Brown's interpretation is questioned in a *New York Times Magazine* article by the "On Language" columnist, William Safire. He writes, "Villagers did not become villains because the church feared them; more likely, it was just that the lords of the manor looked down on the lower classes and equated their coarse manners with loose morals." There is a definite class distinction here. The feudal lords who lived in the countryside were not known as villains. The first form of the word *vilein,* French, refers to the serfs in the medieval feudal system.

Brown also does a short riff on the linguistic history of the word *venereal,* suggesting it has something to do with the goddess of love, Venus. Sounds logical, but according to the *Oxford English Dictionary (OED),* this heritage may be incorrect. The *OED* cites the word as coming from the Latin word *venerābilis,* meaning "honored." Although there may be a possible connection between the worship of Venus and the Latin word for honor, the *OED* does not make the leap.

Brown makes an interesting point about the history of the English word *sinister.* In Latin, *sinistra* originally meant left-handedness. Left-handedness was often considered unlucky. As Brown states, this had much to do with the church's early decision to associate left with female. In the alleged effort by the church to cover up the role of the sacred feminine in the origins of the early church and to emerge as a more patriarchal culture, the word for *sinister* became very negatively charged. (A number of experts believe Leonardo da Vinci was left-handed. Several clues in the novel emphasize the impression that Jacques Saunière was left-handed, as well.)

The phrase *sub rosa* also figures prominently in *The Da Vinci Code.* Sophie tells Langdon about the meetings that her grandfather used to have under the sign of the rose, which Saunière (and Latin language evolution) suggested meant "in secrecy." As William Safire points out, however, Dan Brown may not be correct when he tells readers that the expression *sub rosa* and the technique of using the sign of the rose to signify a confidential meeting originated in ancient times. Safire says, "The earliest citation is in Henry VIII's 1546 State Papers, which in modern English reads, 'The said questions were asked with license, and should remain under the rose . . . no more to be rehearsed.' " However, in a subsequent article, Safire seemed to reverse himself, declaring that millions of Dan Brown's readers knew that *sub rosa* was an allusion to Roman secret meeting practices.

Like other aspects of *The Da Vinci Code,* the Latin derivations are not always a hundred percent correct, but the story gets people talking about ideas, philosophy, religion, history—and even Latin—in an unusually compelling way.

What's Next for Robert Langdon?

By David A. Shugarts

There were probably four million readers ahead of Dave Shugarts when he picked up a copy of *The Da Vinci Code.* He devoured it, he says, as if it were a bag of popcorn at a movie. And he hasn't stopped snacking since. Already known for finding more than 150 plot flaws, small and large, in the novel (see his now legendary collection of plot flaws, page 574), he next turned his attention to the coded message hidden within *The Da Vinci Code* dust jacket, which when solved led him to be the first person to predict that Dan Brown's next Robert Langdon adventure would feature the Founding Fathers and the history of the Freemasons, and that it would be set in Washington, D.C. Subsequently, both Dan Brown and his publisher confirmed (indirectly) Dave's guesses.

What was the key clue? Shugarts found that if you look closely at the flaps of the dust cover, some characters are in slightly bolder type than others. String them together, then separate the string into individual words and, presto, you have the question "Is there no help for the widow's son?" To ascertain the meaning and significance of this sentence, Shugarts delved deeply into subjects related to George Washington, Benjamin Franklin, Paul Revere, and other Founding Fathers. He also looked into interesting connections with Mormons, Gnostics, the Kabbalah, the Tarot, the mystical traditions of major world religions, sixteenth-century Scotland, seventeenth-century England, eighteenth-century France—and especially the development of Freemasonry and its remarkable impact on the creation of American democracy and the birth of the United States. Based on Dave Shugarts's research, the Secrets team came to understand that Dan

---

David A. Shugarts is an award-winning journalist and editor. He has been a major contributor to all the "Secrets" books. This essay is based on research he did for his book, *Secrets of the Widow's Son,* Sterling Publishing Co., 2005.

Brown's newest book, reportedly titled *The Solomon Key*, might do for the early American experience what *The Da Vinci Code* had done for the early Christian experience.

Shugarts has published his most interesting finds in a full-length book, *Secrets of the Widow's Son*. The essay that follows, drawn from that book, is a treasure hunt through the same labyrinthine interconnections of fact, myth, lore, legend, and documentation that Dan Brown is likely to use for *The Solomon Key*. It is not a plot spoiler. It is, in fact, a plot enhancer. For when you finally sit down to read *The Solomon Key* a year from now or whenever it is published, you will understand it much better. More important, if you read the essay, or if you pick up a copy of *Secrets of the Widow's Son*, you will enjoy a stunning, thought-provoking, and utterly surprising new look at our own American historical experience.

The thing all readers know about Dan Brown's books is that fact, fiction, and everything in between is so interconnected that almost any clue by itself could lead you on a frantic scurry through the tunnels and wormholes of history, philosophy, religion, science, art, conspiracies, and centuries of alternate historical narrative. Just when you think you've found the best piece of pungent cheese, there is the far-off fragrance of another, luring you further underground.

So it is with the clue embedded in the dust jacket of *The Da Vinci Code*. The solution to the riddle itself is straightforward enough. "Is there no help for the widow's son?" is a plea for help from one brother Freemason to another. With your arms raised "to the square" you say, "Oh, Lord, my God, is there no help for the widow's son?" The plea is a powerful one. Any brother Freemason is compelled to help you. There are many stories in which combatants on opposite sides in battle set aside their weapons in order to answer this plea. Paul Revere was said to have been spared by a British captain who detained him on the night of his fateful ride, because each recognized certain coded phrases that revealed a fellow Freemason.

But if you are Dan Brown, and fascinated by interconnections, you don't just say, "Oh, that's interesting." You ask the next obvious question: "Now that I know that, what else should I know?" And then you find it relates directly to the central core of Freemasonry: the biblical story of the building of the Temple of Solomon, overseen by an immensely skilled master architect, Hiram Abiff—who turns out to have been the son of a widow. When he is killed by ruffians who try to beat out of him his secrets, legend has it his last words are, "Is there no help for the widow's son?"

The Temple of Solomon, which made an important appearance in *The Da Vinci Code,* has by legend a great treasure stored beneath a nine-vaulted safe. How to enter that safe? With a "key," obviously . . . a Solomon Key. Except no standard key was necessary: the "door" was a massive stone slab.

Now it starts to become a puzzle worthy of Robert Langdon. What other meanings for the word *key* might apply? One worth considering is the key like the legend on a map. Part of the Masonic tradition of hiding things in plain sight was a system of giving coded messages in drawings and engravings, then providing a little symbolic "key" that could be used to decode the message. Another meaning of *key* is architectural, as in *keystone,* the stone that makes a vaulted arch possible. The keystone has a long practical tradition and it has deep meanings for Freemasons.

In work on codes and ciphers, it is common to have a

coded message that might be intercepted, but be difficult or impossible to crack unless you have the decoding key. Dan Brown is enamored of codes in all his novels, and has written specifically about encryption schemes in several of them.

But a very special meaning can be extracted from the device known as a "Lewis key," used to lift massive building blocks. I believe that this could well have been one of the secrets that genuine stonemasons held dear. It's a long shot, but it could give a method for removing the stone locking the treasure vault beneath the Temple of Solomon. (A detailed explanation of the Lewis key, along with a drawing, can be found on page 31 in my book *Secrets of the Widow's Son*).

After completing the book, I stumbled across yet another meaning in a historical legend. In accounts of the destruction of the Second Temple of Solomon in AD 70, the contemporary writer Flavius Josephus said the high priest ran into the burning temple, seized the key that locked the Holy of Holies, and carried it to the top of the temple. He implored God to take it back "until you deem us worthy again." A hand reached down from heaven to take the key.

Building the Virtual Temple

It's the action-adventure part of the story that keeps us turning pages, but the "total experience" of *The Da Vinci Code* is not just to decode the cryptex, but also to absorb history, religion, and philosophy from a variety of ages. Dan Brown's technique of suspending action with each chapter break, combined with a plot that takes place in less than twenty-four hours, is a disguise. It keeps you from noticing how many pages are devoted to descriptions of history or art or religion. But it is this backdrop that makes the reading experience so fulfilling.

To bring these kinds of themes alive for *The Solomon Key,* the novelist is not only likely to use a physical temple, but a virtual one. One not confined to any particular floor plan, historical setting, or architectural style. It is a temple of the mind, with rooms of religion, philosophy, science, and mathematics from all ages, furnished with the powerful themes of Freemasonry: Greek philosophy, science, and mathematics, especially geometry; biblical (especially Hebrew) scripture; Kabbalah, an ancient Jewish system of mysticism; astrology, alchemy, Hermeticism, and an overlay of Egyptian culture.

The inhabitants, to stretch the analogy, are likely to comprise at least three "families," all interconnected for good and for bad, as families are wont to be.

The "Collegians"

What the Renaissance and Reformation were to *Angels & Demons* and early Christianity was to *The Da Vinci Code,* the Enlightenment and the opening of the New World will likely be to *The Solomon Key*—turning points in the struggle between blind faith and reason. And what Newton was to *The Da Vinci Code,* Sir Francis Bacon is likely to be for the new book: a pioneer in the development of the scientific method. But Bacon—not confirmed a Freemason but implicated circumstantially—can be used not just as a metaphorical bridge between religion and science, but as one between the Old World and the New. In his book *New Atlantis* he imagines a utopian society on a remote island. Take Bacon's concept, marry it with a "lost tribe" and you could imagine an interesting new legend: a newly populated land of Chosen People, heir to the Kingdom of God—a "shining city on a hill."

Just a few decades after Bacon's death, a fraternal organization arose among a group of men bonded by their mutual admiration for knowledge gained through "experimental" methods. They called themselves the Invisible College (a phrase that would echo in conspiracy theories for centuries to come). By the time Benjamin Franklin came to England in 1757, the "college" had become the Royal Society, with members like Isaac Newton. Franklin was welcomed with open arms into the Royal Society. Many of these men were fellow Freemasons.

Some of the inspiration that made the early scientists brave enough to challenge religion's domination over knowledge came from sources that were not strictly scientific. One source was Hermeticism, which held that the world below (earth) is patterned after the world above (the cosmos). Further, divine fire (knowledge or enlightenment) flows between the two. It could be taken to mean that man can aspire to be godlike, or "perfectible." (One can imagine how this resonates for Dan Brown.) It could also be interpreted as alchemical, giving veiled instructions about how to create the Philosopher's Stone.

The other source is alchemy, a field not laughed at in those days. Many of the brightest minds among scholars and gentlemen (and early physicians) were attracted to it, not just because of the fabled lure of learning to turn lead into gold. Rather, they also saw it as a way to learn the secrets of the universe. Scientists as diverse as Newton and Franklin were interested in alchemy. Alchemists were, in essence, the first scientists, predating the Royal Society, as seen in the lives of John Dee and Francis Bacon, among others.

The Freemasons

The fact that large numbers of people, educated and not, were beginning to think that man could discover fundamental pathways to "truth" without having to subscribe to a hierarchy like that of the Catholic pope and priests, or of a king under a theory of divine rightness, was a boon to Freemasonry. By the 1730s, Freemasonry was being imported into America, with the founding of the first lodges in New York and Philadelphia. It expanded rapidly.

Many worthy colonists joined Freemason lodges, including a long list of the Founding Fathers, such as George Washington, Paul Revere, Benjamin Franklin, and John Hancock. Thomas Jefferson was not a Mason, but did strongly believe in avoiding a state-sponsored religion. It was no accident that documents like the Declaration of Independence spoke of "Divine Providence" and "Nature's God" instead of a specific deity. (However, there is an ongoing debate about whether this was a Masonic master plan or merely the confluence of fashionable ideas.)

Some conspiracy theorists believe there was a plot at the heart of the Revolution. And they are right! A roomful of men started a big conspiracy in 1776 in Philadelphia, and, yes, it involved Masons. They plotted to overthrow the rule of the king of England and create a new form of government. And, yes, it was secretive. The men in the room all knew that their signatures would get them hanged on the spot if they were captured by the British. For this very reason, although the document itself was read in public on July 8, 1776, the identities of the signers were not revealed until five months later.

There were nine known Freemasons among the fifty-six signers (although some put the number of Masons even higher). The primary writer of the Declaration, Thomas Jefferson, was not a Freemason. The only other signer who became president was John Adams, and he was not a Freemason. Benjamin Franklin was a signer, a Freemason, a wily fellow, and a man of huge importance, but none of his pursuits smacked of a conspiracy to run the new country. So it doesn't make sense to say that the Freemasons took over the United States from the start. But when it's time for Dan Brown to refer to this slice of history in *The Solomon Key,* I am betting he will play up the "Masonic conspiracy" (and probably a fraternity offspring like Skull & Bones, the exclusive and highly secretive society based at Yale that counts both Presidents Bush, father and son, among its members).

The Mormons

Offhand, there would seem to be little connection between this "family" and the two others. But because of the use of the "widow's son" quote, which practically welds the Mormons to the Masons, it seems likely Robert Langdon could find himself dealing with Mormons as representatives of the "conspiracy within a conspiracy." What some people perceive Dan Brown to have done to the Catholic Church, he may be about to do to the Church of Jesus Christ of Latter-day Saints. Their story certainly lends to novelization.

In 1805, only a scant six years after George Washington's death, Joseph Smith was born in Vermont. He grew up within a folk tradition of magic and the occult, including dowsing. While still a youth Smith would allege that an angel gave him the location of certain buried thin plates of gold, on which were written the word of God. After he translated the plates into the Book of Mormon and founded his church, the angel (conveniently) took back the gold plates.

We know now that Joseph Smith borrowed heavily from the Freemasons not only in developing the Book of Mormon, but also in devising his religious rituals and symbology, and in designing Mormon works of architecture. When the first Mormon temple was built, in Nauvoo, Illinois, Masonic symbols such as the sun, moon, and five- and six-pointed stars were placed throughout it. On the weather vane was an angel, supporting a compass and square. Shortly after Smith was made a master Mason himself, he began to outline rituals for initiating his Mormon priesthood that echoed the Masonic rituals.

No virtual or real Temple of Dan Brown would, of course, be complete without a code room. Every one of his first four novels displays his fascination with them. In *The Solomon Key,* with the era of the Founding Fathers as background, there are several codes of note. One, already used several times by Dan Brown, is the "Caesar's box" cipher, which consisted of putting a short message into a square grid of characters. Another was the Culper code, a substitution code used during the Revolutionary War based on a long passage of a mutually available document, in which each useful word was assigned a number. For instance, Washington himself was "711" and New York was "727." Franklin was "72."

Thomas Jefferson, in his role as the third president, kept his diplomatic messages secret by use of a cipher device that he himself designed. It consisted of twenty-six wheeled alphabets on a common axle—a rudimentary form of the famous Enigma machine used by the Germans in World War II. The Jefferson cipher wheel was "reinvented" a couple of times, and saw service as the M-94 coding device from 1922 to World War II.

Building the Physical Temple: Washington the City

Having laid out the groundwork for a kind of cosmic, virtual temple that serves as the background to the plot of *The Solomon Key,* it is now time to look at the physical temple. Robert Langdon has previously hunted for clues in Westminster Cathedral in London, in St. Sulpice in Paris, and the Vatican in Rome. This time it could be an entire city, and there is no better candidate for a temple of codes than Washington, DC.

Washington, DC, is a city with ample symbolism on practically every building facade or cornerstone. Although the Constitution had made it clear there was not to be a state religion, the official artwork, such as the paintings on the Capitol dome and walls, has a profusion of Zodiacs, Greek and Roman gods, Egyptian motifs, Christian references, and numerous images that still defy contemporary critics' ability to understand or decode. And once the visitor begins to look for them, Masonic symbols, particularly the circle and the square, are literally everywhere.

Prime among them, of course, is the Washington Monument, considered Masonic in design for a number of reasons, not the least of which is the form of a pyramid at the top. And if the original plan of having George Washington interred there had born fruition, there would be a large pyramidal tomb in the center of what is now the National Mall. Dan Brown has scattered obelisks and pyramids throughout his Langdon novels.

Other highlights, and perhaps of particular interest to Dan Brown might be:

House of the Temple

About thirteen blocks north of the White House, this is

the home of the Supreme Council 33° of the Ancient and Accepted Scottish Rite of Freemasonry. It has two massive sphinxes guarding the door. The steps are tiered in sets of three, five, seven, and nine—a series revered by Masons.

Once inside, black marble columns support a soaring ceiling in a cavernous temple atrium, leading to a richly appointed lodge room. In a special alcove, the remains of Albert Pike, the revered Mason, are interred. The temple houses a large library full of priceless books of Masonic and other historical significance. Large museum rooms dedicated to famous Masons occupy a labyrinthine basement, with special focus given to the Founding Fathers, Burl Ives, J. Edgar Hoover, and the several U.S. astronauts (Neil Armstrong and Buzz Aldrin, first to set foot on the moon, had a Masonic lodge flag secreted in their inner clothing). In addition, there are other rooms in the basement, crammed with other relics and treasures far too numerous to be displayed. One can only imagine what Dan Brown might conceive of in this "secret" archive.

George Washington Masonic National Memorial in Alexandria, Virginia

If there was ever something that could be described as the Temple of George Washington, this is it. The main hall is a masterpiece of marble columns and murals, housing a massive three-story bronze statue of Washington dressed in full Masonic regalia. Many special symbolic rooms abound, including one devoted to the Knights Templar and another containing a richly detailed replica of the Ark of the Covenant. There is a mural depicting the ruins of the Temple of Solomon, among many dozens of pieces of symbolic art and Washington relics. As such, the George Washington Masonic National Memorial could be a perfect backdrop for Dan Brown's novel, since one can run from room to room chasing the symbolism of ancient history and Freemasonry.

Churches

Since Dan Brown weaves religion into his plots wherever possible, it is appropriate to look around Washington, DC, for a religious setting, of which the most likely candidate would be National Cathedral, prominently placed on a hill northwest of the city's center. It has a rich collection of ornaments and stonework and, like European cathedrals, it has subterranean vaults and crypts reminiscent of catacombs. The cathedral's rich symbology may be interpreted in various ways, including Masonic ones, of course. Gargoyles and grotesques abound (including one of Darth Vader, as you can learn by poking around the National Cathedral website). One could reasonably expect Dan Brown to include at least a chase scene through these American catacombs in *The Solomon Key*.

Artwork

A world-renowned artist has played an important role in both *Angels & Demons* and *The Da Vinci Code*. Who will be the Bernini or Leonardo of *The Solomon Key?* There are a number of good candidates, among the perhaps-too-obvious ones being John Trumbull, Charles Willson Peale, and Gilbert Stuart, all painters who gave George Washington their best shot. In 1840 Albion Hurdle painted a standing, posthumous portrait of Washington in full Masonic regalia. Hurdle, like Washington before him, belonged to Alexandria Lodge 22, where the painting now hangs. It is much revered among Freemasons.

Constantino Brumidi, a renowned artist at the time, created the *Apotheosis of Washington* that dominates the interior ceiling of the Capitol dome. It depicts George

Washington ascending to heaven, godlike, accompanied by heavenly maidens (who, the story goes, were modeled after local prostitutes).

Statue of Albert Pike

Albert Pike has a statue dedicated to him at Third and D Streets, NW, in Judiciary Square. Pike is the only Confederate general to get a full outdoor statue in the nation's capital, but it was his prominence as a scholar and leader of the Freemasons that earned him the spot. Pike's many facets could make him a central figure in *The Solomon Key,* since he combined knowledge of so many arcane subjects—including Freemasonry's deepest secrets—and had so many strange connections historically. Dan Brown used Leonardo da Vinci to create codes and secrets for *The Da Vinci Code;* he could use Pike the same way in *The Solomon Key.*

Monumental Architecture

If we go looking for an echo of the Masonic symbols of the circle and the square in grand buildings, we suddenly see a multitude of structures in which something round is married to something squarish—the pantheon. Arguably the most famous of these is Rome, built in 27 BC, ostensibly as a gesture by Marcus Agrippa to bring together the people of the Roman Empire in the worship of the gods of their choice, since they did not worship the old Roman gods, or did so under different names. The concept of a pantheon is thus a temple for multiple gods.

Shift to the New World, and the most famous and visible pantheon-like structure may be the U.S. Capitol. Originally, Horatio Greenough's statue of George Washington (as Zeus) was to sit at the center of the Rotunda, but it was poorly received and it cracked the flooring. But other statues of great Americans remain in the Capitol, as though in a temple to multiple gods.

Searching for the Solomon Key

The preceding two novels started with a chase for real treasure that then transmogrified into a treasure beyond any price. Think of the antimatter in *Angels & Demons* that could harness all energy (or destroy the world) and that became nothing less than the symbolic truce in the struggle between science and religion. And the Holy Grail in *The Da Vinci Code* transformed into the symbolic womb of Mary Magdalene as a priceless vessel of the holy bloodline.

There are plenty of candidates for a phenomenal treasure of gold and silver that could be tied by Dan Brown to Masonic legends. There is a treasure, for example, and an association with American history, that relates to a Civil War group, the Knights of the Golden Circle. If the plot of Brown's next book were to follow these native "knights"—and their prime protector, Jessie James—the treasure could be a fabulous amount of gold and silver coins and bullion, the entire wealth of the Confederacy at the moment that it decided the cause was lost.

The most serious treasure of all might be the one associated with the Temple of Solomon, which could include not only untold wealth in gold, silver, and gems, but also the Ark of the Covenant. But where to look? One key to the treasure opened by *The Solomon Key* might be a Masonic map overlay to the city of Washington, DC. Finding a perfect overlay is not easy, but the actual resemblance is striking enough, and may very well suit a Dan Brown novel. Among other things, Dan Brown may be able to guide Robert Langdon around the center of town by giv-

The Pagan Ways of George Washington

The connection of our capital with Freemasonry starts with the day Washington laid out the ten-by-ten mile Federal District as a square diamond, with the corners pointing exactly north-south-east-west. Why a square shape? Well, Washington was a former surveyor and a Freemason. If you leave a Freemason alone to doodle, you will probably get either a square or a circle out of him.

Even more startling is the story of the dedication of the Capitol Building. You will not find it in history texts or books about the Founding Fathers on bestseller lists. As on any such occasion, a grand procession of dignitaries attended. But in this case, the dignitaries marched to the building site in full Masonic regalia, with drums and trumpets.

Presiding over the laying of the cornerstone was George Washington, who not only was president of the United States, but in this ceremony was known as the Grand Master of the Masons pro tem, as well as the Worshipful Master of his lodge, Alexandria No. 22. Washington spread mortar with a silver trowel that had been made for the occasion, and the cornerstone block, suspended from a wooden tripod, was lowered into place. There were moments of prayer and silence, but a highlight of the service was when Washington did something most Americans would consider very odd: he anointed the cornerstone

(*continues*)

ing him clues as though they were positions in a Masonic lodge.

There is another intriguing possibility: the literal center of Washington, DC. It is generally assumed that it is the

The Pagan Ways of George Washington *(continued)*

with "corn, wine, and oil." This is an essential Masonic rite, but I consider it also to be an adaptation of an ancient system of consecration representing libations to the pagan gods of earth, air, fire, and water. (In European Freemasonry, salt is the fourth element.) They also represent the four directions of the compass, i.e., the four winds.

This symbology goes back further than the Greeks or the Romans or the Egyptians. It goes back to the time before the gods even had individual names. And coming forward in time, the twelve signs of the Zodiac were subdivided into three groups of four, assigned aspects of earth, air, fire, or water. They first were fundamentals of ancient astronomy and astrology, then were adapted into their roles as gods and goddesses.

In *The Da Vinci Code,* Dan Brown explains that paganism is not a lack of religion; it merely is a religion other than Christianity. By this definition the U.S. Capitol cornerstone ceremony was about as pagan as a ceremony can be. And this very ceremony, with only slight variations, has been part of practically every cornerstone laying of every major historic building in the United States. This is hugely significant for an author such as Dan Brown, who is always looking for the deeper, pagan meaning of symbols in plain sight.

—DAVID A. SHUGARTS

Washington Monument, admittedly a fine candidate, albeit an obvious one. But in actuality, the Washington Monument is only at the illusionary center (as a Robert Langdon—or a real-life observant tourist—would see), built there because the original ground turned out to be a marsh. The actual cross point between the four key monuments is just northwest of the monument, placed there in 1804 at the behest of Thomas Jefferson. The "Jefferson Stone," as it has come to be called, is a much smaller obelisk—about knee height! A squat stone with a blunted top, with a cross cut into it. Jefferson had decided it would indicate the U.S. prime meridian, the zero longitude for all of our maps for many years thereafter.

Perhaps the leading contender for "the clue" is found in the codes embedded into the statue of Kryptos, located at CIA headquarters. Not only are there clues about it on the dust jacket of *The Da Vinci Code* and on the Dan Brown website, but there is a growing buzz about it on the Internet. Kryptos, which means "hidden," was created in 1990 by artist James Sanborn. The "statue" is actually a series of objects, the biggest of which is a scroll-like copper screen pierced by 865 characters of a coded message, divided into four parts. The codes are so complex that it took eight years before a CIA analyst, David Stein, solved the first three parts. Will Robert Langdon solve a puzzle that has mockingly challenged America's best spies and code breakers, who walk by it regularly?

So what treasure will these clues reveal? Here is my modest guess: it is the modern, scientific incarnation of the ancient term alchemy. I think it is probably something related to the genome of Jesus, as carried through the vessel of Mary Magdalene, which figuratively is the Holy Grail. From *The Da Vinci Code* we know that Sophie Neveu is a descendant of this bloodline and therefore a "goddess" as well as a "chalice." It also could be that some form of cloning, or manipulation of DNA, will provide the right amount of the nanotechnology that Dan Brown tends to need in a novel as well. Additionally, I would expect that the treasure would also be portrayed as having a value beyond reckoning. Could it be that the genome carries the potential for immunity from all known diseases, for instance?

As to where to find the treasure, there is one other place to consider. The last time Sophie Neveu and Robert Langdon are together in *The Da Vinci Code,* they are at the famed Rosslyn Chapel in Scotland. This is known as the "Chapel of the Codes" because of the many symbols carved into its stones. Since Rosslyn was built by the Templars and was a showpiece for the craft of masonry, it is a natural anchor for Dan Brown's story of Langdon as he returns to America for his next adventure.

Lo and behold, if one stands atop the Capitol Building looking west, past the Washington Monument, past the Lincoln Memorial, to the opposite bank of the Potomac, one's gaze falls on the suburb in Virginia known as Rosslyn! This "suburb" actually comprises a cluster of steel towers housing the headquarters of some major corporations. Could this be more than coincidence, or will Dan Brown plant a clue or a treasure in this New World version of Rosslyn?

We can even pursue some coincidences a little further. Within sight of Rosslyn lies a small island in the Potomac. From its purchase in 1717 through the 1790s it was owned by the family of George Mason, a very prominent Virginia patriot who has only recently gained the honor he deserves. It was George Mason's writing that contributed some of the most eloquent phrases in the Declaration of Independence, brazenly borrowed by Thomas Jefferson from Mason's Virginia Declaration of Rights, penned only a few months earlier.

The island in the river was long known as Mason's Island. This could give us a pun, since George Mason was not a Freemason. The island later fell into government hands and eventually was set aside as a hiking and picnic park in which to honor Theodore Roosevelt—who was a Freemason. A massive bronze statue, memorializing Roosevelt in the middle of a fiery speech from his bully pulpit, stands in a cool grove of trees at the highest point of the island. Notably, the bridge that crosses the Potomac north and west of the island is Key Bridge, named after Francis Scott Key, a Freemason, who wrote our national anthem.

I found this place by thinking of three words—*Rosslyn, Mason,* and *key*—many months before Dan Brown's publisher announced the title *The Solomon Key.* I visited it on a hot summer day and found the setting to be downright temple-like. Will Dan Brown have us follow clues like "a key" and "a Mason's isle" to reach a staging point in our scavenger hunt? Is the treasure buried where Roosevelt is gazing? (Will I find a hole there the next time I visit the spot?)

In addition, I believe I have found yet another eerie coincidence. A small, friendly memorial has recently been erected to George Mason in a little garden in the shadow of the much bigger Jefferson Memorial, not far from a bridge that most Washingtonians call the Fourteenth Street Bridge, but which is formally the George Mason Memorial Bridge. The memorial consists of a cluster of benches upon which sits a bronze statue of George Mason. In an amiable gaze, Mason looks off in a northerly direction—vaguely toward Mason's Island.

So I would urge everyone to treat the city of Washington, DC, as a giant hide-and-seek playground, and look for clues in all the buildings and all the symbols and codes.

9 "Code Hot, Critics Hotter"

"Code Hot. Critics Hotter." So headlined the *New York Daily News* in its not atypical sassy style. The first newspaper and magazine reviews of *The Da Vinci Code* in the early part of 2003 were enthusiastic, encouraged by an unusually aggressive marketing strategy by Doubleday, the publisher, an imprint of Random House. It was reported at the time that Doubleday had distributed an uncommonly high ten thousand complimentary copies of the book to stoke the fires of the buzz machine.

Janet Maslin of the *New York Times* called *The Da Vinci Code* a "gleefully erudite suspense novel." Patrick Anderson, writing in the *Washington Post,* declared it "a theological thriller that is both fascinating and fun." These initial reviews were written by people who review fiction for a living, not by medievalists, Gnostic document specialists, or art historians. Many of the first group of reviewers were bamboozled by Dan Brown's assertions about the factual nature of the elements of his novel. They didn't know if the Priory of Sion was real or not—but it certainly sounded real in Brown's description.

But the first impression, nudged along by Doubleday's PR efforts to paint Dan Brown as a writer who had done "meticulous research" to discover previously unknown facts from ancient history, soon began to come under attack in the second wave of reviews. Religious groups took angry offense at what they believed was Brown's desire to attack or defame Catholicism or Christianity. They began publishing lengthy articles and even books to critique what they variously termed Brown's errors, mistakes, blasphemy, or heresy.

As *The Da Vinci Code* became the biggest bestseller in adult fiction history, critics who usually don't write book reviews about action-adventure novels started to comment. Various experts began to separate Dan Brown's facts from his fiction. The game of "gotcha" was afoot. Now, three years after its initial publication, we can safely say that, with the possible exception of the Harry Potter series—which *The Da Vinci Code* resembles in many ways—no pop novel in modern times has engendered such a wide range of criticism. In this chapter, we present a small sampling of some of the more interesting of these critiques.

The Da Vinci Con

By Laura Miller

In *The Da Vinci Code,* Sophie Neveu is surprised to discover that the book *Holy Blood, Holy Grail,* another of the many real-life works on Leigh Teabing's library shelves, was an "international bestseller," yet she had never heard of it.

"You were young," Teabing tells her. "This caused quite a stir back in the nineteen eighties. To my taste, the authors made some dubious leaps of faith in their analysis, but their fundamental premise is sound, and to their credit, they finally brought the idea of Christ's bloodline into the mainstream."

It is an ironic statement for many reasons. First, Teabing himself is a composite character modeled on the real life trio of authors who wrote *Holy Blood, Holy Grail.* Indeed, his first name derives from Richard Leigh and his surname is an anagram of Michael Baigent. By openly declaring that "to my taste, the authors made some dubious leaps of faith in their analysis," Teabing (and his creator, Dan Brown) seem to be signaling that they know about the issues of questionable research in *Holy Blood, Holy Grail,* as well as all the allegations of hoax and fraud that have surrounded the modern-day desire of Pierre Plantard and several other French citizens to declare themselves to be the Priory of Sion and that of a number of writers to conjure up a Priory of Sion directly descended from the Templars and the Merovingian kings.

Despite Teabing's expressed concern about dubious leaps of faith, there is no doubt that *Holy Blood, Holy Grail* figured prominently in Dan Brown's thinking as he wove the plot for *The Da Vinci Code.* To help readers of *Secrets of the Code* better understand the arguments of *Holy Blood, Holy Grail,* we have excerpted a section from it, which appears in Chapter 5. Below, however, Laura Miller, writing in the *New York Times Book Review,* takes issue with *Holy Blood, Holy Grail* and the role of its arguments at the center of *The Da Vinci Code*'s plot.

The ever-rising tide of sales of *The Da Vinci Code* has lifted some pretty odd boats, and none odder than the dodgy yet magisterial *Holy Blood, Holy Grail,* by Michael Baigent, Richard Leigh, and Henry Lincoln. A bestseller in the 1980s, *Grail* is climbing the paperback charts again on the strength of its relationship to Dan Brown's thriller (which has, in turn, inspired a crop of new nonfiction books coming out this spring, from *Breaking the Da Vinci Code* to *Secrets of the Code: The Unauthorized Guide to the Mysteries Behind* The Da Vinci Code). *The Da Vinci Code* is one long chase scene in which the main characters flee a sinister Parisian policeman and an albino monk assassin, but its rudimentary suspense alone couldn't have made it a hit. At regular intervals, the book brings its pell-mell plot to a screeching halt and emits a pellet of information concerning a centuries-old conspiracy that purports to have preserved a tremendous secret about the roots of Christianity itself. This "nonfiction" material gives *The Da Vinci Code* its frisson of authenticity, and it's lifted from *Holy Blood, Holy Grail,* one of the all-time great works of pop pseudohistory. But what seems increasingly clear (to cop a favorite phrase from the authors of *Grail*) is that *The Da Vinci Code,* like *Holy Blood, Holy Grail,* is based on a notorious hoax.

The back story to both books, like most conspiracy theories, is devilishly hard to summarize. Both narratives begin with a mystery that leads sleuths to vaster and more sinister intrigues. In Brown's novel, it's the murder of a curator at the Louvre; in *Grail,* it's the unusual affluence of a priest in a village in the south of France. In the late 1960s, Henry Lincoln, a British TV writer, became interested in Rennes-le-Château, a town that had become the French equivalent of Roswell or Loch Ness as a result of popular books by Gérard de Sède. De Sède promulgated a story about parchments supposedly found in a hollowed-out pillar by the town priest in the 1890s, parchments containing coded messages that the priest somehow parlayed into oodles of cash. Lincoln worked on several *Unsolved Mysteries*–style documentaries about Rennes-le-Château, then enlisted Baigent and Leigh for a more in-depth investigation.

What eventually emerges from the welter of names, dates, maps, and genealogical tables crammed into *Holy*

Blood, Holy Grail is a yarn about a secret and hugely influential society called the Priory of Sion, founded in Jerusalem in 1099. This cabal is said to have guarded documents and other proof that Mary Magdalene was the wife of Jesus (who may or may not have died on the Cross) and that she carried his child with her when she fled to what is now France after the Crucifixion, becoming, figuratively, the Holy Grail in whom Jesus' blood was preserved. Their progeny intermarried with the locals, eventually founding the Merovingian dynasty of Frankish monarchs. Although deposed in the eighth century, the Merovingian lineage has not been lost; the Priory has kept watch over its descendants, awaiting an auspicious moment when it will reveal the astonishing truth and return the rightful monarch to the throne of France, or perhaps even a restored Holy Roman Empire.

All the usual suspects and accouterments of paranoid history get caught up in this thousand-year jaunt. The Cathar heretics, the Knights Templar, the Rosicrucians, the Vatican, the Freemasons, Nazis, the Dead Sea Scrolls, the Protocols of the Elders of Zion, the Order of the Golden Dawn—everyone but the Abominable Snowman seems to be in on the game. *Holy Blood, Holy Grail* is a masterpiece of insinuation and supposition, employing all the techniques of pseudohistory to symphonic effect, justifying this sleight of hand as an innovative scholarly technique called "synthesis," previously considered too "speculative" by those whose thinking has been unduly shaped by the "so-called Enlightenment of the 18th century." Comparing themselves to the reporters who uncovered the Watergate scandal, the authors maintain that "only by such synthesis can one discern the underlying continuity, the unified and coherent fabric, which lies at the core of any historical problem."To do so, one must realize that "it is not sufficient to confine oneself exclusively to facts."

Thus liberated, Lincoln et al concoct an argument that is not so much factual as factish. Dozens of credible details are heaped up in order to provide a legitimizing cushion for rank nonsense. Unremarkable legends (that Merovingian kings were thought to have a healing touch, for example) are characterized as suggestive clues or puzzles demanding solution. Highly contested interpretations (that, say, an early Grail romance depicts the sacred object as being guarded by Templars) are presented as established truth. Sources—such as the New Testament—are qualified as "questionable" and derivative when they contradict the conspiracy theory, then microscopically scrutinized for inconsistencies that might support it. The authors spin one gossamer strand of conjecture over another, forming a web dense enough to create the illusion of solidity. Though bogus, it's an impressive piece of work.

Finally, though, the legitimacy of the Priory of Sion history rests on a cache of clippings and pseudonymous documents that even the authors of *Holy Blood, Holy Grail* suggest were planted in the Bibliothèque Nationale by a man named Pierre Plantard. As early as the 1970s, one of Plantard's confederates had admitted to helping him fabricate the materials, including genealogical tables portraying Plantard as a descendant of the Merovingians (and, presumably, of Jesus Christ) and a list of the Priory's past "grand masters." This patently silly catalog of intellectual celebrities stars Botticelli, Isaac Newton, Jean Cocteau, and, of course, Leonardo da Vinci—and it's the same list Dan Brown trumpets, along with the alleged nine-century pedigree of the Priory, in the front matter for *The Da Vinci Code,* under the heading of "Fact." Plantard, it eventually came out, was an inveterate rascal with a criminal record for fraud and affiliations with wartime anti-Semitic and right-wing groups. The actual Priory of Sion was a tiny, harmless group of like-minded friends formed in 1956.

Plantard's hoax was debunked by a series of (as yet untranslated) French books and a 1996 BBC documentary, but curiously enough this set of shocking revelations hasn't proved as popular as the fantasia of *Holy Blood, Holy Grail,* or, for that matter, as *The Da Vinci Code.* The only thing more powerful than a worldwide conspiracy, it seems, is our desire to believe in one.

Looking for the Grail of Truth in *The Da Vinci Code*'s Version of Early Christianity

BY BERNARD HAMILTON

Among the more erudite of Dan Brown's critics is Bernard Hamilton, Professor Emeritus of Crusading History at the University of Nottingham, England. A leading Medievalist, he is the author of *The Leper King and His Heirs* and *Crusaders, Cathars and the Holy Places.*

Hamilton takes the influence of Dan Brown's pop pastiche seriously enough to do real battle with it. Here he jousts with Brown

---

Published as "Truth and Falsity in *The Da Vinci Code,*" July 10, 2005. (www.the-tls.co.uk)

over the story of Jesus and Mary and their possible offspring, the Gnostics, early Christian scriptures, the Templars, the Priory of Sion, Merovingian kings, and the origins and meanings of Holy Grail legends throughout the centuries. Hamilton reveals the little details of history that call into question Dan Brown's credibility as a "fact"-based writer. He notes, for example, that it is hard to swallow the idea that the Priory of Sion is dedicated to honoring the cult of the sacred feminine since this organization, supposed to have continued until the present day, hasn't had a female grand master since the death of Iolande de Bar nearly six hundred years ago. Why her—and why never another woman?

Still, Hamilton likes a good grail romance as much as the next member of Western civilization. So he gives *The Da Vinci Code* grudging credit for being a "congenial" kind of grail-related story and sharing certain stylistic elements—hardship, obstacles, confusion—with the archetypal grail journeys of history, literature, and the human spirit.

The Da Vinci Code is a theological thriller, which makes it an unlikely bestseller in what is often said to be a secular age. Like that other bestseller, *The Lord of the Rings,* this book is almost completely lacking in love interest, or, indeed, in sex of any kind. A rite of *hieros gamos,* sacred marriage, which took place some years in the past, is briefly and almost clinically described; and the hero and heroine indulge in only one, very seemly, embrace.

But bestseller it is, indeed, one of the best-selling books ever. Before considering what makes it so popular, it may be helpful to [consider some of the historical "facts" upon which Dan Brown constructs his novel. Of course,] *The Da Vinci Code* is a novel and it might seem pedantic to point out that the account of Church history given by some of the characters is misleading. But Dan Brown has prefaced his book with this statement:

> Fact: The Priory of Sion—a European secret society founded in 1099—is a real organization. . . . The Vatican prelature known as Opus Dei is a deeply devout Catholic sect that has been the topic of recent controversy due to reports of brainwashing, coercion and a dangerous practice known as "corporal mortification". . . .
>
> All descriptions of artwork, architecture, documents and secret rituals in this novel are accurate.

In Teabing and Langdon's account, however, the information which they give about Jesus' original teaching and the way it was radically changed by Constantine the Great is seriously flawed. Brown's characters assume that the pre-Constantinian Church was a single community, that all its members shared the same beliefs, and that dissenting groups only sprang up when Constantine forced that Church to change its teachings and some members refused to do so. In fact, there were as many different Christian sects in the centuries before Constantine as there are today. The largest of them called itself the Great Church, or the Catholic, that is universal, Church, and that was the one which Constantine favoured and ultimately joined. Its members certainly believed in the divinity of Christ long before Constantine's day and were, indeed, persecuted by the Roman authorities for doing so. The fullest surviving account of the baptismal rite for adults in that Church is found in The Apostolic Tradition, written by St Hippolytus of Rome in c. 220 AD a hundred years before the Council of Nicaea. Among the questions which candidates were asked by the officiating minister was this: "Dost thou believe in Jesus Christ, the Son of God, who was born of the Holy Spirit and the Virgin Mary, who was crucified in the days of Pontius Pilate, and died, and rose the third day living from the dead and ascended into the heavens?" The Council of Nicaea, convened by Constantine the Great in 325, was not concerned with establishing whether Jesus was divine, because there was no disagreement about that among the members of the Great Church, but with debating whether the divinity of Jesus the Son of God differed from that of God the Father (they decided that it did not). Moreover, although the full canon of the New Testament was not finally agreed until later in the fourth century, the Great Church had accepted the four Gospels of Matthew, Mark, Luke and John as the sole authentic accounts of Jesus' life in the course of the second century.

Teabing is correct in asserting that there were other Gospels available in the early Christian centuries. Although most of these were already known before the Nag Hammadi documents were discovered in 1946, those codices in many cases provide fuller and better versions of the texts. Broadly, the texts fall into two groups: those which set out to fill in gaps in the New Testament narrative (e.g., accounts of the childhood of Jesus, or of the later activities of the Apostles), and those which claim to represent the true teachings of Jesus, which the Great Church has misrepresented. The latter group are normally referred to as Gnostic writings because the authors claim a special knowledge (*gnosis*) of Jesus' teaching which the Great Church lacks. These writings, like the four canonical Gospels, do not date from the time of Jesus, as Teabing implies, but were all written down much later. Teabing cites passages from two of them in support of his views about Jesus' true teaching—the Gospel of Philip and the Gospel of Mary (i.e., Mary Magdalene), of which only a fragment survives. Both quotations are accurate, but they do not support the inferences which Teabing (and the Priory of Sion) wish to draw from them.

The Gnostic Churches, which considered that these writings represented Jesus' authentic teaching, did indeed claim that he had given a more prominent place to women among his followers than the tradition of the Great Church was prepared to admit, and that Mary Magdalene was the recipient of at least one special revelation from Jesus after he had returned to his Father.

Gnostic Christianity existed in a wide variety of forms, but all Gnostics shared a common world-view: that the phenomenal universe had come into being as the result of a cosmic accident, which had trapped spiritual souls in physical bodies and cut those souls off from participation in the Pleroma, the fullness of the Godhead. The Gnostic symbol for the human condition was "gold in the mud": gold was the soul, and mud the human body. All Gnostics also agreed that Jesus, far from being an ordinary human being, was a divine messenger, sent from the Pleroma to give men the knowledge (*gnosis*) of their true spiritual condition and how to overcome it. The Gnostic Gospels give no support to the view that Christ was simply a human teacher who preached the importance of the sacred feminine. (There are many other instances of wrong information about Christian doctrine and early Church history in *The Da Vinci Code* and the interested reader should consult Bart D. Ehrman's *Truth and Fiction in* The Da Vinci Code, 2004.)

A Bloodline?

There is no evidence in the Gnostic Gospels, any more than there is in the canonical Gospels, to support the view that Jesus fathered a child. The idea that Jesus was descended from the royal house of David is, of course, found in the New Testament, but the belief that he and

Mary Magdalene produced a royal bloodline would seem to derive from Michael Baigent, Richard Leigh and Henry Lincoln in *The Holy Blood and the Holy Grail*. This book was much hyped, by the BBC among others, when it first appeared, but the authors adduced no evidence about the bloodline of Christ which would satisfy standard historical criteria.

Teabing and Langdon in *The Da Vinci Code* have to offer to Sophie, and to the reader, an explanation about how the royal bloodline of Jesus and knowledge of it has been transmitted to the present day. Their account is reminiscent of one of the exam questions in the book *1066 and All That:* "Fill in two of the following: Blank, Blank, Simon de Montfort." After the Crucifixion, the widowed Mary Magdalene fled to France, where she gave birth to Jesus' daughter, whom she called Sarah. This is simply an adaptation of the medieval legend of how Mary, with her sister Martha, her brother Lazarus and their servant Sarah came to Provence. St. Sarah is still venerated by the Gypsies of Provence. Each year they attend a festival of re-enactment, organized by the Catholic clergy, at the place where the saints are said to have landed, during which they ride into the sea and carry a statue of St. Sarah ashore. Teabing then moves on several hundred years and relates how a descendant of Sarah married a Merovingian King of France, so that for a time the royal bloodline occupied a position of earthly power. The Merovingians were overthrown in 751 by Pepin, the father of Charlemagne, and Teabing skims over another 450 years to reach 1099, when the First Crusade captured Jerusalem and Godfrey of Bouillon became ruler of the Holy City. Teabing claims that he was a descendant of the Merovingian Kings, and therefore of Jesus, though in fact, Godfrey was, through his mother, a descendant of Charlemagne whose father overthrew the Merovingians.

Godfrey of Bouillon, we are told, founded the Priory of Sion in 1099 to preserve the secret knowledge that had hitherto been preserved in his family as an oral tradition. Some thirty years later the Order of Knights Templar was founded and it is implied that they were subordinate to the Priory of Sion. They made their headquarters on the Temple Mount, and conducted excavations on the site of Solomon's temple where they found four enormous trunkloads of documents, dating from before the time of Constantine the Great. These authenticated the Priory of Sion's version of the life and teachings of Jesus, and were shipped back to their headquarters in Europe. In 1291, the Crusader Kingdom was lost to the Saracens, and the Priory of Sion and the Knights Templar withdrew to the West. There, in 1307, the Templars were arrested and put on trial on the orders of Philip IV of France, with the connivance of Pope Clement V, and their Order was suppressed in 1312. The Priory of Sion was, however, able to take charge of the vital trunkloads of documents which the Templars held and also to protect the sacred bloodline.

This account of the historical transmission of the secret teaching is not very satisfactory. The view of the Templars' role in preserving the secret teachings of Jesus and his bloodline described in *The Da Vinci Code* has no support in medieval sources, but is a modern variation of nineteenth-century conspiracy theories about the Order of the Templars.

There had been a Priory of Sion in the Crusader Kingdom. When the First Crusade captured Jerusalem in 1099 they found the church of Our Lady of Sion in ruins.

At some point before 1112 it was rebuilt and a community of Austin Canons was endowed to serve it. The church stood on what was thought to be the site of the house in which Jesus had celebrated the Last Supper, and the Cenaculum, the chapel of the Upper Room, built by the crusaders in c. 1180 to commemorate this, may still be seen there. After the loss of the Holy Land in 1291, the Austin Canons of Mount Sion retired to their estates in Europe, and their headquarters were at Orléans until 1619, when the Priory was suppressed and Louis XIII transferred their property to the Jesuits. The modern Priory of Sion is an esoteric society which has no connection with the Austin Canons of Crusader Jerusalem. Although documents detailing its earlier history have been deposited in French archives, these also appear to be modern. Certainly none of them has been examined and authenticated by professional historians. The claims made by the Priory about historical continuity with the crusader Priory of Sion, and the list of famous Grand Masters, remain uncorroborated.

The Basis for the Popularity of the Novel

In *The Da Vinci Code* the Catholic Church is cast as the implacable enemy of the Priory of Sion and its secret teaching down the ages. Not merely did the papacy ruthlessly suppress the Knights Templar, it also showed its hatred of the sacred feminine by persecuting witches, but "those deemed 'witches' by the Church included all female scholars, priestesses, gypsies, mystics [and] nature lovers," so Robert Langdon claims. They are all said to be victims of the papal Inquisition, but that is patently untrue, for Protestants persecuted witches with as much zeal and as little discrimination as Catholics did. (There was no papal Inquisition at work in Salem in 1692.) This passage is typical of Brown's approach to Church history. There is a notable absence of any reference to Protestantism in the book. As Protestants share with Catholics a belief in the divinity of Christ and the authenticity of the canonical Gospels their reaction to the secret of the Priory of Sion would be as hostile as that of the Vatican—though this is a possibility which Brown seems anxious not to explore. When talking about the Catholic Church in the present day, the hostility of Brown's characters is directed chiefly at its conservative wing and particularly at Opus Dei, which is treated as a sinister organization, though one which admittedly performs many good works. Brown's approach to it resembles that of Alexandre Dumas to the Jesuit Order in his historical novels.

Although some readers may identify with the anti-Catholic prejudices of Langdon and Teabing, I suspect that this has had little to do with the book's popularity. *The Da Vinci Code* belongs to the genre of occult mystery novels, which range from Bulwer Lytton's Zanoni to the works of H. P. Lovecraft and Dennis Wheatley. The only difference is that Dan Brown is dealing with a "white" mystery—the secret teachings of Jesus. Such works, always popular, appeal to the Gnostic which is lurking in many of us, the desire to be part of an elite with privileged information.

There are two other reasons why this book might attract a large readership. First, it is constructed as a series of interconnected puzzles. The solution to one set confronts the investigators with another. Readers are not asked to solve the clues, but if reasonably well educated they will get satisfaction from understanding them: Leonardo's diagram of Vitruvian man, the epicene figure of St. John in his *Last Supper,* the significance of the Fibonacci sequence of numbers, the male and female quantities of poetic scansion. A reader who does not know about some of these points will almost certainly have friends who do, or, if not, will be able to surf the internet for answers. On one level the book is a kind of intellectual game, and will appeal to the many people who enjoy quizzes.

The second reason is very different. Although it starts as a thriller, the book develops into a Grail Quest. The Holy Grail has been a potent force in the Western imagination ever since Chrétien de Troyes wrote his *Perceval* in c. 1181. While the young hero is sitting at dinner in the castle of the Fisher King, a procession enters, led by a page carrying a lance from which blood drips, followed by two squires with golden candlesticks, followed by a maiden, holding aloft a Grail, made of gold, studded with jewels and giving out "so brilliant a light that the candles lost their brightness." Although Perceval later learns from a hermit that the Grail contained a eucharistic host with which the Fisher King's father was fed, Chrétien died leaving the story unfinished, so we never learn what precisely the Grail was. This uncertainty is compounded by the fact that Wolfram von Eschenbach, writing a generation later, claimed that Chrétien had falsified the Grail story, but that he had learned the true version from Guiot the Provençal. Wolfram's Grail is a stone, brought from the Earthly Paradise, the spiritual powers of which are renewed every Good Friday when a heavenly dove lays a eucharistic Host upon it. Thus although in many later versions the Grail is treated as the chalice of the Last Supper, the descriptions given in the two earliest sources and the divergences between them have left space for alternative interpretations.

In *The Da Vinci Code* we are told that the chalice of the Grail signifies the womb, and in particular the womb of St

Mary Magdalene, which transmitted the royal bloodline of Jesus, son of David. In that sense the Holy Grail (or San Greal) would signify a person, someone who carried in themselves the royal blood (or Sang réal). The statistical probabilities are that if Jesus really had had a daughter who had issue, thousands of people would be able to claim descent from her 2,000 years later, but the elitist Priory of Sion seems to envisage that there will only be one descendant. The Grail in *The Da Vinci Code* is said also to be the tomb of St Mary Magdalene, in or beside which the Priory had deposited for safe keeping the four trunks of documents brought back by the Templars from the Holy Land, which proved the authenticity of her cult. The second half of the book is a Grail Quest in which Langdon and Sophie hunt for the shrine. It is surprising, though, that the professor of religious symbology at Harvard did not know that the same legend which reports that Mary Magdalene ended her days in France also says that she is buried in the basilica of Vézelay near Auxerre, where, indeed, her shrine may still be seen.

A Medieval Tale of the Grail Transposed?

There is no obvious attempt to model *The Da Vinci Code* on a medieval Grail romance; nevertheless, there are certain parallels. The Grail quest is an individual adventure in search of spiritual fulfilment, and those who undertake it encounter a series of seemingly irrelevant obstacles and difficulties. Not the least of these is the fact that the Grail castle is very difficult to find. Langdon and Sophie experience the same problem. The final clues which they solve lead them to the Rosslyn Chapel near Edinburgh, but in the best medieval quest tradition they discover that although it had once been there, the Grail is there no longer. They come then to realize that: "You do not find the Grail. The Grail finds you." At the very end of the book Langdon believes that he does experience the Grail in the form in which he understands it: "For a moment he thought he heard a woman's voice . . . the wisdom of the ages . . . whispering up from the chasms of the earth." The phrase is more reminiscent of Rider Haggard's *She* than of *The High Quest of the Holy Grail,* but that may be part of Dan Brown's appeal.

During the Middle Ages people could see the chalice of the Last Supper in the cathedral of Genoa, where it had been deposited by crusaders from the Holy Land. Similarly the Holy Blood, which according to some versions of the legend the Holy Grail was said to contain, was preserved in reliquaries at Bruges and at Westminster Abbey; while the eucharistic Host, present in the Grail in other versions, was to be found on every Catholic altar when Mass was said. But the Grail itself could not be found in one place, having an independent life in the Western religious imagination which the Church authorities could never fully control, and of all the symbols from Christian tradition it is perhaps the one which can most easily be transposed into a post-Christian context. According to recent religious surveys, some 70 percent of the population of Britain claims to value spirituality but to have no religious affiliation. Although such people would probably be unimpressed by the religious ideas of the Priory of Sion, they might well find the Grail quest symbolism congenial.

The Vatican Code

By Maureen Dowd

Maureen Dowd, winner of the 1999 Pulitzer Prize for distinguished commentary, has been a columnist on the *New York Times* op-ed page since 1995. Best known for her provocative, witty, take-no-prisoners views on the White House—and most especially the current occupant thereof—she is also a leading commentator on hot-button cultural issues, from feminism to the role of religion in politics. Here, in a column written two years after the novel first appeared on bestseller lists, Dowd, a Catholic, skewers the Vatican and its Cardinal Bertone for urging the faithful not to read or buy *The Da Vinci Code.* In a neat twist, however, she goes on to say that if the Vatican had actually read the book, they would have praised it because, contrary to the prevailing wisdom, Dan Brown actually has written a book that is both anti-feminist and pro-Catholic.

Some may mock the Vatican for waiting until everyone on earth has read *The Da Vinci Code* to denounce *The Da Vinci Code.*

I am not one of them. It's Easter, and I don't want to blot my catechism.

It's a little late, now that the two-year-old thriller by Dan Brown is a publishing miracle—with 25 million copies sold in 44 languages, a cascade of other books inspired by the novel and a movie with Tom Hanks set to start filming this spring—for Cardinal Tarcisio Bertone to intone on a Vatican radio broadcast: "Don't read and don't buy *The Da Vinci Code.*"

But when you think of the history of the Catholic Church, the Vatican is acting with lightning speed. It took the church more than 350 years to reverse its condemnation of Galileo. The Vatican only began an inquisition of the 16th-century Inquisition in 1998. It wasn't until the reign of Pope John Paul II that the Vatican apologized for the crimes of the Crusaders and offered contrition for the silence of Catholics in the Holocaust. The church has still not apologized for shameful dissembling by its hierarchy on the sex abuse scandal. And America's Catholic bishops only last week announced they were finally going to get serious about opposing the death penalty.

The 70-year-old cardinal assigned by the Vatican to exorcise the success of the novel is the archbishop of Genoa, a former soccer commentator and a contender to succeed the ailing pope. "There is a very real risk that many people who read it will believe that the fables it contains are true," he told *Il Giornale.*

It evokes the Dan Quayle–Murphy Brown flap for a Vatican official to slam Dan Brown's fictional characters, but a former Vatican reporter explained it this way: "The church is founded on a story that some people believe and some people don't, so the Vatican tends to get very threatened by other versions of that story, especially racier ones."

Mr. Brown's zippy version has Jesus and Mary Magdalene marrying and having children. This "perverts the story of the Holy Grail, which most certainly does not refer to the descendants of Mary Magdalene," Cardinal Bertone said. "It astonishes and worries me that so many people believe these lies."

The novelist is not the first one to conjure romantic sparks between the woman usually painted as what one writer calls "the Jessica Rabbit of the Gospels" and the eligible young Jewish carpenter and part-time miracle worker.

For years, female historians and novelists have been making the case that Mr. Brown makes, that Mary Magdalene was framed and defamed, that the men who run Christianity obliterated her role as an influential apostle and reduced her to a metaphor for sexual guilt.

The church refuses to allow women to be ordained as priests because there were no female apostles. So if Mary Magdalene was a madonna rather than a whore, the church loses its fig leaf of justification for male domination and exclusion.

It's obvious that Vatican officials did not read to the end of Mr. Brown's novel or they never would have denounced it.

(*Caveat lector:* If you have somehow missed reading the blockbuster or are one of the thrifty souls waiting for the paperback to finally come out, do not read further.)

After whipping you into a feminist frenzy over the hidden agenda of the church's unjustly perpetuating itself as an all-male, all "celibate" institution—precepts that have clearly led to some unnatural perversions and attracted a disproportionate number of priests fleeing sexual confusion—Mr. Brown abruptly deflates you at the end, going along with the notion that women should stay silent and submissive, letting the men who run the church continue to run the church with men.

The woman who is the descendant of Mary Magdalene and Jesus tells Robert Langdon, Mr. Brown's Harvard symbologist hero, that the secret saga of how the church smeared her ancestor as a slut and swindled all women out of serious roles in the church does not need to be aired. It can continue to remain a secret.

"Her story is being told in art, music and books," the woman says, adding that things are gradually changing for women: "We are beginning to sense the need to restore the sacred feminine."

No whistle is blown. No alarm is sounded. Talk about an anticlimax for a fantastic ride. As it turns out, Mr. Brown is not the tormentor of the Vatican, but an ally.

Religious Fiction

BY DAVID KLINGHOFFER

David Klinghoffer is a columnist for the *Jewish Forward* and writes frequently for a variety of other publications. Former literary editor of *National Review*, he is the author of a spiritual memoir about becoming a Jew, *The Lord Will Gather Me In*, and of a widely praised biography of the Biblical patriarch Abraham, *The Discovery of God*.

When a novel has stuck around the top of the *New York Times* bestseller list for half a year, there is something interesting going on. Such a book has set off a pretty loud pealing of the electric chimes at the front door of the culture. In the case of Dan Brown's *The Da Vinci Code*, what's so special exactly? That depends on what makes conspiracy theories so fascinating.

The conspiracy theory at the heart of Dan Brown's huge bestseller was not invented by him (it has been kicking around for years), but it's a juicy one and he's made the most of it, creating a story with a very effective cliffhanger at the end of almost every one of his 105 chapters. You are

---

This article originally appeared in the *National Review*, December 8, 2003. It is reprinted by permission of *National Review*, 215 Lexington Avenue, New York, NY 10016.

pulled along relentlessly—a feat of narrative art that really does deserve to be called art, no matter what Yale literary critic Harold Bloom said recently in mocking the "immensely inadequate" Stephen King (a similarly gifted writer) when the latter won a lifetime achievement literary prize. If you don't believe writing in this vein merits appreciation, try thinking up a plot like the one in *The Da Vinci Code* yourself. Since Brown's novel is a novel, it can more forthrightly take advantage of the tension inherent in unlocking ancient doors that perhaps should never be opened. He's witty, succinct, and smart—though the reader will have to be prepared to encounter the phrase "the sacred feminine" more than once, and if that makes you extremely queasy, you had better leave this book alone.

But the best thing about *The Da Vinci Code* is that the conspiracy is just an awfully neat one. What makes for an outstanding conspiracy? It doesn't have to be real, as this one is surely not, despite Brown's inclusion of a preface boldly headlined "FACT." One requirement is a complex array of lore. Brown has that: he provides many fascinating historical and quasi-historical tidbits—like the symbolic significance of the figure of a rose, the mathematical phenomenon called the Fibonacci sequence, the ancient Hebrew coding sequence called *atbash,* and much more—with an emphasis on the cryptic meanings of the paintings and drawings of Leonardo da Vinci, all artfully woven into the plot.

Above all, a worthwhile conspiracy needs to explain something that previously you didn't know needed explaining, something also that links to a truth, or at least a pseudotruth, of deep significance. Again, pseudodepth will do fine—we're talking about entertainment, after all. *The Da Vinci Code* has this.

But this book is certainly not for everyone, for the following reason. In this sort of thriller, there has to be something urgently important at stake should the conspiracy be revealed. What's at stake in *The Da Vinci Code* is nothing less than traditional Christianity itself. The Holy Grail, we are told, is not a holy cup but rather holy blood, the lineage of Jesus of Nazareth: the founder of Christianity had a daughter, Sarah, by Mary Magdalene. If true, this theory would overturn some of the central beliefs of Christians.

As a believing Jew, I certainly can't be accused of special pleading on behalf of Christian dogma. This should give me credibility when I say that this "holy blood" theory—of Jesus having descendants—is too nutty to merit serious consideration; any suggestion that such a fact could have been kept secret for two millennia is absurd. Brown does acknowledge that there is some merit—some truth and beauty—in Christianity; but such merit as he sees is very far from the faith of actual Christian believers. Any Christian who is offended by fiction that directly contradicts his faith should certainly avoid this book.

If I were a Christian, though, I think I would find it a little disturbing that some fellow Christians do in fact view this novel as a threat to their faith. Some Catholic magazines have published detailed refutations of *The Da Vinci Code;* that they believe this is necessary indicates that many Catholics, and many in the general reading public, are taking this book far more seriously than they ought to. This also suggests that the problems in Catholic religious education are every bit as severe as Catholic conservatives have been alleging for some time now. If the professional educators were doing their job, any believing Catholic past elementary-school age would know that Brown's book is a total falsehood.

What about the book's influence in the broader culture? Here, I am calmed by the reflection that there's something profoundly religious about conspiracies in the first place, even fictitious ones. Think about this next time you are at the beach in chilly weather. Though the sky is cloudy and a cold wind is up, you'll see people sitting on blankets in the sand just staring out to sea. Why? Because when you look at the ocean you get the intuition that just under the surface resides a vast hidden world of exotic, usually unseen creatures. The realization that there's all that life underneath—in some ways a mirror of our own world on dry land but in others dramatically different—is simply thrilling. It's what keeps people's eyes glued to the ocean even when there is ostensibly nothing going on out there.

This, too, is what makes a conspiracy thrilling, the revelation of concealed complexity all around. Likewise, it's what attracts many of us to thinking about spiritual matters—the gut-level perception, powerful if unproven, of an existence beyond the one of our mundane daily lives. *The Da Vinci Code* may be silly, but in its fashion, it's also thrilling. If its popularity means people are thinking about invisible realities, that's good news.

Broken Promises

Deciphering the Success of The Da Vinci Code

BY CURTIS WHITE

Curtis White has made something of a name for himself as a social critic with a nonconventional perspective on whatever subject he touches. He kicked up a storm with a controversial essay in *Harper's Magazine* in 2002 by attacking National Public Radio's Fresh Air host Terry Gross—seen by many as the best interviewer on radio—as a "schlock jock." He later expanded that article into a book called *The Middle Mind: Why Americans Don't Think for Themselves,* an attack on the pseudo-intellectual tendencies of mainstream America that is critical of the rise in aesthetic and cultural interest on the part of ordinary people over the last few decades. One might easily assume that White would feel *The Da Vinci Code* and all the hoopla surrounding it to be the ultimate expression of his "middle mind" thesis. But, surprisingly, this is not his point. Instead, he sees value and meaning in Dan Brown's novel that even its biggest enthusiasts are hard-pressed to understand, let alone recognize.

In the following essay, which originally appeared under the title "Faith-off—Broken Promises: Deciphering the Success of *The Da Vinci Code*" in the *Village Voice Literary Supplement,* White argues that the book intrigues us not because it's a good yarn or because Dan Brown is right about Leonardo da Vinci or the sins of the Catholic Church, but because the novel allows us to flee the fraudulent culture that dominates our lives, and embrace—albeit temporarily—a different, secret, and erotic spirituality. That is a mouthful for those of us White might see as "middle minds," but White's argument is certainly unique in the world of *Da Vinci Code* criticism.

"Faith Off—Broken Promises: Deciphering the Success of *The Da Vinci Code*" first appeared in the Fall 2004 *Village Voice Literary Supplement.* Reprinted with permission.

As everyone knows by now, Dan Brown's *The Da Vinci Code* is about a detective hero (Harvard "symbologist" Robert Langdon), a murder, and a freightload of arcane and sensational speculations about secret societies (Opus Dei, the Knights Templar, the Priory of Sion) and their mischievous, malicious role in world history. The novel also seeks to educate its readers about the (factual) role of gnosticism in the early Christian church and the (dubious) erotic relationship between Jesus and Mary Magdalene. This narrative line culminates in the notion that the Holy Grail is actually a metaphor for the holy bloodline created by Christ and Magdalene and perpetuated in the descendants of the Merovingian kings. Thus the novel's most sensational suggestion (aside from fantasies about Jesus and Mary *in flagrante*) is that people still walk the earth with the messianic DNA.

What *The Da Vinci Code* has created should interest us, but not because Brown is right about Da Vinci or the infamies of the Catholic Church or powerful secret societies or the real role of Mary Magdalene as apostle and lover to the Christ. *The Da Vinci Code* is important as an expression of a desire for a spirituality that cannot be had within the confines of the institutionalized church. More simply yet, it is the popular expression of a desire for a kind of meaningfulness to life that is missing for most of us. And certainly, it is the scandalous expression of a willingness to be disobedient to achieve the heretical end of a salvation outside the confines of the church. Through this novel we express our fundamental disgust with our institutionalized lives, and we suggest shocking things that we might previously have imagined were unsayable. The novel offers the unexpected opportunity to flee the dominant culture of Truths-That-Make-No-Sense for the Secret, the Unsayable, and the True. From my point of view, there's nothing wrong with imagining that something's fraudulent about the way our lives are ordered, nothing wrong with wanting to go beyond the illusory in order to know the truth. Beyond the scandal and the sensation and the heavy-handed fiction, it is this assumption of our shared sense of spiritual fraud and the assumption that we're willing to think heretically in order to escape that fraud that makes Brown's deepest appeal to his readers. He promises us liberation, and our eagerness to take up his offer reveals much about our spiritual as well as our political condition.

In other words, the interest in gnosticism and alternative forms of Christianity that *The Da Vinci Code* has stimulated holds the possibility for a kind of seriousness that few other creations of popular culture can claim. But as with most "serious" matters in mass culture, the opportunity to have real consequence is abolished in the same moment that it is extended. The *Code* and its many commentaries (like Dan Burstein's *Secrets of the Code*) offer two contradictory possibilities. It is the expression of an authentic longing, and it is the incredulous insistence that we can't really mean what we seem to be saying. To really mean this business about the hidden history and the unconfessed malice of the Catholic Church, about the relationship of a secret society like Opus Dei to the administration of the federal government, is too scary to be taken entirely seriously. So our anxiety about seriously proposing the critique as an alternative to the religio-corporate present is immediately effaced by the assurance that—not to worry!—it's just pulp fiction. It's just a scandal/commodity. It obliges us to nothing more than a familiar and ephemeral enthusiasm and a willingness to stimulate a "market" (in this case, the ever beleaguered book market that staggers from year to year only on the strength of the next Harry Potter adventure, novelistic sensations like the *Code,* and tell-alls by disgraced politicians and celebrities).

Let's take, as an instance of the *Code*'s ambiguity, the revelations about Mary Magdalene and her sexual relationship with Jesus. She represents, on the one hand, a critique of the church's misogynist and patriarchal past. Moreover, she offers not only a secret history but also a secret and erotic spirituality. But she also represents the scandalous and merely lurid idea that she and Jesus did the nasty together. Which option is it that has the greater power to explain the interest in a book like *The Da Vinci Code?* In some ways, the two aspects work together, entertaining and instructing as Horace put it in his *Ars Poetica*. But I would contend what Horace never suggested: The entertainment makes the instruction possible, but it also destroys its meaning. *The Da Vinci Code* makes political and spiritual notions of great potential power broadly available but only with the tacit assurance that these theses will not be made real. They will never be nailed to a church door. It's like the *Mission: Impossible* message that self-destructs after a first reading. It's the cultural equivalent of computer code on a CD that makes it possible to play the CD but not to reproduce it. Cultural meaning is created but only on the condition that its impact will be carefully limited.

Let me put this another way. The authentic social function of the imagination operating through the arts (especially the novel) is to submit to destruction the standing assumptions of the moment but then to redeem that destruction through a process of rebuilding and reimagining. That's what art does. As Wallace Stevens put it,

"Poetry is a destructive force." It destroys and redeems, wipes the slate clean and then re-creates. But a work like *The Da Vinci Code* does just the opposite. It first holds out the possibility of a vast reimagining only in order to betray it in the end through a re-establishment of the familiar (in this case, the jaded world of the bourgeois scandal/commodity). In short, it suggests redemption without ever having the courage to destroy anything. In the end, its real formal function is to reassure, to console, to make one comfortable not with the new and blasphemous but precisely with the most familiar: the pulp of the pleasure-commodity.

Thus, *The Da Vinci Code*'s seriousness is deeply unserious. Its promise of truth is broken in the moment it is made. The culture's habit of finding "seriousness" acceptable only if offered by people who are finally not serious is yet another way that the culture makes certain that nothing alarming will come of our newfound interest in heretical ideas. On the other hand, this is all only as it should be in a culture that believes it can learn about theology by reading a pulp novel.

Ah, dysfunction.

The Cardinal and the Code

By Dan Burstein

Don't buy this [book]. Don't read this because this is rotten food.

—Cardinal Tarcisio Bertone,
Archbishop of Genoa

In an unending stream of novels, films, and plays, writers manipulate the figure of Christ under cover of imaginary and nonexistent new documents and discoveries. . . . Our time, obsessed as it is with sex, seems unable to portray Jesus in any other way than as a homosexual, or as one who taught that salvation is to be found in uniting with the feminine principle and gave the example by marrying Mary Magdalene . . . It is trading on the vast resonance of the name of Christ and on all that he means to a large part of humankind, to achieve wide publicity at very little cost . . . this is literary and artistic parasitism.

—Raniero Cantalamessa,
Preacher to the Papal Household

[Dan Brown] knows that he is doing wrong and that he is deceiving the people.

—Bishop Javier Echevarría,
Prelate of Opus Dei in the United States

When I face almighty God at my final judgment, as we all will, I can say I did try my best. I did try my best to protest.

—Sister Mary Michael,
who knelt in prayer for twelve hours at Lincoln Cathedral to protest *The Da Vinci Code* movie being filmed there

Christianity is not about forgiveness to the point of insulting Jesus Christ.

—Father Abdou Abu Kasm,
President of the Lebanon Catholic Information Centre

I was not born with the luxury of absolute certainty or absolute faith. I have a lot of questions. I've written a novel in which fictional characters ask some of those questions and offer possible answers . . . Readers are smart people, capable of deciding for themselves how much of this novel makes sense to them and how much they want to believe. And as for whether or not we're all getting a little too worked up over this book, a very wise British priest was quoted recently that "Christian theology has survived the writings of Galileo and the writings of Darwin." Surely it will survive the writings of some novelist from New Hampshire.

—DAN BROWN, novelist, addressing the New Hampshire Humanities Council, 2005

For nearly two years after it was published, the Vatican had nothing official to say about *The Da Vinci Code.* Senior church officials remained silent even as the book sold millions of copies, not only in the United States, where it first created a sensation, but in countries with majority Catholic populations, like France, Spain, Brazil, Mexico, Portugal, and Italy.

In the meantime, the rest of the church—laity, priests, theologians—seemingly *couldn't* stop talking about it. From California to Connecticut, some priests urged their parishioners to read the book, join church-sponsored book discussion groups, and even go to weekend retreats devoted to the issues raised by it. While most Catholic leaders were critical of the novel and the way it treats theological issues as well as matters of Christian history, some also asked, Doesn't the book serve to humanize Jesus? Doesn't Mary Magdalene's role as a prominent follower of Jesus—and not as a repentant prostitute—deserve more attention in this day and age? A few even wondered out loud if there was anything wrong with speculating on the possibility that Jesus and Mary might have been married and even had a child or children. There were also plenty of fierce critics of *The Da Vinci Code* in the Catholic community, some of whom wrote blistering and detailed critiques in Catholic magazines, but the standpoint in these articles was one of recognition of how widespread the book's popularity was, and the need to engage its readers in discussion and debate.

The Right Reverend Tom Wright, the Anglican Bishop of Durham and a leading UK theologian, summed it up well for many theologians when he said, "*The Da Vinci Code* has a great deal to say about where our culture currently is and which myths our culture is eager to buy. It comes in on the tide of the New Age postmodern hunger for spirituality which assumes that spirituality is a good thing but also assumes that the one place you will not find it is mainstream Christianity." Like many other Christian leaders of various denominations, Wright thinks the most effective theological riposte to *The Da Vinci Code* is to engage its fundamental ideas in robust argument and present meaningful alternatives from within traditional Christian belief.

After publication of *Secrets of the Code* I was invited to speak to many religious groups, including Catholic institutions that ranged across a wide gamut, from the College of Saint Mary in Omaha (a wonderful four-year Catholic college training young women for careers as teachers and nurses in Catholic hospitals and schools) to the Pope John Paul II Cultural Center in Washington, DC, which is essentially a museum of the Catholic experience in America. At these and numerous other events at Christian churches, Jewish temples, and religious cultural institutions of all kinds, I found extraordinary interest in the issues at the heart of *The Da Vinci Code,* and a real passion for discussion. Frequently audiences stayed long after the formal program had ended to ask their questions and express their opinions.

At the 92nd Street Y in New York City (a Jewish cultural organization), I appeared on a panel together with a representative of Opus Dei and subsequently got the chance to meet a number of Opus Dei members. While they were severely critical of *The Da Vinci Code* and the way Opus Dei is portrayed in the book, the people I came to know in Opus Dei took the position that the book was just a novel and that it shouldn't be taken as factual. Some Opus Dei members even told me that they enjoyed the book at the level of a good beach or airplane read. To the degree anyone had come to take the ideas in the novel seriously, Opus Dei members felt that their organization should try to have a seat at the table of discussion to set the record straight from their point of view. Indeed, Opus Dei in the United States published a detailed set of FAQs on their website with their reactions to specific ideas presented by Dan Brown in the novel. (See page 283 for a sampling of these Opus Dei FAQs.)

In the fall of 2004, I visited Rome and Vatican City for my research for *Secrets of Angels & Demons,* which dealt with the novel Dan Brown wrote just prior to *The Da Vinci Code.* Brown's *Angels & Demons,* published in 2000, five years before the death of Pope John Paul II, is set in the Vatican against the backdrop of the death of a pope and the unfolding of the papal succession process. During my research, I found that the Italian version of *The Da Vinci Code* was on sale everywhere in Italy, even in the bookshops of Vatican City. A few weeks later, when Pope John Paul II's health began to decline markedly, I heard that the Italian version of *The Da Vinci Code* was even on sale in the bookshop of the hospital where he was being treated.

After all of these experiences, I began to draw the conclusion that church leaders were handling the debate thoughtfully and appropriately. They were criticizing the book in forums where it was appropriate to do so, but not launching any kind of campaign against it that would make them look as if they were on the defensive, or as if they took the book too seriously, or that would inadvertently call even more attention to it and make more people want to read it. Whether one agreed or disagreed with Vatican policy on these matters, the church seemed to be playing it cool and smart.

But as it turned out, that conclusion was a bit premature. Suddenly, in early 2005, two full years after *The Da Vinci Code* had first burst upon the world scene, Cardinal Bertone, the seventy-year-old archbishop of Genoa, issued a most surprising statement in which he called for banning the book. Bertone's outspoken comments made headline news around the world. Among the more virulent sound-bites:

"The book is a sackful of lies against the Church, against the real history of Christianity and against Christ himself."

"We can't keep quiet about the truth when faced with all the lies and all the inventions in this book . . . I'm really shocked that a book founded on so many errors and on numerous lies could have such success."

"I would ask the author of this book and similar ones to be more respectful because freedom of expression has limits when it does not respect others."

"This book is everywhere. There is a very real risk that many people who read it will believe the fables it contains are true."

"He even perverts the story of the Holy Grail which most certainly does not refer to the descendents of Mary

Magdalene. It astonishes and worries me that so many people believe these lies."

"There is nothing more false than the need to rediscover a—how can I say it—an 'amazon' Mary Magdalene in order to recuperate the presence of women [in the church]."

"What would have happened if a book like this had been written, full of lies, on the Buddha or Mohammed or even, for example, if a novel had been published that manipulated the history of the Holocaust?"

"Not selling [*The Da Vinci Code*] in Catholic bookstores would be a good first step."

"Don't buy this [book]. Don't read this because this is rotten food."

Seeking to "discourage" the reading of books deemed heretical is not new. For the better part of five centuries, the church maintained a list of books—the *Index Librorum Prohibitorum*—that were to be banned or shunned. Flaubert's *Madame Bovary,* Stendhal's *The Red and the Black,* as well as the complete works of Jonathan Swift, John Locke and Jean-Paul Sartre were included in the *Index* at various times. The church's willingness to use extraordinary means to suppress books it deemed heretical has a long, painful, and unfortunate history, punctuated by well-known incidents—from the Inquisition, to burning the philosopher-scientist Giordano Bruno at the stake, to the trial and house arrest of Galileo.

The practice of attempting to control the ideas and cultural works to which Catholics are exposed through the official or semiofficial banning of books was discontinued in the 1960s. This was a time in church history characterized by a new kind of modern enlightenment, when steps toward the democratization of church organization and belief were taken. (In this same time period, the Vatican acknowledged that Mary Magdalene should not be confused with the repentant prostitute mentioned in certain gospel passages.) Over the past few decades, with church leaders officially criticizing past policy on matters such as the trial of Galileo, and seeking ways to reconcile Genesis and the theory of evolution, it appeared that the church was developing a more open approach to discussion, debate, and criticism.

This recent background made Cardinal Bertone's comments all the more surprising. In attacking *The Da Vinci Code* and calling for Catholic bookstores to stop selling it, Bertone seemed to be suggesting a return to a time when church leaders believed they could win intellectual and philosophical debates by simply banning or suppressing certain ideas.

Few of the faithful seemed particularly moved by Bertone's ban. Even some high-ranking church officials chose to distance themselves from Bertone. For example, Monsignor Jose Maria Pinheiro, Bishop of Sao Paulo, one of the largest Catholic communities in the world, took an explicitly different view. He counseled "prudence," encouraged readers to distinguish "fact from fiction" in *The Da Vinci Code,* and suggested that it was *not* necessary to prohibit anyone from buying or reading this novel.

Other Vatican experts pointed out that if he had wanted to, Pope John Paul II had almost two years to speak out against *The Da Vinci Code* before he lost his voice and his health. He was a pope who often commented on popular culture. In his youth, he had written plays and poems. So it would not have been surprising if he had said something about *The Da Vinci Code.* But he never did. (Incidentally, Dan Brown was once part of a small group that had an in-person audience with Pope John Paul II.) So why was Cardinal Bertone so exercised about this novel?

As it turned out, Bertone was on some people's lists as a possible successor to Pope John Paul II. Bertone's outburst against *The Da Vinci Code* occurred at a moment in time when it had become clear that John Paul II's health was in rapid decline and that a conclave to select a new pope was in the offing. The cardinals follow a strict code of conduct during these transitional times that forbids anything that smacks of campaigning. But speaking out on issues, even though it can be a thinly veiled form of electioneering, is acceptable. By condemning *The Da Vinci Code,* a number of experts believe that Cardinal Bertone was calling attention to the need to strengthen the purity of church doctrine by selecting the new pope from among those in his conservative faction.

Just a few weeks later, the German cardinal Joseph Ratzinger, with whom Bertone was closely allied, would in fact be selected to become Pope Benedict XVI. It was one of the most curious cases of life imitating art: Dan Brown, the Protestant pop novelist from New Hampshire, whose earlier book *Angels & Demons* had dealt with all manner of secrets, conspiracies, theological issues, and Machiavellian plots within a fictional papal selection process, became himself a factor in the real-life papal selection process of 2005.

10 Plot Twists

The spectacular publishing success of *The Da Vinci Code* has generated millions of satisfied readers, fans, and enthusiasts on the one hand, and a wide variety of vociferous critics on the other. In this chapter we reach beyond both camps to take a road that offers some unique perspectives. We divide them into two categories. The first might be labeled "Before there was a *Da Vinci Code,* there was *my* work." The second is "The French Connection."

We know Dan Brown has openly and publicly expressed his debt to those nonfiction authors whose ideas and books he liberally used in developing the concepts for *The Da Vinci Code.* Many of the pioneers in the study of the symbols heretofore "hidden in plain sight" were readily acknowledged with a bibliographical listing on Brown's website, and even in the book. Some of these now familiar names include the authors Margaret Starbird (*The Woman with the Alabaster Jar* and *The Goddess in the Gospels*), Timothy Freke and Peter Gandy (*Jesus and the Lost Goddess*), Lynn Picknett and Clive Prince (*The Templar Revelation*), and Michael Baigent, Richard Leigh, and Henry Lincoln (*Holy Blood, Holy Grail, The Messianic Legacy*). What we wanted to know was, what is it like, for better or worse, to see one's ideas used by Dan Brown to build his blockbuster novel? To find out, we first turned to Lynn Picknett and Clive Prince, whose *Templar Revelation* presented much of the Leonardo–Last Supper–Mary Magdalene thesis that is recapitulated at the center of Dan Brown's novel. It turns out that while Picknett and Prince were flattered that their work is cited specifically in *The Da Vinci Code,* they have also found themselves critics of the book.

Lewis Perdue, a writer not cited by Dan Brown, is the author of two novels drawn from his own fascination with the concepts of the sacred feminine and the alternative history of the early church (*The Da Vinci Legacy* and *Daughter of God*). Let's just say he does not believe imitation is the sincerest form of flattery. Perdue wrote these books years before *The Da Vinci Code,* yet, as he is quick to point out, both Dan Brown's book and his own contain remarkable similarities: a deep dark secret from early Christian history involving a Gnostic female messiah named Sophia, dead art curators, Swiss banks, Leonardo da Vinci, Mary Magdalene, discussion of goddess cults, and much more. So specific were the comparisons, felt Perdue, that he began to claim he was plagiarized, and ended up in court to try and prove it. Thus far, the courts have rejected his claim. But the unfolding story, told in Perdue's own words, is fascinating not only for the intellectual property battle, but even more for what it tells us about the trip through the same mythopoetic fields of mystery and history that Dan Brown and many others have taken. (Interestingly, the authors of *Holy Blood, Holy Grail*—whom Dan Brown openly acknowledges with specific references in *The Da Vinci Code* and on his website—are also pursuing plagiarism charges in a UK court.)

Turning to our French connections, David Downie, an American travel writer living in Paris, gives us a wry touristic look at the Parisian sites that are the backdrop for Robert and Sophie's excellent adventures. Elizabeth Bard gives our readers the wonderful "Code"–related tour they would get if they were with her in person in the

Louvre, absorbing more than two thousand years of iconographic art and walking down the famed Grand Galerie—being careful, of course, to avoid dead curators sprawled out in good Virtuvian Man style. Amy Bernstein, meanwhile, takes us from the mysteries of the *Dossiers Secrets,* through the machinations of Pierre Plantard and the Priory of Sion hoax he perpetrated. Her "French Confection" piece dissects the ultimate urban legends about the ultimate shrine of occult thinkers: Rennes-le-Château. This small French town seems to have a vastly disproportionate market share of baffling legends about the Knights Templar, Mary Magdalene, and the Holy Grail. Dan Brown is far from the first to mine this highly questionable history in novel form. Nor is there any sign he will be the last!

The Real Da Vinci Code

BY LYNN PICKNETT AND CLIVE PRINCE

We asked Lynn Picknett and Clive Prince, the London-based coauthors of *The Templar Revelation* (which figures by name in *The Da Vinci Code*), to contribute this commentary on their reaction to being linked directly to Dan Brown's novel.

We must say that *The Da Vinci Code* was an intriguing 2003 birthday present for one of us. From its opening sequence in the Louvre, like millions of others, we were hooked, breathlessly turning pages, riding high on the sheer fun of it all.

But unlike those other page-turning fans, we had an extra reason for being intrigued: it's not every day that we see the title of our 1997 book, *The Templar Revelation,* embedded in the pages of an international bestselling thriller as one of its four major sources. So we weren't just more or less happy to be whirled along with the action. However, because of our involvement, there in black and white on the page, from the very beginning, we were also *critics.*

Certainly Brown fleshes out the whole concept of the underground society, the Priory of Sion, with its alleged secrets about the bloodline of Jesus and Mary Magdalene, into a dark and turbulent story. Laudably, he's brought these very alternative ideas, which first saw the light of day in *Holy Blood, Holy Grail* back in 1982, to a whole new, excited audience who would probably never have picked up the original. However, it must be remembered that Brown's book is *fiction* and that it draws heavily on other works—not only our own, but also, primarily, *Holy Blood, Holy Grail* by Michael Baigent, Richard Leigh, and Henry Lincoln. This drew on material issued by the enigmatic secret society, the Priory of Sion, indicating that it was the guardian of some great mystery connected with the Merovingian dynasty of Frankish kings and Mary Magdalene. The authors claim that this secret is that Jesus and Mary Magdalene were married and had children who grew up in France and whose descendants founded the Merovingian line.

Although most people believe this is what the Priory of Sion claims, in fact, it is Baigent, Leigh, and Lincoln's own interpretation. The idea was explicitly disavowed by the Grand Master of the Priory of Sion, Pierre Plantard, to whom the importance of the Merovingians is that they are the rightful heirs to the throne of France (assuming that France ever decides to have kings again).

We are far from convinced about the holy bloodline theory. While we accept that there is abundant evidence that Jesus and Mary Magdalene had a physical relationship, which may or may not have resulted in offspring, there's too much ingenuity involved in crowbarring them into the Merovingians' history. But, in any case, even if there were descendants of Jesus around today, why should they be special? Theologically, Jesus was unique, the one and only Son of God. Therefore, his children and their children throughout the generations could have nothing divine about them.

Many people, caught up in the excitement and romance of all this, have assumed that if there were descendants of Jesus around today, there must be something intrinsically special about them. In fact, this *isn't* what Baigent, Leigh, and Lincoln ever claimed. For them, it was the fact that these descendants would be legal heirs to certain titles and powers, such as the throne of Jerusalem, which was important. And the reason these descendants have had to be kept secret from the church is because their very existence would prove that Jesus was nothing more than a mortal man.

A great many people have missed this point, and this has led to theories that there is something inherently, perhaps even genetically, different about this bloodline. Indeed, we regard the notion as potentially dangerous, just like any elitist system that upholds certain people for their physical characteristics over all others. This may take the form of Hitler's master race or white supremacists or those who believe some carry the Jesus bloodline gene, making them automatically superior to the rest of us.

The holy bloodline aspect of Dan Brown's book may be founded on sandy ground, but we agree that the "great heretical secret," so loathed and feared by the church, is indeed sexuality as a sacrament, the sacred feminine. That *was* a secret that had to be protected by the church and it *did* involve Mary Magdalene and Jesus. Her true role as priestess is the key that, if known, would have allowed people to deconstruct the church's teaching, particularly about the place and worth of women. There is even a case for the Magdalene being the most important woman who ever lived, simply because, out of hatred and fear of her real power, as evidenced in the lost, Gnostic Gospels, the church repressed generations of women and degraded the whole of sexuality in her name.

But *The Da Vinci Code* centers on the paintings of Leonardo da Vinci, another area, in our view, in which Dan Brown misses the mark. By trying to combine our discoveries about da Vinci's "code" and the central theory of *Holy Blood, Holy Grail,* Brown has allowed a much more amazing and even shocking revelation to fall between the cracks. The *real* da Vinci code takes us into a much darker and intensely challenging world.

Brown summarizes our discovery of the weird symbolism in Leonardo's *Virgin of the Rocks* (the Paris version; there is another, less interesting one in London's National Gallery) whereby, instead of the infant Jesus being with his mother and young John the Baptist being with his traditional protector, the archangel Uriel, the children, apparently, are with the wrong guardians. This is particularly interesting because the scene is taken from a story the church invented to circumvent the embarrassment of the fact that when John baptized Jesus, he must have had the authority to do so. This scene depicts the moment, or so we are led to believe, that little Jesus bestows this authority on little John for later life. Indeed, the child with Uriel raises his hand in blessing on the other baby, who kneels submissively. However, what happens if the children are with their *correct* guardians? As Brown points out, John would be blessing Jesus, and Jesus would be kneeling submissively to John. Indeed, there are many other elements in the painting that confirm this interpretation. But how would this Johannite (pro John the Baptist) interpretation gel with Brown's basic thesis about the holy bloodline? It doesn't. It stands out like a sore thumb. That's what comes of trying to lever undigested Leonardo secrets into the wrong context.

In over a decade of research, we have found, time after time, evidence that wherever he could, Leonardo da Vinci elevated John the Baptist over Jesus, showing that he regarded the Baptist as superior to Christ. For example, in Leonardo's famous preliminary work of *The Virgin and Child with St. Anne* (ca. 1499–1500) in London's National Gallery, the group consists of the Virgin Mary, Jesus, St. Anne, and a young John the Baptist. But when Leonardo painted the final version, *St. Anne with the Virgin and Child* (1501–07), we find the Baptist's place taken by a lamb, which Jesus seizes so roughly by the ears that we used to joke it should be called *Pulling the Ears Off a Lamb.* In fact, Jesus also has one chubby leg locked around the lamb's neck, visually *severing* it. But as Jesus is called the "Lamb of God" by the Baptist in the New Testament, why has Leonardo represented John himself as a lamb? Perhaps the secret lies in the tradition among the Knights Templar of honoring the Baptist and representing him as a lamb (as in the Templar seal of the knights in southern France, for example). It must be stressed that this is extremely telling: few non-Templars would dream of representing John as the lamb. So, was Leonardo some kind of Knight

Templar, even around two hundred years after the order was brutally suppressed?

Perhaps he was. Certainly we know that the inner circle of the Templars maintained an enormous—many said heretical—reverence for the Baptist, which is reflected in many more of Leonardo's works. The last thing he ever did, for his own benefit entirely and not as any commission, was his darkly strange *St. John the Baptist,* which—together with the *Mona Lisa*—adorned the walls of his death chamber in France in 1519. And his only surviving sculpture, a joint work with Giovanni Francesco Rustici (a known and somewhat sinister alchemist and necromancer), is of John the Baptist, which now stands above an entrance to the baptistery in Florence. The Baptist was everywhere in Leonardo's life, by accident or design. Even if his commissions did not require John to be included, somehow Leonardo always managed to sneak in some Baptist symbolism, such as the carob tree—a traditional association with John—in his unfinished *Adoration of the Magi* (ca. 1481), which is being worshipped by bright, healthy young people, while the holy family is being clawed at by a group of hideous ancient figures like the undead. And the young man standing radiantly close to the roots of John's carob tree is making what we have come to call the "John gesture"—raising the right forefinger heavenward. Leonardo's sculpture is also making this gesture, as is his last painting, *St. John the Baptist* (1513–16)—clearly it is used to represent or symbolize the Baptist, who may or may be not be present in the work himself. One of the figures in his world-famous wall-painting *The Last Supper* (1495–97) is also making the John gesture almost threateningly right into Jesus' face. (This may be at least partly a reference to a relic that is said to be possessed by the Templars, allegedly of the forefinger of John the Baptist himself, which was kept at the temple in Paris. But the gesture here could well have at least a double meaning.)

Leonardo, we discovered, was not alone in his Johannitism. In fact, rather than being basically Christian, the Priory of Sion, however much their beliefs are embroidered with the Magdalene romance, also reveal a similar fascination with the Baptist. Indeed, as the Priory claims Leonardo as one of their own, this struck us as being too much of a coincidence. Their fascination with the Baptist was drawn to our attention by our first Priory contact, known only as Giovanni (John!) in 1991. We even managed to trace this belief in their documents, the most obvious example being the fact that their Grand Masters always take the name John (or Jean or Giovanni)—Leonardo was, according to their own list, John IX. (And is it merely a coincidence that "Sion" itself is Welsh for John?) More intriguingly, the Priory started the count from John II; John I, as Pierre Plantard said, "being symbolically reserved for Christ." But why should Christ be called John? Could it be that to Johannites, John the Baptist is the true Christ—which, after all, means simply an anointed or chosen one?

There is more of this deeply disturbing Johannitism embedded in a Priory-backed publication of 1982, in which the Templars are described as the "Swordbearers of the Church of John," while declaring that they and the Priory were once more or less the same organization.

Thanks to dangerously heretical Leonardo—not to mention the Priory of Sion, whatever they may really be—we found ourselves drawn into some very deep water indeed. Soon we were faced with the extraordinary revelation that there was an ancient tradition in which John the Baptist was revered—and Jesus was regarded as a lesser being, sometimes even reviled.

This Johannite Church, with branches not only in heretical Europe but also in a Middle Eastern tribe, has been largely ignored both by academics and alternative researchers alike. Yet it has always been there, under the surface, its secrets finding form in perhaps many ways, but certainly in the works of the great Renaissance maestro, Leonardo da Vinci. And whatever one's reaction to such irredeemable heresy, his true "secret code" is considerably more exciting and challenging than even the idea that Jesus and the Magdalene had children.

Why does the baby Jesus' leg apparently sever the lamb's neck? *Why* is he pulling the ears off the lamb? *Why* is a disciple raising the John gesture threateningly into Jesus' face in *The Last Supper? Why* are the worshippers of the holy family in *The Adoration of the Magi* evil-looking half-dead wrecks, while those worshipping John's carob tree are bursting with health and youth? Is there any connection with the somewhat different interpretation of Jesus and John's relationship that many modern theologians are now quietly admitting?

The Case of the Purloined Plot?

An Interview with Lewis Purdue

In one novel the heroine is named Sophie, in the other a pivotal character is named Sophia. In both, a major figure in the art world is killed, leaving a mysterious last clue, and there ensues a headlong search for the dark secrets from the past that have been covered up by the Catholic Church—secrets so explosive they could destroy Christianity. And both claim to be based on fact.

But one was published before the other. And therein lies the basis of a courtroom drama featuring Lewis Perdue, author of *Daughter of God* (2000) and *The Da Vinci Legacy* (1983), against Dan Brown, author of *The Da Vinci Code* (2003). As described by Mr. Perdue in the interview below as well as in general news accounts, he began to hear from fans of his books that parts of *The Da Vinci Code* sounded awfully familiar. Soon Perdue himself began to publicly cite what he deemed "powerful evidence of similarity."

Lewis Perdue brought his concern to the attention of Doubleday in the spring of 2003, writing the publisher of *The Da Vinci Code* a letter citing what he thought might be similarities between Brown's book and his own works, and asking for comments. Perdue says that at the time he had no lawyer, had not consulted one, and had no intention to sue. He sought only recognition for his writing. According to court documents, Doubleday rejected his claim as "unfounded," and warned Perdue that if he took legal action, he would be punished with legal costs and fees. At about the same time, the media began to pick up the story. Mr. Perdue provided colorful quotes, particularly after John Olsson, head of the Forensic Linguistics Institute of the UK, concluded that, in his opinion, this was the most "in your face" case of plagiarism he had ever seen.

Perdue told the *San Francisco Chronicle* in March 2004, for example, that "there are far too many parallels between my books and *The Da Vinci Code* for it to be an accident. . . . I feel terribly violated."[1] Later that year he was quoted on the Celebrity Justice website as saying, "Without my writing, *The Da Vinci Code* would never have existed."[2] On the legal front, Mr. Perdue wrote Random House again in September 2004, this time through his lawyer. (Random

1. Adair Lara, "'One 'Da Vinci' Has Sold Millions, the Other Is Little Known. Lewis Perdue Alleges the Popular Novel Has His Book to Thank." *San Francisco Chronicle;* posted on SFGate.com on March 30, 2004.

2. http://celebrityjustice.warnerbros.com/news/0412/15b.html.

House is the corporate parent of Doubleday, publishers of *The Da Vinci Code.*) According to court papers later filed by the publisher, "Perdue's counsel wrote to Random House threatening to file suit unless Brown and Random House agreed to an immediate settlement."[3]

But Perdue says that he has never made a demand for money and that then, as now, he has been willing to resolve the issue in exchange for an acknowledgment that *The Da Vinci Code* used his material. Perdue maintains that the lawsuit and even the publicity resulting from Random House's rejection of his first private letter could all have been avoided with a civil conversation.

The publisher's response to Perdue's letter sent through the lawyer was to file a lawsuit, asking the court to declare Mr. Perdue's claims baseless: ". . . Perdue cannot come close to showing the requisite 'substantial similarity' in protectable expression between his books and Brown's. . . . All of the alleged similarities amount to nothing more than abstract ideas, stock elements common to mysteries and thrillers, or the use of similar factual theories." Perdue's claims, the lawsuit went on to say, were being made only so he could "exploit *Da Vinci Code*'s success."[4]

Perdue then countersued. His expression of the divine feminine and its suppression by the Catholic Church as portrayed in *Daughter of God,* he maintained, was the same as Brown's: "notions of a divine feminine, the unity of male and female in pagan worship, the importance of Sophia, the 'Great Goddess' of the Gnostic Gospels," and more.[5] Not only were there similar themes, Perdue argued, but many common details. Some examples: "the role of the female . . . the physical evidence of the divine feminine . . . similarities between

---

3. Dan Brown and Random House, Inc. vs. Lewis Perdue, February 25, 2005.

4. Ibid.

5. Memorandum Opinion and Order issued by Judge George B. Daniels of the U.S. District Court.

Opus Dei and [my] Congregation for the Doctrine of Faith . . . the fact that both novels incorporate the use of a gold key. . . ."[6]

Six months later, a federal judge sided with Random House and denied a trial on the facts. In a decision handed down in August 2005, Judge George B. Daniels stated, "Both *The Da Vinci Code* and *Daughter of God* involve the unprotectable idea of a mystery thriller set against a religious backdrop . . . [their] total concept and feel, theme, characters, plot, sequence, pace and setting," are not substantially similar. "Any slightly similar elements are on the level of generalized or otherwise unprotectable ideas," he concluded, describing Brown's book as "an intellectual, complex treasure hunt focusing more on the codes, number sequences, cryptexes and hidden messages left behind as clues," whereas Perdue's is "more action packed, with several gunfights and violent deaths" and "sex scenes."[7]

Just as the theological and historical debates about *The Da Vinci Code* have not abated, so Mr. Perdue has not given up. He has filed an appeal and vowed to take his case to the Supreme Court. We interviewed Mr. Perdue to hear about his experience firsthand, and also to find out when and how he first got fascinated with the subject of the "secret" religious and historical themes that run counter to the orthodox version of history.

Lewis Perdue is a *New York Times* bestselling author of twenty books. Something of a polymath, he has taught college-level journalism courses; founded two technology firms, a publishing company, and a wine-importing firm; been a top political aide to a senator and a governor; and has written for the *Washington Post, Los Angeles Times, Nation, Washington Monthly, Forbes, Barron's,* CBS *Marketwatch,* and *Wall Street Journal Online,* among many more.

---

6. Ibid.

7. Ibid.

In your book Daughter of God, *the early Catholic Church doesn't just suppress female deities and women, it has a teenage female messiah murdered. Your modern-day heroine and her detective stumble across this secret, and a fierce and deadly struggle ensues between them and a splinter group from the church, as well as other villains, when they try to expose it.* The Da Vinci Legacy *also deals with the sacred feminine and other religious themes. When did you begin having an interest in these ancient stories about the feminine side of religion?*

I was born in Mississippi. I grew up in a culture that is filled with religion. It took me until my adolescence to recognize that religion, particularly as it was practiced in the South and around the world, was a great tool for oppression. The church said if you were a woman or a black, you were a second-class citizen. That was astonishing to me; I was very influenced by the feminist movement. Then, in college, I studied the origins of religion and the history of religion and found that God the Creator was viewed as female from the earliest prehistory and didn't really begin to be viewed as a male until four thousand to five thousand years ago. I did not only a lot of research but some writing in *Daughter of God* to explain why our vision of God changed from female to male.

For example, there are famous verses in the New Testament used to support women's inferiority—especially those in Timothy and the Corinthians. These are forgeries and not actually written by the apostle Paul. These were books that were added to support that particular viewpoint!

According to Bart Ehrman, author of *Lost Christianities,* and in my opinion the most objective biblical scholar alive today, I Timothy, 2:12–15, which states, among other things, that "I do not allow a woman to teach, nor to exercise authority over a man" is probably a fake.

Ehrman writes, "Most critical scholars think that I Timothy is pseudonymous: its vocabulary, writing style, theological modes of expression, and presupposed historical situation all differ significantly from what can be found in Paul's authentic letters."

Ehrman and most biblical scholars also believe the same holds true for I Corinthians 14:34–35, which seems to have been added to support the anti-woman sentiment penned by the forger who created I Timothy.

Your messiah figure is named Sophia; presumably after the Sophia that appears in the Gnostic gospels?

What I did in *Daughter of God* was create a view of Gnosticism which is really kind of my own. I imagined a school of Gnosticism built around a cult of a flesh-and-blood female messiah, named Sophia.

Actually, in the Gnostic texts, Sophia appears in only one of the codices whose Greek name is "Trimorphic Protennoia." It's a creation myth. In it, Sophia is the daughter of the Great Goddess and she is sent down to earth in a kind of Prometheus-type role. Not strictly that, but enlightening people.

The Trimorphic Protennoia is about ten pages long, out of five-hundred-some pages of alternative gospels that were found in 1945. So Sophia plays a relatively small role in the Gnostic gospels. You'd think from reading my stuff or Dan Brown's that Sophia dominates them, but she doesn't.

Now, in the Old Testament Sophia narrates the entire book of Proverbs. Since Sophia means wisdom in

Greek, and proverbs obviously are words of wisdom, it's really interesting to compare the Trimorphic Protennoia Sophia with the Sophia of the Proverbs, chapter 8, verse 22, where she says, "The Lord possessed me in the beginning of his way, before his works of old. I was set up from everlasting, from the beginning, or ever the earth was. When there were no depths, I was brought forth; when there were no fountains abounding with water."

By comparison, in the Trimorphic Protennoia she says, "It is I who am hidden within [radiant] waters. I am the one who gradually put forth the All by my Thought. It is I who am laden with the Voice. It is through me that Gnosis comes forth."

Clearly, here are some of the last pieces of the divine feminine that the gospel authors didn't edit out or revise away for the sake of dogma or orthodoxy.

From the way you talk about these issues, you clearly have studied them in great depth. What sources in particular have you found useful?

My research over the past twenty-five years encompasses several hundred books and thousands of articles. It includes multiple readings of the world's major sacred scriptures, among them the Christian Bible (including the Catholic Apocrypha), the Jewish Bible (Tanakh), the Quran, the Nag Hammadi Library, the Dead Sea Scrolls, the writings of the gurus of Sikhism, many Hindu scriptures, and more.

Although your main plot in the Daughter of God *deals with the church's role in the murder of the teenage female messiah in AD 325, one of your subplots concerns Hitler. In your novel he knows about the church's order to murder her and uses this to blackmail Pope Pius XII into silence about the Holocaust. Is there any historical evidence for this?*

No. However, there is a large amount of historical data that Pope Pius XII knew the Holocaust was taking place and did nothing to stop it. See, for example, *Hitler's Pope* by journalist and historian John Cornwell. The church is currently trying to rehabilitate Pope Pius XII, who was probably an anti-Semite and silently allowed the Holocaust to happen. Still, who knows what is in the Vatican secret archives?

On your website and in the suit brought against you by Random House, the publisher of The Da Vinci Code, *you have claimed there are major plot similarities between* Daughter of God *and* The Da Vinci Code. *Some of these, you say in the Random House lawsuit, include a slain collector of art who leaves behind a gold key, a relic named for the divine feminine, a heroine who is a symbol of the divine feminine, a complex secret container that holds clues that send the hero and heroine to a foreign country, and so on. When did you begin to feel that these were more than just similarities?*

The similarities you mention above are general titles that apply to lengthy strings of specific expressions and sequences. Generalities are not protectable, but specific expression is. I maintain that *The Da Vinci Code* duplicates my specific expression in most of *Daughter of God*'s and *The Da Vinci Legacy*'s key elements—even the mistakes. I said Leonardo wrote on parchment, but the great artist never did. He wrote on linen. *The Da Vinci Code* repeats that mistake. It's all there in my legal documents. But to answer your question, readers of my books began to send me emails commenting on the similarities, some of them even saying, "You've been plagiarized." I was in the process of finishing *Perfect Killer,* my new book, and I didn't pay too much attention because I happen to agree that different writers can pick up on the same themes and write perfectly good pieces.

I was not myself completely convinced that there was infringement until John Olsson, one of the world's top forensic linguists, showed me his analysis of the three books. He did this out of the goodness of his heart. I know this contradicts the holding of the federal judge about a lack of similarity, but people can make their own judgment about this professional analysis. It is on the Web for anyone to see [www.davincilegacy.com]. I still believe [my characters and his] were essentially the same people doing the same things with the same motivations.

The judge found all your copyright infringement claims to be unfounded, whether on plot, on characters, on themes, and even total concept and feel. Will this be the end of it, or do you intend to keep pursuing your claims?

We have filed an appeal. The judge didn't permit a jury trial, he didn't allow in our expert testimony; he refused to allow a trial on the facts. We will take it to the Supreme Court if necessary. We're not going to give up. It'd be the wrong signal to send to my kids. You don't run from a bully.

Why did the judge in his ruling compare Daughter of God *to* The Da Vinci Code *and not, as you had wanted him to, your earlier novel,* The Da Vinci Legacy, *to which he referred only in a footnote?*

I think his not dealing with *The Da Vinci Legacy* is another ground for appeal. We were very specific in our written and oral arguments that we had not abandoned our claims there. The court imposed a length limitation of forty pages on the documents we could submit, and there were so many infringements in *Daughter of God* that we couldn't include the rest from *The Da Vinci Legacy.*

And what is it about The Da Vinci Legacy *that makes you believe Dan Brown used it?*

There are a hundred or more similarities, too numerous to go into here. But I feel his characters were too close to mine. For example, in *The Da Vinci Legacy* a secret group called the Elect Brothers of St. Peter, with which Leonardo and many other famous people were associated, held a secret that would destroy the Catholic Church if revealed, which is that they are the bloodline of St. Peter. They hold St. Peter's bones and are essentially dedicated to the continuance of the bloodline. Also, they attempt to regain rightful control of the Vatican. The only difference here, as far as I'm concerned, is that in *The Da Vinci Code,* the Elect Brothers of St. Peter have been replaced by the Priory of Sion.

So how would you summarize your overall approach to writing about these complex and controversial issues in religion and society?

What's key to my writing about religion and society is how it has twisted scripture and dogma to fit political purposes. I have now done three books exploring these themes. It started with *The Da Vinci Legacy,* continued with *The Linz Testament,* and then *Daughter of God. Daughter of God* in particular tracks my fascination with the lost feminine and builds on the Catholic

Church's abuse of dogma and theology for its own purposes. All three books have the same theme and build on each other and, my lawsuit maintains, were borrowed inappropriately for *The Da Vinci Code.*

Postscript: In late 2005, news accounts emerged saying the authors of the 1980s historical potboiler *Holy Blood, Holy Grail* are also suing Dan Brown with similar claims. This is the book Sir Leigh Teabing lifts off the bookshelf at his château to back up his revelation that Jesus married Mary Magdalene, saying, "The authors made some dubious leaps of faith in their analysis, but their fundamental premise is sound." According to these reports, the authors now charge that Brown stole their idea that Christ's marriage to Mary Magdalene founded a royal dynasty. The trial is slated to begin in England in 2006.

French Confection

BY AMY BERNSTEIN

Amy Bernstein is an expert on French Renaissance poetry. For *Secrets of the Code,* she reviewed the recent French literature and public discussion about the debate over whether the Priory of Sion, the secretive organization that underlies so much of *The Da Vinci Code's* plot, is a real organization or a twentieth-century hoax. Her report follows.

Like a perfect *île flottante,* which upon tasting reveals itself to be mostly air, the Rennes-le-Château–Prieuré de Sion (Priory of Sion) story is a magnificent French confection of pseudo history built on a delicately thin substructure of truth. Many people have analyzed the set of facts and legends involved in this story. My conclusion from reviewing the most credible among them is that beginning in the 1950s, a small group of men with neo-chivalric, nationalist, and sometimes anti-Semitic leanings was able to perpetrate what is almost certainly a marvelously intricate hoax that still draws people in today.

The history of this hoax is better than any bestselling thriller. It is no surprise then, that *The Da Vinci Code*—set for the most part in present-day France—draws heavily from details of the Priory of Sion–Rennes-le-Château affair described in the 1982 bestseller *Holy Blood, Holy Grail.* By introducing murdered museum director Jacques Saunière in the first chapter of *The Da Vinci Code*—a character who shares the same surname as the central figure in the Rennes-le-Château enigma—Dan Brown picks up where the original tale leaves off. In doing so, he is just one more of the many in France and England who have made a cottage industry out of an obscure provincial drama that took place over a hundred years ago. Here are the basic outlines of the original Rennes-le-Château–Prieuré de Sion story.

In 1885, the abbé Bérenger Saunière, an educated young man from a local bourgeois family, became the parish priest of the church of Saint Mary Magdalene in Rennes-le-Château, an isolated town in the department of Aude in southwestern France, not far from Le Bezu, a local mountain peak (from which was undoubtedly derived the name of the judicial police chief, Bezu Fache, in *The Da Vinci Code*).

The year of Abbé Saunière's appointment as parish priest was also marked by national political elections, with candidates taking an obligatory position on whether France should return to a pro-Catholic monarchy or remain a republic with a constitutional separation of church and state. During the election period, Bérenger Saunière became embroiled in this debate, earning a reputation as a fiery preacher supporting the return to a pro-Catholic monarchy. As a result, he gained the protection of the Countess of Chambord (widow of the pretender to the throne of France), who is said to have given him 3,000 livres to renovate his church.

In the late 1880s, during the course of the renovation of his dilapidated church, Saunière is said to have discovered some coded parchments hidden in a hollow pillar supporting the church's altarpiece. Advised by his bishop, Félix-Arsène Billiard, Saunière reportedly brought the parchments to Paris to show them to experts. While in Paris, he is reported to have made the acquaintance of a circle of occultists and esoterics, among them Emma Calvé (with whom he supposedly had an affair). Upon his return from Paris, he suddenly—and for no apparent reason—gained access to large sums of money with which he financed a number of building projects. These included the renovation of his ancient parish church and the construction of a large house (the Villa Bethania) and a tower (the Tour Magdala) which he used as his study and library for his increasingly large collection of books. He was able to maintain a lavish living style, despite the meagerness of his priestly income. He is said to have conducted numerous nightly excavations in and around his church. It was rumored, but never proven, that he had found treasure hidden in various spots within the church precincts.

Eventually it came out that the abbé Saunière was selling mass indulgences by mail all over Europe, which offered a plausible explanation for his wealth. He was removed from his position as parish priest and prohibited from saying Mass, and later tried and convicted for trafficking in masses by the diocesan authorities in Carcassonne. He died on 22 January 1917, leaving his house and tower to Marie Dénardaud, his lifelong housekeeper and companion (and, some say, his mistress). Interest in the local legend of the buried treasure endured, however, and an article about it appeared in the newspaper daily, *La Dépêche du Midi,* in 1956.

Enter the Priory of Sion.

In that same year, in another part of France, a small group of friends formed a recreational club on 25 June 1956, in Annemasse, Haute-Savoie, which called itself the Priory of Sion—apparently after a nearby mountain, the Col du Mont Sion. It was disbanded the following year, but soon morphed into a second, politicized incarnation under the direction of Pierre Plantard. Drawing on the neo-chivalric, utopian, nationalist, and anti-Semitic principles of Paul Le Cour, who had exercised a major influence on Pierre Plantard in the 1930s and '40s, the Priory of Sion began publishing a periodical called *Circuit,* which appeared on and off during the 1950s and 1960s.

Plantard had a history of involvement since the 1930s with anti-Masonic and anti-Semitic nationalist organizations. He first attempted to establish an association called The French Union in 1937 "to engage in purifying and renewing France." This group was conceived in opposition to the leftist Popular Front government of Leon Blum, the first Jewish prime minister of France. In 1941 Plantard attempted to start another organization under the name of "French National Renewal," but was again denied official permission by French authorities. By this time, Plantard was already deeply involved with the Grand Order of the Alpha Galates. According to H. R. Kedward, professor of history at Sussex University, the Alpha Galates were part of "a fringe right-wing society with an emphasis on tradition, chivalry, Catholicism, spiritualism and what can only be called a kind of occult nationalism . . . one of the very many 'Occident' movements which pitted what they saw as authentic French history and culture against the 'Freemasonic and Jewish Orient' . . . They all flowered in the spring of Vichy (1940–41), began to lose momentum in 1942 and mostly lost all political significance in the declining years of 1943–44."

Plantard's shadowy activities with right-wing and nationalist organizations continued after the war up to the founding of the Priory. During all that time, he did not seem to have had any means of employment. He served four months in Fresnes prison in the early 1950s, convicted of fraud and embezzlement. In 1958, during the political crisis in France over the war for independence in Algeria, Plantard claims to have been a member of the Committees of Public Safety, using the pseudonym "Colonel Way."

At the beginning of the 1960s, Plantard launched a concerted effort to forge a trail of documentation to support his bogus claim of being a descendant of the Merovingian royal line, and to establish the bona fides and pedigree of the Priory of Sion. The story of Rennes-le-Château was little known at that time but it dovetailed conveniently with his own fictions, given the abbé Saunière's right-wing political leanings and his links with an occult circle in Paris. In fact, it served as a convenient point of departure for Plantard's fertile imagination.

During the 1960s, a number of fake documents were deposited at different times in the Bibliothèque Nationale in Paris by Pierre Plantard and his associates under various pseudonyms. The first set, composed in 1965 and fabricated by his accomplice, Philippe de Chérisey, included parchments supposedly found by Bérenger Saunière in Rennes-le Château, as well as other documents concerning the Priory of Sion and genealogical documents of the Merovingian kings. Members of the Priory of Sion were listed, including figures such as Leonardo da Vinci, Isaac Newton, and Jean Cocteau. The next part of the hoax was to spin and disseminate the fairy tale.

One of the authors whose services were enlisted to tell the fabulous story was named Gérard de Sède, who, it seems, was a willing pawn of the Priory. He published two books concerning the *dossiers secrets* and the tales of Rennes-le-Château: *L'Or de Rennes ou la vie insolite de Bérenger Saunière, curé de Rennes-le Château,* (René Juilliard, Paris, 1967), and in expanded form, *Le Trésor maudit* (Editions J'ai Lu, Paris, 1968). In his first book, de Sède reproduced the two coded parchments found by Bérenger Saunière, one of which was signed "PS," linking them to the Priory of Sion. As the journalist Jean-Luc Chaumeil later remarked, "The books of Gérard de Sède were, generally speaking, only the text, the basic tools of Pierre Plantard."

After these books were published, however, Plantard and de Sède had a fight over royalties from *L'Or de Rennes,* and Plantard and de Chérisey began to tell people quietly that the parchments had been faked. But the word leaked out very slowly. About this time, Robert Charroux participated in the filming of a documentary for ORTF (the French National Film Organization), and in 1972 published a book about Rennes-le-Château, entitled *Le Trésor de Rennes-le-Château,* which continued the fiction about the parchments. By 1973, however, Jean-Luc Chaumeil, the journalist who had become deeply involved with Pierre Plantard, wrote a story claiming that the secret dossiers were a hoax.

As interest in Rennes-le-Château deepened—replete with secret symbolic codes in the paintings of Poussin and Teniers and clues to the location of the Holy Grail—historians and journalists began to dispute other parts of the story as well. In 1974, René Descadeillas, a bona fide historian, began the debunking of the story of the treasure of Rennes-le-Château in a book entitled *Mythologie du trésor de Rennes, ou l'histoire véritable de l'abbé Saunière curé de Rennes le Château,* saying that Saunière had amassed his wealth through trafficking in mass indulgences. The following year, Gérard de Sède responded with *Le vrai dossier de l'énigme de Rennes: Réponse à M. Descadeillas,* in which he made the point that the cost of saying a mass was so little, and the time it took to say a mass so long, that the abbé Saunière could never have amassed much money, adding, "Descadeillas's fairytale of trafficking in masses, as we can see, is nothing more than the most fantastic nonsense."

A British film producer, Henry Lincoln, became interested in the Rennes-le-Château story and did a series of three documentaries for BBC-TV: *The Lost Treasure of Jerusalem* (1972), *The Priest, the Painter, and the Devil* (1974), and *The Shadow of the Templars* (1979). None of these dealt seriously with the possibility that the Priory of Sion documents were an elaborate hoax, even though by then, their authenticity was subject to widespread questioning as well as allegations of out-and-out fraud. As a result of the enormous interest engendered by the BBC programs, Henry Lincoln and two others involved in the documentaries (Michael Baigent and Richard Leigh) came out with their book, *Holy Blood, Holy Grail,* which discussed not only the mysteries surrounding Rennes-le-

Château, but also the claim that the Merovingian kings of France were the descendants of Jesus and Mary Magdalene. The book went on to become a bestseller, an enduring international sensation after it was first published in 1982 in England, and of course, one of Dan Brown's basic texts for developing the storyline of *The Da Vinci Code*. The British bestseller was translated and appeared in France as *L'énigme sacrée* (Editions Pygmalion, Gérard Watelet, Paris 1983).

Back in France during the late 1970s and '80s, the early debunkers of the authenticity of the parchments came out with their own clarifications on the subject. Jean-Luc Chaumeil, in *Le Trésor du Triangle d'Or* (A. Lefeuvre, Nice, 1979, p. 80), included de Chérisey's confession that his parchment forgeries were copied from an ancient text found in the *Dictionnaire d'archéologie chrétienne et de liturgie* (15 vols., ed. Fernand Cabrol, Paris, Letouzey et Ane, 1907–53). Similarly, Pierre Jarnac in his *Histoire du Trésor de Rennes-le Château* (Cabestany, 1985, pp. 268–69) includes a copy of a letter from de Chérisey from Liège, Belgium, dated 29 January 1974, confessing that he had indeed forged the parchments.

Long after the unmasking of the hoax, Gérard de Sède finally came out with his book, *Rennes-le-Château: Le dossier, les impostures, les phantasmes, les hypothèses* (Les Enigmes de l'univers, Robert Laffont, 1988), in which he essentially admitted that the dossiers were forged and that the Merovingian line does not exist today. In 1997, BBC-TV also produced another program admitting that the story was not true. But the myth lives on, mostly because people want it to; and the list of French books on Rennes-le-Château and related subjects—not to mention the burgeoning bookshelf and Internet world of English-language commentaries—continues to grow. Back in

1974, René Descadeillas summed it up well, when he commented in his above-mentioned book as follows:[1]

> The legend of the treasure of Rennes derives—no more and no less—from something that happened one day, in this poor, half-ruined village, to a priest whose calling was not very much in line with his natural inclinations.
>
> And so, because of all this, we've been regaled in turn with the treasure of Queen Blanche of Spain, of the Cathars, of the Temple and of Dagobert, all jumbled up with the secret archives of goodness knows how many different sects. After assembling and confusing all these different treasures, people then ask us to believe that the soil of Rennes hides the evidence of a conspiracy aimed at regenerating the government and the political life of France! Countless men and women have visited Rennes. Some have even brought expensive equipment with them. . . . They've torn tiles off walls, sounded out rocks with electronic probes, dug holes in the streets and squares, and excavated tunnels.
>
> The church has been turned inside out no fewer than four times and the cemetery has been desecrated. Graves have been opened, corpses have been exhumed. Reams and reams of paper have been covered in scribbles. Newspapers and magazines have been inundated, tracts and leaflets printed, two films made and three books written. . . . Hordes of journalists have gathered—from France, England, Germany, Belgium, Switzerland and elsewhere. . . . People have gone all the way back to Benjamin, the Jews and the Scriptures, passing by Titus and Dagobert, the sack of Rome, the Visigoths and Blanche of Castile on

1. Translation from Paul Smith's *Priory of Sion Archives,* priory-of-sion.com/psp/id129.html.

the way to Peter the Cruel, Nicolas Poussin and Superintendant Fouquet. They've tried to drag in emperors, kings, archdukes, princes, archbishops, the Grandmasters of every conceivable Order, magi and alchemists, philosophers, historians, magistrates, and humble monks and priests. . . . They've brought into existence people whose existence is far from certain and have given birth to others who never existed in the first place. They've touted magicians, paraded mediums in front of us, conjured up spirits and interrogated clairvoyants. They've fabricated books of magic spells, family trees and wills, and have uncovered illegitimacies, murders and assassinations. They've lied to the point of absurdity and have even—surely the ultimate in ridiculousness—invoked the name of the Devil!

And what for may we ask? For absolutely and precisely nothing!

Paris

In the Footsteps of The Da Vinci Code

BY DAVID DOWNIE

David Downie is a Paris-based freelance writer, editor, and translator. His latest book is *Paris, Paris: Journey into the City of Light.* In this piece, he takes readers on a quick tour of Paris landmarks, symbols, and signposts that have attracted new tourist interest since the publication of *The Da Vinci Code.*

This article originally appeared in the *San Francisco Chronicle,* January 25, 2004.

What do Place Vendôme, the *Mona Lisa,* astronomer Louis Arago and a medieval bishop named Sulpicius have in common? Simple: *The Da Vinci Code,* Dan Brown's breathless, five-hundred-page quest for the Holy Grail, set primarily in Paris.

The thriller's hero, professor Robert Langdon, is a Harvard "symbologist" lucky enough to be lodging at the $1,000-a-night Ritz on elegant Place Vendôme when foul play begins nearby at the Louvre. The museum's director, the Grand Master of a secret society charged with protecting the Grail, is murdered thirty yards from Leonardo da Vinci's enigmatic *Mona Lisa,* one of the tale's keys. An invisible north-south line bisects the Louvre and a church south of the Seine, Saint-Sulpice. The line is the Paris Meridian, first plotted in 1718, then recalculated with precision in the early 1800s by Arago. It predates the Greenwich Meridian and since 1994 has been marked with 135 brass disks.

Other sights scattered around the book's somewhat surreal Paris cityscape include the Palais-Royal, Champs-Elysées, Tuileries Garden, Bois de Boulogne parklands and Gare Saint-Lazare train station.

But it's the blood-soaked Louvre and looming Saint-Sulpice, and the treasure hunt for brass "Arago" disks, that are currently attracting squadrons of Grail seekers, many of whom travel with dog-eared copies of *The Da Vinci Code.*

Until 1645, a Romanesque church and graveyard stood where the imposing, colonnaded pile of Saint-Sulpice rises today, between the Left Bank's Luxembourg Garden and Boulevard Saint-Michel. . . . Long known for its towering 6,588-pipe organ, and Eugène Delacroix's gloomy *Jacob Fighting an Angel,* Saint-Sulpice has roughly the same footprint (360 feet long by 184 wide and 108 tall) as

Notre Dame cathedral. Grail pilgrims now flock here to admire the astronomical gnomon that features prominently in the book. Its significance is twofold, revealing the location of a secret keystone and introducing readers to the Paris Meridian. The author dubs the meridian a "rose line." Apparently roses are symbolic of the Grail and therefore of Mary Magdalene.

Designed to calculate the spring equinox (and from it, Easter), the gnomon's brass strip crosses the transept's floor, then climbs a stone obelisk along the north-south axis. At noon the sun's rays passing through an oculus on the transept's south wall focus on the strip, giving the solar calendar date. Easter (a movable feast with pre-Christian roots) falls on the first Sunday after the equinox, so the gnomon accurately establishes the holiday's date.

In Brown's bestseller, a murderous albino monk named Silas breaks the tiles at the obelisk's base while searching for the keystone, then batters to death a nun assigned to protect it. On a recent visit to the site, Grail pilgrims could be seen prostrate, rapping the floor in front of the obelisk. Others listened to church guides explaining how the gnomon works, or searched for the luckless nun's upstairs rooms.

In reality, the Paris Meridian passes nearby but does not actually correspond to the gnomon's axis. No mention is made in the book of Sulpicius' tomb in the provincial French city of Bourges, which the meridian does traverse.

Church sacristan Paul Roumanet discounts Brown's claim that a temple of Isis lies beneath the sanctuary. On a Sunday afternoon tour of the crypt, attended by a clutch of thriller readers, no ancient temple could be discerned, though Romanesque walls and columns remain.

However, conspiracy theorists may be pleased to learn

that a subcrypt containing five tombs is off-limits to the public. Further, according to the *Guide de Paris Mystérieux,* it was in the Romanesque church's graveyard that in 1619 three witches attempted to evoke the devil, and for many years, local residents held "macabre dances" on the toppled tombstones.

The brass Arago disks are a work of installation art titled *Hommage à Arago,* by Dutchman Jan Dibbets. Following an imaginary meridian, they lead north from No. 28 Rue de Vaugirard (near Saint-Sulpice) to Boulevard Saint-Germain, Rue de Seine, Quai Conti and Port des Saints-Pères. Across the river at the Louvre, three disks traverse the museum's Denon Wing (in the Roman Antiquities section, on a staircase and in a corridor). Five others stipple the Cour Carrée behind the main glass pyramid designed by I. M. Pei at the behest of former French president François Mitterrand.

(Warning! If you haven't read *The Da Vinci Code* yet, you might want to stop here. What follows gives away some key plot points.)

In the book's epilogue, Professor Langdon feels the Arago disks pull him south across the Palais Royal into the Passage Richelieu, eventually converging on the pyramid (which, Brown says, has 666 glass panes, a number symbolic of Satan). It's here that the "rose line" turns due west and runs through the Louvre's subterranean Carrousel shopping concourse to an "inverted pyramid" hanging from the ceiling.

In the protagonist's mind, this upside-down pyramid is a metaphorical chalice or grail, symbolizing the "sacred feminine," first venerated here in the Earth goddess rites of antiquity. On the floor beneath the skylight stands a small stone pyramid, symbolic of a blade or phallus. The tips of the pyramids point at each other, hinting that underneath a hidden vault might just contain chests of ancient documents, and the tomb of Mary Magdalene—the Holy Grail.

Ninety percent of the Louvre's annual 6 million visitors make a beeline for the Mona Lisa, making it difficult to spot Grail pilgrims looking for bloodstains or messages near the celebrated painting. But the many budding "symbologists" counting panes in Mitterrand's pyramid, or genuflecting by the inverted skylight, do attract attention.

Were it not for the author's claim that "all descriptions of artwork [and] architecture . . . in this novel are accurate," it might be unsporting to reveal that the number 666 can't be divided evenly into four sides of a pyramid. Similarly, pagans never danced around the Carrousel, and there is no chamber beneath the phallus. The miraculous "rose line" capable of a 90-degree turn is none other than the so-called "Triumphal Way," a perspective laid out in 1670 by Louis XIV's royal landscaper Le Nôtre.

However, there may yet be material in Paris for a Grail sequel. The Triumphal Way runs past an ancient Egyptian obelisk in the Place de la Concorde, and Mitterrand might well have belonged to a secret society or two. Who knows what the symbologists will discover when the Louvre's subterranean concourse is remodeled in 2007 to further speed access to museum shops and the *Mona Lisa?*

Cracking *The Da Vinci Code* at the Louvre

By Elizabeth Bard

Elizabeth Bard is a journalist, art historian, and an expert guide for Paris Muse, a group of Paris-based art historians offering private tours in the city's museums. Since they began offering their "Cracking *The Da Vinci Code* at the Louvre" tour in February 2004, Bard and her colleagues have led more than a thousand visitors in the footsteps of the novel.

"Is this where that curator's body was found?"

"I read that there are heretical codes and messages in Leonardo's paintings. Is that true?"

Although our company, Paris Muse, had been leading private tours in the Louvre for some time, in the spring of 2003 we began to hear these same curious questions over and over again. There was clearly a new "buzz" at the museum, but we were puzzled by the source. Then one of our guides picked up a copy of *The Da Vinci Code* in the airport on the way back to France after summer vacation. Now that we understood where the questions were coming from, we could begin to develop the answers. We also had a great idea for a new Paris Muse tour: "Cracking *The Da Vinci Code*™ at the Louvre."

As art historians, we wanted to give our clients more than a glorified plot summary. For us, the Louvre is much more than a chance to walk in the footsteps of the novel. As a group, we've spent hundreds of hours exploring its labyrinth of galleries, and the treasures within.

We decided to develop a tour that would explore the Louvre's collections through the lens of the novel's themes. Beyond the obvious choices of the plot-related paintings by Leonardo da Vinci (several of whose most famous works are in the Louvre's collection), we chose works of art that would help us explore the controversial questions raised by novelist Dan Brown. How did ancient peoples worship the sacred feminine? Did Christianity entirely obliterate these practices? How do signs and symbols evolve over time? Did Christianity really "steal" things from pre-Christian traditions? What do images of Mary Magdalene tell us about her changing role and her relationship with Jesus? Are there subversive "clues" buried in Leonardo's paintings? We realized that not only could we answer the questions people were already asking—we could expand the discussion, allowing the works of art themselves to have a say in the debate.

"Cracking '*The Da Vinci Code*' at the Louvre" immediately became Paris Muse's most requested tour. Part of its appeal for our visitors is that it offers a fun and focused way to navigate what can be an overwhelming museum. Some of them are excited to see the actual locations described in the book. For many, the story has sparked new ways of thinking about art and religion; they come to see for themselves if they are convinced by Dan Brown's theories.

We first meet our visitors under Napoleon's Arc du Carrousel, just outside the museum. It's a fitting place to begin, since Napoleon's famous quip—"What is history, but a fable agreed upon"—is one of the book's most memorable lines. It also says a lot about Paris Muse's approach. We get up close to the Louvre's collections and find out how one work of art can tell many different stories, depending on who's doing the telling, and when!

The Sacred Feminine

Our first stop inside the Louvre is the collection of terracotta sculptures from ancient Greece. Perhaps the nicest part of taking a wider view of the book is that we can get off the main tourist track. We often have these galleries, with their great view of the Cour Carré, the Louvre's central courtyard, all to ourselves!

Many of the figurines displayed here are *kourotrophos,* dating from the fourth to sixth centuries BC. Kourotrophos are commemorative statues that worshippers would have brought to the temples as offerings, a parallel to the practice of lighting a votive candle in church. They give our visitors a more concrete idea of what the "sacred feminine" might look like in the history of art.

Some of these female figures depict draped mothers holding their babies on their laps—an image that bears a striking resemblance to later Christian images of the Madonna and Child. But these particular sculptures were used to worship the primary goddesses of ancient Greece: Venus, the goddess of love and beauty, Demeter, the goddess of agriculture, and Athena, the goddess of wisdom. These goddesses express many of the basic needs of ancient women—to bear healthy children, have plentiful harvests, and make wise decisions. The figure of the mother and child will follow us throughout the history of art—from the ancient Egyptian goddess Isis with her son Horus, to the tender paintings of mothers and children by the late-ninteenth-century American painter Mary Cassatt.

The *Bell Idol* (700 BC) from Thebes is one of the most captivating sculptures in these galleries. She is in the form of a woman, but she also has an elongated neck, hollow center, and dangling legs that recall a bell. Because her body also emulates the shape of an inverted chalice, visitors see a very early example of one of the central metaphors in Brown's book: the idea of the woman's body [i.e., Mary Magdalene] as a sacred vessel. Just like our *Bell Idol,* this is a metaphor with legs. It has followed us all the way from ancient Greece to the *New York Times* bestseller list!

We also look closely at how the *Bell Idol* was decorated by its anonymous artist. There are dancing women painted on her skirt, and holes in her ears where gold earrings once hung. She also has a geometric motif on her neck that, because of its misleading similarity to the Nazi swastika, people are often shocked to find on a sculpture made over 2,700 years ago. Tracing this symbol's complex history is a great opportunity to talk about Robert Langdon's fictional job description—professor of symbology at Harvard University. Although academics might not use that term, Brown has picked up on a key tool of art historians. We call it iconography, the study of signs and symbols and how they develop over time.

Cultural Recycling: Paganism and Early Christianity

The second part of the tour takes us downstairs to the Louvre's Roman sculpture collection, housed in what were once the sumptuous summer apartments of Anne of Austria, mother of Louis XIV. Here we begin looking at art of the early Christian period (first to fourth century AD) to see if we can identify exchanges between early Christianity and pagan religions.

"Nothing in Christianity is original." This controversial claim of Teabing's is the starting point for our discussion here. Visitors learn that there are indeed elements of pagan religion—symbols, rituals, even dates—that are shared with Christianity as it develops from an upstart religion in the first century AD to the official religion of the Roman Empire under Constantine in the fourth century AD.

A double-sided Mithraic relief (second to third century AD) is a particularly striking illustration of a complex process *The Da Vinci Code* calls "transmogrification," a fancy word for cultural recycling. The sculpture was made for followers of the Mithraic cult, a religion that developed alongside Christianity. The cult of Mithras was adapted from an ancient Persian religion, based on a Supreme Being. It spread to Rome and even as far away as Britain, since it was popular with military men who brought their beliefs with them as they traveled through the empire.

This particular relief depicting Mithras was found in Rome; it tells us quite a bit about the Mithraic cult's mythology and rituals. On one side, the central deity Mithras is shown sacrificing a sacred bull, whose blood gives eternal life. Beneath Mithras a dog, symbol of goodness, and a serpent, symbol of evil, vie to drink the blood. The narrative is not unlike the story in Genesis, where good and evil (also represented by the serpent) battle for eternal life.

Mithras also has quite a lot in common with the figure of Jesus. They are both referred to in their own traditions as the Son of God and Light of the World. They are both born on December 25. As the approximate date of the winter solstice, this was an important festival for many pagan religions, and was likely adopted by early Christians because no birth date for Jesus is specified in the New Testament. Both Mithras and Jesus are said to have died and been resurrected after three days.

On the other side of the relief, we see the figure of the Supreme Being presiding over scenes of worship. He has the rays of the sun around his head, which recall the halo we see in Christian art to identify holy figures. Throughout the history of art, one culture or tradition will make use of existing signs and symbols, adding their own layer of meaning.

This side of the panel also shows us two figures of Mithras, one accepting symbolic nourishment from the Supreme Being, the other preparing a ritual sacrifice. Because the Mithraic cult was an all-male religion, it was kind of like an American college fraternity—you had to go through initiation rites to prove that you were man enough to belong. The relief illustrates two of those rites: drinking the blood of a sacrificed animal and the symbolic eating of the body of the Supreme Being.

Of course, these rituals immediately recall for visitors the Christian practice of Holy Communion. This is not to say that early Christianity "stole" the idea of communion from the Mithraic cult. Rather, the point we encourage visitors to consider is that there were elements of god-eating rituals in many religions of this period. In fact, many rituals and symbols we think of today as exclusively Christian have roots in earlier religious traditions.

The Mithraic relief is a highlight for many visitors interested in the idea of religion as a constantly evolving process, rather than a fixed group of texts or rituals set in stone.

Leonardo in the Louvre

Stepping into the Grande Galerie is often the moment when the events of the book snap back into focus for our visitors. This is where Jacques Saunière, the fictional cura-

Paris Muse FAQs

Where's that famous bathroom in the Louvre where Robert Langdon and Sophie Neveu huddle to plot their escape?

There are actually two bathrooms along the length of the Grande Galerie, one in the middle (off in a hallway) and one at the far end. Unfortunately, neither of them has access to the exterior of the building for Sophie to break the window and throw out the security tag embedded in the bar of soap. No actual bars of soap either—just those plastic liquid soap dispensers.

Are there containment gates inside the Grande Galerie?

The end of Grande Galerie is a high wooden doorway—no gate in sight. But the new Salle des États where the *Mona Lisa* is displayed, which opened in April 2005, has what look like metal doors that could seal off the room in the event of a fire.

Is Leonardo's Last Supper *at the Louvre?*

If only! It would be wonderful to be able to view all of the major works discussed in the book under one roof. But *The Last Supper* is in Santa Maria della Grazie in

(*continues*)

tor, is murdered, and where Robert and Sophie find their clues tucked away behind Leonardo's paintings. While we do point out these plot points, we also tell visitors a bit about the rich history of the building, before it became the backdrop of a bestselling novel and Hollywood film.

This imposing gallery was the grand entertainment space of the French kings when the Louvre was a royal palace, and it was the first part of the building to open to

Paris Muse FAQs (*continued*)

Milan. Our solution is to carry around a color reproduction, so we can answer questions about Dan Brown's hypotheses and how they differ from traditional art historical interpretations. We use visitors' observations about paintings by Leonardo in the Louvre to help them judge Brown's theories about *The Last Supper.*

What about the book's ending at the inverted pyramid? Does that really exist?

The inverted glass pyramid, where the book ends, is just outside the corridor of the Louvre's gift shops, at the entrance to the commercial shopping mall (look for the Virgin Megastore). Brown suggests the smaller marble pyramid is in fact the top of a burial chamber where future generations may find the Holy Grail. A provocative proposal, though the smaller pyramid seems to rest firmly on the floor. I guess we will have to wait for the Louvre's next big construction project to find out for sure. . . .

—ELIZABETH BARD

the public when the palace became a museum in 1793. Today, this fifteen-hundred-foot hall is the nerve center of the Louvre, home to the Italian Renaissance collection, including five paintings by Leonardo.

The Grande Galerie is also the busiest part of the museum. A typical weekday afternoon can look like rush hour at Grand Central Station, so part of our challenge here is to carve out a contemplative experience for our visitors. The Louvre is rapidly approaching eight million visitors a year, and 90 percent of them pass through the Grande Galerie on their hurried trek to the *Mona Lisa*.

We let the crowds sprint by us, stopping to take in works by lesser-known artists. We also look closely at all of the other Leonardo paintings in the collection, so by the time we get to the *Mona Lisa,* visitors know enough about his style to approach his most famous work with confidence.

The *Mona Lisa*'s knowing smile presents a direct challenge to the viewer—and to us as guides. How do you intelligently "explain" the world's most talked-about work of art? As we try to do with all of the works on our tour, we engage the visitor's own observations in front of this painting. We ask them what they think. As *The Da Vinci Code* makes clear, there are many competing interpretations to negotiate. We try to separate fact from fiction, art history from popular legend.

The *Mona Lisa* is usually dated between 1503 and 1506, though there are scholars that believe Leonardo may have continued to work on it as late as 1513 or 1514. One thing is sure—the sitter never received her painting. Leonardo kept it with him until the end of his life. After his death, the painting passed into the French royal collection, which became the national collection after the French Revolution of 1789.

Dan Brown gives us a quick summary of the different theories about the *Mona Lisa* during a fictional art history class that Robert Langdon teaches at a Boston prison. One racy option, according to Langdon, is that *Mona Lisa* is a self-portrait of Leonardo in drag. In 1910 Sigmund Freud wrote an article suggesting that Leonardo was homosexual. This fuelled speculation that some of Leonardo's drawings, once thought to be self-portraits, may have been studies for the *Mona Lisa*. There are even scientists who have done computer morphing to match the bone structure and facial features of these drawings with that of the *Mona Lisa!* In fact, we have no firmly established likeness of Leonardo in his own hand—although art historians continue to argue this point, so the self-portrait theory of the *Mona Lisa,* as appealing as it may be, doesn't hold a lot of water.

Dan Brown adds his own bit of speculation to the search for her identity. He doesn't think she is a real woman at all, but rather a combination of the ideal masculine and the ideal feminine—"Mona Lisa" becomes an anagram for Amon and Isis, the Egyptian fertility gods. As other *Da Vinci Code* commentators have pointed out, this, too, is implausible, since the painting was not known as the "Mona Lisa" in Leonardo's lifetime, nor is it known as the "Mona Lisa" in French or Italian today.

Once again, we ask visitors to consider this theory against the likeness they see in front of them. We also let them know that Leonardo scholars have identified the sitter as Lisa Gherardini, wife of the wealthy Florentine silk merchant Francesco del Giocondo. The "Mona" of the painting's title—adopted only in the nineteenth century and therefore not Leonardo's choice—is actually short for "Madonna" ("Madame" or "Mrs." in Italian). Her famous smile may also be a nod to her married name. "Giocondo" means "joyful" or "jovial" in Italian; an increasing number of scholars think that her smile may be a pun on her last name. That's why the French call her La Jaconde—the smiling one!

Drag queen or Florentine matron, in the end what really matters is what resonates with what we can actually see. Visitors enjoy testing out Brown's theory of an uneven horizon line in the background of the painting. We test to see whether or not it makes *Mona Lisa* "look more majestic from the left," as Brown says, favoring the side of the painting historically associated with the feminine. The two halves of the landscape do tend to strike visitors as uneven. But if you look carefully, the horizon line actually runs straight across the upper reaches of the painting, near her eye level. Leonardo is always leading us toward her face, particularly her expressive eyes—"the window of the soul." The background itself is an idealized fantasy, a mixture of actual Florentine landscapes, allegorical symbols, and Leonardo's lifelong obsession with botanical and topographical drawing. This mixture of the specific and the universal tells us something very important about the way that Leonardo worked. He was always searching for the ideal through the real.

Mary Magdalene: The Harlot and the Hermit

After the crush of crowds in front of the *Mona Lisa,* it's a relief to escape downstairs to the ground floor, into the cool and echoing hallways of what used to be Napoleon III's stables. We look at several paintings of Mary Magdalene on the tour. Some suggest a prostitute, others a pious disciple; there is even one where she has what could be argued as a look of wifely devotion.

In fact, we end not with a painting, but with a sculpture of Mary Magdalene. But unlike the typical image of the "scarlet harlot" that we see in so many of the late medieval and early Renaissance paintings upstairs, here we find a beautiful and very secular-looking nude with long flowing blond hair and a serene expression. She looks more like Botticelli's Venus rising out of the sea than the lamenting woman often depicted at the foot of the cross.

This sculpture takes us out of Italy and into the early German Renaissance, around 1515. The sculptor, Gregor Erhart, worked in and around Augsburg. His Mary Magdalene has been carved out of a single piece of wood and delicately painted.

When we see Mary Magdalene like this, wearing her hair and nothing else, it illustrates legends about her life as a hermit, which pick up where the Bible leaves off. The legend tells us that Mary fled Jerusalem after the crucifixion. She sailed across the Mediterranean Sea in a rudderless boat, landing on the southern coast of France. From there, she went to the caves at St. Baume where she lived for thirty years as a hermit, doing penitence for her sins. She survived without food, water or clothing—just a choir of heavenly angels to lift her up to Christ during her prayers. In fact, this sculpture was originally meant to be hung from the ceiling. She would have been surrounded by a group of sculpted angels to show us the moment when Mary Magdalene ascends to Christ through her prayers.

We close our tour with this exquisite German sculpture because it highlights the main ideas that visitors take home after looking at many images of Mary Magdalene in the Louvre: the understanding of her role in Christianity has evolved, and will continue to do so. Whether or not we believe Brown's theory that Mary Magdalene was the *literal* wife of Jesus, in Western art she has definitely represented both a spiritual and a more worldly love for Jesus. We see how beautiful her nude body is here, and are reminded that sensuality is very much of this earth. But her peaceful gaze is meant to convey a higher, more spiritual type of beauty.

One thing is certain: anyone who thinks that Goddess worship is dead in Christianity has never seen this!

11 Sophie's Library

Welcome to Sophie's Library, housing one of the world's great virtual collections of specialized knowledge relating to *The Da Vinci Code.* We can imagine several types of surroundings. It could be reminiscent of the old-world library created by Sir Leigh Teabing at his seventeenth-century Château Villette. Or something more contemporary, such as the Louis Kahn–designed library on the campus of Phillips Exeter Academy, Dan Brown's alma mater, with its more than 140,000 books and symbolic architectural motifs hinting at the Vitruvian Man and some of the Masonic symbols of *The Da Vinci Code.*

Today we will visit but two of its many rooms. (For others, see www.SecretsOfTheCode.com) We first visit the reading room, with its large collection of news clippings that reflect the impact *The Da Vinci Code* has had on our public life in ways both large and small. Here we find the factoids, the ephemera, the numbers, and the other evidence of attempts—from the halls of Congress to the kitchen of a bakery—to hitch a wagon to this cultural comet.

Then we find our way to the Shugarts Archive, with its storehouse of knowledge relating to nearly each and every physical, fact-based plot point in the novel—at least those presented as such. Plot flaws? You mean there are plot flaws and inaccuracies in the novel that's supposed to be based on facts? Yes, but like everything else in

The Da Vinci Code, even its plot flaws and erroneous facts are interesting—and, in many cases, debatable.

Leaving our virtual library, it's time to go home, find a comfortable chair and open *The Da Vinci Code* once more—maybe just to reread that part about the Louvre's artworks. Or the eye-opening trip to England. Or follow once again the arcane clues that lead to the evidence of the holy bloodline. Well, maybe we had better start at the very beginning again. Let's see, "Renowned curator Jacques Saunière staggered through the vaulted archway . . ."

Hidden in Plain Sight

The Da Vinci Code *Effect*

By Arne de Keijzer

The Da Vinci besteCode has taken the publishing world by storm. At last count, the novel has sold more than forty million copies and has been translated into forty-four languages. It has spent some 137 weeks atop the *New York Times* bestseller list and continues to be a bestseller worldwide. And now comes the film, likely to be one of the highest-grossing movies in history. Numbers do not tell the whole story, however. The fact is that *The Da Vinci Code* is not just a book, but a worldwide cultural phenomenon. It has penetrated every seam of our culture. In ways large and small, significant and petty, the book has set off a national dialogue about the great themes of history and religion. It has also set off a rush to cash in.

A gaggle of experts undoubtedly could shed some light on the phenomenon—and they have done so throughout this book. Still, sometimes it is the brief impression, the little snippet of information, the random piece of ephemera, the intriguing quote that floats by that will give us the clear insight. Here, in a series of bite-sized portions, are what could be called the "leading indicators" of *The Da Vinci Code* effect.

Clues to the Codex: Playing the Numbers

1 Rank of the book among the fastest-selling adult novels of all time.

$1 billion Estimated size of the *Da Vinci* industry, including Dan Brown's earnings as well as all the books, movies, CDs, documentaries, and other spin-off products that have followed in the novel's wake.

$5 million Dan Brown's reported initial pay package for the movie rights to *The Da Vinci Code.*

$40 million Tom Hanks's reported pay package for *The Da Vinci Code* movie.

22% The number of people who believe the book is proof of "anti-Catholic" prejudice, according to an MSNBC poll conducted after the network broadcast a report about Cardinal Bertone's campaign to ban *The Da Vinci Code.*

112 The population of the hamlet of Rennes-le-Château.

$20 million The amount of money the town fathers of Rennes-le-Château say was pumped into the village by tourists in 2004 because of its ties to *The Da Vinci Code* story.

$175,000 The amount of money the producers of *The Da Vinci Code* movie were willing to pay Lincoln Cathedral after the Westminster Cathedral, the actual location for an important scene in the novel, refused permission for filming there.

$2.2 million The amount Dan Brown and his brother and sister donated to Phillips Exeter Academy in honor of their father, Richard Brown, who taught mathematics at the school for thirty-five years.

1950 The year in which "Mona Lisa," a ballad sung by Nat King Cole in tribute to the painting, reached number one on the hit parade and went on to sell three million copies.

$2 Admission paid by fans of the book who wanted to catch a wax-figure display of *The Last Supper* at a mall in Port Charlotte, Florida.

22–24 The number of paintings Leonardo is said to have completed during his lifetime.

15 × 29 The size, in feet, of *The Last Supper* fresco.

$47 The per-person cost of a two-hour discussion on *The Da Vinci Code* over tea at the Hotel Ritz in Paris.

$55,000 The cost of a weeklong *Da Vinci Code* tour with lodging at the fifteen-bedroom, 240-acre seventeenth-century Château de Villette (breakfast included). Owned by San Francisco super real estate agent Olivia Hsu Decker, she rewards favored clients like Sharon Stone and Andre Agassi with weekends at her pied-à-terre.

187 The number of men to avoid, in a book of humorous one-liners (e.g., "Men who stir-fry") written by Dan Brown under the pen name Danielle Brown in 1993.

976-LOVE Title of a song by Dan Brown about paid phone sex, written in the late 1980s, a time when he was striving to become a singer-songwriter.

127 The number of pages produced by Opus Dei

on its U.S. website and related links as its response to *The Da Vinci Code* as the result of being depicted as an extremist cult.

$3.6 million The salary given up by Ricky Williams, star Miami Dolphins running back, when he decided to take a leave from his team. "I thought, 'Oh my gosh, he got injured,'" said his agent Leigh Steinberg, "but, no, he wanted to talk about *The Da Vinci Code*."

16% The percentage of Canadians who are estimated to have read the book.

33% The percentage of Canadians who have read the book and believe there are descendants of Jesus alive today and a secret society exists dedicated to keeping Jesus's bloodline a secret.

1993 The year Dan Brown read Sidney Sheldon's pulp novel *Doomsday Conspiracy* and said, "I can do that."

12 Ranking of Dan Brown in *Forbes* magazine list of the "most powerful celebrities" in 2004.

213 The number of cubes in the stone ceiling of Rosslyn Chapel holding mystical symbols "of great spiritual significance" that revealed a coded six-minute piece of music for thirteen medieval players.

4516 The Hollywood Boulevard address of the Ecclesia Gnostica center, home of the Gnostic movement in the United States for twenty-seven years.

2005 The year in which Mr. and Mrs. Oliver Lawn, formerly of Her Majesty's World War II code-breaking squad, deciphered an inscription on the Shepherd's Monument in Shugborough, England, long thought to contain a definitive clue to the location of the Holy Grail. The code decoded: "Jesus (As Deity) Defy." He says, "It's connected with the Priory of Sion." She says, "No, it has nothing to do with Jesus, it's a love poem."

120 The number of photographs based on documents and paintings by Leonardo gathered with the aim of "reassessing and disclaiming" *The Da Vinci Code* at a mock trial in Vinci, the artist's hometown.

35% The average number of acceptances to the University of Virginia for the class of 2008 from among those who applied.

67% The average number of acceptances to the University of Virginia among those who wrote about Vladimir Nabokov on their application essays.

24% The average number of acceptances to the University of Virginia of those who wrote about *The Da Vinci Code.* "Several of the admission staffers were mad because they were reading the book and didn't want the plot spoiled," said the senior dean of admissions.

5.4 million The number of "hits" on Google for a search on *The Da Vinci Code.*

Why Has *The Da Vinci Code* Achieved Such Runaway Success? And What's Wrong with Society that Allowed It to Happen?

I really got the sense that people were ready for this story. It was the type of thing that people were just ready to hear.

—Dan Brown, in a 2003 interview

The idea of the "Sacred Union" of Christ and Mary Magdalene at the heart of Christianity apparently resonates at a very deep level. At this point of crisis in the Roman Catholic Church, it is clear to many that the institution has a fundamental flaw—the dissociation of its doctrines and hierarchy from the Feminine.

—MARGARET STARBIRD,
author of *Magdalene's Lost Legacy*

The answers "range from the moral bankruptcy of public life in the developed world and its concomitant preoccupation with conspiracy theories as a search for meaning beneath sordid reality, to the appeal to women of a book that strips Christianity deliciously naked of patriarchal clothing and the gathering evidence that popular culture plays (at times) a big role in shaping theology."

—MICHAEL VALPY,
senior writer for Toronto's *Globe & Mail*

What's so special exactly? That depends on what makes conspiracy theories so fascinating . . . [and] what makes for outstanding conspiracy? Many fascinating historical and quasi-historical tidbits. . . . Above all, a worthwhile conspiracy needs to explain something that previously . . . didn't need explaining, something also that links to a truth, or at least a pseudotruth, of deep significance . . . [and] the revelation of concealed complexity all around. If the book's popularity means people are thinking about invisible realities, that's good news.

—DAVID KLINGHOFFER,
columnist for the *Jewish Forward*

We are supposed to live in a skeptical age. In fact, we live in an age of outrageous credulity. The "death of God" or at least the dying of the Christian God, has been accompanied by the birth of a plethora of new idols. They have multiplied like bacteria on the corpse of the Christian Church—from strange pagan cults and sects to the silly, Christian superstitions of The Da Vinci Code. *It is amazing how many people take that book literally, and think it is true.*

—UMBERTO ECO, author of *Foucault's Pendulum,* a book that has been described as "the thinking man's *Da Vinci Code*"

Literary critics have a technical term for novels like this: enjoyable crap. Yet anybody with an interest in the culture of our age should read The Da Vinci Code, *a book that is genuinely remarkable, less for what is in it than for what so many readers have chosen to take out of it. No novel of modern times says so much about the strange, paranoid, conspiracy-worshipping age we live in.*

—BEN MACINTYRE, novelist

In the United States, East Coast liberals are reading The Da Vinci Code *while the conservative evangelicals are reading the eschatological* Left Behind *novels, and women are responding to DVC's pre-Christian feminist themes and loving the fact that Pope Gregory wrongly labeled Mary Magdalene a prostitute.*

—IAN MARKHAM,
professor of theology and dean of Hartford Seminary

There's an element of reading Da Vinci *and being made to feel like a more interesting person. It's also a book that people want to talk about. Word of mouth went like wildfire."*

—BILL SCOTT-KERR,
publisher, Transworld Publishers (UK)

The Da Vinci Code *is an excellent candidate for "the worst novel ever written."*

—SALMAN RUSHDIE, novelist

So why are people buying The Da Vinci Code, *if not for its literary refinements? The obvious answer is that, like Harry Potter books that are so popular with adults, it is a hugely accomplished escapist narrative. Brown knows exactly what he is doing, what he wants to say and how to say it. [And] . . . it has something else to offer: it is a fascinating political text, underscored by an intense eschatological anxiety."*

—JASON COWLEY, in the *New Statesman*

It's the Harry Potter of adult fiction."

—RON BERNSTEIN, book agent for International Creative Management

I believe myths, tales, and folklore have always competed with "official" religion. The only difference between now and 500 years ago is the sheer scale of popular culture and its globalization. . . . The book promotes debate, that's it. Its ideas will have no lasting impact on the church or theology.

—CANON MARTYN PERCY, principal of Ripon College, who is cited by name in the novel

It seems different from what I was taught as a good Catholic girl."

—SHAMA, New Age Reader

The Religious Perspective: Not Exactly Ecumenical

I was not born with the luxury of absolute certainty or absolute faith. I have a lot of questions. I've written a novel in

which fictional characters ask some of those questions and offer possible answers.

—DAN BROWN, in a speech, October 2005

Gnostics: It's fiction! It's subversive! It's trash!

Stephan Hoeller, bishop of the Ecclesia Gnostica, the U.S. arm of the Gnostic religion:

Although I'm delighted by the interest in Gnosticism it's stirred up, and by its part in restoring Mary Magdalene to her place at the side of Jesus, I must confess my regard for The Da Vinci Code *is considerably less than for* The Matrix. *Mr. Brown seems to have an agenda . . . deliberately courting . . . conspiracy buffs, enthusiastic but badly informed Goddess worshippers and almost anyone who harbors a grudge against the Christian faith.*

Protestants: It's fiction! It's subversive! It's trash!

The Rev. James L. Garlow, coauthor of *Cracking Da Vinci's Code,* and pastor of the evangelical Skyline Wesleyan Church in San Diego:

It don't think it's just an innocent novel with a fascinating plot. I think it's out there to win people over to an incorrect and historically inaccurate view, and it's succeeding.

Rev. Steven Murray of St. Matthew's United Methodist Church in Sandown, New Hampshire, who wonders why Dan Brown, a Christian, would want to lead people down the wrong path:

. . . people's eternal fate could be affected.

David Neff, editor of ChristianityToday.com, wrote this in his Editor's Bookshelf column on "Da Vinci Dissenters":

Dan Brown promotes . . . a sexual agenda. Modern sexual

libertinism is blended with themes from ancient fertility cults to argue that everyone has access through sex to a direct, unmediated experience of the divine. [On a visit to the temple of Cybele, in Turkey I had an "aha" moment and it] came when the senior archeologist excavating the site pointed to niches in the wall behind the alter, places where male worshippers who had emasculated themselves in an ecstatic frenzy would deposit their testicles as an offering. Of course, that is not what today's sexual and spiritual left want us to remember about goddess worship.

Catholics: It's fiction! It's subversive! It's trash!

Sandra Miesel, one of the first to write a detailed critical analysis of *The Da Vinci Code,* and coauthor of *The Da Vinci Hoax,* was moved to protest because her daughter read the book and started to ask questions. . . .

I am avenging my daughter's waste of time and money. I needed to respond because it is so stupid and wrong and people are taking it [as] truth."

Darrell Bock, research professor of New Testament Studies at Dallas Theological Seminary, and author of *Breaking the Da Vinci Code:*

The issues of faith and relationship to God are too important to be left to the confusing category of "historical fiction."

Father Abdou Abu Kasm, president of Lebanon's Catholic Information Centre explaining why the book had to be banned in that country:

Christianity is not about forgiveness to the point of insulting Jesus Christ.

Veni, vidi 'Da Vinci'

On the occasion of the second anniversary of the publication of *The Da Vinci Code,* and to properly celebrate its phenomenal success, Celia McGee of the *New York Daily News* suggested this "party list."

Number of candles on the birthday cake: 10 million, for the American copies in print. Or 44, for the number of translations.

Honored guests: Jason Kaufman, the young editor who brought the author with him when he moved to Doubleday. Suzanne Herz, mastermind behind the "Code" publicity campaign. Tour operators booking various "Da Vinci Code" trips to Paris, Rome, and the south of France.

Dress code: For women, scanty, as in the girly posters Brown claims Robert Langdon noticed in most Harvard male undergraduate dorm rooms. One of many factual errors. For men, dress preppy like Brown—but leave home your spiked belt like the one Brown's murderous Opus Dei members wear.

Working in the kitchen: Author Brown has been accused of, ahem, reading too closely: Lewis Perdue (*Daughter of God*), Michael Baigent (*Holy Blood, Holy Grail*), Lynn Picknett (*The Templar Revelation*), and Jane Stanton Hitchcock, whose *The Witches Hammer* is being reissued as a reminder.

Not invited: Contributors to the anti-"Code" publishing industry.

Suggested gifts: A plane ticket to Paris so Brown can count the panes of glass in I.M. Pei's Louvre pyramid. He writes that there are a Satanic 666, but there are 678. Not planning to spend that much? Any valuable religious knickknack—Brown uses them to decorate his sumptuous New Hampshire home.

Father Raniero Cantalamessa, whose official title is "Preacher to the Papal Household," said this to the faithful during a sermon:

It is trading on the vast resonance of the name of Christ and on all that he means to a large part of humankind, to achieve wide publicity at very little cost . . . this is literary and artistic parasitism."

Wait! Hold On! There May Be Something to Be Learned Here!

Right Reverend Tom Wright, bishop of Durham (UK), lecturing on the Bible and postmodernism at the Scottish Bible Society:

The Da Vinci Code *comes in on the tide of the New Age postmodern hunger for spirituality which assumes that spirituality is a good thing but also assumes that the one place you will not find it is mainstream Christianity.*

Reverend John H. Sewell, Christian scholar and rector of St. John's Episcopal Church in Memphis, Tennessee, after being astounded that nearly seven hundred people showed up at a church meeting to discuss the book:

If I had said to people, "Come to a church meeting and let's talk about issues of faith and religious history," who would have come? But with this very popular novel, we got people to our meeting who hadn't been in church for years. And some of them stayed.

The Da Vinci Code Effect and the Political Process

Learning the Code I:
The DVC as a Metaphor for Cover-Up and Deceit

The Senate intelligence committee report is the Da Vinci Code *of the Iraq war. Some of the clues are in plain sight, but unless one knows how to read them they remain cryptic. Deletions, covering one-fifth of the report, and omissions, stretching endlessly, are as significant as what's included. The storyline is jumbled into incoherence, the main characters are often spectral, and it's all extremely dangerous.*

—SIDNEY BLUMENTHAL,
former senior adviser to President Clinton and Washington bureau chief of Salon.com, invoking the "*DVC*" word in his scathing commentary on pre-Iraq war intelligence assessments

Learning the Code II:
The DVC as a metaphor for winning elections

As the Democratic Party goes through its quadrennial self-flagellation process, the same tired old consultants and insiders are once again complaining that Democratic elected officials have no national agenda and no message. Yet encrypted within the 2004 election map is a clear national economic platform to build a lasting majority. You don't need Fibonacci's sequence, a decoder ring, or 3-D glasses to see it. You just need to start asking the right questions . . . The answers to these . . . are the Democrats' very own Da Vinci Code*—a road map to political divinity.*

—DAVID J. SIROTA, writing in the *American Prospect*, December 2004, on why he believes the route to the Holy Grail for the Democratic Party should be with paved with populism

Learning the Code III:
The DVC as a metaphor for the feeble-minded

Over the past month, I have hardly been able to open my e-mail without a flood of similarly portentous tripe [as is in The Da Vinci Code*] concerning the "Downing Street*

Memo(s)." This time, it is not the interior of a Templar Church but the style of a clerk in the British Foreign Office that furnishes "the key to all mythologies." . . . The outrage about the nondisclosures in the Downing Street memos has led Congressman Walter Jones of North Carolina to demand that we tell the al-Qaeda forces in Iraq exactly when we intend to give up. . . . They illustrate exactly how the credulous search for Da Vinci codes is the sign of feeble minds.

—CHRISTOPHER HITCHENS, writing in June 2005 on Slate.com about a recently leaked British memo which purportedly revealed that President George W. Bush had already decided to overthrow Saddam Hussein in the summer of 2002

Learning the Code IV: The DVC as a Metaphor for an Unwillingness to Face Facts

It used to be that the longest border was that between the United States and Canada. Today it's the one between fact and fiction. . . . More than 60 percent of the American people don't trust the press. Why should they? They've been reading The Da Vinci Code *and marveling at its historical insights. I have nothing against a fine thriller . . . [but] if one more person talks to me about Dan Brown's crackerjack research I'm shooting on sight. [Across all media, from newspapers to books to Wikipedia to TV], we're happier to swallow a half-baked Renaissance religious conspiracy theory than to examine the historical fiction we're living (and dying for) today.*

—STACY SCHIFF, Pulitzer Prize–winning historian, writing in the *New York Times*

The *DVC* Movie: Scenes from the Cutting Room Floor

I'll Have Nun of It, Thank You Very Much

Sister Mary Michael, sixty-one, knelt in prayer outside the Lincoln Cathedral where scenes for the *Da Vinci Code* movie were being shot to protest it as "heresy." Asked if she thought the people making the film would care about her protest, she said: "I don't suppose they do, but that doesn't matter a tuppence to me. It matters to me what God thinks, not what the film crew think. . . . When I face Almighty God, at my final judgment, as we all will, I can say, I did try my best, I did try my best to protest."

I Think It Meets My Code Very Well, Thank You Very Much

Dan Brown, speaking in October 2005: "The novelist is always the adaptation's most skeptical audience, but I've got to tell you, I think this movie will blow people away. The script has emerged as powerful and thought-provoking . . . [and] I believe moviegoers will come out of the theater feeling like they've just watched the novel."

The Da Vinci Con: Actress Merges Fact and Fiction

Seven-year-old Daisy Doidge-Hill convinced the film's director, Ron Howard, that she was fluent in French at her audition—yet she can barely speak a word of the language. She had learned one phrase for her audition: "*Je m'appelle Daisy. J'ai sept ans et j'habite a Falmouth,*" and claimed her father was French. Howard hired her on the spot to play the role of the young Sophie Neveu. Said Daisy's mother: "I couldn't believe she actually lied to Ron Howard. Daisy has been to France a few times but that's it."

The Da Vinci Grail, Act I: Ensuring a Treasure for Hollywood

Word is that screenwriter Akiva Goldsman (*A Beautiful Mind, Cinderella Man*) is making plenty of changes [to the movie script]—and that downplaying Brown's anti-Catholic theme is one of them. For example, the Catholic organization Opus Dei will not play a significant role in the movie, according to one of the select few who have read one of the carefully numbered scripts. "They're not out to make a religious movie," he says.

Controlling that controversy will be the key for Sony in protecting its investment, say some Hollywood experts. That's why its team of PR experts is sending the message that it will be an enjoyable "popcorn" fiction.

And if Columbia Pictures plays its cards right, it could be a journey to box-office heaven.

The Da Vinci Grail, Act II: Ensuring a Treasure for Hollywood

"The question I was asked was, 'Can you give them some things they can do to change it, to make it not offensive to the Christian audience?'" said Barbara Nicolosi, executive director of Act One, an organization that coaches Christians on making it in Hollywood. She said she was approached by Jonathan Bock, a marketing expert hired by Sony for his knowledge of Christian sensibilities. "We came up with three things," Ms. Nicolosi said: a more ambiguous approach to the central premise, the removal of Opus Dei, and amending errors in the book's description of religious elements in art. "The phrase I heard used several times was '*Passion* dollars'; they want to try to get '*The Passion*' dollars if they can," said Ms. Nicolosi, referring to her conversations about the film. "They're wrong," she added. "It's sacrilegious, irreligious. They're thinking they can ride the '*Passion*' wave with this. And I said, 'Are you kidding me?'"

The Da Vinci Grail, Act III:
Getting an Autograph from Tom Hanks

One of the intrepid reporters from the *Scotsman,* which includes Rosslyn Chapel in its beat, reports this from the front line: "'Balmoral hotel?'" frowns Carol Honeyman, one of a knot of seasoned autograph hunters trying to decode the clue that will lead to Hollywood A-lister Tom Hanks. 'Naw, we tried that last night—nine hours waiting in the rain!' She shakes the rain off a cardboard placard that reads: Tom Hanks Please Stop and Sign! then says: 'If he doesn't come out soon you can tell him I'm boycotting the film.' Jim Munro, the chairman of the Friends of Rosslyn and a local independent tour guide, is phlegmatic. 'Would we know these people if we saw them in the street?' he says. 'Apparently I once showed Brown around the chapel, but I can't remember him.' He shrugs and beckons us inside the Balmoral to share the haggis. 'We don't need Hollywood to enjoy ourselves. To hell with 'em.'"

The Da Vinci Welcome: Not Exactly a Scottish One

A descendent of the family that founded Rosslyn Chapel has condemned the trustees of the medieval church for allowing it to be used in the film of *The Da Vinci Code.* Dr. Andrew Sinclair, a descendant of the St. Clairs of Rosslyn, has claimed this will damage the reputation of the fifteenth-century building outside Edinburgh by giving credence to the "preposterous" claims made in Dan Brown's book. "As far as I'm concerned it is a load of rubbish," he said. "It's appalling. What it says about the grail and Rosslyn is absolute invention."

The Da Vinci Fish Story

But the last word should be reserved for Simon Beattie, director of Rosslyn Chapel, the epicenter of the world's "grail questers." Admitting thorough excavations have found nothing, Simon said, "I think it's very much in kin with the Loch Ness Monster. It's a hugely good story—tourists love the story. Scotland is built on many of these stories [but] proving them is another kettle of fish."

Ten Clever—and Too Clever—Attempts to Ride the Coattails of *The Da Vinci Code*

The Dick Cheney Code, a topical parody in which the heroes stumble on an "explosive and frankly preposterous centuries-old secret that plunges them into a plot-crammed, prose-swollen Washington intrigue." Winner of the (fictional!) "1.1" rating in the *Fibonacci Report.*

A *Da Vinci Code* game that takes people from pub to pub in Norwich, England, until they crack the code. "It's also about not just going out drinking. People can learn about Norwich and its history and more about all the different pubs," said Giles McCathie, the brains behind the liquid-treasure hunt.

Breaking the Code, a book by teenagers Lara Fox and Hillary Frankel on how parents should cope with their set: "Don't flip out about Cheetos and smoking. You've got to pick which issues is [sic] more important." And parents should also know: "We acknowledge we're manipulative."

The Asti Spumanti Code. Toby Clements, heretofore a literary editor for a prestigious London paper, says he tried for ten years to write a "sensible" book; this *Da Vinci Code* parody took him a month and gained him international notoriety.

The Givenchy Code: An Homage and a Parody by E. R. Escobar, who shamelessly plugs his book as "the most salacious writing since Dan Brown's *The Da Vinci Code* hit the stalls." The book's publicist "warns" the Catholic Church it is in for another shocker: "There is also definitely the potential here that readers may take *The Givenchy Code* 'secret' as fact and may become profoundly troubled by it."

The Oyster Code? "After reading the blockbuster book *du jour*—Dan Brown's *Da Vinci Code*—my interest in the sultry subject of aphrodisiacs have been awakened," said food writer Jo Ewarts, who finishes this verbal hot flash with a recipe for grilled oysters, spinach, and hollandaise sauce.

A *Last Supper* fashion ad, plastered all over New York and Paris. A French fashion house recast the scene with an almost all-female cast, clad in the company's casual chic. One man, John the Apostle, sits on a woman's lap, his torso bare and jeans riding low. The city fathers of Milan have banned it, but not before describing it in enticing terms: "One of the women apostles is kissing the naked torso of a man . . ." The company responded by saying, "It's a tribute to women, and we simply took our inspiration from Dan Brown's bestseller *The Da Vinci Code*."

The Lost Chimes of Eda Vinci, a leadership training program for executives offered by Four Seasons Event Management. Said David Mold, "After I read *The Da Vinci Code,* I was inspired to create a new team-building event, incorporating intrigue and fun into an exhilarating learning day."

Even sober scientists use the book as a talisman: "*The Da Vinci Code* may also be linked someday to the solving of a scientific mystery as old as Leonardo Da Vinci himself—friction," reported a group of top scientists in the journal *Science*. "We have used Da Vinci's principles of friction and the geometric oddities known as quasicrystals to open a new pathway towards a better understanding of friction at the atomic level."

The Diet Code: Revolutionary Weight-Loss Secrets from Da Vinci and the Golden Ratio. Stephen Lanzallota, a baker in Portland, Maine, was losing half his business to the low-carb craze in 2003. Inspired to reinvent himself, he came up with *The Diet Code,* and the marketing copy tells us it is all "based on the mathematical principles of the golden ratio: bread, fish, cheese, vegetables, meat, nuts and wine." Warner Books reportedly gave him a six-figure advance. The book's cover promises to make the diet fun: "Eat bread, drink wine, and lose weight."

The Plot Holes and Intriguing Details of *The DaVinci Code*

BY DAVID A. SHUGARTS

FACT: The Priory of Sion—a European secret society founded in 1099—is a real organization. In 1975 Paris's Bibliothèque Nationale discovered parchments known as Les Dossiers Secrets, *identifying numerous members of the Priory of Sion, including Sir Isaac Newton, Botticelli, Victor Hugo, and Leonardo da Vinci. . . . All descriptions of artwork, architecture, documents, and secret rituals in this novel are accurate.*
—DAN BROWN, *The DaVinci Code*

David A. Shugarts is an award-winning journalist and editor with thirty-six years' experience, and a major contributor to both *Secrets of the Code* and *Secrets of Angels & Demons.* He has also recently published *Secrets of the Widow's Son,* an intriguing look at Dan Brown's next novel.

The above statement from Dan Brown has wielded an enormous power of suggestion over readers. *The Da Vinci Code,* after all, is a novel. In other words, it is a work of fiction. Every detail is not supposed to be factual and accurate in fiction. Indeed, fiction is supposed to be the province of the authorial imagination. Everyone who buys the book knows this. And yet, somehow, the combination of the extremely well-sculpted and detailed realism of many passages, the big events and issues from history that every reader feels he or she should know more about but doesn't, and the compelling logic of conspiracy theory (i.e., the reason you don't know something is that powerful forces have intentionally kept you in the dark about it) have all worked together to cause readers to take this particular work of fiction very seriously—as seriously as if it were a work of nonfiction.

The reader's fascination with trying to separate fact from fiction has turned deciphering *The Da Vinci Code* into its own Holy Grail hunt. To add value to the hunt, *Secrets of the Code* made up a list of typical reader questions about *The Da Vinci Code* and turned the list over to investigative journalist David Shugarts, a writer with an extremely keen eye for detail, who was fascinated by *The Da Vinci Code,* but troubled here and there by annoying plot details that didn't seem quite right to him. Shugarts combined the search for answers to readers' questions with his own questions, and set off like a bloodhound to track down answers.

Let us make this caveat at the outset: we know that *The Da Vinci Code* is a work of fiction. We fully appreciate the creative mind of Dan Brown that has woven so many interesting facts and historical concepts into the murder mystery–action thriller–potboiler genre. But given the author's opening claim about the factual nature of the material, and given how seriously the debate generated by the novel has been taken by some, we thought it would be fun to share with our readers the many plot holes and flaws that Shugarts has uncovered. For more of Shugarts's findings beyond what is presented here, visit our website at www.secretsofthecode.com.

One note: The page numbers in this commentary refer to the U.S. English-language hardcover edition of *The Da Vinci Code,* published in 2003, although Shugarts's scrutiny starts before the numbered pages begin—with the dust jacket of the book. We have noticed a few subtle differences in various U.S. hardcover editions, details of which are covered in Shugarts's piece. So every reader should be able to follow along with any edition.

Dust jacket: Is there a secret code on the book's dust jacket and does it indicate what Dan Brown's next book will be about?

Yes, and here's our take on it. If you look closely you will see that some characters are in slightly bolder face than others on the dust jacket flaps. If you find all of these and string them together, they spell out "Is there no help for the widow's son?"

It only takes a moment to search and find out that this sentence refers to the Book of Enoch, where a favorite Dan Brown theme arises, about the lost treasure of the Temple of Solomon. There are many allusions to Enoch. Genesis implies that he was a mortal who walked with God and was seen no more because God took him. The mystery surrounding Enoch was a subject for writers in Hebrew apocrypha even before the time of Christ.

"Is There No Help for the Widow's Son?" was the title of a talk given before the Mormons in 1974, which purportedly established a connection between Freemasonry and the founder of the Church of Latter-day Saints, Joseph Smith.

It is said that Smith not only used lots of Mason symbology, but also wore a talisman containing mysterious symbols. Further, that there are Mormon-identified locations in the United States that lie due west of the Temple of Solomon (by no coincidence, of course).

The talk goes on to describe the Illuminees, who are female Masons of two types—the righteous and the voluptuous. So another Dan Brown theme, of the male hierarchy's suppression of the sacred feminine, is suggested.

Some of this territory has been covered already by the veteran sci-fi and fantasy novelist Robert Anton Wilson, including a novel in his Illuminati trilogy called *Widow's Son*. Many Masonic lodges have "widow's son" events and rites to this day.

The content of the Book of Enoch has multiple aspects that would attract Dan Brown's attention. These range from references to the angel Uriel (who Brown shows interest in with regard to analyzing Leonardo's *Virgin of the Rocks*) to material said to be from the lost Book of Noah.

But the most prominent, widespread use of the Enochian legend descends to us through Freemasonry, originally a brotherhood of English and Scottish gentlemen that styled itself after ancient principles taken from many cultures and philosophical streams. Because these influences are confluent with Rosicrucianism and with the Enlightenment, there is an immediate connection to the principles of Revolutionary America.

Many Founding Fathers were Freemasons, and the brotherhood has an inexhaustible supply of arcane symbols, some of which found their way into American symbolism and the architecture of public buildings. The city of Washington, DC, by layout and in many of its structures, is highly Masonic in design. Not the least of the symbols is the Washington Monument, honoring the greatest of American Freemasons. It all fits for the setting of the next Langdon escapade.

There are several other codes on the dust jacket of *The Da Vinci Code,* and they tend to point to an enigmatic statue, Kryptos, by the artist James Sanborn, dedicated at the CIA New Headquarters Building in 1990. Sanborn encrypted certain codes into Kryptos. A portion of the codes remains unsolved to date, and some of the decoded passages relate to the first gaze of archeologist Howard Carter into the tomb of Tutankhamen. This offers plenty of possibilities for incorporation into Dan Brown's next novel.

Dan Brown's publisher has revealed that the new book will be called *The Solomon Key.* This can spark a new series of associations, encompassing everything from medieval grimoires, or books of magic, to biblical tales of Solomon's Temple (again, a theme revered by Freemasons).

In the last pages of *The Da Vinci Code,* Dan Brown showed the unification of two equilateral triangles, representing the "chalice" and the "blade," into a symbol, a six-pointed star. This symbol is typically called the Star of David and thought of as Jewish, but it can also be called the Seal of Solomon, with many significances.

Page 3: Silas has "ghost-pale skin and thinning white hair. His irises are pink with dark red pupils." Does this describe an albino?

Albinism is a pigmentation deficiency affecting about one in seventeen thousand Americans. Although this can take many forms (and skin colors), society tends to label people, so albinos are often portrayed with white skin and hair, and pink eyes.

According to the National Organization for Albinism and Hyperpigmentation (NOAH), "A common myth is that by definition people with albinism have red eyes. In fact there are different types of albinism, and the amount of pigment in the eyes varies. Although some individuals with albinism have reddish or violet eyes, most have blue eyes. Some have hazel or brown eyes."

Almost universally, the disorder causes poor eyesight or even legal blindness. "In less pigmented types of albinism, hair and skin are cream-colored, and vision is often in the range of 20/200. In types with slight pigmentation, hair appears more yellow or red-tinged, and vision often corrects to 20/60," according to NOAH. Thus, Silas perhaps ought to be portrayed as having difficulty with vision, perhaps wearing thick glasses.

NOAH has been steadily calling attention to the stereotypical Hollywood portrayal of albinos as nonhuman, evil, or deranged. *The Da Vinci Code*'s Silas is a perfect example. Incidentally, one of the reasons the organization uses the acronym NOAH is that the Noah character of the Bible is believed by some to have been an albino.

Page 3: Silas shoots Saunière in the dark at fifteen feet. Is this likely, given Silas's visual acuity?

It would be extremely lucky for anyone to shoot someone in the dark with a pistol, but Silas is not likely to be able to do it without his glasses, which are never mentioned. It is extremely rare for an albino to have good vision.

Page 4: Silas fired once and hit Saunière in the stomach. He took dead aim at Saunière's head and pulled the trigger again but "the click of an empty chamber echoed through the corridor." Silas "glanced down at his weapon, looking almost amused. He reached for a second clip, but then seemed to reconsider, smirking calmly at Saunière's gut."

Silas has killed three people earlier this evening. All were presumably surprised by their assassin. His gun is a thirteen-shot Heckler and Koch USP 40 (see DVC, p. 73). The company name is actually Heckler & Koch. But the real question is, how come the "clip" (magazine) is empty? Does it take twelve rounds to kill three old men, or did he begin the evening with a weapon only half loaded?

No explanation is given by Dan Brown. But perhaps Silas is making up for his poor eyesight by firing more rounds.

Page 4: Saunière is shot several inches below the breastbone. Because he is "a veteran of la Guerre d'Algérie," he knows "for fifteen minutes, he would survive as his stomach acids seeped into his chest cavity, slowly poisoning him from within."

Is this really how people die with gunshot wounds in the stomach? Could a man this age survive for fifteen or twenty minutes with this injury?

We consulted medical literature. The overall mortality rate from gunshot wounds to the abdomen is approximately 12 percent. However, in the absence of vascular injury, the mortality rate is less than 5 percent. This includes a wide range of organs that could be injured. The most frequently injured organs from anterior abdominal gunshot wounds are small bowel, colon, liver/biliary system, spleen, vascular system, stomach.

Death is very dependent on which organ might be struck by the bullet. If, for instance, an artery is struck or the spleen damaged, rapid loss of blood can cause shock and death.

But perforation of the stomach alone does not kill a person quickly. It could take many hours. If Saunière is a fit person and has no other injuries, there would be no reason why he should not live until the security guards could open the gate. By the same token, he probably does have sufficient time (and not just fifteen minutes, which seems improbable) to stagger around the Louvre and leave secret messages.

Page 4: Saunière is "a veteran of la Guerre d'Algérie." At age seventy-six, could he have served in the Algerian War?

Yes. The war for Algerian independence lasted from 1954 to 1962. If *The Da Vinci Code* takes place in 2001 or 2002, Saunière would have been born in the mid-twenties. He would have been in his late twenties to late thirties during the course of the war.

Page 15: The crisp April air is whipping through the window of the Citroën as Langdon is taken from his hotel to the Louvre. What day in April does the action take place on and what year is it supposed to be?

The clues are contradictory. One hint lies in Dan Brown's previous book, *Angels & Demons.* That book also takes place in a twenty-four-hour time period in a month said to be April—in this case, in Rome. Robert Langdon, whose life as a Dan Brown character began with *Angels & Demons,* recalls in *The Da Vinci Code* that the prior experience was "a little over a year ago" (page 11). That would place the action in *The Da Vinci Code* later in the month of April than *Angels & Demons* since it is "a little over" a year ago. We also assumed that the action is in the latter part of April because

Easter arrived in early April of 2001 and would have affected any mentions of crowds, traffic, and the like.

April 2001 looks good for a number of reasons. We will learn later that it has to be substantially past the turn of the millennium—probably by a year. This is because the plot instigated by Teabing and carried out through manipulation of Opus Dei and the Vatican, as we will come to find out, arose in a meeting of Aringarosa and churchmen at Castel Gandolfo during the previous November (page 149). The motivating reason for Teabing's actions was that the Priory of Sion, expected to reveal the Grail secret around the turn of the millennium, had failed to do so.

September 11, 2001, was a worldwide shock, and it had a profound effect on security arrangements throughout Europe. Dan Brown would have had to treat the subjects of terrorism, religious fundamentalism, religious tensions in the Middle East, and all the many complexities of September 11 had he consciously been trying to set the action of the book in April 2002, when the memory of September 11 was still so fresh all over the world. Certainly, we would not have seen the same permissive attitude by customs officials allowing Teabing into England, for instance. Many other aspects of the plot, from how Swiss bank vaults are treated to security precautions in public buildings, would undoubtedly have been affected.

But the book has contradictory evidence as well. Langdon has euros in his pocket. This monetary unit was not released as currency and coin until January 1, 2002, which would argue for April 2002. Another item: the article in the *New York Times Magazine* about the art diagnostician Maurizio Seracini (mentioned in *DVC* on page 169) was a real-life article about the secret meanings of some of Leonardo da Vinci's works—and it was published on April 21, 2002. So Langdon could not have known about it the year before.

So does the action take place in April 2002, with the noted symbologist simply ignoring the signs and symbols of the September 11 tragedy that has happened so recently (there is not one direct reference to it in the book)? Or is *DVC* set in April 2001, with the noted symbologist having premonitions of the euro coins and the *New York Times Magazine* article to come a year in the future?

Page 15: The night breeze is scented with jasmine blossoms. Does jasmine grow in the area and does it bloom in April?

There are jasmine shrubs in the nearby Tuileries, but jasmine is a summer-blooming plant, starting around July and reaching a peak of fragrance around August.

Page 15: The Citroën "skimmed south past the Opera House and crossed Place Vendôme." Is this possible?

No, to leave the Ritz Hotel on place Vendôme and pass the Opera House, you must go north, not south.

Page 15: The Citroën goes south on rue de Castiglione and turns toward the Louvre. It "swerved left now, angling west down the park's central boulevard." Is this possible?

No, you would be going east after turning left to go to the Louvre.

Page 18: It would take a visitor an estimated five weeks to "properly appreciate the 65,300 pieces of art in this building" (the Louvre museum).

Think about it. If you spent an average of one minute per piece of art, and did not sleep, it would still take forty-five days of twenty-four hours each. This would hardly be called "properly appreciating" the artwork. Luckily, not all 65,000 pieces are on display, so you don't have to try. The number on display is nonetheless formidable—approximately 24,400 works. If you put in six eight-hour days a week looking at one piece of art per minute, this would still be more than eight weeks.

Page 21: Langdon says that "at President Mitterrand's explicit demand" the new Pyramid monument at the entrance to the Louvre had been constructed of exactly 666 panes of glass." It was a "bizarre request that had always been a hot topic among conspiracy buffs who claimed 666 was the number of Satan." How many panes are actually in the Pyramid?

For this answer, we contacted the offices of the architect, the renowned I. M. Pei. A spokeswoman said the Pyramid actually contains 698 pieces of glass, as counted by one of the architects who worked on the project. She said the notion that President Mitterrand had specified the number of panes is "not based in fact."

She also said the 666 rumor was published as fact by some French newspapers in the mid-1980s, commenting: "If you only found those old articles and didn't do any deeper fact checking, and were extremely credulous, you might believe the 666 story."

We also contacted Carter Wiseman, whose biography of I. M. Pei is among the works cited on Dan Brown's bibliography. Wiseman points out that I. M. Pei is an architect interested almost exclusively in geometric patterns and abstractions. To think he was concealing symbolic content in his work would be to miss the whole point of his aesthetic, says Wiseman.

Page 25: Fache wears a crux gemmata. *What is the origin of this term?*

It is a cross with thirteen gems, described by Brown as "a Christian ideogram for Christ and his twelve apostles." In many places, orthodox Christianity calls for a plain wooden cross, or a cross with the body of Christ depicted. Gem-encrusted crosses arose in some medieval churches and were interpreted as signs of the resurrection. However, a *crux gemmata* can be seen as a sign of pride, power, and wealth as much as devotion.

Page 26: Brown says the Louvre security cameras are all fake, and most large museums use "containment security." True?

False. The concept of the gates that drop down and trap a thief comes from *Pink Panther* or *The Thomas Crown Affair*–type movies, not from reality. The Louvre not only believes in security cameras but, in fact, it recently made a major upgrade of its security system using the French conglomerate Thales, and video cameras are a big part of the system. Thales Security & Supervision is managing "a total of 1,500 proximity access control readers, 10,000 contactless secure badges, 800 video surveillance cameras, including 195 with digital recording systems, and more than 1,500 intrusion alarm points," according to the company.

Page 27: Langdon notices that the security barricade "was raised about two feet. . . . Placing his palms flat on the polished parquet, he lay on his stomach and pulled himself forward. As he slid underneath, the nape of his Harris tweed snagged on the bottom of the grate and he cracked the back of his head on the iron." Is this likely?

No. In *Angels & Demons,* Langdon is said to have "the body of a swimmer, a toned, six-foot physique that he vigilantly maintained with fifty laps a day in the university pool." A fit individual would be only about nine or ten inches thick, back to front. If he put his stomach on the floor and slithered, it would be unlikely his jacket or head would be touching the bottom of a grate that was a full two feet off the ground.

Page 28: Brown says Opus Dei has its world headquarters at Murray Hill Place, 243 Lexington Avenue, New York City. Built for $47 million, 133,000 square feet, red brick and Indiana limestone. Designed by May & Pinska, with over a hundred bedrooms, six dining rooms, and chapels on the second, eighth, and sixteenth floors. Seventeenth floor entirely residential. Men enter through the main doors on Lexington Avenue. Women enter through a side street and are "acoustically and visually separated" from the men at all times within the building. True?

Close enough. According to another source, Opus Dei "had just 84,000 members worldwide—three thousand in the U.S.—but its new $55 million, seventeen-story building in midtown Manhattan reflected a power far beyond its numbers."

Page 29: Brown says Opus Dei founder Escrivá published The Way *in 1934, with 999 points of meditation for doing God's work in one's life. He says there are now over four million copies in circulation in forty-two languages.*

Generally accurate. Actually, the original title in 1934

was *Spiritual Considerations.* It was revised a number of times. According to an Opus Dei website (www.josemariaescriva.info), the book "has been translated into forty-five different languages and has sold more than 4.5 million copies worldwide." *The Way* does indeed have 999 points.

Page 30: Brown writes about an organization that monitors Opus Dei's activities called the Opus Dei Awareness Network (www.odan.org). Does this group exist?

Yes. ODAN exists and that is their website.

Page 30: Brown says FBI turncoat Robert Hanssen was a prominent member of Opus Dei.

True. Bonnie Hanssen's brother is an Opus Dei priest in Rome whose office is mere steps away from the pope. One of Bob and Bonnie's daughters is an Opus Dei numerary, a woman who has taken a vow of celibacy while remaining a layperson.

Bob Hanssen befriended bestselling espionage author James Bamford and, after pumping him for information about interviews he had had with Soviet leaders, would invite him to join him at Opus Dei meetings. "He was a little obsessed about it. Bob would rant about the evil in organizations like Planned Parenthood and how abortion was immoral," Bamford recalled.

Page 32: Fache and Langdon begin at the east end of the Grand Galerie and pass the fallen Caravaggio painting nearby. Is this where the Caravaggios hang?

No. They are hundreds of feet down the Grand Galerie, not far from Saunière's corpse.

Page 35: Saunière used his left index finger to draw the pentangle on himself. Is he left-handed?

Yes. Throughout the book there are clues that Saunière is left-handed. This supports a supposed affinity with Leonardo da Vinci, whom some experts think was left-handed (see *Secrets of the Code,* Chapter 8).

Page 35: Brown says, "A white Ku Klux Klan headpiece conjured images of hatred and racism in the United States, and yet the same costume carried a meaning of religious faith in Spain." True?

Long dark robes and hoods are worn by penitents during Holy Week throughout Spain, but nowhere so spectacularly as in Seville. Thousands of penitents representing some fifty-seven fraternities form a candlelight procession in honor of the Virgin Mary and in recognition of the suffering of Christ. They are hooded because no one is meant to be able to guess the identity of sinners who are seeking forgiveness. Each of the fraternities chooses their distinctive colors of hoods and robes. Ku Klux Klansmen typically have white hoods, but not quite as pointy as the Spanish penitents. It is unclear whether there is any connection between the two.

Interestingly, the KKK was founded in Polaski, Tennessee, in 1866, by six Confederate officers. One of them, the first imperial wizard of the KKK, was a former Confederate general and Freemason, Nathan Bedford Forrest. Oddly, Forrest was written into the book *Forrest Gump* by Winston Groom, which was made into an Oscar-winning movie in 1994. The book's hero is said to be a namesake of Forrest, a distant relative.

Page 36: Langdon says the pentacle is "representative of the female half of all things—a concept religious historians call the "sacred feminine" or the "divine goddess." True?

No. The pentacle represents both male and female, exactly as does yang and yin.

Page 36: "As a tribute to Venus, the Greeks used her four-year cycle to organize their Olympic Games. Nowadays, few people realized that the four-year schedule of the modern Olympics still followed the half-cycles of Venus. Even fewer people knew that the five-pointed star had almost become the official Olympic seal but was modified at the last moment—its five points exchanged for five intersecting rings to better reflect the game's spirit of inclusion and harmony." True?

Partially true, partially false, and much more complicated. The Greeks did not use their Olympics to pay tribute to Venus. The Olympics were dedicated to Zeus.

Instead of a decade, the Greeks had calendar cycles of eight years. Each cycle was called an *octaeteris,* and this was later divided into four-year periods called olympiads.

The primary reason for the eight-year cycle was that the Greeks observed a close fit between ninety-nine lunar cycles and eight earth cycles. More than any other heavenly body, the moon is likely to govern what a month is in any ancient culture. (However, they also did know that Venus completes five synodic cycles in the same eight-year period.) The ninety-nine/eight coincidence allowed them to make five years of twelve months and three years of thirteen months—the added months coming in the third, fifth, and eighth years. As the Greeks improved their calendar, they could divide the octaeteris into two parts, of fifty and forty-nine lunar cycles, which became known as olympiads. It wasn't perfect, but it was a calendar!

The average Greek would not have been able to detect it, but a patient astronomer would be able to take note of the five nodes of Venus's travel in the sky. From the latitude of Greece, this would have made a very irregular pentacle.

The five rings are a modern symbol. They were invented in 1913 by Pierre de Coubertin, president of the International Olympic Committee. He originally intended them to signify the first five games, but the interpretation was later amended to have the rings represent the five original continents.

The five-ring symbol was mistakenly ascribed to ancient origins when a Nazi propaganda filmmaker for the famous 1936 games (attended by Hitler) had a five-ring stone carving made and filmed it against the backdrop of Delphi.

Page 37: Langdon says, "Symbols are very resilient, but the pentacle was altered by the early Roman Catholic Church. As part of the Vatican's campaign to eradicate pagan religions and convert the masses to Christianity, the church launched a smear campaign against the pagan gods and goddesses, recasting their divine symbols as evil."

Brown conveniently disregards the fact that Christian emperor Constantine, who elsewhere in the book is treated as the enemy most responsible for wiping out Gnostic, goddess, and pagan traditions, used the pentagram, together with the Chi-Rho symbol (formed from the first two letters, *X* and *P*, of the Greek word for Christ), in his seal and amulet.

Page 45: Brown says Leonardo had an "enormous output of

breathtaking Christian art . . . accepting hundreds of lucrative Vatican commissions, Da Vinci painted Christian themes not as an expression of his own beliefs but rather as a commercial venture—a means of funding a lavish lifestyle." True?

Not true. Leonardo's output was not enormous. He characteristically had trouble finishing works and they would drag on for long periods. The number of paintings he finished is extremely small compared to most great figures in the history of art.

Page 52: Sophie's personal code for her answering machine is 454. Is this number significant to Dan Brown or a random number?

We don't know, but the hardcover book does end on page 454.

Page 55: Silas leaves home at the age of seven after his father kills his mother and he kills his father. He is imprisoned at age eighteen and freed by an earthquake at thirty. Aringarosa dubs him "Silas." According to Dan Brown, he has forgotten "the name his parents had given him."

Hard to believe that he has truly forgotten his name. Anyway, what did he call himself for twenty-three years? What did the authorities call him when they decided he was too dangerous to remain in Marseilles and when they imprisoned him? What did his jailors call him for twelve years?

Page 58: Brown says chapter 16 of Acts speaks of Silas as a prisoner, naked and beaten, lying in his cell, singing hymns to God, when an earthquake frees him. By coincidence, the albino has been freed by an earthquake, so the bishop names him Silas. To what does this refer?

In the Book of Acts, both Paul and Silas were imprisoned together, by false accusations. The earthquake freed all the prisoners, but Paul and Silas did not leave. Instead, they first converted their jailer to Christianity and baptized him, then they refused to leave until their accusers came and apologized and led them out of the prison.

Page 60: Sophie decrypts the numerical series and comes up with 1-1-2-3-5-8-13-21, which she says is the Fibonacci sequence, "one of the most famous mathematical progressions in history." Is she accurate?

Not completely. Mathematicians agree that the Fibonacci sequence includes 0, making the full sequence 0-1-1-2-3-5-8-13-21 . . . Note that a math sequence is properly written with an ellipsis at the end, indicating that the series continues indefinitely.

Page 65: Sophie tells Langdon about the "GPS tracking dot." It is described as "a metallic, button-shaped disk, about the size of a watch battery." Sophie explains that it "continuously transmits its location to a Global Positioning System [GPS] satellite that DCPJ can monitor. It's accurate within two feet anywhere on the globe." Does such a system exist?

Yes, but it's much larger than the unit that Sophie describes. For instance, units that help in tracking wild animals have been fashioned into somewhat bulky dog collars (or bird or fish collars). They recognize their position via GPS, and transmit to satellites—but these are not GPS satellites. Rather, they are Argos or GlobalStar satellites. (GPS satellites do not receive signals from GPS receivers.) Unfortunately, you cannot use an Argos satellite continuously at any one point on earth, since it orbits and goes out of sight.

But smaller units for continuous tracking can be constructed, if you accept that they do not need to transmit to satellites. These have small radio transmitters, good up to fifteen miles, and if you stay within range, you can track them 24/7. The smallest of these units is still about ten times the size of the so-called GPS dot that Sophie describes.

All of these units require antennas, and there is a relationship of antenna size to receiving sensitivity or transmitting power. So you might require a two- or three-inch antenna even if you could make the transmitter into a dot.

Page 78: The men's room window looks out of the "westernmost tip of the Denon Wing" of the Louvre. Sophie looks out and sees that "Place du Carrousel ran almost flush with the building with only a narrow sidewalk separating it from the Louvre's outer wall. Far below, the usual caravan of the city's nighttime delivery trucks sat idling, waiting for the signals to change." Is the view correct?

The men's room is not located at the western tip of the Denon Wing and this part of the building is not open to the public, but let's assume it was. The place du Carrousel is not almost flush with the outer wall. Nor is it a major truck route with caravans of trucks idling in line.

Page 79: Sophie says the U.S. embassy is "only about a mile from here." True?

Close. It's about 4,100 feet, and you can see it from the posited location of the men's room window, but Sophie will still miss it when she goes to drive there!

Page 82: Fache has a Manurhin MR-93 pistol. Is this used by French authorities?

Yes, this is the weapon of the French police. It is an extremely rugged revolver with distinctive styling.

Page 85: Brown says, "The last sixty seconds had been a blur." He then describes action beginning with Sophie throwing the GPS dot out the window. Since this includes Fache sprinting the length of the Grand Galerie, how fast was Fache as a runner?

Sign him up for the French Olympic team! He could be a sub-four-minute miler!

Page 85: Brown says that the "twin-bed Trailor delivery truck" traveled from the Louvre, south on the pont du Carrousel (crossing the Seine) and then turned right onto pont des Saints-Pères. Can this be done?

No. If you cross the pont du Carrousel southward, you must turn right onto quai Voltaire, a one-way street going west. This takes you away from pont des Saints-Pères, not toward it. Also, pont des Saints-Pères is one-way going north.

Page 86: Brown says the trailer truck drove to within ten feet of the end of the building (the west end of the Louvre's Denon Wing). It heads south across the Seine. By tossing the GPS dot, contained in a bar of soap, into the truck, they make the French police believe that Langdon has jumped out the window into the truck. Is this possible?

No. First of all, the public restrooms of the Louvre's Grand Galerie are not at the end wall of the building, and the Louvre's restrooms have liquid soap, not bars of it. But even if we pencil in a men's room there, the place du Carrousel is more than fifty feet away from the building's wall. No one could jump and reach the street, even its nearest edge. By law, they drive on the right side of the street in Paris, so the southbound traffic would be farthest from the Louvre, adding another twenty feet or so. We doubt that Fache is going to believe Langdon jumped.

Page 92: Brown says Tarot cards come in a deck of twenty-two and have a suit called Pentacles, as well as three cards named the Female Pope, the Empress, and the Star. Does this accurately describe a Tarot deck?

Yes and no. For a guy who is supposed to be into the occult, Brown misses key facts here. There are actually seventy-eight cards in the most common Tarot decks. There are the twenty-two cards of the Major Arcana, and then the fifty-six cards of the Minor Arcana. The Major Arcana can be thought of as Trumps, but literally, the divisions are Major Secrets and Minor Secrets.

The four suits are Wands, Cups, Pentacles, and Swords. The suit called Cups, unmentioned by Brown until later in the book, is a clear reference to chalices.

The complete tale of Tarot, which can be embellished at will by anyone, will include (at least) Freemasonry, Gnostics, the Female Pope, the Holy Grail, and much more, but not always interconnected in the way *The Da Vinci Code* portrays. The card in the Major Arcana now commonly known as the High Priestess stems from an early deck and the legend of the Female Pope, or Pope Joan.

According to a widely told medieval legend, a woman named Joan disguised herself as a man, rose in the priesthood, and actually became pope. But she became pregnant by another priest and not only could not hide it, but came to give birth in the streets, whereupon a crowd recognized her deception and tore her to pieces. There is another story suggesting an Italian female pope closer to the era of the Renaissance.

In any event, around 1450, several decks of *Tarocchi* (Tarot) cards were commissioned by the great Visconti family, including one widely recognized as one of the earliest extant decks, the Visconti-Sforza deck. An early Female Pope card is found in this deck.

Page 93: Brown uses a classroom setting to talk about the Divine Proportion. He congratulates a student who recognizes the number 1.618 as PHI (pronouncing it "fee"). Is this correct?

Somebody must have told Dan Brown that there are two numbers, one uppercase and the other lower, and he took them to mean PHI and phi. But in fact, the numbers are written out as Phi to mean the Divine Proportion, and phi to mean its reciprocal. In English, it is pronounced "fye" to rhyme with "pie."

But we are astounded that a famous symbologist such as Robert Langdon would not use the symbols for this number pair, the Greek uppercase Φ and lowercase ϕ. With all the other symbols in the book, couldn't Doubleday have gotten the Greek letters set into type?

The true statements are that the number Phi can be derived from the Fibonacci sequence, is found often in nature, math, and architecture, and has names like Golden Mean, Golden Ratio, etc.

Phi is an irrational number (goes on forever after the decimal point). If you want it longer, just do the math—1.618033988 is Phi at nine decimal places, for instance, and some people have calculated it out to thousands of decimal places.

Page 94: "Hold on," said a young woman in the front row. "I'm a bio major and I've never seen this Divine Proportion in nature."

"No?" Langdon grinned. "Ever study the relationship between females and males in a honeybee community?"

"Sure. The female bees always outnumber the male bees."

"Correct. And did you know that if you divide the number of female bees by the number of male bees in any beehive in the world, you always get the same number?"

"You do?"

"Yup. Phi."

Honey is golden, but do the bees follow the Golden Ratio?

Brown bumbles badly. The population of a hive changes throughout the seasons, and the seasons change throughout the world, so there can be no time when all the beehives in the world have the same ratio of male to female population. Bad news for the guys: in the fall, practically all the drones (males) are driven out of the hive to die, so the male population approaches zero.

In the spring and summer, there will be drones. But bee experts have counted hive populations and the numbers they use are nothing like a Divine Proportion. For instance, an average active hive will have one queen, about three hundred to one thousand drones (males), and fifty thousand workers (females). If you do what Langdon says and divide the female number (50,001) by the male number (we'll use one thousand), you get fifty—not even close to 1.618.

Page 98: Brown says, "French kings throughout the Renaissance were so convinced that anagrams held magic power that they appointed royal anagrammatists to help them make better decisions by analyzing words in important documents."

We don't think there were French kings that were gung-ho for anagrams "throughout the Renaissance," a period that lasted from around 1483 to 1610. But one king, Louis XIII, who reigned from 1610 to 1643, was famous because he appointed a royal anagrammist, Thomas Billon. But there's not much evidence to suggest Billon had a big role in decision making. It was said Billon's function was "to entertain the court with amusing anagrams of people's names."

This citation is found everywhere that anagram aficionados refer to their history. Louis XIII ascended to his throne at the age of nine, but we don't know when the appointment of Billon occurred. The young king was initially governed by his mother, then later heavily influenced by advisors such as Cardinal Richelieu.

Page 98: Brown says, "The Romans actually referred to the study of anagrams as ars magna—'the great art.'"

Did the Romans speak English? *Anagrams* is the English word that can be rearranged to make *ars magna*. The Latin word for anagram is *anagrammat*, or *anagramma*, modified from earlier Greek terms.

Page 99: Saunière once wrote the word "planets" and told Sophie "that an astonishing ninety-two other English words of varying lengths could be formed using those same letters." True?

It's astonishing that Saunière did not pose a higher number. We can think of 101 words and we're not that smart.

Page 106: Brown says, "To this day, the fundamental

navigational tool was still known as a Compass Rose, its northernmost direction still marked by an arrowhead . . . or, more commonly, the symbol of the fleur-de-lis." Is this factual?

Perhaps you've seen a movie where the compass rose has a big fleur-de-lis at the top on a treasure map. You'll want to believe it's on modern maps but, no, it's not. It's hard to say which of the compass roses in use on today's charts and maps is the most common. But we can answer for the standard U.S. aviation and marine charts. They don't have a fleur-de-lis.

The air charts have a simple arrow for north, and they are already oriented for magnetic north. The nautical charts have a prominent marker for true north on the outer ring, and a smaller simple arrow for magnetic north on the inner ring. The true north marker? A five-pointed star, oddly enough. Mariners readily recognize its symbology to mean the North Star, Polaris.

Since most people don't use a compass for navigating on road maps, which are perhaps the most common maps, they don't have compass roses. They usually just have north arrows. Old charts and maps—particularly charts drawn by those master cartographers, the Portuguese—commonly do have a fleur-de-lis for north. Interestingly, they also often have a cross—typically a Maltese cross—for east. This is because east was thought of as being "toward Jerusalem." So Dan Brown missed his chance to remark on yet another usage of the Knights Templar symbol.

Page 106: Brown says, "Long before the establishment of Greenwich as the prime meridian, the zero longitude of the entire world had passed directly through Paris, and through the Church of Saint-Sulpice. The brass marker in Saint-Sulpice was a memorial to the world's first prime meridian, and although Greenwich had stripped Paris of the honor in 1888, the original Rose Line was still visible today."

Paris was not the site of the world's first prime meridian. Not by about fourteen hundred years. The first known attempt to establish a prime meridian came in the second century BC, when Hipparchus of Rhodes proposed that all distances be measured from a meridian running through the island of Rhodes, just off the southern coast of Turkey. But perhaps a stronger attempt was made by the Greek Ptolemy, writing between AD 127 and 141. His prime meridian went through the Canary Islands. Ptolemy's works, as revived by the German Benedictine monk Nicholas Germanus around 1470, were hugely influential and became the inspiration for Christopher Columbus.

As many countries established claims throughout the world through voyages of exploration, they often attempted to establish their own prime meridians. There were hundreds of years of confusion on this point, but England emerged as the world's technical leader in cartography and navigation. What it came down to is, if you printed the best charts, you got to say where the zero lines began.

The hubbub came to a head in 1884 when President Chester A. Arthur called a conference in Washington, DC, to get international agreement on a prime meridian and a universal twenty-four-hour day. At the time, ships attempting to get their bearings at sea were confronted with a total of eleven national prime meridians: Berlin, Cadiz, Copenhagen, Greenwich, Lisbon, Paris, Rio, Rome, St. Petersburg, Stockholm, and Tokyo. But by then, some 72 percent of commercial shipping recognized Greenwich, while only 8 percent used Paris.

The twenty-five nations voted twenty-two to one to make it Greenwich. Abstaining were Brazil and—you guessed it—France. France clung to the Paris meridian as a rival to Greenwich until 1911 for timekeeping purposes and 1914 for navigational purposes.

Page 120: Professor Langdon refers to the artist as "Da Vinci." Is this correct?

No. It grates on the nerves of everyone who is knowledgeable about art. His actual name is Leonardo di ser Piero and he was from the town of Vinci, so he was thus Leonardo di ser Piero da Vinci (from Vinci). Throughout the art world, his shortened name is Leonardo.

Page 121: Professor Langdon "reveals" Leonardo's secret joining of male and female in the Mona Lisa by rearranging the name to become Amon L'Isa, a putative androgynous union. Could Leonardo have intended such a pun?

This all relies on the painting being called the *Mona Lisa.* Since Leonardo never called it *Mona Lisa,* this is completely absurd. In Leonardo's lifetime, the painting had no title. It was referred to by a variety of names, including "a courtesan with a gauze veil."

Page 121: Brown says, "At first Langdon saw nothing. Then, as he knelt beside her, he saw a tiny droplet of dried liquid that was luminescing. Ink? Suddenly he recalled what black lights were actually used for. Blood." Plausible?

Dan Brown, if you're going to watch *CSI,* ya gotta pay attention! Blood doesn't luminesce in black light without some chemical help. If you use Luminol (a *CSI* favorite) you don't need special light, just a darkened room. That's because the reagent triggers chemiluminescence, giving off its own somewhat eerie glow.

If you use Fluorescein (an alternative preferred for faint latent blood traces), you do need an ultraviolet light. But first you spray the area of interest with a freshly made batch of Fluorescein solution, and then with a hydrogen peroxide solution. Sophie didn't have the time or materials to do this.

Page 124: The message scrawled in front of the Mona Lisa *says, "So dark the con of man." Langdon sees this as a perfect expression of a fundamental Priory of Sion philosophy, that the powerful men of the early Christian church conned the world with a bunch of lies.*

As a classical scholar, Langdon should not jump to the meaning of *con* as in confidence game or confidence man, involving cheating and swindling. This term came into use around 1886, relatively late. The Shakespearean-era term *con* meant "to know or learn" or "to commit to memory." To a scholar, the most likely meaning of the phrase would be "So dark the knowledge of man."

Page 128: Dan Brown has Silas look up Job 38:11 in the Bible at the altar in Saint-Sulpice. "Finding verse number eleven, Silas read the text. It was only seven words. Confused, he read it again, sensing something had gone terribly wrong. The verse simply read: 'Hitherto shalt thou come, but no further.'"

There are more than seven words in the verse. The King James Version gives these seventeen words as the complete verse 11: "And said, Hitherto shalt thou come, but no further: and here shall thy proud waves be stayed?"

It is also highly doubtful that Silas would be reading an English-language Bible at the altar of a venerable French cathedral in the heart of Paris.

Page 131: Sophie gets the key from the back of the painting Madonna of the Rocks *by Leonardo. Brown's description: "The masterpiece she was examining was a five-foot-tall canvas." Later, he says that Sophie "had actually lifted the large painting off its cables and propped it on the floor in front of her. At five feet tall, the canvas almost entirely hid her body. . . . The canvas started to bulge in the middle . . . The woman was pushing her knee into the center of the canvas from behind!"*

This painting is not five feet tall. It is about six feet six inches tall, not including the frame. Also, it is four feet wide. Sophie would have to be a giant to be visible behind it, and she would have to be unbelievably strong to pull it off the wall and set it down without wrecking it.

Page 137: "The vehicle was easily the smallest car Langdon had ever seen.

'SmartCar,' [Sophie] said. 'A hundred kilometers to the liter.'"

Sorry. The Smart Car is nifty and thrifty. It gets great gas mileage, but not a hundred kilometers to the liter—not even close! Your mileage may vary, but perhaps a typical figure is nineteen kilometers per liter. For several years, Smart Car has been the rage in Europe, built in Germany and France and now owned by DaimlerChrysler under the Mercedes-Benz brand. To see some examples, go to daimlerchrysler.com.

There are a series of two-seat versions of the Smart Car with hip styling (originally provided by Swatch). At eight feet long, two can fit in a normal parking space. You can't buy the two-seaters in America, except through very special arrangements. The new four-seater versions were to be brought to the U.S. market sometime in 2006, but at press time this plan had been delayed indefinitely. A rumored "SUV" version (with four-wheel drive) was in the wind for the American market for 2007.

Page 138: The destination is the American embassy. Sophie drives north to the rue de Rivoli, and west on Rivoli a quarter mile to a "wide rotary." Coming out the other side of the "wide rotary," she is heading out the wide Champs Élysées and now the embassy is "only about a mile away," according to Brown. Sophie turns hard right, "cutting sharply past the luxurious Hôtel de Crillon" and into the diplomatic neighborhood. Suddenly, they discover themselves one hundred yards short of the police blockade at the avenue Gabriel.

Sophie needs a better map. When she was headed west on Rivoli and reached the area of the "wide rotary," she had found place de la Concorde, a huge open square that is the centerpiece of Paris. On the north side of this square is the Hôtel de Crillon. Nearby is the American embassy, where rue de Rivoli becomes avenue Gabriel. If you have found one, you have found the other. (One attraction of rooms at the Crillon is the view of the embassy.)

Page 147: The destination is the Gare Saint-Lazare. As Sophie leaves the area of the rue Gabriel, stymied by the police blockade, she heads back west onto the Champs

Élysées, going to the Arc de Triomphe and taking a street going north from the rotary there (most likely, the avenue de Wagram). She goes north a few blocks, then turns hard right onto the boulevard Malesherbes. Eventually, with another turn or two, she ends up at the train station.

Once again, Sophie needs a better map. As she leaves the rue Gabriel, she is only about a quarter-mile away from the Gare Saint-Lazare, if she would only head north. Instead she goes a long way west, then north, then back south and east, to reach the same point after a trip that is roughly one and a half miles longer than it needs to be. Maybe she just wants to get to know Langdon a little better?

Page 148: Dan Brown says, "Architectural Digest *had called Opus Dei's building 'a shining beacon of Catholicism sublimely integrated with the modern landscape.'" Is this an accurate quote?*

We queried *Architectural Digest* about this. They replied tersely, "*Architectural Digest* has never featured the headquarters of Opus Dei."

Page 153: Aiming to leave Paris, Sophie directs the taxi driver and they head north on rue de Clichy. Out the window to his right, Langdon sees Montmartre and Sacré-Coeur.

Yes. This is a plausible view.

Page 154: While going north on rue de Clichy, Sophie discovers that the address on the key is 24 rue Haxo. The taxi driver tells Sophie that rue Haxo is "out near the [Roland Garros] tennis stadium on the western outskirts of Paris." . . . "Fastest route is through Bois de Boulogne," the driver says.

The taxi driver, too, needs a better map. You do not have to meander through the park called the Bois de Boulogne in order to get to the tennis stadium. There is a high-speed, limited-access artery, the boulevard Périphérique, which will take you right to the stadium.

But there is a big discrepancy here, because the rue Haxo is not in this western region of Paris. In fact, it is on the east side of the city.

Page 155: Fache learns that Langdon bought train tickets. "What was the destination?" he asks. "Lille," says Collet. "Probably a decoy," says Fache. How can he be so sure?

Perhaps because he knows that trains for Lille do not depart the Gare Saint-Lazare. The Lille train departs the Gare du Nord. On page 152 in some earlier editions of *The Da Vinci Code,* Langdon and Neveu buy tickets for the 3:06 a.m. train from the Gare Saint-Lazare to Lyon. In later editions, it is from the same station and at the same time, but to Lille. In general, one would not use Gare Saint-Lazare for either route.

Page 157: Sophie asked Langdon to tell her about the Priory of Sion.

" 'The brotherhood's history spanned more than a millennium,' he mused . . ."

" 'The Priory of Sion,' he began, 'was founded in Jerusalem in 1099 by a French king named Godefroi de Bouillon.' "

Well, if it was founded in 1099, how could its history span "more than a millennium"?

Page 157: Dan Brown says the park called Bois de Boulogne was known by Paris cognoscenti as "the Garden of

Earthly Delights" because of its "hundreds of glistening bodies for hire, earthly delights to satisfy one's deepest unspoken desires—male, female, and everything in between."

Our French friends don't call it the Garden of Earthly Delights; maybe that was just an excuse for Brown to introduce an allusion to Hieronymus Bosch and his painting of the same name. It is, however, a fact that the park is teeming with male and female prostitutes and transvestites at night.

Page 160: Langdon describes the plot formulated by Pope Clement V and King Philippe IV of France to arrest and execute the Knights Templar in a coordinated effort starting at dawn on Friday, October 13, 1307. This is said to be the actual, direct source of the modern superstition about Friday the thirteenth.

This is only one of a variety of explanations for the superstition about Friday the thirteenth being unlucky.

Page 166: Bishop Aringarosa asks Silas, "Were you not aware that Noah himself was an albino?" Does it make sense for the bishop to say this?

The Bible does not say Noah was an albino, but the Book of Enoch—one of the apocryphal books that was omitted from the Bible—does have this description of the birth of Noah:

> Unto Lamech my son there hath been born a son, the like of whom there is none, and his nature is not like man's nature, and the colour of his body is whiter than snow and redder than the bloom of a rose, and the hair of his head is whiter than white wool, and his eyes

are like the rays of the sun, and he opened his eyes and thereupon lighted up the whole house.

But this is actually a kind of glued-on appendix to the Book of Enoch. And in any case, it is hard to imagine that a mainstream Opus Dei supernumerary such as Aringarosa would subscribe to scriptures from the alternative camp.

Page 168: Sophie takes over the driving and soon has the car "humming smoothly westward along Allée de Longchamp, leaving the Garden of Earthly Delights behind."

Sophie says the taxi driver had said the destination, rue Haxo, is "adjacent to the Roland Garros tennis stadium" and she is confident of finding it. "I know that area," she says.

Sophie needs a better map. Allée de Longchamp runs north-south and is one-way going north. The tennis stadium is not west of the park, but south of it. As we said before, rue Haxo is on the east side of Paris, miles away.

Page 169: Leonardo's famed Adoration of the Magi *was sketched by the master, but filled in by some rogue artist who modified the composition. This was revealed by X-rays and infrared reflectography. Italian art diagnostician Maurizio Seracini discovered the secrets of the painting and the story was published in the* New York Times Magazine.

All true. Seracini is a genuine, renowned art diagnostician. The article was written by Melinda Henneberger and published April 21, 2002. Ms. Henneberger is researching a book on Seracini's main quest, to find the lost Leonardo fresco, *Battle of Anghiari*.

Page 172: The Zurich bank signage reminds Langdon that the Swiss national flag contains an equal-armed cross.

Not only is the cross equal-armed, but the official flag of Switzerland is unusual in being a perfect square (not a rectangle), further accentuating the symmetry.

Page 176: Is there really a Depository Bank of Zurich?

If you Google it, you will find a website that looks for half a second like it could be real. Then you will discover it is part of the Dan Brown–Random House treasure hunt. It is a fun site to visit with a lot of inside jokes for readers of the book. Also try Googling Robert Langdon, and you may find a similarly amusing faux site.

Page 181: Collet is at the Gare du Nord when Fache calls him. Why is he there?

Fache had told Collet to "alert the next station, have the train stopped and searched." He sent Collet off to supervise. Fache has apparently forgotten that Lille trains don't depart the Gare Saint-Lazare, so Gare du Nord is not the "next station." It is even more implausible for Collet to have gone to the Gare du Nord in the earlier editions of the book, where Sophie and Robert have bought tickets for Lyon, far south of Paris.

Page 184: Vernet tells Sophie she needs to know her ten-digit account number. "Ten digits. Sophie reluctantly calculated the cryptographic odds. Ten billion possible choices. Even if she could bring in DCPJ's most powerful parallel processing computers, she still would need weeks to break the code."

There are at least a couple of things wrong with Sophie's assessment. First, the basic task of getting a computer to run through all ten billion possible numbers isn't at all difficult and any of today's ordinary computers can do it in minutes. You don't need parallel processing or huge computers. Admittedly, if you insist on printing out all the possible numbers, you will be in for a long wait at the laser printer and will face a huge bill for paper and toner.

But it has been a long time since a professional security system was built that would allow the user to make endless attempts to guess the passcode. Recognizing that people often slip on the keyboard, some systems allow up to three attempts, but the Depository Bank of Zurich has a stricter policy—you only get one try, as Sophie learns on page 188.

Page 201: Sophie muses about the cryptex: "If someone attempted to force open the cryptex, the glass vial would break, and the vinegar would quickly dissolve the papyrus. By the time anyone extracted the secret message, it would be a glob of meaningless pulp."

This isn't plausible to us. Papyrus itself is made from matted strips of the papyrus plant, layered with a flour paste (to which a dash of vinegar was added during manufacture). The fibers are mostly cellulose, an extremely durable material that doesn't instantly dissolve in vinegar. If we were told that the message on the papyrus is written in ink that dissolves with vinegar, we would be much more inclined to believe it. Note that the cryptex would probably contain papyrus that

Saunière had obtained, manufactured during his lifetime, not five hundred years earlier.

Page 201: The cryptex has five dials with twenty-six letters each. Sophie does the math: "That's 26 to the fifth power . . . approximately twelve million possibilities."

Yes, it's 11,881,376, to be exact.

Page 218: Langdon begins to speak of Sir Leigh Teabing's estate, which he says is "near Versailles." Later (page 220), Dan Brown describes it as follows: "The sprawling 185-acre estate of Château Villette was located twenty-five minutes northwest of Paris in the environs of Versailles. . . . The estate fondly had become known as la Petite Versailles." Is the Château Villette real and is it near Versailles?

The real-life Villette is up for rent to any tourist who can pay five thousand dollars a night, and has been kicking around the Web for some time as a kind of vacation rental listing. The California-based rental agent's ad copy says Villette is "near Versailles, northwest of Paris." The history of the house told in *The Da Vinci Code* matches the history on the rental agent's site, including the seventeenth-century involvement of Le Nôtre (designer of many of the gardens at Versailles) and Mansart. This is clearly a beautiful and historic house.

However, we would not call it "near" Versailles, except in real estate business jargon. Versailles is about ten miles west of the center of Paris and three miles south. Villette is about twenty miles west of Paris and ten miles north. The road distance between them is about nineteen miles.

Page 224: Vernet phones and instructs the bank's night manager to activate the armored truck's "emergency transponder." The manager goes over to the bank's LoJack panel and does so, warning that it will also alert the police. Vernet remains on the phone in order to hear the location of the truck. Is this how LoJack works?

Not exactly. In France, LoJack is called Traqueur. It requires a call to the police in order to activate the vehicle transmitter. Once this is done, it is the police, in their cars and helicopters, who use tracking gear to find the vehicle. You do not get an instant position report unless the police are ready to spring into action and coordinate their tracking efforts. It may take hours. (If you wanted instant results, you would need a system that reports its own GPS coordinates—like the "GPS dot" on *DVC* page 65, for instance.)

Traqueur has a number of advantages, however. First, it is thoroughly entrenched in France, which has more or less blanket coverage with over twenty-three thousand police cars and forty-two helicopters (far more comprehensive coverage than in the United States, in fact). Second, its discreet, coded signal allows the police to prepare quietly to make the arrest, rather than issuing a signal that can be decoded by anyone.

Page 227: Gargoyles! Flashback to Saunière taking young Sophie to Notre Dame in a rainstorm. The gargoyle rainspouts are gurgling. "They're gargling," her grandfather told her. "Gargariser! And that's where they get the silly name 'gargoyles.'"

No. *Gargariser* is current French for "gargle." The term that both gargle and gargoyle stem from is not *gargariser* but *gargouille,* an old French word meaning "gullet" or "throat." But the etymology is much more interesting than that! According to myth, in the seventh century a dragon rose up out of the River Seine. But rather than breathing fire, this dragon gushed forth water. His name was Gargouille, or Throat. He proceeded to drown the towns around Paris, until he was confronted and tamed by St. Romain, the archbishop of Rouen, who made the sign of the cross with his two index fingers. Throat was led tamely back to Paris, slain, and burned, but not before they cut off his head and mounted it on a building.

Many buildings, old and new, have scary creatures adorning them. Strictly speaking, only those creatures that are part of the gutter systems, spouting water, are called gargoyles in honor of Gargouille. All the other creatures are called grotesques.

Page 227: Sophie says she "studied at the Royal Holloway." Is that a place to learn cryptology?

Yes, the Royal Holloway is a part of the University of London and has respected undergraduate degree programs in mathematics and computer science. It offers M.Sc. and Ph.D. degrees and is host to the Information Security Group, a graduate-level conclave of scholars known for cryptology work.

Page 233: "Hold on," says Sophie. "You're saying Jesus' divinity was the result of a vote?" "A relatively close vote at that," Teabing added.

Holy hanging St. Chad, Batman, let's see the Supreme Court settle this one! The vote was 316 to 2. Teabing calls this close? By the way, there really was a St. Chad. He humbly stepped aside in AD 669 when a dispute arose as to who was properly ordained as the Bishop of York.

Page 234: Dan Brown says, "The Dead Sea Scrolls were found in the 1950s hidden in a cave near Qumran in the Judean desert."

The year was 1947. Some Bedouin herders were searching for a lost goat and found the cave with jars containing ancient scrolls. Initially, seven scrolls were brought out, but further searches yielded thousands of scroll fragments over the next decade or so.

Page 234: "Because Constantine upgraded Jesus' status almost four centuries after Jesus' death, thousands of documents already existed," Teabing says (referring to the Council of Nicea).

Fuzzy math again: If Jesus died around AD 30 and the Council of Nicea met in AD 325, how many centuries elapsed in between? We think it rounds off to three centuries, not four.

Page 243: "Our preconceived notions of this scene are so powerful that our mind blocks out the incongruity and overrides our eyes," said Teabing.

"It is known as scotoma," Langdon added.

Interesting syndrome, but not quite right. What Teabing has said does not correctly describe scotoma, which is a real visual defect or disease, not a mere perceptual quirk.

The definition of scotoma is "a blind spot or dark spot in the visual field." Medically speaking, "Scotomas may be central, if caused by macular or optic nerve disease, or peripheral if the result of chorioretinal lesions or retinal holes." There is even a phenomenon associated with migraine headaches called scintillating scotoma, where the blind spot pulsates and has ragged edges.

True lacunae buffs take note: in the first hardcover edition of *The Da Vinci Code,* this word is misspelled as skitoma.

Page 246: Sophie recalls that "the French government, under pressure from priests, had agreed to ban an American movie called The Last Temptation of Christ."

The French government did not ban the movie. The 1988 film, directed by Martin Scorsese, was based on a 1955 novel by Nikos Kazantzakis, who is also known for writing *Zorba the Greek.* It did indeed portray Jesus (Willem Dafoe) as lusting after Mary Magdalene (Barbara Hershey).

When the novel was published, it triggered protests and some bannings (the Vatican, most notably), but not in France. The Greek Orthodox Church excommunicated Kazantzakis, who was nominally a member. When Scorsese's movie opened, there were protests practically everywhere, including the firebombing of a theater in Paris, as well as attacks on movie houses elsewhere in France. There were incidents of violence throughout the world. In the United States, a protester crashed a bus into a theater lobby. At least two governments did ban the film—Chile and Israel—but not France.

By the way, if Saunière is supposed to be keeping a low profile, why is he writing such a letter? And if Sophie is supposed to be thirty-two at the time of the novel, making her born around 1969–70, why is she talking to her grandfather about the 1988 movie in the discussion represented on page 247, with childlike naiveté, wondering if Jesus had a girlfriend?

Page 251: Aringarosa "had a chartered turbo prop awaiting

him" at Ciampino Airport (page 251). But on page 272, he is found in a "chartered Beechcraft Baron 58."

The Beech Baron 58 is not a turboprop. It has piston engines and burns gasoline. A turboprop has turbine engines that drive propellers and it burns jet fuel.

Page 271: The police find Silas's Audi. "It had rental plates. Collet felt the hood. Still warm. Hot even." What are rental plates?

There isn't a special plate for rental cars, but there is a coding system that sometimes gives away the information that thieves, for instance, might be seeking. Each region (department) of France has a code assigned to the last two digits of a license plate. Taxes vary with different departments, so the rental companies became known for plates ending with ninety-two, fifty-one, or twenty-six, where they registered their cars because taxes were lowest. The rental car companies have been phasing out this practice. Insiders can still readily identify a plate as nonlocal, however.

Page 272: Aringarosa is racing "northward" over the Tyrrhenian Sea on a flight from Rome-Ciampini to Paris.

If you go due north from Rome, you will not reach the sea. You must go northwest or west.

Page 279: On page 220, Langdon brought the armored truck to a shuddering stop at the foot of the mile-long driveway. Now, on page 279, "a sea of blue police lights and sirens erupted at the bottom of the hill and began snaking up the half-mile driveway."

Leigh Teabing has a long driveway. But is it a mile or half a mile?

Page 280: Here, we learn that "Collet and his agents burst through the front door . . . They found a bullet hole in the drawing room floor, signs of a struggle . . ." But a few pages later, on page 296, we find out that "Collet was grateful that PTS had located a bullet hole in the floor, which at least corroborated Collet's claims . . ."

Gee, you would think that Collet would have told the PTS people that he had found the bullet hole, but maybe he let them discover it on their own.

Page 281: Here we read this description: "Collet ran to the door, trying to see out into the darkness. All he could make out was the faint shadow of a forest in the distance." But two pages later, on page 283, Rémy "was doing an impressive job of maneuvering the vehicle across the moonlit fields."

Perhaps the moonlight was different at one end of the field than at the other?

Page 293: "The Hawker 731's twin Garrett TFE-731 engines thundered."

We understand what airplane Dan Brown is probably talking about, but practically no one would call it a "Hawker 731." It is a Hawker-Siddeley HS-125 with Garrett 731 jet engines, a representative model being an HS-125-400-731. This was originally built by de Havilland, then British Aerospace, and now is under the Raytheon banner.

Page 300: Dan Brown describes the $30.8 million purchase by Bill Gates of "eighteen sheets of paper" comprising the Leonardo notebook known as the Leicester Codex.

The eighteen sheets are two-sided and fold in half, creating a seventy-two-page booklet. The wealthy Armand Hammer bought the codex in 1980 for $5.2 million and renamed it the Hammer Codex, but Gates restored its name to Leicester Codex. Its home is the Seattle Art Museum, but it has toured the world and has been made into an interactive CD.

Page 332: The police were "awaiting the moment when the plane's engines powered down. The instant this happened, a runway attendant would place safety wedges under the tires so the plane could no longer move."

Practically the whole world over, the "safety wedges" are called "chocks." In England, Dan Brown's "runway attendant" would be called a "marshaller."

Page 332: "The Hawker's engines were still roaring as the jet finished its usual rotation inside the hangar, positioning itself nose-out in preparation for later departure. As the plane completed its 180-degree turn and rolled toward the front of the hangar. . . ."

No jet pilot would attempt this maneuver. Pilots simply do not operate planes inside hangars. The jet vortices would make lethal projectiles out of anything not bolted down in the hangar, and the thrust would very likely blow the hangar's walls out. A Biggin Hill pilot told us this would be "a sackable offense."

Page 343: The Temple Church survived "only to be heavily damaged by Luftwaffe incendiary bombs in 1940," according to Dan Brown.

The incendiary bombs actually fell on the night of May 10, 1941.

Page 343: As Teabing and company arrive at Temple

Church, "the rough-hewn stone shimmered in the rain." A minute or two later, inside, "Teabing pointed toward a stained-glass window where the breaking sun was refracting through a white-clad knight riding a rose-colored horse."

We guess that this was the only ray of sun on an otherwise cloudy, rainy morning. Throughout the book's activities in London during the morning, it is raining—sometimes heavily.

Page 346: Teabing once had to lie on stage for half and hour "with my todger hanging out." What's a todger?

British slang for penis.

Page 347: Teabing has spoken of Temple Church as housing "ten of the most frightening tombs you will ever see" a few pages earlier. Now, on page 347, inside Temple Church, Langdon sees "ten stone knights. Five on the left. Five on the right. Lying supine on the floor, the carved, life-sized figures rested in peaceful poses. The knights were depicted wearing full armor, shields and swords . . . All of the figures were deeply weathered, and yet each was clearly unique."

But they are all surprised to find that "one of the knights is missing."

There isn't a knight missing. There are just nine carved knights in effigy. This should be no surprise to anyone who knows the Temple Church.

One of the main reasons for the weathered look of the knights is the damage caused by falling debris in the incendiary bombing by the Germans on May 10, 1941. The roof of the Round Church burned first, followed eventually by all the wood throughout the church.

Page 360: Legaludec's pistol is a "small-caliber, J-frame Medusa." What is this?

This appears to be a confusion of two weapons. The J-frame is commonly associated with a series of snubby revolvers in the Smith-Wesson lineup, such as the Model 60, a five-shot .357.

The Medusa is a very special weapon made by Phillips & Rodgers that does not confine itself to one caliber. Instead, it accepts a wide range of ammo from the same approximate caliber, such as .357, 9 mm, and .38 rounds. It is a small six-shot revolver. Interestingly, at the request of forensic scientists, the gun is made with nine rifling lands and grooves, making it probably unique among handguns.

Page 365: In the barn loft at Villette are examples of a listening system that the French police consider "very advanced . . . as sophisticated as our own equipment. Miniature microphones, photoelectric recharging cells, high-capacity RAM chips. He's even got some of those new nano drives." They discover a radio receiving system and they agree that the remote bugs are "voice-activated to save hard disk space, and [they] recorded snippets of conversation during the day, transmitting compressed audio files at night to avoid detection. After transmitting, the hard drive erased itself and prepared to do it all over again the next day." Collet now looks at a shelf containing "several hundred audio cassettes, all labelled with dates and numbers." What's wrong with this picture?

Quick! Find any ten-year-old kid and ask him or her whether it would make sense to store MP3 files on audio cassette tapes! (Just to be fair, first explain to the kid what a cassette tape was and what the player used to look like!)

For those who can't get the story from a kid, the compressed audio files can be played right on the computer and stored right on the computer's hard drive, or transferred to a CD or DVD for safekeeping. It would be time-prohibitive and unnecessary to make audio tapes. By the way, what are nanodrives? We are students of nanotechnology developments, and can imagine many things there may be in the future, but we're not sure what Dan Brown is talking about here, except to sound futuristic.

Page 367: Langdon and Sophie "hurdled the turnstile at the Temple tube station" on their way from Temple Church to the library of the Institute of Systematic Theology. Does a tube ride make sense for this trip?

No. There are two problems with this trip. If you wish to find the Institute of Systematic Theology, you will need to go to Room 2E of the Cresham Building on Surrey Lane (on the day when the institute's scholars meet). If you run to the Temple tube station, you are only half a block from the Cresham Building and there is no need to go into any station.

But the octagonal room that is described as the library of the institute won't be found in the Cresham Building. In all likelihood, this is really the Round Room, which is in the Maugham Library of Kings College. To get there from Temple Church, you just go north, cross the Strand, and go up Chancery Lane. It's only a block. If you ran to the tube station, you would be going the wrong way.

Page 377: Dan Brown says there is a "Research Institute in Systematic Theology" at King's College in London. Is this real?

Yes. The respected institute is run by the college's Department ofTheology and Religious Studies. However, it is really just a conclave of scholars who meet regularly in a seminar room and often host conferences on theology.

Page 377: Dan Brown says the Kings College Research Institute in Systematic Theology has a primary research room that is a "dramatic octagonal chamber." Sophie and Langdon arrive just as the librarian is making tea and settling in for the day. Does that sound right?

The room he describes does exist as part of Kings College, but it is in the Maugham Library on Chancery Lane. It doesn't belong to the Research Institute. It does not open until 9:30 a.m. on Saturday, and we estimate that Sophie and Langdon would reach it sometime around 8:30 at the latest (even after getting lost a bit).

Page 379: Dan Brown says the Kings College Research Institute on Systematic Theology for two decades had used "optical character recognition software in unison with linguistic translation devices to digitize and catalogue an enormous collection of texts—encyclopedias of religion, religious biographies, sacred scriptures in dozens of languages, histories, Vatican letters, diaries of clerics, anything at all that qualified as writings on human spirituality." The data is said to be accessible via a "massive mainframe" computer that can search at five hundred MB/sec through a "few hundred terabytes" of information. Does this exist?

No. We contacted the faculty of the Research Institute. They were surprised and amused to learn about their putative huge computer and database.

One professor told us, "Our computing facilities are the staff desktops [currently G3 iMacs]." He said,

"We do not, unfortunately, have any computing resources devoted to assembling 'a huge [or even modest] database of theological works.'" He added, "I once tried using optical recognition software, but it was such a disaster that I typed the piece in myself instead."

Page 392: In seeking "a knight A. Pope interred," Langdon obtains this "hit" on the Research Institute computer: "Sir Isaac Newton's burial, attended by kings and nobles, was presided over by Alexander Pope, friend and colleague, who gave a stirring eulogy before sprinkling dirt on the tomb." Did Pope really preside and read a eulogy?

No. Newton's funeral on March 28, 1727, was remarkable in the lofty honor afforded Sir Isaac. He was considered almost a deity. According to a chronicle of the time, his body was brought from the Jerusalem Chamber of Westminster Abbey by pallbearers that included a lord, two dukes and three earls. The chief mourner was Sir Michael Newton, and the bishop of Rochester read the service.

Although Alexander Pope was probably the preeminent poet of the time, his role came later, when a number of people decided to erect a monument to Newton about four years after his death. Because Pope had a reputation for writing outstanding epitaphs (and earned a good income from it), he was selected to write the epitaph that appears on the monument. It became one of the most famous of all time:

ISAACUS NEWTONUS:
Quem Immortalem
Testantur, Tempus, Natura, Caelum:
Mortalem
Hoc marmor fatetur.

Nature and Nature's Laws lay hid in Night.
God said, Let Newton be! and All was Light.

Page 393: Sophie and Langdon seemed to have arrived at the King's College institute library around 8:00 a.m. on a Saturday morning, yet they find it open and staffed by the friendly and efficient Pamela Gettum. This seems improbable. What time do these early birds get to Westminster Abbey and is it open?

Our calculations show that they probably arrive at Westminster Abbey at about 8:45 a.m. Although they move right into the abbey without problem, the fact is that it doesn't really open until 9:30 a.m. This is just one of several problems we have identified with the timeline of *The Da Vinci Code*'s action. Another is with the air travel of Bishop Aringarosa. The bishop's travels are inconsistent with the rest of the timeline, in our opinion. In the extreme possibility, it seems he could be airborne about six hours from Rome to Biggin Hill, with intermediate points that do not fit the trip. But further, if events were taken in sequential order in the book, he would instantly arrive at 5 Orme Court to be shot by Silas, when it should require about fifty minutes to get from Biggin Hill to London center.

Following the Rose Line

By Dan Burstein

Our extremely able tour guide, David Shugarts, has brought us to this juncture. He has led us through four hundred pages of *Da Vinci Code* plot details and plot flaws.

An amazingly jam-packed eight hours has passed from 12:32 a.m., the time the phone awakened Robert Langdon from his reveries (no doubt of the sacred feminine) in his comfortable bed at the Ritz Hotel in Paris, to this moment, at approximately 8:45 a.m., when Robert and Sophie are arriving at Westminster Abbey. At this point, some of the biggest plot mysteries jump out from behind their gargoyles. The story of the Teacher falls apart. His motives for setting this whole plot in motion prove irrational and implausible. The Priory of Sion appears to wimp out on the legacy that has occupied so much of the book. And the fearsome Opus Dei seems humbled and unlikely to launch new conspiracies and intrigues. The strong allusion that is made to the ultimate resting place of the Holy Grail seems silly to many readers.

With a lot to choose from, however, what follows is my personal favorite example of a plot flaw: everything has led us to believe that Sophie, aka Princesse Sophie, the hothouse grandchild of Grand Master and Grand-Père Saunière, is the twenty-first-century descendant of the royal bloodline flowing from the union of Jesus Christ and Mary Magdalene. We were thrown off the scent briefly in the middle of the book when Sophie begins to get the inkling that she might be the modern-day bearer of the bloodline of Jesus. But Langdon tells her that since Saunière is not a Merovingian name, and since no one in her family is named Plantard or Saint-Clair, "it's impossible" that the auburn-haired Sophie is the modern-day descendant of Mary Magdalene and Jesus Christ.

Yet by the end of the book, Dan Brown will let us know he was just tossing us a red herring. Marie Chauvel, Saunière's wife and Sophie's grandmother, is explicit when she tells Sophie the truth: her parents were both descended from Merovingian families—"direct descendants of Mary Magdalene and Jesus Christ." Sophie's parents had changed their names from Plantard and Saint-Clair long before, for protection. "Their children represented the most direct surviving royal bloodline and therefore were carefully guarded by the Priory."

Powerful dark forces (presumably of the church) conspire to kill Sophie's family and to eradicate this sacred bloodline once and for all. But Sophie and her brother survive the car accident that was intended to wipe out the entire family. The parents are dead, and Saunière must act precipitously in the face of great danger. He separates the survivors, moves Sophie in with him, sends his wife and Sophie's brother to live secret, separate lives in Scotland (at the Rosslyn Chapel), and cuts off virtually all communication between the Paris grandfather-granddaughter pair and the Scotland grandmother-grandson pair. After taking all these elaborate precautions to keep the future bright for these last descendants of the royal bloodline, Saunière sets about raising Sophie and training her for her future role.

Then, the unfortunate primal scene takes place when Sophie visits Saunière's country house on an unannounced early return from college. She is so traumatized by the *hieros gamos* rite she briefly witnesses that she refuses to speak to Grand-Père ever again, she refuses to read the letters he sends her, and she refuses every effort he makes to explain. But how can the brilliant Saunière, a modern-day Leonardo da Vinci and grand master of the great Priory of Sion, not be able to get through at all to the granddaughter he loves? Crusades have happened, wars have been fought, people have been massacred, believers have been tortured to death, all to protect the secrets of the Priory of Sion. Now Saunière can't find a way to communicate these secrets to his granddaughter?

Moreover, if bloodline is so important, and if *sang real*—royal blood—is what the Holy Grail is really all about, as we are told so often in the novel, how is it that both Sophie and her brother—the two last descendants on earth of Jesus Christ and Mary Magdalene, whose families and secret society protectors have withstood every effort to extinguish their line for two millennia—are so blithely unmarried, unengaged, and without even a hint of a girlfriend or boyfriend? Sophie is said to be thirty-two when the action of the book takes place. Her biological clock is definitely ticking. And yet, she is childless. This, to me, is a massively glaring plot hole. Does it all come to an end here?

Well, not exactly. Langdon invites Sophie to join him next month in Florence, where he will be lecturing. They can spend a week in a luxury hotel that Langdon calls the Brunelleschi. (Dan Brown presumably gives the hotel this name as an allusion to Brunelleschi's dome, the centerpiece of Florence, and arguably the ultimate architectural metaphor for the female breast.) Sophie wants no museums, no churches, no tombs, art, or relics. Langdon wonders what else they will do? At which point they kiss—on the mouth—and he is reminded of what else one can do in Florence for a week. Thus, we leave Sophie and Langdon dreaming of Florence, the city of Leonardo da Vinci, and the hotel room that awaits them.

Assuming Langdon is not overcome by performance anxiety at the thought of making love to a woman descended directly from Jesus Christ—and there's no reason to believe that he would be, given his belief in the sacred feminine—there may be progeny yet. We'll have to wait for the sequel.

Acknowledgments

Two years ago, for the hardcover edition of this book, we began the acknowledgments with these words: "Special thanks and deep appreciation are due to a stunning array of people who became excited about the project of assembling this book and leaped with us over the chasm of all the obstacles to get it done in record time." That sentiment has not changed now that we are bringing you the revised and substantially updated edition of *Secrets of the Code*.

We originally developed the concept for *Secrets of the Code* in an inspired and creative partnership with Gilbert Perlman, Steve Black, and their colleagues at CDS Books. They moved mountains and made things happen on a schedule we have never seen before in two decades of writing and publishing books. David Wilk has proven to be the best friend authors could have for both editions, twice coordinating the nearly infinite number of fibers involved with this project into a cohesive piece of papyrus.

CDS has since been acquired by the Perseus Books Group. David Steinberger, president and CEO of Perseus, has welcomed us and become our reliable North Star, continuing to help us navigate the complex cosmology of the publishing universe for our "Secrets" titles and other books. Thanks, also, are due to many publishing professionals at both CDS and Perseus who worked on either or both editions of *Secrets of the Code:* Lane Jantzen, Elizabeth Whiting, Matty Goldberg, Stephen Bottum, Robert Kimzey, Kerry Liebling, Kate Greder, Kari Stuart, Hope Matthiessen, and Kipton Davis. An added salute to Christine Marra, den mother for this edition.

We could not have produced this book without a terrific team of consulting and contributing editors, as well as research and editorial associates. We owe a special clear and uncoded message of thanks to David A. Shugarts, our indefatigable investigative reporter and code breaker, for his many contributions to this and all our "Secrets" series books. For the new edition, we add Paul Berger to a supporting cast that includes Jennifer Doll, Kate Stohr, Nicole Zaray, John Castro, Brian Weiss, and Peter Bernstein and Annalyn Swan of ASAP Media LLC.

As we have worked on revising and updating *Secrets of the Code*, we have also been working on a documentary film based on the book. Our thanks go out to the terrific team of filmmakers and investors who have helped us bring the ideas in these pages to the screen as well.

We also want to extend our thanks and appreciation to Danny Baror at Baror International, who has introduced *Secrets of the Code* and the other titles in the "Secrets" series to publishing partners in more than twenty-four countries. With two million copies now in print worldwide, "Secrets" books have appeared on bestseller lists in markets that range from France to Poland, and Portugal to India.

On the production side, we have been blessed with much talent and many people who perform with grace under pressure. We want especially to thank Leigh Taylor, as well as the team on the first edition: George Davidson, Lee Quarfoot, Nan Jernigan, Gray Cutler, Suzanne Fass, David Kessler, Mike Kingcaid, Ray Ferguson, and Jane Elias. We will always remember Jaye Zimet's contributions to the look and feel of *Secrets of the Code*.

Our families provided intellectual, artistic, and moral support throughout our journeys of the last two years. Love and lasting gratitude to Julie O'Connor, Helen de Keijzer, Hannah de Keijzer, David Burstein, and Joan O'Connor.

Numerous friends and professional colleagues championed the project, pitched in when the going got tough, helped us with key bits of information, gave us new ideas about how to tell the story, or generally helped us manage the rest of our lives while we were trying to put this book together: Ann Malin, David Kline, Sam

Schwerin, Peter Kaufman, Marty Edelston, Judy Friedberg, Carter Wiseman, Stuart Rekant, Ben Wolin, Bob Stein, Gregory Rutchick, Cynthia O'Conner, Chuck Hirsch, David Balter, Jen Prosek, Meryl Moss, and Lottchen Shivers. Best wishes for a cancer-free life to Craig Buck and Phil Berman.

Elaine Pagels, one of the leading scholars in the field of Gnostic and alternative gospels, provided encouragement and support to us at the very beginning of this journey. She is a true Renaissance woman. We also want to thank all of our other authors and contributors, who, after all, have provided the fascinating insights for both editions that are the backbone of this project: Diane Apostolos-Cappadona, Michael Baigent, Elizabeth Bard, Amy Bernstein, Esther de Boer, Denise Budd, Michelle Delio, Keith Devlin, Maureen Dowd, David Downie, Betsy Eble, Bart D. Ehrman, Riane Eisler, Glenn W. Erickson, Brian Finnerty, Marcia Ford, Timothy Freke, Peter Gandy, Deirdre Good, Bernard Hamilton, Collin Hansen, Susan Haskins, Stephan A. Hoeller, Asher Jacobson, Katherine Ludwig Jansen, Karen L. King, Gwen Kinkead, David Klinghoffer, Matthew Landrus, Richard Leigh, Henry Lincoln, Diane Maclean, James Martin, Richard P. McBrien, Craig McDonald, Celia McGee, Cathleen McGuigan, Brendan McKay, Laura Miller, Anne Moore, Sherwin B. Nuland, Craig Offman, Lance S. Owens, Lewis Perdue, Lynn Picknett, The Prelature of Opus Dei, Clive Prince, James Robinson, John Saul, Margaret Starbird, David Van Biema, Curtis White, and Kenneth Woodward.

—*Dan Burstein and Arne de Keijzer*

King James Version gives these seventeen words as the complete verse 11: "And said, Hitherto shalt thou